the
best
of
fact:

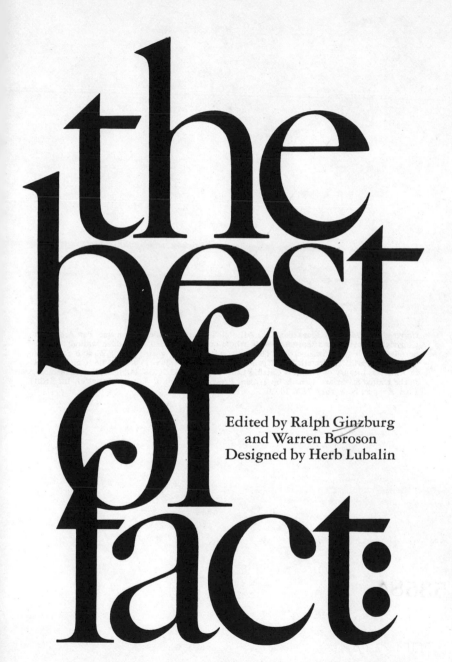

the best of fact

Edited by Ralph Ginzburg
and Warren Boroson
Designed by Herb Lubalin

Trident Press New York 1967

From the masthead
of the
first issue of FACT,
published on
January 1, 1964:

This magazine is dedicated to the proposition that a great magazine, in its quest for truth, will dare to defy not only Convention, not only Big Business, not only the Church and the State, but also—if necessary—its readers.

Introduction

According to a few rumors that have been floating around, *Fact* Magazine was bankrolled at a meeting between Adam Clayton Powell, Jimmy Hoffa, Tim Leary, Elizabeth Taylor, and Fu Manchu in an LSD session at THRUSH headquarters in Passaic, New Jersey.

According to Ralph Ginzburg, however, the man who began the magazine, *Fact* is the Son of Eros—an assertion that may be slightly closer to the truth.

In 1961, the U.S. Post Office, in its finite wisdom, concluded that *Eros*, the first magazine that Mr. Ginzburg published, was obscene and could not be sent through the mails. Only Volume 1, Number 4, which contained photographs of a white woman and a Negro man together, unclothed, was singled out for this attention, so he could of course have gone right ahead and published Volume 2, Number 1, which was already at the printer's. But Mr. Ginzburg's lawyers warned him that if Post Office censor-morons were to be kept at bay, all further issues of *Eros* would have to be about as ballsy as *Godey's Lady's Book*. After due reflection, he decided to stop publishing *Eros*, confidently awaiting victory in the courts.

Meanwhile, *Eros* still had a staff of eager workers, a floor of offices near the New York Public Library, and a large number of subscribers who were wondering where their magazine was. Now, for many years Mr. Ginzburg had been thinking of launching another publication, a magazine of dissent, a magazine that would print those articles other magazines are too timid, or too corrupt, to print. Thanks to the U.S. Post Office, here was his opportunity. So in late 1962, he and I began sending out brochures describing a new muckraking magazine; money flowed in; with the money, *Fact* was born.

* * *

One of the assumptions behind the magazine was that advertising overtly and covertly castrates content. Therefore *Fact* would take no advertising. We wanted to be perfectly free to rough up powerful and sacrosanct institutions when they deserved roughing up, and free to explore topics considered taboo by most other magazines and the big advertisers that support them.

A second assumption was that *Fact* would be a *professional* magazine, one that profited from the skills of modern journalism. Manuscripts, if unclear, would be made clear— "translated into English," as H.L. Mencken used to say. Formless, discursive manuscripts would be organized, preferably around one central theme. Manuscripts written ploddingly would be brightened up and tightened up.

A third assumption was that *Fact* would be a *magazine,* a storehouse, and not just a house organ for anyone's pet ideas. Articles in *Fact,* if they were responsible and cogent enough, did not have to coincide with the views of the editors. To be sure, *Fact* would have a "personality": It would be tough-minded, rationalistic, progressive, and psychologically oriented. But it would not preach political liberalism and practice intellectual totalitarianism.

Finally, there was the assumption embedded in the name itself. It was called *Fact* because the magazine would concentrate on articles grounded in personal experience and scientific research. Most people's opinions, the editors believe, are the products of their personalities—their emotional needs and desires. To a degree, this makes their opinions suspect. In *Fact,* we hoped, all opinions expressed would be corroborated not only by independent research, but by personal, experiential familiarity with the subject. The ivory-tower "expert" would be regarded with a little skepticism: There always seems to be a professor of astronomy at Harvard who is convinced that the world is flat. *Our* expert would be a man who had not only read the leading works on (say) employment agencies, and who had not only sought out the views of insulated experts, but had also actually worked for an employment agency. Furthermore, by personalizing articles in this way, we could do what every new magazine, and every new art movement, should do: get closer to current, everyday reality.

In sum, we wanted *Fact* to have the lucidity of the *Reader's Digest,* the cleverness and wit of *Time,* the intrepidity of the old *American Mercury,* the integrity of the *New Yorker,* and the factual foundation of *Scientific American.*

* * *

The topics *Fact* would cover, and has covered, are almost unlimited—from *Mad* Magazine to Warren Gamaliel Harding's alleged Negro ancestry. Yet *Fact's* articles are linked, on the one hand, by a critical, personal, and psychological approach, and on the other by the fact that other magazines usually shy away from such articles—because the topics may be depressing (like an examination of life on Welfare), emotionally charged (like miscegenation), fiercely controversial (like the campaign to tax the churches), or deeply disquieting (like the mental condition of Presidents and would-be Presidents). Most American magazines, emulating the *Reader's Digest,* wallow in sugar and everything nice; *Fact* has had the spice almost all to itself.

Although it was not deliberate, *Fact's* articles have come to revolve around certain themes, themes that may represent the key problems faced by this country in the 1960s.

First and foremost is America's obsessive and paranoid anti-communism. Communism, like all forms of totalitarianism, should be condemned and opposed, just as the United States should condemn and oppose all totalitarian regimes—in Haiti, South Africa, Rhodesia, Spain, Portugal, and Mississippi. That a totalitarian regime happens to be communist doesn't make it any worse. And just as we manage to get along with Haiti and South Africa, we must learn to live with China, Cuba, and a communistic Vietnam. For if a country like Vietnam voluntarily casts its lot against us, we must accept that decision—and learn the bitter lesson that our support of dictators like Diem, and now Ky, is self-defeating. Today the survival of civilization seems less endangered by communism's purported aggressiveness than by our own bellicose, paranoid anti-communism. *Fact* has been trying to explore the underlying reasons behind this obsession, and more important, trying to transform *Anti-Communism!* into plain, ordinary anti-communism.

A second theme is also not new: briefly, it is our neglect of the public sector of the economy—our cities, schools, hospitals; and especially our neglect of "deprived institutions"—prisons, mental hospitals, welfare departments—the victims of which are inarticulate and their sufferings little publicized. We are, true enough, making headway: Today there is serious talk, for example, of a negative income tax. But when are we going to place the public welfare above such goals as reaching the moon, or being able to kill everyone on earth a few dozen times?

And then there is what A.J. Liebling called the Press Mess. American journalism, like American medicine, is the best in the world, and it is very bad. Our newspapers, magazines, and TV stations are afraid of advertisers, afraid of pressure groups, afraid of controversy. But their timidity is a minor fault compared with their corruption. The great contribution America has made to mass communications is impartiality, the objective reporting of notable events. Yet this ideal is being flagrantly violated right and left, especially right, and principally by two of this country's leading magazines. One is the *Reader's Digest,* which piously claims to be impartial but in reality deals a stacked deck; the other is *Time* Magazine, which reports the news at the same time that it colors the news. To *Time,* "interpretive" reporting means interpreting it your way. When the fear of Henry Luce's empire finally abates, he will be remembered as the man who dirtied the mainstream of American journalism.

A fourth theme of many *Fact* articles concerns the need for more and stronger countervailing powers in American society, especially to protect the weak, naïve consumer against predatory producers. The poor American consumer may drive a car that is unsafe, take drugs whose pernicious side-effects he is unaware of, buy insurance that gives him shoddy coverage, get a job through an employment agency that charges excessively, patronize travel agencies that don't tell him what he is paying for, and smoke cigarettes because he wasn't warned soon enough and forcefully enough about the harm smoking causes. As for reforms, the producers themselves sing the refrain, "I'd rather do it myself." They haven't, they won't, they can't. We need, therefore, strong outside agencies to fight for the average American citizen—agencies that will police TV stations, advertisers, drug companies, utilities, and, of course, police the police.

And yes, we confess it: Another *Fact* theme has been sex, or better, taboo topics in general. Sex is taboo perhaps because the subject automatically arouses neurotic worries; or it arouses guilt and shame associated with almost-forgotten fantasies, impulses, and deeds; or just because of the common confusion of reproduction with excretion. Whatever the causes, anti-sexuality seems to be one of the most widespread neuroses in American society. After all, it cuts across party lines: You can be a political liberal, like I.F. Stone, and at the same time a sexual Fascist. We probably need new classifications, like Up for the sexually enlightened and Down for the sexually repressed. But the real tragedy is that anti-sexuality creates misery and unhappiness not only for the afflicted, but for innocent bystanders—the women who want legal abortions, the youngsters who should have proper sex educations, and the writers, artists, and publishers who want to treat the subject honestly and responsibly.

One last theme I will mention is psychology. Perhaps *Fact*'s most pressing campaign has been to have the leaders of our country, and eventually of other countries, periodically examined by psychiatrists, as a step toward preventing future Hitlers and Stalins. But we have also attempted to use the insights of psychology, psychiatry, and psychoanalysis to understand and cope with various problems and puzzles of our civilization, from the rumors about Kennedy's assassination to the revulsion commonly inspired by the thought of miscegenation, from the effects of circumcision to the irrational reasons behind America's foreign policy.

*   *   *

Fact has had many things going for it. We have had, of course, the freedom to write about any subject at all, frankly and fully. Thus we were the first major magazine to publicize the scandalous hazards of American cars—in 1964, in an article researched by a then-unknown Ralph Nader. We were the first major magazine to warn that the Ku Klux Klan was riding again—again in 1964. Our exposé of the inhuman conditions at Bellevue Psychiatric Hospital in 1966 had something to do with the speeding of emergency financial assistance to the hospital. Our first issue, in January-February of 1964, featured a first-person account on the effects of LSD.

We have had other, more subtle advantages, too. We publish about nine articles every 2 months, and therefore have been able to pick and choose. By and large, *Fact* has avoided the superficial, ephemeral articles that *The New York Times Magazine,* for example, is cursed with, and has probed the root causes of long-lasting controversies. Thus this book could easily have been doubled in size simply because *Fact* articles do not date readily.

Another advantage is that our staff is young and has the enthusiasm and the imagination of youth, and our staff is small, so we don't suffer from the committee decisions that kill all projects except the most bland and seemingly safe. The average age of *Fact*'s editors is about 33. The average age of editors of the *Reader's Digest,* I would guess, is 82. Among *Fact*'s editorial innovations: the periodic study of recent joke-patterns as an indication of what the public may be really thinking; occasional symposia of well-known people's opinions on some controversial issue, symposia that usually confirm that, indeed, personality forms opinion; and the publishing of wildly illogical, fiercely emotional letters to the editor, instead of only the more erudite, restrained ones, again as a way of getting *Fact* closer to the world as it really is.

* * *

The circulation of *Fact,* in 3 years, has zoomed to 250,000, easily surpassing the circulations of such established periodicals as the *New Republic,* the *Progressive,* the *Nation, Ramparts, Evergreen Review,* and a host of others. Among the authors who have written for us are Arnold J. Toynbee, Bertrand Russell, Mary Hemingway, Irwin Shaw, Sen. Ernest Gruening, Kenneth Rexroth, and Dr. Benjamin Spock. The Nobel Prize-winning biologist Hermann J. Muller has said that *Fact* is filling a needed role, and filling it well. Han Suyin has praised *Fact*'s "courage." Bertrand Russell has said that *Fact* is "well-prepared, irreverent, and serious." The Rev. William Glenesk has written: "Yours is the toughest meat in print since Upton Sinclair's *Jungle* or even the sharp pen of Jonathan Swift."

We must be doing *some*thing right.

We do things wrong, too. But perhaps not as wrong as some of our critics think. *Fact* has been called sensational—and, in a sense, it is. We publish articles about miscegenation, the pathologic personalities of many nuns and priests, the opinions psychiatrists have about a Presidential candidate who had two nervous breakdowns, the teratology of drugs purchased in supermarkets. We offer a forum to such cultural nonheroes as Stokely Carmichael, a dead communist named Robert Thompson, the leader of the Society for Sexual Freedom, and assorted John Birchites. Of course *Fact* is sensational. So were the muckraking magazines of the early 1900s.

Many of our critics seem to be people who think in clichés. A new magazine that treats sex and other taboo subjects frankly, that skins fatcats and scalps big-wigs, that stirs up trouble—well, it must be out for a fast buck, or it must be full of falsehoods, or it must be communist-inspired. The one thing that many of *Fact*'s critics seem to have in common is that they haven't read *Fact* Magazine very carefully.

But the longer any magazine exists, the more likely it will receive proper consideration. The same is true of individuals. In his young manhood, when Frank Lloyd Wright ran away with someone else's wife, he was a pariah. Decades later, when his hair had turned white and his architecture was at last being appreciated, he became a Grand Old Man. Even with time, *Fact* will never become part of the Establishment, but someday it may get a better press. The *New York Post* may lift its embargo on the mention of *Fact*'s name, *The New York Times* may write objective stories about us, and even *Time* Magazine—no, I almost got carried away.

This hostility is the burden of being a troublemaker. Orrin E. Klapp, professor of sociology at San Diego State College, points out in *Heroes, Villains, and Fools* that most Americans condemn five types of "villains": the flouter, the rogue, the rebel, the outlaw, and the troublemaker. The troublemaker's "typical mischiefs," Professor Klapp writes, "are to arouse discontent and conflict, disturb status, 'rock the boat,' and make a nuisance of himself. . . . He is the opposite of the smoothie and good Joe, doing the very things they would avoid." Whereas Americans seem to have conflicting feelings about flouters, rogues, outlaws, and rebels, they are virtually unanimous in their dislike of troublemakers. After all, it *is* painful to have to doubt and re-think one's cherished opinions and one's comfortable view of the world.

* * *

Fact owes a good deal of gratitude to many people. To its readers, of course. (Someone once sent us a letter saying, simply, "I appreciate what you are doing." Enclosed was a check for $500.) To Sloan Wilson, not only for the many fine articles he has favored us with, but for his unflagging encouragement and enthusiasm. And, naturally, to the employees—past and present—who have worked so hard: Iswar Subramanya, Rita Brenig, Miriam Fier, Paul Feingold, Marie Uddgren Sutton, Rufus Causer, Norman Moskowitz, Suzanne Aimes, Linda Broder, Barbara Quinn Smukler, Betty Feist, Arthur Whitman, Robert E. Lee, Henry Cojulun, Rosemary

Latimore, Myra Shomer, John Dempsey, and Sandy Russo.

Finally, a few words about *Fact*'s appearance. Herb Lubalin, voted Art Director of the Year not long ago by the National Society of Art Directors, and the man who art-directed *Eros*, was given carte blanche in designing *Fact*. He designed a magazine with large, easy-to-read print, together with an illustration facing every article—a splendid balance of art and text. He also originated the idea of assigning every issue to a different illustrator; using letters-to-the-editor as "fillers" after articles; and having the cover lines read out after the logos, "fact:". Mr. Lubalin's design has won the Award of Excellence from the Society of Publication Designers for both 1964 and 1965, and quite as flattering, his design has been imitated piccemeal and wholesale thoughout the publishing world.

Warren Boroson
NEW YORK, JANUARY, 1967.

Contents

the best of fact

Some Debatable Points in American Foreign Policy

By Arnold J. Toynbee

The Administration at Washington is showing signs that it resents criticism of its foreign policy, a foreign policy that is causing increased anxiety all over the world.

From an American's point of view, however, if the Administration is claiming the right to make life-and-death decisions in private, this is a new departure in American political life. The publication of political facts and the public discussion of political issues seem to be key parts of the American political tradition, and it seems improbable that the American people are going to renounce traditional rights that are of the essence of democracy.

But what about world opinion?

Probably there are many Americans, besides President Johnson and his advisers, who feel that United States policy is exclusively the American people's affair. This too is a traditional attitude, one not confined to the United States. It is bound up with the concept of local sovereign independence. A sovereign country has been held to have a right to go its own way as it chooses. But today every country in the world, including the most powerful, is dependent on the behavior of other countries. And this means that no country any longer has a moral right (if it ever had one) to act just according to its own sovereign will and power. And therefore an enormous degree of responsibility rests upon the two countries—the United States and the Soviet Union—that now possess effective atomic armaments. Deliberately to escalate a "conventional" war is knowingly to increase the risk of this rankling into an atomic war. And the threat of an atomic war legitimately concerns the whole human race.

Naturally, America's and Russia's allies and satellites would all try to jump clear of entangling alliances before any Russo-American duel started. And we would be morally justified, because we should have had no voice in the decisions that had led up to the catastrophe. We might or might not succeed in avoiding belligerency, but none of us could escape the damage that a Russo-American war would do. In other words, such a war would not be just a Russian and American catastrophe; it would be a world-wide catastrophe.

This is a point Americans ought to bear in mind if they find themselves resenting foreign criticism of the United States Government's policies. The 85% of the human race that are neither Russians nor Americans have the same life-and-death interest that the Russians and the Americans have in the consequences of Russian and American policy. And we do not even have a vote. The American voters do have a say, if only a rather small one, in decisions about their own fate. The rest of us have no say.

This is an intolerable position for human beings to find themselves in. It is bound to bring world-wide odium on the United States or the Soviet Union if either shows any inclination to abuse its life-and-death power. These two super-countries have a super-obligation to the rest of the human race to use their power responsibly. They have no right to claim exemption from criticism on the part of the unenfranchised 85% of mankind. Since we do not have the vote, the only way open to us of keeping some control over our fate is to exert some influence on the American and Russian governments and peoples.

The nonvoter can express his pique by sticking pins into Goliath between the joints of the giant's armor. This is President de Gaulle's way of expressing his feelings. He is adept at this. But it is childish self-indulgence, for a very likely response to this pin-sticking is the stiffening of the Administration's inclination to turn a deaf ear and to forge ahead. What the nonvoter must do is offer some alternate policy that is obviously preferable, and at the same time, obviously practicable.

The first thing that foreign critics of the Administration at Washington must try to do is put themselves in the Administration's shoes. Is the following account of the Administration's standpoint approximately correct?

President Johnson believes that the United States is confronted with a Communist movement, unitary and world-wide, that aims at converting the whole world to Communism—by force if persuasion does not succeed (and, in Mr. Johnson's view, no country has ever turned Communist voluntarily). This aggressive, monolithic Communism, the President believes, is making the war in South Vietnam. The people of South Vietnam are thought to be united in opposing the Communist attempt to subvert the anti-Communist regime in South Vietnam from outside. They are also thought to be united in wanting to remain separate from Communist North Vietnam. The United States, in intervening militarily in South Vietnam against the Vietcong guerrillas on the invitation of successive anti-Communist governments at Saigon, is (in President Johnson's view) defending freedom and self-determination and, in the process, doing something necessary for her own national security.

In opposing world-wide Communist aggression, President Johnson claims the right—at his country's own discretion and without first obtaining a mandate from the United Nations—to intervene militarily in any foreign country, anywhere, for either of two purposes: to keep *in* power an existing non-Communist government, or to keep *out* of power a government that, even if not itself Communist, might open the way for a Communist take-over.

If this account of President Johnson's views is approximately correct, he is claiming, in effect, that the only alternative to Communist domination of the world is American domination of the world. For the universal interest in opposing Communism (and, as President Johnson sees it, this is a universal interest) is identical with the United States' interest.

3

And if the two interests, together, justify the United States' present intervention in Vietnam, what country in the world can feel sure henceforward that it will not find the United States intervening in its domestic affairs as a result of a unilateral decision of the United States Government? Vietnam is a test case. For Vietnam is as remote from the United States as any spot on the earth can be. If the United States' presence in South Vietnam were to be replaced by a Communist regime there, and if all the rest of Southeast Asia as well were then to go Communist, the security of the United States would not be impaired—if the notion of security is interpreted in its traditional sense of security against an attack on one's own national territory.

* * *

The subversion of President Arbenz's regime in Guatemala by the United States in 1954, and the United States' opposition to Colonel Caamaño's regime in the Dominican Republic, suggest some home thoughts to an English mind. According to what seems to be President Johnson's doctrine, the government of a foreign country cannot justify its existence in the eyes of the United States Government merely by virtue of being constitutionally elected, or of being representative of a majority of its people, or of being non-Communist. It must be sufficiently anti-Communist to satisfy the United States Government that it will not serve unwittingly as a "Trojan Horse" for a Communist take-over. Now, President de Gaulle has stigmatized Britain as the United States' "Trojan Horse" for the take-over of Europe. But suppose President Johnson happened to form the opinion that Britain was playing the "Trojan Horse" role, *not* for the United States, but for Communism. Would the President then contemplate dictating to the British people which members of the Labor front bench might not be included in the membership of a Labor Government in Britain? Britain is not so close to the coasts of the United States as Santo Domingo is. However, Britain is very much closer to the United States than Vietnam, and she is also very much more important than Vietnam for the United States' military security. And though the idea of American intervention in Britain's internal affairs is at present chimerical, the disturbing feature about President Johnson's whole present policy is that it is *a policy of escalation without any foreseeable limit*.

Even as it is, President Johnson's claim to a right to intervene, as exemplified by the United States' present intervention in Vietnam and Santo Domingo, has already begun to produce something like a world-wide reversal of sympathies. People who previously thought President de Gaulle's denunciation of the United States ludicrously wide off the mark are now beginning to wonder whether de Gaulle, after all, may not have been prescient. People who have regarded the Soviet Union and China as archaggressors and bullies are now beginning to wonder whether the United States is becoming the world's No. 1 aggressor and bully.

In the United States today, there is a current of opinion which holds that America is in a position to do whatever she chooses in the world. Her military might, it is argued, is so overwhelmingly greater than the military might of all the other countries in the world put together that even the Soviet Union and, a fortiori, China would not dare challenge the United States by resort to arms, however much these powers might dislike what the United States was doing.

This doctrine is surely proved fallacious by experiences in our own lifetime. It was the German Government's line of reasoning before the outbreak of both the first and second world wars, and both times it proved fallacious. Germany's opponents were certainly conscious of her military superiority to them, and they certainly did yield to Germany once and then once again. But just because they had now yielded twice, they felt that they could not afford to yield a third time. Even the worm turns at last, and Germany's assumption that the worm would behave as before for any number of times running proved a miscalculation that, for Germany, was disastrous. In both world wars it was mighty Germany that went down to defeat. Her superiority in material armaments had been overwhelming, and yet this apparently decisive advantage was canceled out by unforeseeable and imponderable factors—and the most potent was the alienation of world opinion by Germany's reliance on her military might for arbitrarily imposing her will.

Before the American people advance any farther along this same forbidding road, it would be a wise precaution for them to re-examine the picture of the facts on which President Johnson's policy appears to be based.

* * *

Is there, in truth, a unitary world-wide Communist movement working methodically to make Communism prevail all over the globe? What *is* true is that the conversion of all mankind is one of Communism's official objectives. But the conversion of all mankind is one of the official objectives of Christianity, too (Christianity gave Communism the idea). And it is also one of the objectives of Islam and of Buddhism. On the other hand, these movements for the conversion of the world have rarely been centrally directed. Islam in its early days, and Communism before the Communists came into power in China, are examples of militant missionary movements under unitary control. But to maintain that there has been a monolithic Communist movement since China went Communist is fantastic.

Communist China and Communist Russia are not a monolithic bloc, any more than capitalist America and capitalist France are. Suppose that a Communist were to maintain that there is a unitary capitalist conspiracy to suppress Communism, and that de Gaulle's pretense of a feud with the United States is a piece of play-acting arranged between Washington and Paris in order to throw dust in the Communists' eyes. If a Communist were to tell us that, we would laugh. It is just as fantastic to believe that the Russo-China feud is a piece of shadow-boxing. It is a quarrel in deadly earnest, and this quarrel is one of the most important current international facts. China and Russia have quarreled because their views of their respective national interests have led them to pull in contrary directions. In this, human nature is uniform. Capitalists and Communists resemble each other in all being nationalists first and foremost.

To ignore this conflict between Communist China and Communist Russia is perverse; to base a policy on deliberate refusal to recognize an important fact is to ask for trouble. One of the unfortunate effects of the United States Government's present militant policy in Vietnam is that it is forcing Russia and China back into each other's arms. Washington is, in fact, doing its best to turn the imaginary bogy of Communist solidarity into a real menace. But there is still time to relax the present American pressure on Russia and China. And then they will certainly fly apart again, for nothing but American pressure is holding these two nationalist-minded Communist powers together now.

* * *

Then there is the thesis that the war in Vietnam is being made solely by Communist intervention from without. This does not explain the existence or the tenacity of the Vietcong. These guerrillas are not Russian or Chinese or North Vietnamese. They are South Vietnamese. And the cause for which they are fighting must be one they have very much at heart because they are accepting severe privations and heavy casualties. There is no mystery about what this cause is. The Vietcong South Vietnamese guerrillas are fighting for national liberation and national unity—causes for which other peoples, including Americans, have also fought stubbornly in the past.

For about 2000 years the Vietnamese resisted being dominated by the Chinese. For a hundred years they resisted being dominated by the French. Now they are resisting being dominated by the Americans. American intervention in Vietnam is not only preventing the South Vietnamese from expressing their national will and from establishing a regime that represents the majority of the people; American intervention is also preventing the two severed halves of Vietnam from uniting. And every partitioned nation wants to reunite.

In refusing to recognize that the Vietcong represents a national liberation movement made by the South Vietnamese themselves, and in attributing the war wholly to Communist intervention from outside, the United States is unintentionally

7

making herself the heir of European colonialism in Asia. While she believes herself to be opposing Communism in South Vietnam on behalf of freedom, she is actually opposing national self-determination there. This is colonialism. And American colonialism in Vietnam has begun in the way most of the now-liquidated European colonial empires started: By supporting an unrepresentative local government dependent on the colonial power because it would be overthrown if outside support were withdrawn.

In thus resuscitating colonialism, the United States is challenging one of the most powerful political forces in the present-day world—a force stronger than either Communism or capitalism. She is challenging the Asian, African, and Latin American determination—the majority of mankind's determination—to recover equality with the Western minority. This Western minority, for the last two or three centuries, has been able to dominate the majority thanks to its temporary lead in technology and therefore in weapons. But technological superiority is a wasting asset. The European ex-colonial powers have seen the red light and have cleared out. The United States has jumped in—and this at a stage in history when colonialism is no longer practical politics.

The present foreign policy of the United States Government is based on ignoring the Russo-China feud and on ignoring the true nature of the Vietcong. It is also based on ignoring China, and this is the third of America's refusals to face realities. It was possible to ignore China in the age of colonialism. It is no longer possible to ignore China, and China's destiny in Eastern Asia is as manifest as the United States's destiny is in the Western Hemisphere.

*   *   *

If one thinks that the United States' present policy is a mistaken one, based on a serious misreading of the facts, what policy suggests itself as an alternative? I will offer some suggestions at my peril.

First, I suggest that Americans discard the myth of a

8

monolithic Communist world conspiracy and, instead, deal realistically with each of the Communist countries. By this I mean taking account of their respective national interests—interests that often conflict as sharply as the interests of capitalist countries.

Second, I suggest that Americans recognize that the successive governments they have been supporting in Saigon are not representative of the wishes of the majority of the South Vietnamese people. They should now stand aside and allow self-determination in Vietnam to have free play—even if this leads, as it most certainly will lead, to the reunification of the two artificially sundered parts of Vietnam under a Communist regime. This would, anyway, come a good deal nearer to fulfilling the political wishes of the majority of the Vietnamese people than the present state of affairs in Vietnam does.

In the third place, I suggest that the United States confine her anti-Communist intervention in the internal affairs of foreign countries to cases where it is clear that a very great majority of the people are anti-Communist, and where the United States is invited to intervene by a local, stable government that clearly represents the majority of the people. Cases in point would be Canada, Australia, and New Zealand. If any of those three countries were to ask for American help against aggression by a Communist country—or by an aggressive non-Communist country, for that matter—the United States could come to their assistance without any misgivings whatsoever.

In the fourth place, I suggest that the United States not only recognize continental China but deal with her on a footing of absolute equality.

The chief obstacle to the making of the changes in American policy suggested above is, I believe, American pride. The American people, as well as their government, seem reluctant to admit making a mistake and paying for this mistake by accepting a reverse. This is, as I see it, a wrong kind of pride—a kind that is a symptom not of moral strength but of moral weakness. In private life, when someone will not face the truth that he has done wrong and must change his behavior, we do not admire him for his obstinacy. We judge that he is giving in to moral cowardice. And human psychology and morals are the same in public life as in private life.

Although President de Gaulle can be annoying, especially to the Americans and the British, he is a great man in spite of this. And one of his greatest and bravest acts was to stop the war in Algeria and to withdraw the French army without its having won a military victory over the Algerian nationalist forces—the counterparts, in Algeria, of the Vietcong. Has France lost or gained prestige by this act? It is undeniable that she has gained prestige. She has been admired for having had the strength to do a difficult thing because it was right.

But can the United States afford to take this risk? Suppose that she withdraws from Vietnam and does lose prestige by doing right—contrary to what happened to France when she withdrew from Algeria. My answer would be: America can take it. Her conscience will be clear. Her prestige can look after itself.

The Man Who Thinks Goldwater Is a Communist

By Ralph Ginzburg

Way out at the extreme right—and nearly invisible— end of the American political spectrum sits George Lincoln Rockwell, head of the American Nazi Party. From his perch, nearly everything appears to be tinged with red and tainted by Communism: the N.A.A.C.P., the United States Navy, even Barry Goldwater. To find out, firsthand, how the mind of an American extremist works, I phoned Rockwell from New York and arranged to interview him at his headquarters in Arlington, Virginia, the next day.

"Are you sure you can make it?" I asked. "Remember, it's Yom Kippur."

"Save your friendly hanky-panky for other Jew-Communists," he said. "Don't try to get friendly with *me.*"

Rockwell's retort surprised me. I had seen him described in newspapers as a harmless crackpot with a good sense of humor, and his reaction to my jest certainly did not fit that description. Anyway, I flew to Washington with my wife, Shoshana, took a cab to Arlington (which lies across the Potomac from the national capital), and arrived at 928 North Randolph Street, headquarters of the American Nazi Party. Across the face of the two-story white building a huge red sign shrieks, "White man, fight! Smash the black revolution!" Bullet holes in the sign and paint splatterings across the façade of the building give evidence that not everyone in Arlington relishes Rockwell's company.

My wife and I entered Rockwell's office, located just inside the front door. The 45-year-old Führer of the American Nazi Party was seated at his desk. He did not look up. I was immediately struck by his resemblance to Rudolf Hess. He had the same strong features, swarthy complexion, and wavy black hair.

"Hello there," I said, breaking the silence. Rockwell refused to greet me. Finally, after a few more moments of silence, Rockwell rose, signaled to a guard at the door, and, looking me square in the eye, said, "I want it clearly understood that I think you are *vile* and a *louse!*"

The guard shouted to the "barracks" up on the second floor (where Rockwell and his storm troopers live) and down came 12 burly young men in suntan uniforms, paratroop boots, and red, white, and black swastika armbands. My wife and I sat down across the desk from the Führer, and the storm troopers surrounded us. Rockwell ordered his aide—who had a remarkably pretty face and dainty mannerisms—to set up a tape recorder and he then asked me to sign a typewritten document stating that I would not distort his remarks, and would pay him $10,000 if I did. I signed it. (It also contained a guarantee that I would spell out at the beginning of my article that Rockwell "despised" me as "evil, vicious, and immoral.")

While Rockwell's aide was setting up the tape recorder, I examined the room. Its walls were painted jet black and the only source of light was a spotlight beaming down dramatically on Rockwell's fierce countenance. The room had no windows. The wall behind the Führer was covered by an enormous swastika banner and portraits of Hitler and George Washington. To the left stood a rostrum painted fire-engine red and festooned with swastikas. To the right was a shrine consisting of a badly painted oil portrait of Rockwell and three candles burning in red glasses. Beside the shrine a table was piled high with swastika gummed-stickers and photographs of Rockwell and the late Sen. Joseph R. McCarthy, along with pamphlets titled "Niggers! You Too Can Be a Jew!", "Martin Luther Coon—Black Puppet for Red Jews," and "The Diary of Ann Fink." The room's only exit was behind us. It was now blocked by Rockwell's henchmen. It was then, as my eyes traveled around the room, that I noticed that several of Rockwell's

14

storm troopers were armed with .45s and Lügers and that their Sam Browne belts contained rounds of ammunition. Turning my eyes to Rockwell, I spied a long truncheon lying across the top of his wastebasket, within easy grasp. I suddenly remembered reading an Anti-Defamation League report in which a Washington psychiatrist who had examined Rockwell was quoted as saying that, under certain conditions, Rockwell could become "extremely dangerous." Although I don't think I showed it, I began to feel apprehensive, like a Jew hauled into SS Headquarters in Nazi Germany. Also, I was angry with newspapermen who had described Rockwell as a "buffoon," "vaudevillian," "half-penny Hitler," and "ambulatory farce," when, in fact, it now was obvious that he took his Nazism with a frightening seriousness.

"We will proceed with the interview," Rockwell said as his aide indicated the tape recorder was operating. I thumbed a set of index cards containing questions that I had prepared the night before and it became clear that I would not be able to ask many that were sharply barbed. The threat of violence was too great. (Among my baited questions were: "Are you aware that psychologists believe Nazis have strong homosexual tendencies?" and "Do you find that the American Nazi Party attracts members of the lunatic fringe?") I selected questions less likely to provoke Rockwell and proceeded to interview him as follows:

Q: My first question, Mr. Rockwell, is why do you need all these storm troopers here?

A: I have no objection to them. I have no intention of saying anything to you in private. (*Addressing his storm troopers*) This man is *vile!* For the record, I want to state he publishes *Eros* magazine. He printed pictures of what looked like a Jewish lady, naked, hugging a black man. ("I happen to *know* he's vile," echoed one of the henchmen.) Well, that's why I wanted to have plenty of witnesses here when I talked to him.

Q: As you're probably aware, political surveys indicate that Barry Goldwater has a good chance of getting the Republican Presidential nomination. [This was before the Republican débâcle.] Do you feel Mr. Goldwater would make a good President?

A: Well, I think Mr. Goldwater is more dangerous as President than Khrushchev. If Khrushchev were President everybody would *know* we had a Communist President. Everybody would be on his guard, ready to struggle and fight. But if Goldwater gets in there all the so-called conservatives would relax and say, "Well, thank God. Now we've got one of our people in there," when all the while a Communist would be running the government. This is just like having a firebug in as fire chief . . . a *secret* firebug. Goldwater will betray us.

Q: How?

A: I think he will betray us on the race question. Mr. Goldwater is pro-Negro and pro-Jewish. He *is* Jewish. [In point of fact Goldwater is an Episcopalian, but his father was Jewish.] And when people see how Goldwater deals with the Negroes —just the way Truman did, and just the way Ike did, and Roosevelt did—they'll be *disgusted*. That's the only reason I granted you this interview, vile as you are. I want to go on record, as publicly as I can, as blasting Goldwater, the phony, with everything I've got.

Q: Then you think Goldwater has the coming election sewed up?

A: Oh, no. I'm talking about 1968. The Jews have Goldwater set up this time as a straw man to show the nation repudiates conservatism.

Q: Then how do you explain Goldwater's present popularity?

A: It's a phony popularity, built up by Jew millionaires. They first started grooming Goldwater by having Walter Reuther blast him. Now all the reactionaries who don't like welfare programs and who want to keep their money are backing Goldwater 'cause they think he'll save their money. That's what Goldwater people are mostly after, money.

Q: You mean that Mr. Reuther is really a shill for Goldwater?

A: Yes.

Q: Mr. Rockwell, I am sure you're aware that many people

16

would automatically believe the opposite of anything you say—

A: (*interrupting*) There's a lot of 'em—and Robert Welch of the John Birchers is one of them!

Q: Okay. Well, now I ask you, do you think people will say that by opposing Goldwater publicly *you*, like Reuther, are privately trying to win votes for him?

A: Yes, some people will accuse me of working for the Jews and Communists, and Barry *Morris* Goldwater, but that's why I'm so careful with you here, to be sure there's witnesses, so my true views will be known. I *hate* Goldwater! (*Pounds fist on desk*) Before one of his rallies in New York some of our pickets got him all shook up with our anti-Semitic pamphlets. So he jumped up in Madison Square Garden and said, "I never heard of a Jew who wasn't a patriot!" And some of my guys hollered, "How about the Rosenbergs?" And he hasn't got over that one yet.

Q: Would you care to comment on Harry Golden's statement that "I always knew the first Jewish President would be an Episcopalian"?

A: Well, I think every Jew in the country has a little place in his heart for Goldwater. He figures if the far side has got to get in, let's have it one of our boys. It's pretty clever. The Jews' motto is, "If you can't beat 'em, lead 'em." And that's what they're doing in running Goldwater.

Q: How about other Republican contenders? Has Rockefeller sold out for Jewish money?

A: Ohhh! He's *crawling* with it! Rockefeller has got Javits behind him and that whole gang!

Q: Do you think Rockefeller's divorce will cost him the nomination?

A: Through magazines such as your *Eros* our nation has become so perverted and depraved that I don't think it will make any difference at all. Nobody cares about morals any more. It's considered square now to be moral and clean.

Q: Mr. Rockwell, as you probably know, Senator Jacob Javits, who is a Jew, has written an article for *Esquire* pointing

17

out the tremendous advantages in foreign relations that would accrue to the United States if we elected a Negro President . . .

A: Ho, ho, ho, ho. Well thank gosh. . . . Go ahead . . . Ha, ha, ha, ha . . .

Q: . . . and also, I understand that the Jewish-owned publishing firm of Simon and Schuster has commissioned Jewish author Irving Wallace to write a novel about America's first Negro President—

A: Well, go to it! I hope they do. I hope they have a big hooknosed Jew right on the frontispiece so people will see who's pushing this Negro President idea.

Q: Do you see this as part of a plot?

A: Certainly it's a plot. The Jews have never yet been masters of any nation that's been of the pure, white, Nordic, Aryan race. They're always the Number Two people. The only time they can become masters is to become the man behind the throne. That's why they want a Negro on the throne, so they can tell him what to do.

Q: Well now, in just these few minutes you've knocked an awful lot of men in public life—

A: They need to be knocked! They're cowards! They all should be standing up and fighting for the white race! But not one of them will!

Q: May I finish my question?

A: Shoot.

Q: Is there anyone in public life whom you would regard as worthy of the Presidency?

A: There's only one living American fit to fill the office of President of the United States.

Q: Who's that?

A: Me.

Q: Why do you feel you are qualified?

A: Because I'm not a politician. I'm not afraid to go to jail. We've had a whole bunch of Southern governors that said they'd go to jail before there'd be any Negroes in the schools. There's Negroes in all the schools now and there's not a single Southern governor in jail. And if it comes to going to jail, the

18

people know I have been there before for what I believe in and I'll go there again.

Q: Do you expect to be elected?

A: Yes, in 1972, after Goldwater gives the people a dose of the same form of watered-down Communism they're getting now. Then there'll be no place left for the people to turn to except the American Nazi Party. We'll make it in 1972, after one dose of Goldwater. Goldwater is my ticket to the White House.

Q: Will you run for any other office first?

A: I will be elected Governor of the State of Virginia in 1966. Then I will have power to buy television time. And when George Lincoln Rockwell speaks on TV in front of a swastika I will be heard all over the United States and the world. I'll have the biggest audience ever assembled in the history of mankind!

As Rockwell was delivering this pronouncement, a fat young lady, whose arms and legs were covered with welts, broke through the cordon of storm troopers, approached the nonplussed Führer, and said, "For the record, I would like to say that I admire and respect you, Mr. Rockwell." "Well, I appreciate that very much, ma'am," Rockwell replied, his face reddening slightly. "Let the record show that I think you're *great* . . . I *love* you!" The girl then extended her arms to embrace the Führer. "Now wait, wait. Hold it a minute, please," Rockwell sputtered. "This is an interview. I don't want to have anybody else in on this. If you're going to be here, please be silent. Mr. Ginzburg is a guest and he deserves that much courtesy, vile as he is." The girl then pressed several dollar bills into the hand of Rockwell's aide and tiptoed from the room in an ecstatic trance. "She just came in to visit; I don't even know who she is," Rockwell abjured. "Let's continue."

I then asked Rockwell to describe his life in politics, and he said that for ten years he had been affiliated with such organizations and publications as, reading from Left to Right, William F. Buckley's *National Review* (which Rockwell said he helped to found), the National States' Rights Party, the

American Federation of Conservative Organizations, Russell Maguire's *American Mercury* magazine, the National Committee to Free America from Jewish Domination, the United White Party, and, finally, the American Nazi Party, which Rockwell started in November, 1958. Rockwell said he makes about 50 personal appearances each year on campuses, picket lines, and at rallies. Sometimes, he said, his appearances lead to "mob violence." As for finances, Rockwell said his party was supported by small contributions and by proceeds from the sale of Nazi literature. The annual budget of the American Nazi Party ran to $20,000, he said. I asked Rockwell to define the aims of his party. He said they were to preserve, protect, and defend the white race. He said that surveys by his storm troopers indicate that his election to the Presidency in 1972 is a certainty. The best way to find out what people believe is in bars on Saturday nights when they get brave on beer, he said, and at such times they invariably denounce "race-mixing" and say that the only person left to vote for is Rockwell. Once in the White House, he said, he would obliterate every last trace of Franklin and Eleanor Roosevelt, even burning Eleanor Roosevelt commemorative stamps and melting down F.D.R. dimes. As for Negroes, Rockwell said he would ship them all to Monticello, New York, "to crawl all over the Jews there, who are the most loathsome Jews I have ever encountered anywhere." He expressed disdain for the N.A.A.C.P., which he said was Communist-infiltrated, but said he admired Elijah Muhammad, and the Black Muslims for their policies of apartheid. Asked whether men or women were attracted to his organization in greater numbers, Rockwell said, "Men, because women are not political animals—except Jewish women."

My wife then asked Rockwell what he thought of Hitler's having murdered six million Jews.

A: Ha! You want to tell me about those six million kikes who were supposed to've been gassed? [Rockwell's tone was even more hostile to my wife than it had been to me.] That's the funniest . . . that's the biggest bunch of boloney that has ever been put out.

Q: (by Mrs. Ginzburg) And you never met a concentration-camp victim?

A: I have gotten figures from the Jews that show here that it's mathematically *impossible* for Hitler to have gassed six million Jews . . . or five million . . . or four million . . . or even three million. It's absolutely *impossible!* That whole story was put out by Jews who control show business.

Q: (by Mrs. Ginzburg) You regard Jews as inferior beings?

A: Unhappily, no. I think they're superior. I think Jews, in terms of intellect, are a superior race. They're smarter. They outsmart our people left and right all the time. They've been doing it for thousands of years. They're smart people. They're brilliant. But our people have something that the Jews *don't* have, and this is the main difference between racial, loathsome Jews like yourselves and people like me. And that is *idealism.* Jews just can't believe people are willing to die for something, for an idea. They just can't understand that.

Q: (by Mrs. Ginzburg) Do you intend to exterminate all Jews when you become President?

A: No, not all Jews. Only the ones that are traitors.

Q: (by Mrs. Ginzburg) How many is that?

A: Only about 80 per cent.

Q: (by Mrs. Ginzburg) Are there any Aryan traitors?

A: Of course! Because a man is a white, Protestant American doesn't mean he's automatically to be trusted. Take Alger Hiss. He's worse than any kike traitor. A Jew when he's a Communist is at least fighting for his race. I have that much respect for him. But a Gentile who fights for Communism is not even fighting for his own. He is nothing but a white Gentile swine!

I then asked Rockwell about his personal life. He said he was born in Bloomington, Illinois, on March 9, 1918. His father, vaudeville star "Doc" Rockwell, is still living but refuses to have anything to do with him, Rockwell said. The Führer was raised and educated in Maine, completed two years at Brown University, entered the Navy as a pilot during World War II, rose to the rank of Commander, and was later booted out of the Naval Reserve because of his Nazi activities. Rockwell expressed great bitterness over this and blamed Commu-

21

nists and Jewish War Veterans for it. After World War II, Rockwell said, he knocked around as a printer, cartoonist, and advertising copywriter, unable to hold a job for very long and failing in several business ventures "because power-hungry partners squeezed me out." Rockwell said he had been twice married, twice divorced, and was the father of seven children. He freely admitted having been a poor provider. He said he loved his children and wives—particularly his second wife— "but in ordinary, everyday responsibilities, such as earning a living, I am a positive flop, and this makes me difficult to live with. I am only interested in the extraordinary, in the things that most people consider 'impossible.' Only when faced with enormous challenges do I become deeply interested. The driving force of my life has been a deep satisfaction in defying overwhelming odds." As Rockwell talked about his personal life it became clear to me that, when off the subject of Nazism, he was a human being.

Rockwell handed me a copy of his recently published autobiography, *This Time the World*. He said it had been modeled after *Mein Kampf* and had been put out by a New York firm called Parliament House. (I later learned that there was no such firm and that Rockwell had laboriously turned the book out himself on a small offset press, gluing and binding copies together by hand with the aid of his storm troopers.)

Rockwell was called out of the room to take a "confidential" long-distance telephone call and I perused *This Time the World*. I was impressed by the candor of several passages. The first, on page 95, described the night of Rockwell's first wedding, at the Statler Hotel in Boston, in April, 1943. The sight of a negligée and contraceptives in his wife's valise, when she opened it, greatly upset him:

I wound up crying—and so did she. I struggled out of the room and spent hours loading up on beer in the Silver Dollar Bar, and trying to understand what was wrong with the world.

The second passage—which I found interesting mainly because it tended to support Freud's thesis that homosexuality and anti-Semitism are intertwined—appears on page 128:

At the risk of being accused of fruity tendencies, I must insist that, as a work of straight art, the well-muscled male figure is far superior to that of the blubbery-looking female.

The third passage described Rockwell's intense passion for Hitler. It appears on page 308, just after Rockwell tells how he was "cruelly" abandoned by his second wife:

I went to the post office one morning and found a big carton waiting for me. It was from James K. Warner, one of my first supporters. Inside I found, lovingly folded, a huge Nazi flag, eighteen feet long.

I went home and hung the beautiful banner completely across the living-room wall. In the center, I mounted a plaque of Adolf Hitler. Then I placed a small book-case under it, and set three candles to burning in front, to make a holy altar to Adolf Hitler.

I closed the blinds, lit the candles, and stood before my new altar. For the first time I experienced the soul-thrilling upsurge of emotion which is denied to our modern, sterile, atheist "intellectual" but which literally moved the earth for countless centuries: "religious experience." I stood there in the flickering candlelight, not a sound in the house, not a soul near me or aware of what I was doing—or caring.

But as I looked at the stern face of the greatest mind in twenty centuries, I felt the unbelievable flood of "religious" power pouring into me which would be easily understood by an Indian savage standing on a mountain top at sunrise and communing with the Great Spirit before battle—but which the intellectuals have denied themselves because of their conceit that they can "know" everything.

I was moved beyond the power of words to describe. Goosepimples rose all over me, my hair stood on end, my eyes filled with tears of love and gratitude for this greatest of all conquerors of human misery and shame, and my breath came in little gasps. If I had not known that the Leader would have scorned such adulation, I might have fallen to my knees in unashamed worship—but instead I drew myself to attention, raised my arm in the eternal salute of the ancient Roman legions, and repeated the holy words, "HEIL HITLER!"—meaning every tiny syllable with all my heart and mind and soul.

Rockwell returned from his telephone call in the next room and I continued with my questions as follows:

Q: Mr. Rockwell, it has been said that two-thirds of the world live by the tenets of three Jews: Karl Marx, Sigmund Freud, and Jesus Christ—

A: (*angrily*) The hell they do! That's a lot of boloney. They may go around mouthing such beliefs, but they don't really believe in them. Take Jesus Christ. First of all, I think he was a myth. I have never met anybody that I would call a Christian. I couldn't understand that boloney when I was a kid and they took me to church. These people would tell me how to believe in all this morality stuff and they wouldn't do it themselves.

Q: You are an atheist?

A: No, an agnostic. I think an atheist and a religious person are both conceited. The Christian says, I have examined the entire universe and I find that the only true religion is this. And the atheist says, *I* have examined the universe and there ain't no God. And I don't think you can make either one of those statements. I think both of them are conceited. My statement is, I don't know. I don't know how I got here and I don't know where I'm going, or if I'm going anyplace.

Q: Mr. Rockwell, what do you regard as the purpose of life?

A: . . . The purpose of life . . . (*Rockwell paused, for the first time during the interview*) . . . is to struggle as hard as you can for what you believe in . . . and to enjoy the struggle. I'm a Dionysian. I believe life *is* struggle. Even to stand up is a struggle against gravity. I think that the joy of life is in the struggle itself. You've got to find fun in the fight to live.

Q: And there are no pure, unalloyed joys?

A: Even the joy of thinking, the effort to avoid chaos, is a struggle.

Q: Do you believe that there can be a positive relation between two human beings called love?

A: Certainly. I have experienced it.

Q: And you find love a struggle, too?

A: Indeed. It's a struggle to control yourself and to systematize your emotions so that you don't hurt the person you love with things that you can't help sometimes doing.

Q: Do you believe man is inherently hurtful?

A: People are not inherently bad. When they do bad things it is usually because they are afraid and they lash out wildly and foolishly like a terrified cat, scratching and biting everything in sight.

24

I decided to end the interview with that observation, but could not resist getting in one last, slightly-loaded question.

Q: Mr. Rockwell, is it possible that in refusing to have your storm troopers leave this room during our interview, and in keeping a truncheon by your side, and in berating all Jews and me personally, that perhaps you are lashing out wildly and foolishly like a terrified cat—as a result of your own insecurities and fears?

A: Let's not be absurd, you wretch.

Q: I have no more questions.

* * *

The interview over, I quickly packed my notes into my attaché case, eager to leave. Rockwell's inflammatory words had worked his storm troopers into a state of near-frenzy. They stared at my wife and me transfixed. "You can *smell* they're Jewish," one muttered to another. Had he chosen to do so, Rockwell could have brought his men pouncing down on us with a snap of his fingers. Although it may not be evident from the transcript, Rockwell is a master at appealing to man's baser emotions. He is an exceptionally forceful speaker and his phrases ring with conviction. That his "facts" may be cock-eyed, that his logic may be nonexistent, that his delusions of grandeur may be colossal, that, as has been chanted at some of his rallies, he may be "Sick! Sick! Sick!," is all beside the point. The fact is that George Lincoln Rockwell is a formidable and frightening figure. Newspapers that continue to portray him as a harmless clown are doing our country a great disservice. I was angry for the mistaken impression they had given me. It seemed clear to me that, given the kind of panic that gripped the nation during the McCarthy era only ten years ago, George Lincoln Rockwell could rise to power. The old alarmist phrase "It *can* happen here!" kept running through my mind and I had just met the man who could make it happen.

A Psychiatric View of the Cold War

By Benjamin Spock, M.D.

People ask me why a children's doctor is working for disarmament. My answer is that I think it's no longer enough to protect children just from ordinary diseases and stresses—other dangers loom greater now. And if we do not help reduce these new dangers, our children and grandchildren will either grow up in an increasingly fearful world, or will be destroyed in a nuclear disaster.

Nowadays the chance of a 1-year-old's being killed by disease or accident before reaching the age of 21 is less than 1½%. Does anyone think that the risk of nuclear destruction —through brinkmanship or insanity or mistake—is as small as 1½%? True, we've survived 21 years of the atomic age. But the weapons are still being piled up—bombs on planes, missiles on submarines, land-based missiles—and the danger keeps increasing in proportion. And now China, which is much more belligerent and much less fearful of the consequences of atomic war than Russia and the United States, is also producing these weapons.

But I want to concentrate on the emotional consequences of Cold War tension, because I believe that unless this tension is reduced our children's outlook on life will be more and more distorted and their ability to see where America's best interests lie, when they become adults, will be greatly impaired.

Several recent studies have shown how much our children are troubled by Cold War anxieties. Between 25% and 50% of them, in different schools, believe there *will* be a nuclear attack. The younger ones worry about being separated from their parents in a disaster and about the death or maiming of

27

their parents or themselves. Adolescents speak with bitterness about the possibility of having no future, or of giving birth to deformed children. Some of them ask, "What is the use of studying hard?" More disturbing to me are the evidences of an unwholesome, passive fear of the malevolence of Communists. A fifth-grade class, for instance, was looking at pictures of the Russian countryside. One picture showed a tree-lined road. A child asked what the trees were for, and two other children made prompt suggestions. One said, "So that the people can't see what's going on on the other side of the road." The other said, "To make work for the prisoners." These are morbidly suspicious attitudes for children to be acquiring.

We have instilled into past generations of American children the belief that they could cope with whatever life offered, and as a result they have usually succeeded; we've brought them up with a natural confidence in their ability to deal with all kinds of people, and they've impressed the world with their assurance and friendliness. But if increasing numbers are now going to reach adulthood believing that Communists are supernaturally clever, evil people who are likely to outwit us and destroy us, they will end up with impaired personalities. They won't be able to think positively about what they and America should be doing to solve the world's problems. They'll be less effective at their jobs. An unstable leader will find it easy to lead them into war. They will be ready to be stirred up into a wholesale suspiciousness of fellow-Americans far worse than what occurred in the McCarthy period.

* * *

I believe that when we teach our children modern history, at home and in our schools, we should certainly tell them about the unprincipled and aggressive actions of the Communist nations, including their annexation or occupation of neighboring states, their brutal suppression of the Hungarian revolt, and so forth. But I think we should deliberately avoid alarmist phrases like "world-wide conspiracy to destroy us," which imply much more unity, power, and ferocity among the Communist nations than exists, phrases intended to arouse fear and hate. We should always be careful to interpret the actions of Communist nations in the *least* alarmist way possible—not to be generous toward them, but to give our children the confidence that we will be able to understand our adversaries; to deal with them in the future as we have in the past; and even reach mutually advantageous agreements with them.

I'd let our children realize that capitalist nations too have sometimes annexed their neighbors in the past, under the delusion that this would make their borders more secure. I think it will help our children become realistic voters and provident leaders if they know that part of the aggressiveness of the Soviet Union and China is due to fear, brought about by the long hostility of many capitalist nations; if they know that the United States, with her World War I allies, even intervened on the White Russian side in 1918–20, before the Russian revolution was over; if they know that the United States refused to recognize the new government for a decade and a half.

It's reassuring and educational for children to hear about the peaceful intentions of the Russians, to learn that the Russians feel so urgently the need to avoid major wars (barring "wars of liberation") that they have split the Communist world down the middle on this issue. I would tell my children and grandchildren that my friends who have been to the Soviet Union have found the ordinary people and the professional people almost universally friendly—despite decades of anti-American propaganda—and a lot more friendly, in fact, than the people of some of the countries allied with us. I'd tell them how the Russians gave the piano prize to Van Cliburn, and how they cheered for *Porgy and Bess* and for the Oberlin Choir.

To keep our children's fears to a sensible minimum is only half—the negative half—of the Cold War problem. Children, like adults, function better during stress when they see a positive course of action and can participate in it, preferably side-by-side with their parents. And there is no lack of goals to strive for. In school and at home they should hear and talk about the gradual expansion of the peace-keeping functions of the United Nations, and of the proposals for strengthening it

29

until it becomes a world government. With their teachers and parents they should take a personal interest in plans for disarmament and for East-West political agreements.

They also should recognize America's responsibility for helping the underdeveloped regions of the earth out of their poverty and chaos. And they should learn that even in our own country, with all its luxuries, there are expanding areas of blight, in mining areas and in the centers of our cities, where chronic unemployment produces poverty, disorganization of families, neglect of education, and unfitness for the jobs that are available—a vicious spiral downward that shows no signs of being checked and that will destroy the fabric of our society through rot or riot if we don't find solutions.

In our adults we have already seen some of the results of the fear and suspicion of Communists that we are imbuing in our children. At the extreme end of the scale are the paranoid haters who think there are subversives even in the Supreme Court and in the White House. In a milder form, this distortion of reality—in which we see the Communist nations as always in the wrong and ourselves as always in the right—has already affected a lot of us and hurt our country. It is an example of a general human mechanism latent in all of us: to excuse ourselves from uncomfortable guilt by blaming others. In a number of international situations, this distortion has misled us into policies that were intended to be anti-Communist but which have alienated our allies and the neutrals and have hurt us more than our adversaries.

More dangerous still is the paranoid mechanism by which we manage to *deny* the hatred we feel for our adversary. We project it all onto *him*. We see him as hating and threatening us. We cling to this self-deception because it allows us to retaliate without guilt. Then, when our hostility begins to provoke him into countermeasures, we welcome this as evidence we were right in suspecting him in the first place! This is a deadly pattern that keeps escalating suspicion and animosity. We've seen it played out endlessly between the United States and the Soviet Union, and between the United States and China.

30

Still another source of danger is the denial of the danger itself. In medicine it often happens that when there is a threat of death or permanent disability, the patient and his family are unable to face up to the truth. They don't hear what the physician says, or they brush aside his warning. Instead they displace all their anxiety onto some minor condition and keep asking treatment for *that*.

Most of us, I think, succeed in ignoring the appalling nuclear dangers that surround us. We focus instead on the immediate Communist threats in such areas as Berlin and Southeast Asia. We don't face the terrifying fact that the present accumulation of weapons and mutual suspicion makes it quite possible that one act of miscalculation or fanaticism will destroy our world. We didn't see the tens of thousands of burned corpses in Hiroshima and Nagasaki, nor the other tens of thousands dying with vomiting and diarrhea.

Another source of danger is the relationship between the head of a state and the people. A leader who may be quite mature in his ordinary dealings may, when feeling threatened in an international crisis, announce an inflexible determination to impose his will on the adversary. This is partly his fear of being considered timid, which is ingrained in every male beginning at the age of 3 and which automatically colors his actions the rest of his life. But for a leader, the compulsion to appear strong is enormously magnified: He must try to intimidate the officials of the other country, he must show his own people that he is up to the task of protecting them, he must prove to the political opposition at home that he is not guilty of softness. Even Nehru, who preached to the world the absolute evil of the use of force, yielded to the fear of seeming weak by sending his army into Goa.

Equally dangerous is the inclination of the majority of people of any country to surrender their moral judgment to their leader. They assume his course is right because he *is* the chief, just the way children feel about their parents.

And once the officials of a government have publicly committed themselves to a policy, it is hard for them, as it may

31

not be hard for honest individuals, to admit they are wrong. They may change the policy if there is a good excuse. But better to risk disaster than confess a real mistake.

* * *

Part of the explanation for our present predicament, then, lies in some primitive aspects of human nature. Another part, I believe, comes from the insensitive and cocky aspects of our American character.

We Americans have strengths in our national character —resourcefulness, flexibility, friendliness, and a spirit of co-operation with each other—that help account for our extraordinary progress. But we have faults too.

Most of us are insensitive to the feelings of people unlike ourselves. We robbed and betrayed the Indians. We treated badly wave after wave of immigrants. We've continually abused and humiliated Negroes.

We have also taken pride in our lawlessness. In some frontier regions the individual relied entirely on his own pistols; vigilantes dispensed justice. Our fascination with violence has persisted right up to the present. Our adults and children have watched brutality on television for two decades without having enough; the proportion of war toys in our stores keeps increasing; our rates of crime and delinquency show no sign of leveling off after 20 years of steady rise. Lynchings, the bombings of Negro churches, the kind of hatred and obscenity spewed out in court by the attorney for the man tried for the murder of Mrs. Liuzzo in Alabama would be inconceivable in any other nation calling itself civilized. So would the cheering of some school children when President Kennedy's assassination was announced. We Americans must face the disturbing fact that we are only half-civilized in these respects. This is particularly dangerous for the country that is the world's mightiest.

European nations, having all been defeated in wars as often as they've won, have been chastened of any delusion of omnipotence. We have won all *our* wars, and this seems to have convinced many of us that we are not only unbeatable, but that this is because we are always *right*.

We are not good losers. In the Olympic games a few years ago, when the Russians first began to beat us by the official system of scoring, our sports writers emphasized the American scoring method—to keep us ahead. When the Russian sputniks first went up, our officials sneered at them as unimportant playthings. It is revealing to read in newspapers these days the letters to the editor that state, "We must teach the Communists a lesson in Vietnam," or "We should clean up the mess in Cuba," as if no one's wishes count but ours, as if we have the right and the ability to impose them by force.

Until a few years ago, America's influence in the world was always in the ascendancy. Whatever we set our minds to—whether it was expanding our exports, helping to win wars, developing the atomic bomb, rehabilitating Europe with the Marshall Plan—we accomplished. But in recent years we've run into repeated conflicts with the Communists, and sometimes we have had to be satisfied with stalemates. In certain psychological respects, we have reacted neurotically to these setbacks. Instead of calmly pursuing the course that would serve our longtime aims, we have seemed obsessed with the fear of what the Communists would do to us. A more disturbing reaction, to me, is that of the citizens, editors, and legislators whose only recommendation is more suspicion, more threats to the opponents, more arms.

Why has America been so much more fearful of Communism than European nations that have been closer to it? Why are so many of us ready to launch a holy war against any Communists anywhere in the world? I don't know all the reasons. But I can see that we are reaping the harvest from the suspicions sowed for years by politicians like McCarthy, who built their careers this way, by the House Un-American Activities Committee, by the FBI, by the publishers who advocate belligerence as the solution for all foreign problems.

* * *

Now our government has succumbed to such an unhealthy distortion of reality that it imagines dangers that don't exist, fails to see actual dangers that are truly serious, and creates dangers that never needed to be. It violates international agreements, jeopardizes the very existence of the United Nations, alienates its allies, antagonizes the neutral nations, and is ready to attack or intervene in any small country by which it feels threatened. Our country has become like a bull that will lower its head and charge—without discrimination, without insight, without even an elemental sense of where its self-interest lies—whenever it thinks it sees Red. In various parts of the world its actions are being compared with the suppression of the Hungarian revolt. What a disgrace for the country of Washington and Lincoln!

Now, I'm all for standing up firmly to Communist bullying when our cause is just. I believe that we had to go to war when the North Koreans invaded South Korea, and that we had to be ready for war during the arbitrary threats to Berlin. But it is necessary to explain to people that there is a profound psychological difference between firmness and hostility. In civilian life this shows up with particular clarity in rehabilitation work with a juvenile delinquent. If one submits timidly to his unreasonable demands, this only makes him more of a bully. The real job consists in offering him friendship, recognizing his legitimate human needs and helping him to satisfy them, and showing appreciation of his good qualities. Any person will respond to acceptance with a somewhat greater degree of cooperation. Then successive layers of mutual confidence can be built up, though this takes a long time. But if the rehabilitation worker is too insecure to trust himself or his patient, if he angrily loses his head when frustrated, if he becomes chronically hostile, he not only fails to help his aggressive patient but he stirs up new waves of suspicion and belligerence. The same principles are the basis of good or bad relationships in the family, in the community, and in international affairs. In dealings between nations, just as between neighbors, we must recognize that belligerence provokes belligerence, friendliness creates

34

friendliness, trust builds trust. As Lincoln said, "The best way to destroy an enemy is to make a friend."

Then too, I believe that a very basic reason why this Administration's foreign policy has gone wrong—unlike its domestic policies—is that the high officials of the State and Defense Departments and the C.I.A. have conceived of our relations with the Communist nations as essentially a cold-blooded game of power politics to be played in terms of armed forces and weapons, threats and bluffs. It has ignored such human matters as people's loyalty to leaders who seem to share their aspirations, and their resentment against foreign intervention. Our government must think about *people,* feel for *people,* act for the benefit of *people*—in Vietnam, in all parts of Latin America, all over the world. It sounds simple. It could be simple.

The path to the salvation of the world can be defined more simply still. Christ said: Love thy neighbor. That means stop killing. It means stop hating. It means stop the hypocrisy of saying our hearts bleed for the poor people of Vietnam while we bomb their homes and bridges, burn their fields, and kill and maim them and their children. They have done nothing to us to deserve this barbaric cruelty.

Yet the obstacles sometimes appear overwhelming. America, unlike the Soviet Union, has the industrial capacity to maintain a high average standard of living, pile up arms, and still have unemployment and underutilization of plants. It is the job of the armed services, the Atomic Energy Commission, and the Central Intelligence Agency to always be pessimistic about the adequacy of our power. Industry, along with labor, now has a tremendous stake in more and newer weapons, as President Eisenhower himself has warned. Congressmen and Senators are concerned not only with defense itself, but with defense contracts for local industries. The press is also sensitive to the need of local industry for defense contracts. These one-sided pressures all converge on the President in particular, and on Congress.

Who is to speak up for those who believe there could be

greater safety and a better future in a vigorous pursuit of disarmament and accommodation? Only the citizens who feel moved to do so. And it seems unlikely that they will prevail unless they can convince a majority that this course is the wise one.

* * *

Today, I believe our country is in greater danger than at any other time in its existence. Our ruthless disregard for the rights of other nations—as evidenced in Vietnam—is earning us animosity throughout the world. And all of us will continue to be partly responsible until we can bring this madness to an end. If each of us will voice his displeasure now, and every time there is news of escalation, we will eventually make an impression on the officials who are leading us step by step to destruction.

We may not have time to wait until a new generation of healthy Americans can bail us out of our difficulties.

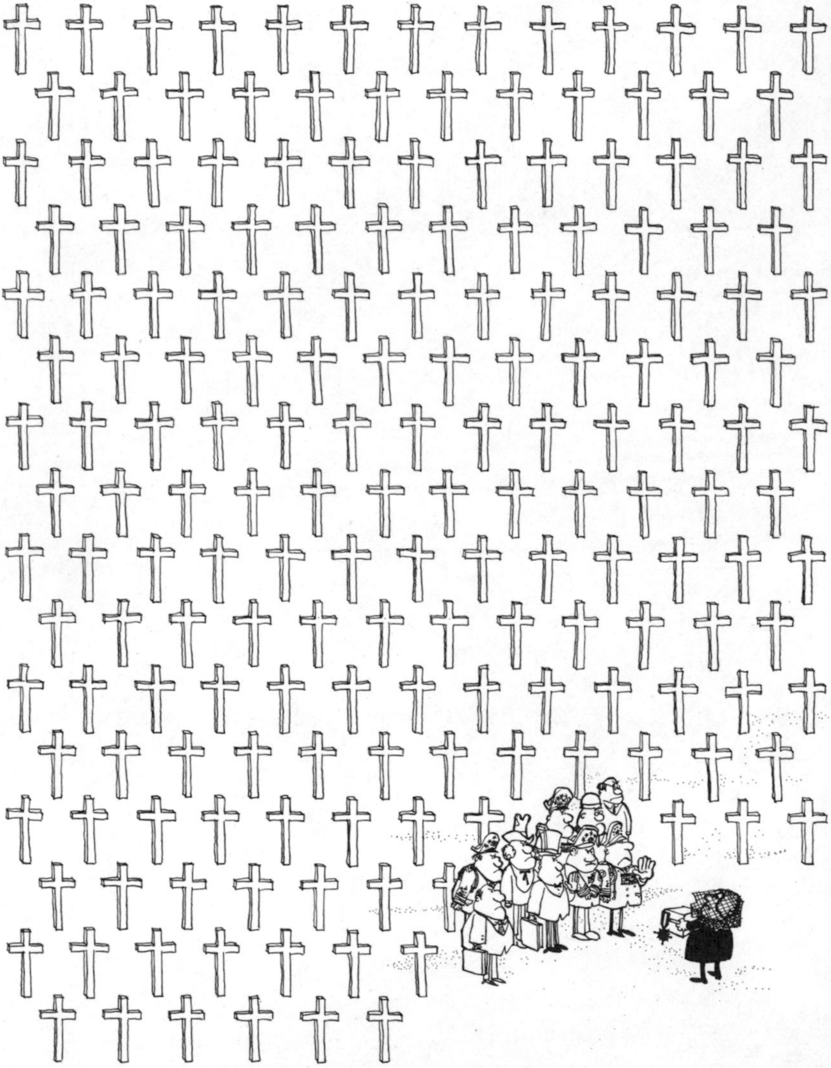

My Husband, the Communist

By Sylvia Thompson

y husband, Robert Thompson, died of a coronary occlusion at the age of 50 in our Manhattan apartment on Saturday morning, Oct. 16, 1965. Bob was a veteran of World War II and had won the Distinguished Service Cross, which is second only to the Congressional Medal of Honor, so it seemed to me fitting that he be buried in Arlington National Cemetery, in Washington. I asked the funeral director to send an application there, and over 2 months later, on January 14, approval came through. Bob's ashes would be buried on January 30. The urn was delivered to the cemetery, and I made plans to drive from New York to Washington for the interment.

On January 24, after lunch, I returned to my office in downtown Manhattan, where I work as a secretary, and was told that a Mr. Alfred Fitt had phoned, and wanted me to return his call. I was just sitting down to do that when the phone rang. It was Mr. Fitt, and he identified himself as the general counsel for the Department of the Army. Politely and coldly he informed me that the scheduled burial of my husband had been postponed. The Justice Department, he said, wanted to reconsider whether my husband was entitled to burial in a national cemetery.

I hadn't expected this, but I knew immediately what was going on. My husband was a Communist—a member of the party's national board and a leader of its New York organization. A news item reporting that Bob was going to be buried in Arlington had been published in the *Worker,* the Communist newspaper, and apparently had been seen by professional Communist-baiters. A Southern Congressman spoke out, claiming that Bob's ashes "would despoil Arlington." Others, like the *National Review* editors, said Bob was a "traitor" and a "conspirator." My husband had been persecuted all his life for being a Communist; now that he was dead, he was still being persecuted.

Two days later, I heard from the polite and cold Mr. Fitt again. The Army, he told me, had decided *not* to permit the burial. "Where do you want the urn delivered?" he asked.

The Government's gimmick was this: Bob had been sentenced to 3 years in jail for allegedly conspiring to overthrow the government, and 4 years on charges of contempt of court for not showing up to serve his first jail sentence. According to a new rule, as expounded by Attorney General Katzenbach, anyone sentenced to over 5 years in jail for a crime cannot be buried at Arlington.

I sat at my desk for a while, not able to work. I was angry, and I was stunned. I could not imagine a more vicious, callous insult. Gen. Edwin Walker, when he dies, can automatically be interred in Arlington. Confederate soldiers who fought against the United States are buried there. Arlington also has the remains of at least one German soldier who fought with the Nazis in World War II, a Sergeant named Anton Hilberath, who died in a prisoner-of-war camp in 1946. But a decorated hero who fought against Fascism in World War II was barred . . .

When I telephoned my lawyer, I learned that there was no legal basis for the Government's action. Contempt of court is *not* a crime, but an administrative decision, and the Government itself (as Chief Justice Warren pointed out) has said so. So my husband was eligible to be buried in Arlington after all! Enlisting the aid of the American Civil Liberties Union, I thereupon brought suit against, among others, the superintendent of the cemetery and Secretary of Defense Robert McNamara.

* * *

40

I met Robert Thompson in 1957, at a Thanksgiving party at the home of friends. He was tall, broad, and strong-looking. We talked for 5 or 6 hours, then he walked me home. He struck me as being a quiet sort of person, shy and thoughtful— in fact, I found that in *everything* he did, whether playing chess or considering where to hang a picture, he was thoughtful and deliberate.

I was a widow of 3 years when I met Bob, and he himself had a prison sentence hanging over his head. In 1959 he began serving that sentence, and a year later he was paroled. One week after that, we were married.

It was a rough life, hectic and busy. Bob, who was a good speaker, was always immersed in Communist political activities—he wasn't the type of husband who comes home every night and watches TV. Neither of us earned very much. And though we never got threatening phone calls or heckling visitors, we lived with a vague anxiety in the air. After all, years before our marriage, Bob was once just out walking in Queens and someone knifed him.

Bob was almost entirely self-educated, yet he knew most of the classics. On the other hand, he loved TV Westerns, and the only classical music he ever learned to enjoy was Chopin. During our life together, we played a lot of Scrabble: Bob had a tremendous vocabulary but was one of the world's worst spellers. In his spare time, Bob also would often build things— a hi-fi cabinet, a coffee table, a couch—partly to relax, I guess, and partly to impress me (he once told me he was too old to walk on fences). But even while working on a piece of furniture he would stop for a while to pace back and forth—pacing is a habit many former prisoners carry with them. My husband was a splendid athlete, too, and almost every day he would go swimming at the Y: the two of us, whenever we could, also went fishing in upstate New York. We had only a few very close friends in our own age bracket, but quite often young people would drop in for a game of chess, or to discuss politics and share a meal.

I am writing all this to show that my husband, a Communist, was a human being, a "nice guy." Many Americans some-

41

how seem to think this is impossible. Bob was not a terrorist, nor was he a traitor. As he once wrote, he believed that "The essence of my Party's political program and activities is the defense and extension of the institutions and traditions of democracy in this country, not their overthrow." He believed that "The peaceful coexistence of the capitalist and socialist sectors of the world can be achieved."

My husband was born on June 15, 1915, in Grant's Pass, Oregon. His father, who died in 1943, was a boilermaker and sheet-metal worker. He was also an old-time Socialist, and joined the Communist Party in 1934. Bob's mother was non-political, and didn't understand what her son was doing, but she always backed him up. While Bob was in prison she fell and had a stroke, and for many years she lay in bed on her back, in great pain. I met her once, and was astonished that she never griped or complained; like Bob, she had a lot of spunk. She died only a month before his death.

When the depression came, Bob left high school, at 14, to work in the logging camps and saw mills. In those years the camps were ugly hellholes, and the death and accident rates were high. There were strikes and bloody violence. Bob once said, "I never met any advocates of Gandhiism among those workers."

For a time Bob tried his hand at boxing. "It was a way of getting supper money," he told me. His career was brief. He won two or three fights, then his manager matched him with a veteran left-handed boxer—not telling Bob that his opponent was a veteran, or a lefty. Bob was supposed to lose, and he did. Afterwards, he learned that his manager had bet against him. Bob quietly put on his clothes, straightened his tie, and knocked his manager cold.

In search of steady work, Bob and his family moved to Oakland, California. Bob was 18 then, and he began working as a machinist for the Continental Can Company, for the railroads, and other places. It was then that he started reading Marxist literature, organizing unions, and getting arrested for "labor troubles." In 1933, at the age of 19, a year before his father did, he joined the Communist Party. He felt, as he has explained it, that the working class was forever fighting defensive, disorganized battles against Big Business, and what was needed was an organized frontal attack—and this the Communist Party seemed the most eager and most capable of doing.

In 1935 and 1936 Bob visited the Soviet Union, working in a ballbearing factory. Then, when the Spanish Civil War broke out, he went to Spain with the International Brigade to fight with the Spanish Republic Army against the Fascists. He was wounded at Jarama, one of the war's first major battles. (While he was hospitalized with shrapnel in his knee, he taught himself enough Spanish to read *Don Quixote* in the original.) He returned to battle, and became commander of the Mac-Kenzie-Papineau battalion, at the age of 22.

Bob was a legendary fighter. I remember that one of the soldiers who fought with him described him as a "rare breed. He had no fear. I saw a lot of courage in Spain, but his was the best."

My favorite story is told by a friend who was with Bob at Fuentes de Ebro. He tells it this way: "I got a bullet through my helmet one afternoon while on observation duty. After that, I walked around like a hero, showing off my helmet. Then I noticed Bob quietly standing there, wearing that brown beret he always wore, puffing on his pipe. He had a bullet hole in his beret. But he never said a word about it. After that I shut up."

Bob was wounded again, and came back to the United States. To return to Spain he had to use a false passport. He was arrested in France, and spent 2 months in a French prison. He had made, and lost, many friends in Spain. Of 3000 Americans and Canadians who went to fight, half never lived to return.

* * *

Back in the States, Bob moved to Ohio and became secretary of the Young Communist League. In November, 1941, just 10 days before Pearl Harbor, he was inducted into the Army.

Two years later, my husband was a Staff Sergeant in the 127th Infantry, serving in the Buna region of New Guinea.

Let me quote from the citation he later received for the Distinguished Service Cross, "for extraordinary heroism in action":

Volunteering to lead a small patrol in an attempt to establish a foothold on the opposite shore, Staff Sgt. Thompson swam the swollen and rapid Konombi River, in broad daylight, and under heavy enemy fire. Armed with a pistol and hand grenade, he assisted in towing a rope to the other shore where he remained under cover of the bank and directed the crossing of his platoon. Staff Sgt. Thompson then led the platoon against two enemy machine-gun emplacements which dominated the crossing, and wiped them out. The success of this action permitted the advance of the following units.

Recently, the Akron *Beacon-Journal* published an interview with H.N. Harger, a patent attorney who had fought with Bob in New Guinea. Harger was a Captain then, and First Lt. Tally D. Fulmer was the commander. To quote from the article,

To Harger and Fulmer, both comparatively green, Thompson was a godsend.

He was the gutty, cool, confident type of non-com who makes things easy for his CO. . . .

"Fulmer ran the company and Thompson provided the tactics," said Harger. . . .

He was also a Communist. He didn't talk about it, but everyone knew and no one questioned it.

"He was one of the most unassuming characters I ever met," Harger recalled. "He never talked about himself or his Communist affiliation." . . .

"I don't know of anyone who was more of a hero," said Harger. "He did a fantastic job."

The title of the newspaper story: HE WAS RED BUT GODSEND IN WAR—AKRON GI PAL.

Bob was recommended for a promotion. Gen. R.L. Eichelberger wrote: "Staff Sgt. Thompson has been unusually outstanding in combat. I have personally seen him in action and am convinced that he is a natural leader and will make a very fine officer." But the promotion never came through. "I suspect," Mr. Harger has been quoted as saying, "his associations held him back."

After being discharged because of the malaria and tuberculosis he had contracted, Bob settled in New York. In 1945 he was elected chairman of the State Communist Party. In 1946, he ran for controller on the Communist Party ticket, receiving 80,000 votes.

Two years later, Bob and 10 other national Communist leaders were arrested under the Smith Act, for allegedly conspiring to teach and advocate the overthrow of the Government.

The trial featured two prosecutors, one acting for the Government, the other one named Judge Harold Medina. Judge Medina evidently was determined that no one should think he was "soft on Communists." He kept threatening the defense attorneys with contempt, while continually complimenting the prosecutor, and forever baiting the defense witnesses. To read the court transcript is to get a taste of life in Nazi Germany:

Prosecutor: Do you recall making any radio speeches?

Thompson: I don't recall any radio speeches that I made during this period, although it is entirely possible that I may have.

Judge Medina: You know, that is a regular formula of yours.

Defense Lawyer: Oh, your honor, please!

Judge Medina: Oh, he knows well enough. . . .

Defense Lawyer: I object to what the Court has stated and the manner—

Judge Medina: Object away.

Bob received only a 3-year sentence, because of his war record, while the others were given harsher terms.

* * *

Bob thought deeply about his sentence and chose not to report for that prison term because in jail he could not continue his activities against the McCarthy hysteria and the drift toward a third world war. He went into hiding.

For 2 years Bob went on doing political work, also taking jobs as a construction worker, a high-steel jockey, and a truck driver. In 1953, FBI agents seized Bob and several other Party

45

officials while they were staying in a cabin in California's Sierra Nevada range.

My husband was sent to Alcatraz, and then to New York City, to a jail in West Street. While in West Street, Bob was standing on the food line in the lunchroom. A refugee Yugoslav seaman named Alex Pavlovich, who was awaiting deportation, came up behind him. Picking up a 3-foot long, 2-inch thick iron pipe from a trash basket, Pavlovich crashed it into Bob's skull. Bob fell to the ground. His assailant then bent over his body, shouted: "You dirty Communist, I hope I kill you!" and landed a second blow. Prison guards just watched.

Who, if anybody, put Pavlovich up to it? How did an iron pipe just happen to be lying nearby in a trash basket? It was never explained. Pavlovich got off with a light sentence, and I don't know whether he was ever deported.

Bob, near death, was rushed to Bellevue Hospital for emergency surgery. An operation was performed, and a large metal plate was inserted in his skull.

While he was recovering from the madman's attack, thoughtful prison authorities locked him in the "tank" of the Tombs, the New York City jail. There, in a filthy cell, amid the noisy steady flow in-and-out of addicts and drunkards, Bob struggled to regain his health—and to prepare his defense in court. He wrote a forceful speech about civil disobedience. Part of it went: "Your honor. The motives for my not appearing for imprisonment under the Smith Act have been raised. The government prosecuting attorney has done his best to picture them as secretive and sinister. This is unadulterated nonsense. My motives were political and are openly and frankly declared. . . ."

At the trial, Judge Gregory Noonan sentenced my husband to 4 more years in prison. "I didn't expect a different verdict," Bob said matter-of-factly. And when Bob tried to read his speech, the Judge abruptly cut him off.

Bob spent 4 years in Atlanta Penitentiary, in a top-security cell with seven hardened criminals. He got along well with his fellow-inmates (he could be as tough as they were), and when he wasn't working in the welding shop, he caught up on his reading. When he was released, Bob said he now knew how Rip Van Winkle felt.

The few remaining years of Bob's life were very painful. His war-incurred tuberculosis and malaria had left their effects, and the Government had cut off his 100% disability pension because he had protested against the Korean war. There was hardly an inch of his body that didn't bear scars from battles. And his head, where the metal plate had been inserted, ached and throbbed. Two more operations to adjust the plate were required. Bob once told me that he was like a Model T Ford hanging together with baling wire.

Of course Bob never complained about the pain he endured: He would just sit and clench his fists. And despite his pain, despite all that he had to put up with, Bob never gave in. On the day he died he was planning to march in a parade to protest the Vietnam war, a parade that he himself had helped to organize.

* * *

My husband was a patriot. He had a special love for this country. He loved its plains, its mountains, its teeming cities, and above all, its people. But he was not a tin-horn patriot. He once said, " 'My country right or wrong' is one of the most vicious and harmful slogans ever put forward by man. I hate this slogan because I had to kill too many potentially fine young German, Italian, and Japanese men who were misled by this slogan." A far better slogan, he believed, was written by Carl Schurz: "Our country, right or wrong. When right, to be kept right; when wrong, to be put right."

While my husband was alive, he fought for this country, so valiantly that he was awarded the Distinguished Service Cross. He never denied that he was a Communist, and no one questioned his politics as he swam past enemy gunfire across the Konombi River. In return, the U.S. Government canceled his disability pension; sentenced him to prison for his ideas; bore some of the responsibility for his head having been bashed in; denied him the right to vote after he served time in prison; and for a time even denied him the right to see friends

47

or engage in politics. As Murray Kempton has said, Bob Thompson was "an American who paid everything he owed his country double and never got back a fraction of what it owed him in return."

Now that my husband is dead, I think that the United States should show some elementary decency to this man who served his country so well. A small plot in Arlington is little enough. In the long run, I think we will get it. I am sure that there are enough good-hearted people in this land who are outraged by the Pentagon's decision.

The Americans for Democratic Action has stated: "We can only hope that the Defense Department will realize that one does not defend freedom by denying it, and that the graveyard at Arlington will not be polluted by the ashes of someone who, after all, may have saved hundreds of American lives by defending freedom and the United States in World War II."

The Akron *Beacon-Journal's* executive editor and publisher, Ben Maidenberg, has written: "No one in these parts has ever yelled more about the Communist menace than I have. And I think I'm about as conservative as they come. But this business with Robert Thompson strikes me as a vile injustice."

Most eloquent of all, I think, was Murray Kempton, who wrote:

And so an American who was brave has been judged and disposed of by Americans who are cowards of the least excusable sort, cowards who have very little to fear. Wherever those ashes go, the glory of America goes with them. They belong to every soldier. They are all that remains of that afternoon at Buna, the guns in front and the vulnerable, half-naked body swimming to engage them. Those ashes have done everything for us but disgrace us, and now, by our treatment of them, we have disgraced ourselves.

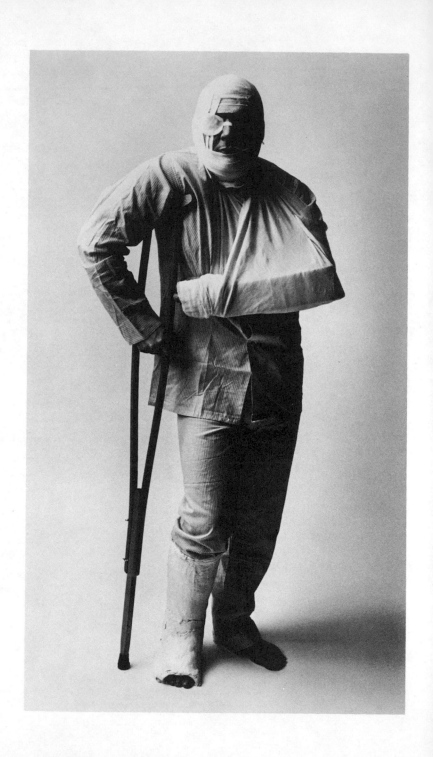

The Man Who Stood Up

By Sylvia Alberts

T he Grand Ballroom of the Waldorf-Astoria is an unusual setting for an act of civil disobedience. Certainly the 1500 guests who assembled there one night in February, 1966, after paying $25 each, were not expecting anything more dramatic than the customary five- or six-course dinner, followed by about the same number of after-dinner speakers. In addition, of course, there was the privilege of being in the same room with the guest of honor, the President of the United States. The occasion was the presentation of the Freedom House Award to Mr. Johnson, and the highlight of the evening was to be his acceptance speech: a seven-page apologia for his Vietnam policies.

In the rear of the ballroom, at table No. 95, one of the dinner guests was sitting quietly. From time to time he glanced at the wall, where plainclothes detectives and Secret Service men stood in pairs only a few yards away. When the speeches began, he hitched his chair around so that a few more feet separated him from the guards. He sat silently through four long speeches. He had entered the ballroom at 7 o'clock; not until 9:30 was the President introduced. The dinner guests rose to applaud, the detectives stood alert. As the applause faded and the audience resumed their seats, the man at table No. 95 climbed onto his chair, took off his jacket, and shouted in a clear voice heard on radio and TV across the country: *"Mr. President, peace in Vietnam! Please, Mr. President, peace in Vietnam!"* For those who didn't hear, the same message was painted on the front and back of his shirt—*Peace in Vietnam*. He was able to shout it twice again before he was seized, handcuffed, and carried from the room. The detectives silenced him by stuffing a napkin in his mouth, cutting his lip and cheek in the process. Afterwards, an official of Freedom House said that the man's act had been very dangerous: Secret Service agents, remembering Dallas, might have shot first and asked questions later. One reporter even asked the man if he meant to harm the President. "Of course not," he replied. "I wouldn't harm anybody. I'm a pacifist."

The man who stood up was Jim Peck. He has been standing up for 30 years now, on picket lines, protest marches, and peace vigils, and he has also sat-in, bussed-in, sailed-in, and been jailed-in. For all of his adult life, Jim Peck has been a fully-committed, full-time pacifist. He has spent 30 years in active service, voluntary and unpaid, in the cause of conscience.

Because of Jim Peck's demonstration at the Waldorf, he was charged with "disturbing a lawful meeting" and "resisting arrest." (His "resistance" consisted of going limp.) He pleaded not guilty and was held in $3000 bail. On March 21, Judge Joseph Martinis (the same Martinis whose son was almost instantaneously acquitted of vehicular homicide a few years ago) found him guilty on both counts. On May 9 he was sentenced to 60 days in jail.

While Peck was in the Manhattan House of Detention, before being sent to jail at Harts Island, his wife went down to ask that her husband's health needs be considered—he had tuberculosis once, and for the past 3 years he's had stomach ulcers. As she tells it: "I had to wait for 25 minutes in front of a window before anyone paid any attention to me. Not that there was any line—nobody was ahead of me. Finally an officer appeared on the other side of the glass—very thick glass. You couldn't make yourself heard through it. He had to turn on some sort of public-address thing before we could talk. I told him my husband is a sick man, that he has ulcers, that the doctors said that he has to have milk. And I also wanted to see if he could get the paper every day—Jim can't get along without *The New York Times*. But the officer just kept saying the same thing over and over—'Lady, this man doesn't *exist*.'"

A few weeks before Jim Peck officially ceased to exist, he sat in his apartment on Riverside Drive and talked to me for an hour or so. Peck is in his 50s, but looks about 45, partly because he has all his hair—light brown and beginning to gray a little now. His face is reminiscent of Bogart's, with the same blurred and battered look. He's about average height, but extremely thin, and his sunken chest and stooped shoulders contribute to an impression of great vulnerability. He talks slowly, in a deep, sometimes hesitant, rather rough-edged voice. He takes his time answering questions, but he's not evasive. You get the feeling that he's incapable of insincerity, that he would answer honestly any question put to him.

His wife, Paula, is a dark, plump, pretty woman with bright brown eyes and a wide and easy smile. She too has the quality of candor, of having nothing to hide. There are two sons—Sam, who's 16½, and Charles, 14—both good-looking boys, lively teen-agers with loose shirttails and tight schedules. How do they feel about their father's activities? Peck says, "Well, they're pretty much involved with their own world, you know. Busy in school—they both go to Fieldston. I think they wish I had an ordinary job like other fathers. No, they're not activists. They haven't joined me on the picket line and they don't have any strong antiwar feelings. I can't insist on these things, you know—you can't force them. But the younger one, Charles, came home one day and showed me an article he'd cut from the *New York Post*—about a Negro soldier who'd been killed in Vietnam, and when the mailman or messenger went to deliver the message to his father down South, he found he was a very poor old man who couldn't read. So the messenger had to read the notification to the father, who broke down. Charles was moved by the story."

Jim Peck was talking to me on April 16, the morning after most citizens part with a certain percentage of their income. On April 15 he was on a picket line in front of the Internal Revenue Service office in lower Manhattan. He always refuses to pay his taxes. The money, he feels, is put to military uses and he will not support the war effort. The government collects by simply attaching a portion of his income from his

53

father's estate. "I'm fortunate in having an independent income," he says. "All the work I've done for civil rights and pacifist organizations has been on a volunteer basis. I've written a couple of books—one of them is out of print, but the other, *Freedom Ride,* is doing pretty well in paperback. My wife is a more successful author than I am, though. She has a cookbook in its sixth edition now, and another one's coming out soon."

Mrs. Peck's kitchen is a wonderful place, filled with a profusion of pots, ladles, bowls, knives—every possible utensil. The living room is bright with travel posters (the Pecks get to Europe for a couple of weeks most summers) and so full of green plants that you feel almost outdoors.

Mrs. Peck believes that one activist in the family is enough, though she too is a pacifist. When a reporter asked her if she didn't think her husband's action at the Waldorf was "a little bit drastic," she responded, "Don't you think *our* actions in Vietnam are a little drastic, too?" Usually her husband is very considerate about telling her beforehand what he's planning to do and whether there will be any trouble, "but he didn't tell me about that Waldorf thing." She is not at all discontent with her husband's activities, though abusive phone calls in the middle of the night can be a problem. "The worst was when I got a crank call that said he was dead. Fortunately, he walked in a few minutes later."

The Pecks' living-room windows face the Hudson and would afford a view of the river if the West Side Highway didn't intervene. As it is, there's a view across the river to Palisades Amusement Park in New Jersey—a view that has, for Jim Peck, many associations.

Palisades Park boasts the largest salt-water pool in the world, but until the summer of 1949 it wasn't big enough to accommodate any Negroes. In those days, a white man who felt like a little "surf bathing" could simply buy a ticket and jump in; a Negro was advised to join the "Sun and Surf Club." If he pursued the matter and made an application to this mythical club, he was told that he would be notified by mail of his admission. That notification never came.

In the summer of 1947, CORE decided to make something of a splash. As Jim Peck tells it in his book *Freedom Ride,*

New Jersey is a long way from Alabama. Yet if an observer had stopped off there on certain summer Sundays and witnessed the violence to which CORE members were subjected, he would have believed himself transported to the heart of the South. . . .

On August 3, seven of our group were beaten by park guards and arrested at the pool ticket booth. Four others were seized as they started to picket at the entrance gate. While police pinned back my arms, a very fat guard beat me, fracturing a rib and making a deep cut over my left eye. . . .

It got so that each Sunday when we went to Palisades, we knew in advance that we would be beaten, arrested, or both. As I stood in the crowded bus climbing the steep hill from the ferry to the park gate, I would gird myself in the same way I do when a dentist is about to apply his drill to an open-nerved tooth.

On one occasion, a park guard approached me and announced, "I'd like to kill you!" The next thing I knew, I was in the police station—20 minutes later. The guard had knocked me unconscious and broken my jaw.

It took two summers of picketing and many lawsuits in both state and Federal courts before the Palisades pool was available to any citizen, regardless of color.

* * *

Where does a man find the courage to stand up to this treatment? For some, the source is religion. Jim Peck is an atheist. For others, it's total commitment to a powerful ideology. Jim Peck is nonpolitical (though he did, ironically, vote for Johnson). His closest philosophical affinity to any social organization, he says, is for the old International Workers of the World, which declined long before he reached his teens. Nor is his crusading inherited from a family tradition. His father died when Peck was 11; his mother was ultraconservative in her views on war, labor, and particularly race. She would not even have a colored maid in the house because she said Negroes were "dirty" and "thieving."

James Douglas Peck was born on December 19, 1914, in New York City, an only child. His father was active in real-estate, a wholesale clothing concern, and other businesses. The family lived in the East 60s—the "best" of the New York neighborhoods. There were servants and there was every possible luxury. Perhaps too much luxury for the solitary boy. He grew up encased in wealth and isolated by it, fatherless and estranged from his mother. He remembers her as a society woman, scornful of all who were not in her immediate circle, and cold. For warmth, the boy turned to one of his mother's servants, a Frenchwoman named Angèle, who remained close to him until her death a few years ago. But for the most part, he remembers his early years as a chilly time.

Back in the early 1930s, when Jim Peck was in his teens, he read a book and a pamphlet. The book was *All Quiet on the Western Front,* and its presentation of the First World War through the eyes of those who had been the enemy was a revelation to him. The pamphlet, "Arms and the Men," was a reprint of an article that had appeared in *Fortune* Magazine. It told in detail how the big munitions-makers had helped promote World War I, then had sold their products to both sides. To Peck, it was concrete proof that war is a ruthless racket.

While he was still an adolescent, his mother sent him to a stuffy prep school, Lawrenceville, near Princeton. There the cautious conformism of both teachers and students repelled him. Next he went to Harvard—he was 16—where his rebellion found a new expression: He took a Negro girl to the freshman dance. She wore, he recalls, a red dress. The sombrely dressed Boston matrons on the sidelines stared and whispered and stared again.

A year at Harvard was enough to convince Peck that his place was in the outside world. He left school, he left home, and went to sea. It was as a seaman that he got his first taste of what was to become for him almost a full-time occupation—picketing. The Seamen's Union was on strike, and Peck marched on the Chelsea piers. He remembers the date—March 22, 1936—(he still has that first picket card) and he remembers, too, the brutality of the police. "Cops just rode their horses into the midst of the strikers and started swinging their clubs," he recalls. "The only other comparable instance

—in the North, I mean (these things happen more often in the South)—was in 1962, when the same thing happened in Times Square. It was a mass demonstration against nuclear tests. I had the experience of being clubbed by mounted police who simply rode, head-on, into the crowds —without provocation."

Experiences such as these strengthened Peck's conviction that nonviolence is the only possible answer to force, especially in a world that, in the late '30s, was growing more and more violent. Then the Spanish Civil War broke out. Here was the clearest possible injustice: reactionary forces, aided by Hitler and Mussolini, against the Loyalists, desperately outnumbered and fighting with a gallantry that aroused freedom-lovers all over the world. Some years after, it was possible for Peck to reflect that a Loyalist victory might have meant a Communist dictatorship rather than Franco's; but at the time he was strongly tempted to go to Spain and volunteer his services as a noncombatant. It was only after much painful thought that he stayed out of the war.

The outbreak of World War II caused him no such ambivalence. To Peck this was another businessman's war. Not that Peck was blind to the menace of Hitler, but the pacifist position is clear-cut: War is a crime against humanity, and to support *any* war is to participate in that crime. From the outset of World War II, Peck knew that he had to be a conscientious objector. He also knew that without religious grounds for his stand, he would be jailed. Nevertheless, on Oct. 6, 1940, the first registration day, Jim Peck wrote on his draft card the words "conscientious objector" and read a statement of his principles to the press. He was given a high draft number and 2 years passed before he received those "Greetings." He replied with the same statement he had made on registration day, and in November, 1942, he was sentenced to 3 years at Danbury.

* * *

The Federal Correctional Institution in Danbury, Connecticut, is surrounded by lawns and flowerbeds. The buildings are modern and light. There are no outer walls, no guard towers, not even bars in the windows. But as the former chief psychiatrist at Sing Sing, Dr. Ralph S. Banay, has said, "Prisons today are in essence still medieval institutions. There has been little change in the mental torment and emotional damage that have always been the lot of those whom society locks away." Jim Peck tells the story of his years spent locked away in his book *We Who Would Not Kill*: "According to my experience, the utter monotony and aimlessness of prison life—month after month, year after year—by itself constitutes considerable 'mental torment and emotional damage.' On the outside a person becomes restless if he has an unoccupied hour to pass between two appointments or waiting for the next train. In jail, even when one is not in solitary confinement, the unoccupied hours to pass are endless. If judges were required to do time, even for a very brief period, as part of their training, they would be far more careful in imposing sentence."

The years Peck spent in prison were not entirely wasted. Along with 22 other C.O.s, Peck participated in a work strike that lasted for 135 days and ended in total victory for the strikers: Danbury became the first Federal prison to abolish segregated seating in its messhall. As Peck wrote: "It seems to me that the campaign against racial discrimination may be counted as one of the most important accomplishments of C.O.s in World War II."

*   *   *

When Jim Peck walked out of Danbury he confronted a number of closed doors. Before being sent to prison, he had worked as a reporter for a news service; he'd been told the job would be available when he came out. It wasn't. On the other hand, he did have some good luck—he began working full-time for the War Resisters League, a pacifist group; and he married a woman who shared his beliefs. Appropriately, they met at a street-meeting during an antidraft demonstration.

During the late '40s, Peck put in a number of miles on picket lines. "At Christmas of 1946," he recalls, "we picketed the White House wearing old-style, black-and-white-striped prison suits. It was to dramatize an appeal for amnesty for conscientious objectors who were still in prison. We'd rented the suits from a theatrical company. Very effective. A year or so later, on the same issue, we picketed in funeral attire carrying a coffin marked 'justice.' And in 1948, when the peacetime conscription bill was pending, we rented Uncle Sam suits and goosestepped in front of the White House with signs reading, 'The Draft Means a Goosestepping U.S.' It's very tiring on the legs, goosestepping, but when we saw the publicity, we figured the demonstration was worthwhile.

"We'd never had a peacetime draft and I knew that it was more than a temporary measure. I knew that once it was signed into law, it would be permanent."

This conviction led Peck to make a dramatic protest in June, 1948. He tells the story in *We Who Would Not Kill*:

A few days before President Truman signed the 1948 draft law, I decided to put on a shirt bearing the inscription "Veto the Draft" and chain myself to the White House steps. I realized that this action might be interpreted as crackpot by some and I saw the danger of the authorities discrediting the demonstration by sending me to an institution for observation. On the other hand, it might prove a forceful protest action which would get plenty of publicity. I decided to take a chance.

An artist friend painted the slogan "Veto the Draft" on my shirt and I bought a chain and padlock at a hardware store. The following morning I took the train for Washington.

My shirt was concealed by a coat and tie. The chain and padlock were hidden by the sleeves of the shirt. I entered the White House with the many other visitors. I went through once to examine the lay-out of the staircase and to choose a place where I would have time to remove my coat and tie and secure the padlock to the bannister before any of the guards could stop me.

I decided on a place about half-way up the staircase. On my second trip, I halted at that place, took off my coat, and secured the chain. For several minutes the guards didn't notice me. Big crowds of White House visitors were streaming up the stairs. I started handing out some anti-conscription leaflets which I had brought along.

After what seemed to be about 5 minutes, two guards came. They started to yank at the chain. It was not sufficiently thick and within a few minutes it parted. The two guards then escorted me down the stairs and across the street to Secret Service headquarters, where I was grilled for a couple of hours on every conceivable topic.

At one point during the questioning, a man who had been looking into a file cabinet across the room swung around and shouted: "Where's your card?"

"What card do you mean?" I asked.

"Your Communist Party card," he growled, and with that he rushed over and started to shake me down like they do in prison. He even looked inside my socks.

Ordinary citizens as well as Secret Service agents tend to confuse all demonstrators with Communists. "Go back to Russia!" is frequently shouted at pickets. One heckler yelled "Go back to Russia!" at Peck while he was picketing the Soviet Embassy in New York protesting the Russian nuclear test in 1962.

In 1958, Jim Peck and four other pacifists set out from Honolulu in a 30-foot ketch they called the "Golden Rule." They were planning to sail to the Pacific island where the hydrogen bomb was to be detonated and risk their lives in protest. The Federal Government got a court injunction to stop the ketch from sailing, but the men managed to get 6 miles out before they were apprehended. They were brought back to Honolulu and given 60 days in jail. Honolulu, now that it's part of the United States, has an up-to-date jail full of the latest modern conveniences. In 1958, the jail was a decrepit antique. Peck contracted tuberculosis during his 60-day sentence. He spent the next year recuperating.

His closest brush with death, however, has come not from microbes but from men. This is how he tells it in *Freedom Ride:*

The most nightmarish day of our 1961 Freedom Ride was Sunday, May 14, Mother's Day. I identify the date with Mother's Day because when Police Chief Connor was asked why there was not a single policeman at the Birmingham Trailways terminal to avert mob violence, he explained that since it was Mother's Day, most of the police were off-duty visiting their mothers. That there was going to be a mob to meet us had been well-known around Birmingham for several days. . . .

However, we did not know in advance that a similar mob was waiting in Anniston, a rest stop on the way. When the first bus pulled into Anniston, it was immediately surrounded by an angry mob armed with iron bars. They set upon the vehicle, denting the

60

sides, breaking windows, and slashing tires. Finally the police arrived and the bus managed to get away. But the mob pursued it in cars, forced it to pull over, and within minutes had hurled a bomb through the broken rear window.

All the passengers managed to escape before the bus burst into flames and was totally destroyed. Policemen, who had been standing by, belatedly came on the scene. A couple of them fired shots in the air. The mob dispersed and the injured were taken to a local hospital. The Freedom Riders were finally transported to Birmingham in cars. . . .

I was on the second bus which arrived in Anniston an hour later. We learned what had happened when eight hoodlums climbed aboard and stood by the driver as he made a brief announcement. He concluded by stating that he would refuse to drive on unless the Negroes in our group moved to the formerly segregated rear seats. They remained quietly in their front seats. The hoodlums cursed and started to move them bodily to the rear, kicking and hitting them at the same time.

Walter Bergman, a retired professor, and I were seated toward the rear. We moved forward and tried to persuade the hoodlums to desist. We too were pushed, punched, and kicked. I found myself face downward on the floor of the bus. Someone was on top of me. I was bleeding. Bergman's jaw was cut and swollen. Mrs. Bergman, who observed the beating, commented later, "I had never before heard the sound of human flesh being hit. It was terrible."

Finally, all of our group had been forced to the back of the bus. The hoodlums sat in the very front. The seats in between remained empty. At that point the driver agreed to proceed to Birmingham. Some of us doubted whether he would really head there or turn up some obscure side road for another mob scene. For the entire 2-hour ride to Birmingham, the hoodlums craned their necks to make sure we didn't move into any of the empty rows of front seats.

Upon arrival in Birmingham, I could see a mob lined up on the sidewalk only a few feet from the loading platform. Most of them were young—in their 20s. Some were carrying ill-concealed iron bars. A few were older men. All had hate showing on their faces. . . .

As we entered the white waiting-room and approached the lunch counter, we were grabbed bodily and pushed toward the alleyway leading to the loading platform. As soon as we got into the alleyway and out of sight of onlookers in the waiting-room, six of them started swinging at me with fists and pipes. . . . Within seconds, I was unconscious on the ground.

61

When Peck regained consciousness, he was alone in that alleyway. "I didn't know," he says today, "whether I would live or die and, frankly, I didn't care. I don't know, maybe because I was so tired. All that blood."

He was on the operating table in Birmingham for 8 hours. It took 53 stitches to close his wounds.

* * *

For many years Peck has been working full-time for the War Resisters League, packing and shipping peace literature and editing the bimonthly *WRL News*. The War Resisters League, founded in 1923, is the American branch of War Resisters International, a world-wide pacifist movement that encompasses 23 nations. The American branch has more than 6000 members, among them A.J. Muste (a man so pacifist he once said, "If I cannot love Hitler, I cannot love at all"), Negro leader Bayard Rustin, and draft-card burner David McReynolds. All members of the League are conscientious objectors and many have served long terms in C.O. camps or prisons.

The W.R.L. headquarters is in lower Manhattan, on the tenth floor of an old office building—the elevator gives out at the ninth floor, and visitors must negotiate the last lap on foot, climbing a narrow wooden stairway to confront a door plastered with signs reading "Committee for Non-Violent Action," "Student Peace Union," "Fellowship of Reconciliation," "Summerhill," "New York Workshop in Non-Violence," and of course "War Resisters League." There is also an admonishment to "Make Love, Not War"; someone has inserted between "Make" and "Love" the word "Free."

When Jim Peck got out of prison, he returned to work here, and with more enthusiasm than ever. The War Resisters League seems to be making headway: According to Peck, "We get letters every day, and phone calls. People come in off the street to ask what they can do." In the last 5 years, membership has doubled.

Jim Peck has excellent qualifications for advising today's conscientious objectors. "Ordinary youngsters can identify with him," says Ralph DiGia, administrative secretary of the

War Resisters League and a man who has known Peck for 20 years. "He's a conscientious objector, but he's not religious. Jim doesn't think a C.O. has to be a saint. He drinks occasionally, and smokes, and has a fine sense of humor. He's a regular guy." In still another way Jim Peck is admirably suited to advise today's conscientious objectors. Once, in a ceremony in front of the White House, Peck and several associates publicly burned their draft cards. The year was 1947.

* * *

Although Jim Peck is really an uncomplicated man, a man intensely preoccupied with one great cause, he is not easy to explain or to pigeonhole. It is true that a person estranged or separated from his parents often develops in unusual ways, because he has no firm model to pattern himself after, and must develop an identity of his own, on his own. It is true that such a man, more than the rest of us, needs approval from within, since he did not, as a child, receive the approval he needed from outside. Still, this does not entirely explain why Jim Peck is the man he is—as a friend of his described him, "a Dostoevsky character," a Prince Mishkin whom virtually everyone considers an "idiot," though in truth he is one of the few really sane people living.

I asked Jim Peck, before he was jailed, "How have you been able to take all these beatings without fighting back?" He conceded that he has almost always felt an impulse to retaliate. "But," he added, "I've found that it can be curbed by a complete realization of the futility of violence. Anger is a natural response to physical pain. But when I'm attacked, my reaction has come to be a sick feeling inside, a sort of overpowering nausea caused by the spectacle of physical violence. During beatings I try to cover my head with my arms as best I can. Afterwards, the sick feeling remains. On some occasions I actually vomited. But on every occasion, I felt that my remaining nonviolent has proved worthwhile."

When I asked him if he considered himself a pessimist, his answer was a reluctant "Yes." He elaborated: "I'd call it more realism than pessimism. Things *do* get better. I *have* seen re-

63

sults. We had the Freedom Rides and now interstate travel *is* unsegregated. There are gains. They may seem small, but they're gains. We've demonstrated against the bomb and we have a test-ban treaty. And there are many more pacifists today than there were in 1958."

Finally, I asked him how he "got that way." To him, it was a matter of chance—and conviction. "I decided a long time ago," he said, "that my principles were important to me, the most important thing I had. I suppose the most valuable people in the world are the creative ones—artists, writers, architects. The rest of us who aren't creative, who don't have talents, ought to do the next-best thing: Work to make the world a little better."

64

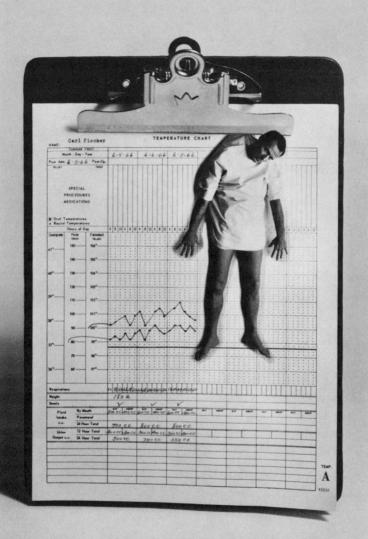

America's Hospitals: Undercure
in an Age of Overkill

By Sloan Wilson

Lately I have been reading a good deal about the crisis of American hospitals. With Medicare, a lot of people are able to afford hospital care who in the good old days died quietly and inexpensively at home. With the cost of living going up, nurses and other hospital employees are getting restless and are joining unions, which proclaim the odd idea that people whose profession is healing should also be allowed to eat well. And patients who find beds crowded in wards and corridors supervised by gruff, overworked people are voicing astonishment that they have not stumbled into some medical utopia of the kind they see constantly depicted on TV. When charged up to $70 a day for medical care that even a layman can tell is lacking, many a middle-class person wonders, What's going on around here?

Well, what is?

One thing not many people realize is going on: Hospitals are much more important to all of us nowadays than they were even 10 or 20 years ago. In the old days most people were, of course, born at home and they died there. Today, not only do most of us begin and end our lives in hospitals, but we go there for diseases that formerly were treated in the local doctor's office or in our own bedrooms. As medical technology becomes more and more complicated, the importance of the hospital keeps increasing. It's a rare person nowadays who doesn't visit a hospital a dozen times during the last third of his life. Hospitals are the settings for our greatest personal tragedies.

Despite the fact that virtually all of us have a hospital in our future, whether we like to think about it or not, hospitals are not a subject that arouses the sustained indignation of most Americans. People tend to be grateful to a hospital if they escape from it alive. If they see conditions that are not right there, they feel embarrassed to comment, because the whole place is under the supervision of physicians, and how can a layman argue with a doctor about how to cure people? As soon as most of us are well, we like to forget hospitals. The very smell of them is enough to bring on the horrors.

Yet sustained public indignation is what is needed if the money and determination to maintain good or even adequate hospitals is to be found.

Now, a good many people tell me I shouldn't write about hospitals because I'm not an expert. I dispute this.

Of course, I'm not a physician, and I'm not a psychiatrist, and I'm not a hospital administrator. I am not, thank God, a nurse, nor have I ever been a nurse's aide, an orderly, or even a volunteer worker in a hospital. In fact, what I've done all of my life is to keep away from hospitals as much as possible.

Unfortunately, almost no one can have a perfect record in this matter. Several times I have been a patient, although by the grace of God, not recently. My four children were all born in hospitals. I have been a visitor in hospitals many times when friends and relatives were being repaired. Two of the people I have loved best in my lifetime learned about their last illnesses in hospitals.

I don't claim this makes me more expert than most people about hospitals, but it does mean that I'm not ignorant. The mechanics of hospital administration may be beyond me, but I know enough to ask six important questions.

* * *

1. Why do hospitals treat their nurses and other employees so badly?

If these people are discontent and harried, the patient cannot hope for much. As things now stand, a lot of the kindness that hospitals are supposed to show patients must, in effect, come out of the hides of the nurses and nurses' aids, who are asked to take care of more patients than any human being can be expected to clean up after, never mind treat according to any prescribed course of medicine. The young women who go into nursing generally have high ideals and a deep fund of human kindness, I believe, but after having been made to run their legs off for a few years, they can hardly help becoming hardened. Dehumanized nurses have a dehumanizing effect upon the patients, who in their hours of pain often need kindness and sympathy more than anything else. Nowadays it is generally easier to find an understanding listener during the rush hour at Grand Central Station than in the ward of a city hospital.

All my life I have heard and read about beautiful, sympathetic nurses. I have even known a few socially, but the nurses I meet on duty in hospitals invariably seem to be trying to act out the stereotyped part of somebody's mother-in-law on the rampage.

"Please be quiet!" they shout at the top of their voices. "Visitors are not allowed now! I'm sorry, but you can't smoke here! Now you listen here, absolutely no drinking is allowed in this hospital! No, the book cart isn't available!"

When they are not talking in these dulcet tones, they sugar their voices with a sickening kind of baby talk that I used to hate when I was 3 years old.

"It's time for our breakfast now!" one nurse said to me every morning for a week.

In a fury I finally asked, "Are you going to climb in bed with me and share the tray?"

"Oh, aren't we funny this morning! I guess we are getting better, aren't we?"

If one stays in a hospital long enough, one may even come to like this sort of talk, compared with the usual lack of any response from the nurses. I have often wondered why they put pushbuttons by hospital beds if nobody ever pays any attention to the bells when they ring. Even when one has private nurses around the clock, it is often impossible to get a nurse until one's thumb turns blue from the pressure.

I don't blame nurses for being cranky, I blame this horrible system of treating the sick that dehumanizes everybody, both patients and nurses. Faced with the conditions most nurses have to live with year after year, I couldn't keep my sanity for more than a month. When faced with too much suffering and too much work, any human being has to grow somewhat apathetic in order to survive. I feel sure that if most of the nurses who charge around hospital corridors with hard faces and strident voices were given a reasonable number of patients to care for, and enough pay to make their own lives tolerable, they might grow to be something like those Angels of Mercy I keep reading about.

Hospital administrators are always groaning about the shortage of nurses, but to my mind the real wonder is that they can get anyone at all to put on that white dress. Lucky to get $5000 or $6000 a year, expected to work all hours around the clock, and required to involve themselves in the most torturous details of life and death, the nurses have to be either starving people who can get hardly any other kind of work, or saints.

The dilemma of the nurses is all the more pitiable because the many saints among them are not given the opportunity to be saintly. The overworked nurse has added to all her other burdens the knowledge that she is doing her job badly. Convinced that patients under her care may die from lack of attention, the nurse often blames not only the system, but herself. Exhausted, guilty, impoverished, our nurses and their even more pathetically underpaid aides are a strange comment on our Great Society.

* * *

2. Why do our hospitals treat the matter of birth so badly?

A lot of people are surprised to find that the United States does not have as good a record in infant mortality as do many other nations. Fourteen other nations have fewer deaths per thousand births than the United States has. Sweden's infant-mortality rate is 12.4 per 1000 births. The State of Washington's rate is 35.2, and New York's is 38.1. One reason is that our prenatal clinics are so crowded, inaccessible, and downright callous in their treatment of people that countless mothers refuse to go to them. An expectant mother who already has one or more children to care for often cannot waste hours standing in line, or reading magazines in a waiting room. Thousands of them just wait at home until the baby starts to come, at which point someone actually has to do something to help.

In my opinion, even those women who can afford the best hospital care get pretty poor treatment when they have babies unless they are both knowledgeable and aggressive.

Most hospitals are hostile to parents who want natural childbirth, and a husband has to fight all kinds of regulations if he wants to stay with his wife through labor. Unless the couple put up a fight, the mother will be heavily drugged almost automatically.

Not all hospitals offer the facilities for keeping an infant next to the mother's bed. Unless a big point is made of the desirability of keeping infant and mother together, the infant is automatically put in a baby ward, where he may or may not receive even basic physical care.

One thing the infant is sure to get, however, is a bottle before he sees his mother. One result is that many an infant declines to nurse vigorously. The whole hospital routine is geared for mothers who expect to put their infants on bottles immediately or after a very brief period. The mother who wants to breast-feed is often regarded as something of an eccentric, and if she doesn't have a great deal of self-confidence, she soon gives up. And when the baby grows into a man he goes around leering mournfully at women with enormous bosoms. It is difficult to understand why our whole medical system, in infant care, seems to be geared to subverting nature.

* * *

3. Why do our hospitals treat children so badly?

Sick children do not like to be abandoned by their parents —one does not have to have a degree in psychology to realize that. A 3-year-old with a broken leg may find the process of being left by his mother in a strange, terrifying building more painful than the aching flesh, and the emotional scar in the long run may be more damaging. Ideally, hospitals should

71

offer rooms for the mothers of sick children. Lacking the physical facilities for that, everything possible should be done to make it practical for parents to visit as often as possible and to stay as long as they can.

Few hospitals are hospitable to the parents of children in the wards, and even when one has a child in a private room, one is rarely given a comfortable chair. Some hospitals are trying to do what they can to make visiting hours flexible, but a great many children's wards are run by harried supervisors who believe that parents just get in the way and may be harmful. Of course, there are some neurotic parents who should be kept away from sick children, but to hear hospital authorities talk, one would think the vast majority of mothers cannot be trusted with their own offspring.

One administrator told me "in strict confidence" that his hospital had to be very careful, because one family of Gypsies in New York City once tried to build a fire on the floor of a room when they were visiting their child and wanted tea. Perhaps this actually happened, but that odd story impressed me less than the fact that the administrator obviously felt those Gypsy parents were somehow typical of most of the great unwashed public that has eternally to be watched, and distrusted.

It would take time and trouble to supervise parents intelligently, but all too few hospital authorities seem to realize that parents are what many sick children desperately need. Even hardened soldiers often cry for their mothers when they are wounded. Can't our Great Society make it possible to grant that request from a 2-year-old close to death?

* * *

4. Why do our hospitals treat dying people so badly?

According to the ethics of the medical profession, people are kept alive as long as possible, even when there is no hope of relieving their pain. If a person is dying, it is widely believed that this should be kept a secret. Perhaps many people do not want to learn they are dying, but other people do want to know, and they don't want to be subjected to the kind of false

72

optimism and phony cheer that are dished out to the dying as a kind of standard farewell ration of our prosperity.

Just as Americans are somewhat batty on the subject of birth, it is my belief that we are very much confused about death. We assume, for one thing, that all people fear death, and want to pretend they are not dying even when their bodies are withering away in the mirror. I suppose some people find comfort in pretense, but I know that some do not. One man I knew was infuriated by the charade that doctors and nurses insisted on playing with him in his last days.

"My, you certainly are looking better today!" one nurse would say every morning, when this man was in the final stages of wasting away.

He knew she was trying to be kind, and endured her.

Dying is, of course, a highly personal act, and my point is that a crowded hospital ward is no place for it.

When a man is sick at home, his relatives can show their love by tidying up the room a little, bringing glasses of water, offering to help with the medicine. At home a sick man can find comfort in the fact that people he loves are in the next room. He does not have to confront them steadily a few feet away for an hour at a time, or know that they have dropped out of his existence. The sounds of a normal household are comforting to a man who is dying, I have been told, and so are the familiar furnishings of his own room.

Of course, dying at home isn't much fun for anyone, either. Unless one can afford nurses around the clock, and find them, emergencies can arise that are painful for relatives. Despite this, the two people I have known well who had fatal illnesses chose to go home to die, and none of their relatives ever regretted it.

When a person is dying in a hospital, I believe he needs a little special consideration, like a private room and facilities that make it possible for his relatives to stay with him in his final hours. I believe he should be able to talk to people about his approaching end if he wishes. There are psychiatrists who know a lot about how to ease the psychic torments of dying,

73

but their advice is rarely known or followed by harried nurses who may have a whole ward of dying people to cope with.

We give a prisoner condemned to death a talk with a chaplain and, supposedly, one last big meal on the house. A dying man or woman who has worked a lifetime for the benefit of his country and family should rate a little more. If he's going to die anyway, hospitals should be geared to give him, within reason, anything he wants in regard to privacy, food, drink, company, and psychiatric or religious counseling.

One reason, I believe, that people so often like to keep approaching death a "secret" from a patient is that then they don't have to do anything special for him. Is our country really so poor that it can't afford a farewell party tailored to the tastes of the person who is departing?

I was with a relative once in the waiting room of a hospital that looked much like a subway station at 5 P.M. A harried physician came in and said, "I am sorry to report that your father has cancer. It's all through him, and there's very little we can do."

There is no way such news can be made pleasant, but the horror of this was increased by the fact that there was no privacy, not even a place to sit down and discuss the matter without being overheard. My relative cried in public with a great many people watching, some with casual compassion, some with complete uninterest.

Receiving news like that is a shock and, like other shocks, should be administered in carefully controlled circumstances. Why in this rich nation can't hospitals have private-consultation rooms where the relatives of the dying can be treated like the injured human beings they are?

* * *

5. Why do hospitals have to be so depressing?

Sickness and death are hardly cheerful, but they can be made even harder to bear when they take place in what looks like a morgue. If one acknowledges the fact that many of our worst emotional crises are going to take place in hospitals, why not fix them up a bit? Psychologists know that color has deep

74

emotional effects on people. Is it necessary to have everything a ghastly white in order to have it clean? If money in this great rich nation were not always a deciding factor in hospital calculations, would it not be desirable to have hospitals that in many ways look like good hotels? Tasteful colors, rugs on the floor, paintings, a little music, nurses in attractive dresses—why are all these things so hard to imagine in a hospital?

* * *

6. Why can't hospitals treat convalescents better?

Is it really necessary to subject most convalescents to a set of petty regulations that would seem normal only to experienced convicts? "Hospital Routine" may be necessary in institutions suffering acute shortages of money and personnel, but we are never going to get better hospitals if we accept "Hospital Routine" as desirable in itself. Just because a person is sick, he doesn't necessarily have to be treated much worse than he ever has been treated while he was well. It does not say in the Bible that a sick person has to wake up at a certain time and go to bed at a certain time and have visitors at stipulated hours. No medical theory demands that sick people be served food they would spurn in their most robust days. Many people have diseases and take medicines that do not make the moderate use of alcohol harmful. Why can't they have a cocktail or a glass of wine with their meals in the hospital?

To many people that sounds fantastic, but this is only because we have settled for the stereotyped idea of a hospital that imposes puritanical regulations on everyone. Even distinguished old men are commonly treated like children, once they are made to don that humiliating, grotesque nightgown most hospitals hand to their patients. Can't the clothes designers of this age of high fashion come up with some practical hospital garment that doesn't make a person feel he is being prepared for a pauper's grave?

Why do intelligent nurses commonly talk to intelligent adults with such condescension, just because the adults are sick? There is probably no place in the world where a rich man with a record of achievement will be treated with less respect than in a hospital, where his ego probably needs more help than it ever did. And the treatment accorded the sick poor is often downright insulting.

Not long ago I visited a ward in a relatively rich hospital in New York. I saw an old man groaning while a nurse's aide was sponging his forehead.

"Aw, shut up," she said casually. "You're all right. . . ."

In a nearby ward, men and women were jammed into beds next to each other.

"We're supposed to have men's wards and women's wards," a nurse with a cheerful voice told me, "but these people are so sick they don't know what they are."

Perhaps it was true, but in a moment of consciousness I would not like to realize I had been shoved into a ward with a lot of old women because I was so sick I didn't realize what I was. And I didn't like the tone of that hard-working, cheerful nurse who seemed to believe she had just made a slightly bawdy joke.

Is it absurd to think that a person convalescing after a serious disease should be treated at least as well as when, say, he's at a summer resort? Which one of us would consider sharing a hotel room with a stranger while we're on a business trip if there were no great emergency? Yet it is considered normal to receive a "semiprivate room" in a hospital, sometimes at $50 a day, and private rooms are considered a privilege for the self-indulgent and pampered rich. (So much are private rooms considered a luxury that their occupants are usually charged far more than cost, to make up for some of the deficits of the wards. I do not doubt that the rich should give to the poor, but I do not think that charity should be forced from them in their own time of need, and I don't think that privacy should be considered a luxury for sick people anyway.) There is, I submit, no such thing as semiprivacy, any more than there is such a thing as semipregnancy. Either one is private or one is not, and just because one does not wish to share a room with a coughing, snoring old stranger, one should not be subjected to a kind of luxury tax.

To sum up, I do *not* think that hospitals treat expectant mothers, infants, children, dying people, the relatives of the foregoing, and convalescents anywhere as well as might be expected in a rich nation in a time of prosperity. What, if anything, do they do well, then?

As far as I can judge, they generally provide good physical care in emergencies, which is all a lot of people expect. As medical technology advances, I have no doubt that all of us will have a better chance of surviving any disease that can be treated quickly by experts. It is when the patient is no longer considered an emergency case that he begins to suffer most. This seems a logical result of a philosophy of medicine that increasingly regards the human body as a machine devoid of emotions, no matter how much the psychiatrists learn.

In a time of emergency, a patient can receive the full blast of attention from highly trained teams of physicians armed with every conceivable kind of machine designed for the preservation of life.

But once the patient is judged no longer to be in acute physical danger, he is wheeled out into wards or rooms where nurses may at heart care a great deal about him, but where the facilities for the expression of that concern simply do not exist.

There are a few hospital people who agree with me that places for sick people do not necessarily have to be like hospitals. The Loeb Nursing Center, which is part of the Montefiore Hospital in the Bronx, is trying to treat patients like people. It keeps one nurse on duty for every two patients, and nurses are encouraged to answer the bell, even if all the sick person wants to do is talk. Nurses don't even wear uniforms at Loeb Center —they sport pretty dresses. There are almost no rules patients have to observe. If a sick person wishes to act in any way injurious to his health, the nurses and doctors warn him, but if he is in full possession of his mental faculties, they leave the decision of what to do up to him. Lydia Hall, the nurse who runs the place, says that if she had her way she would even install a small bar for the use of those patients whose sickness does not preclude alcohol.

The hospital authorities I know smile indulgently when I

77

tell them about the Loeb Center and my ideas for making hospitals fit places for people. It's too expensive, they say. If adequate care is to be given people past the point of acute emergency, many hospital staffs would have to be doubled. If nurses were to be put into a situation where they could give the best care they know how to give, it might be necessary to employ one nurse for every two patients, and that of course would be extremely expensive. As it is, many a man has prayed to die quickly so that his widow would not be left destitute. Many a child has been robbed of a good education because the money had to be spent to cure illness in the family. If we had hospitals that treated patients like people, they would cost even more, so why talk about them.

The other reforms suggested in this article, such as more pleasant surroundings and better food, seem to harried administrators of crowded wards to be fantastic dreams. The kind of hospital I have envisioned would, I am told, cost many billions of dollars in an era when most hospitals have trouble paying their bills without making any improvements at all.

All this is no doubt true. But the gnawing question persists, How can a nation that spends so many billions of dollars on Vietnam, on reaching the moon, and on an arsenal capable of blowing up everybody in the world several times over, talk so poor when it comes to taking care of its own infants, its own sick and dying? In an age of overkill, why so much undercure?

That is, of course, the really big question. It is easy to blame the government, but in this as in so many things, aren't our politicians shrewdly guessing the public will? A lot of people get indignant at the thought of not having enough bombers or enough rockets, but one doesn't hear a great deal of furor over hospitals that are an affront to human dignity. In some strange way the thought of bombers and rockets apparently makes people feel safe and protected, while the thought of hospitals makes them feel threatened, on the edge of death.

I do not think it would do much good to try to tell people that a civilized nation should look to its hospitals as well as to its military defense. The whole tenor of the times is against such a notion. Because of this, I have come up with a modest proposal that just conceivably might offer a ray of hope.

* * *

The way to get better hospitals in this Year of Our Lord is to declare them part of the Defense Program. That, I know, sounds absurd, but do you remember how much support the public schools got when people started saying we needed them to develop scientists and engineers who could compete with Russia? And our highway-building program too gets vast injections of money from the Federal Government because highways have been declared part of our system of defense.

Well, how about hospitals? My best guess is, we'll need them if war ever comes. They are much overcrowded now, and although they handle individual emergencies pretty well, how would they do in a time of real national emergency, when our cities were being bombed?

It is a chilling thought.

Write your Congressman. Tell him it is his patriotic duty to make sure we can cure as well as we can kill. He doesn't have to admit the side-benefits, for they might sound effete to a warlike people, but the happy fact is that hospitals that could cope with war at all could also offer really human conditions in time of peace.

Seduction of the Guilty:
Homosexuality in American Prisons

By Donald Lee

I had been in Western State Penitentiary, in Pennsylvania, for a week when one convict said to me, "This is the second-biggest faggot factory in the State. The biggest is . . . *Eastern* State Penitentiary." I laughed. Later I was to find out he wasn't joking.

At the time I was 30 years old. A few months before, depressed by the death of my mother, I became involved in a check-passing scheme with two other men. I now think that I acted more from confusion than from criminal design. I was not poor and I was a businessman with a good reputation in my community. Even before any charges were brought against me, I made complete restitution on all the checks I had cashed. Nonetheless I was sentenced to 3 to 6 years in the State penitentiary. I served my 3 years, spent a short time on relief, and now I am working as a salesman.

One of the first things I noticed when I arrived at Western State was that the average prisoner was, like myself, in his 20s or early 30s. Though there were a handful of lifers, and a larger number of middle-aged or elderly repeaters, in prisons young men seem to predominate. These are men in their physical prime. They have the same drives that young men on the outside do, but they don't have the same opportunities for satisfaction. They crave sex, but there are no girls. So, of necessity, prisoners turn to each other.

In prison, we lived in a truncated world populated only by men. We ate together, talked to each other in the yard, worked side by side, slept in the same cells. We gambled with dominoes (cards were forbidden), bet on ballgames, ran pools.

81

We lived like rabbits in a warren, our cages rising tier upon tier, the whole a lump of steel and stone. We had no sure freedom from the prying eyes of passing guards or fellow prisoners, not one corner for undisturbed privacy. Always surrounded by the sounds and sighs and the breathing of men, we were never alone except inside ourselves, where the loneliness was terrible.

And the deadening monotony and routine of prison life intensified our lusts. The teen-agers and young men with smooth, firm skin and a trace of baby fat merged with our memories of girl friends and wives. The ready smile of a young man, his puppy playfulness, his high-pitched but pleasant voice, his frank and trusting manner, in time made the rest of us equate all youth with women.

Put a sane person in an insane asylum for a long period of time and he will begin to doubt his sanity. His standard of reference is the society he lives in. There is strong pressure on him to conform, to get into step. The same thing happens in prison. The newcomer may be shocked and repelled at the propositions and the talk and the sexual acts, but the unremitting daily exposure soon conditions him and rubs off the taint of abnormality. Homosexuality suddenly begins to sound normal.

In Western State, the two main subjects of conversation were sex and gambling, in that order. Everybody discussed sex the way people on the outside discussed the weather. "Getting much lately?" was a standard greeting. And it was easy to find a "mate," easy to find someone who would gratify any kind of sex act. If you were young, you were bombarded constantly with suggestions and proposals, you were coaxed and pressured. So it was that the heterosexual swirled into the prison whirlpool and was sucked under.

Sometimes the newcomer was bought. In prison there are two ways to get money: gambling and sex. But they often merged. To gamble you needed a pack of cigarettes. And if you got into debt, the creditor might suggest payment in sex. The debtor might be unwilling, but when the choice was to pay up or get beaten up, he didn't have much choice. Another

82

source of debt was the court costs for filing a writ. Even if an inmate filed *in forma pauperis,* there were court costs to be paid for filing the first writ.

In Louisiana, a young convict was attempting to establish that his trial had been unfair, and he had paid another convict to prepare a writ of habeas corpus. The court ordered the filing fee to be paid by a certain date. The fee, nominal by court standards ($8.50), was almost 3 months of his prison pay ($3.25 a month). To raise the money by the set date, the convict sold himself to all comers and spent almost all of one pre-arranged night getting visitors under his bed. After the men in his dormitory had had their fling, they just refused to pay up. The young convict broke down and told his story to the guard on duty. To his credit, the guard ignored prison rules and announced that any man who did not pay up would be reported to the deputy for disciplinary action. Everybody paid.

Little do judges realize that the fees needed to pay for the writs that they may so casually dismiss have often been paid for by perversion and prostitution.

Sometimes an inmate is even forced to engage in homosexuality. William Remington, the Dartmouth professor convicted of perjury and sentenced to a Federal prison in Pennsylvania, had his head bashed in in 1954 when he spurned a homosexual's advances. Also in 1954, a riot broke out at Western State. It occurred during the winter, and with typical lack of foresight the convicts smashed the windows. In the days that followed they almost froze to death. The riot burned itself out by the second day but the State police—who had taken charge of the institution—took their time about moving in and re-establishing control. They wanted to teach the convicts a lesson, so they let them suffer cold and hunger for a few more days. The cell blocks had been sealed so there was no chance of escape, and for the next 3 days the cons roamed aimlessly and restlessly about the cell blocks. Some of the prisoners, more like beasts than men, roamed in gangs and forced their attentions on whomever they wanted. One kid was ganged up on and raped 23 times. His anus was badly torn. A few of the more responsible convicts, learning of his condition, arranged with the guards outside to transfer him to the hospital. After this, the convicts themselves set up details to patrol the block and prevent any recurrences of the incident. The raped prisoner spent several months in a hospital and then was given a quick parole. Newspapers never learned of the incident—prison authorities are careful to avoid any publicity that would expose them to any criticism, or worse, to an investigation.

Whatever the cause—the need for a sexual outlet, the desire to conform, debts, or the fear of force or actual force itself—almost every man who goes to prison in America today becomes a homosexual, permanently or temporarily. One prisoner I met told me bitterly on the day of his departure, "I was put here because I was a bigamist. Now I'm leaving—a homosexual."

* * *

From the point of view of the out-and-out homosexual, prison life is a paradise. He is much sought after. And the lucky man who finally comes to own him (called the "jocker") looks upon his mate (called the "kid") with a proprietary indulgence, and even makes sacrifices to keep him in cigarettes and candy.

"Pretty Boy" was an unabashed homosexual. He was a Negro in his late 20s, with a soft, handsome face and the sinuous body of a ballet dancer. He was articulate, and had a sharp sense of humor and a fast, snappy comeback. Now, usually a homosexual proposition is done with finesse. A man seeks out his desire and engages him in casual conversation, or a game of checkers, or even a ballgame. He does him little favors, like lending him a book or sharing a bar of candy with him. Then come such gambits as, "Hey, don't look me in the eye like that. I lose my head when you do that!" Or, "Boy, do I get a thrill when you brush against me." Or "When are you going to give me a break? You know I've got eyes for you." Only an angry and absolute No is considered final. If the suitor hears a "Come on, you know I'm not that type," he figures all he has to do is keep trying. Pretty Boy's approach was direct. He used it for shock value, and usually succeeded in getting his way. To a fish (new prisoner), he'd say, "Tell me about the first time you were screwed. . . . Oh, come *on*, baby, don't give me that innocent routine. I'll bet you're *hell* in bed with a man."

In Western State, Pretty Boy had "gotten married" and had settled down, more or less, with a white man named Sammy as his jocker. But even in prison the course of true love seldom runs smooth. Sammy burned while Pretty Boy flitted around from affair to affair. Sammy would take it for so long, then explode, and the two would pummel each other around. At times they'd lose control and even try to injure each other.

Because of their fights, the deputy warden was determined to break up the relationship between Pretty Boy and Sammy. He threw them both into solitary for 2 weeks. When he released them, he warned them that if they so much as talked to each other he'd put them back in isolation for 6 months.

Because the deputy warden came from Alabama, Pretty Boy thought he was prejudiced. He wrote letters to the N.A.A.C.P. and to the Governor complaining that he was being forbidden to associate with a white man. The deputy warden stopped the letters and summoned Pretty Boy into his office. "I don't care if you associate with a white man or a green man or a purple one," he told him, "but you're not going to associate with Sammy and these letters aren't going anywhere."

Lovers don't give in easily. Pretty Boy wrote another letter, this time to his attorney—and this time the deputy warden couldn't interfere. Afraid that the lawyer might cause a stink, the deputy mulled the matter over for a few days, then sent for Pretty Boy and said: "This letter won't be necessary. I'm going to let you see Sammy. But I'm warning you: You're on thin ice. One misstep and you'll sit in isolation until you rot."

* * *

Interracial liaisons, like that of Pretty Boy and Sammy are tolerated by most prisoners, though Negroes prefer that the jocker be the Negro and the kid a white, while whites prefer the opposite. Whatever the color of a kid in an interracial

85

affair, members of his race usually treat him with contempt, or ignore him altogether. A few people deliberately limit their associations to the other race, probably as a form of rebellion, but after a time they find themselves frozen out when members of their own race reject any offer of friendship. The Black Muslims I met in Western State tried to keep their contacts with whites limited, but this didn't seem to apply to sex affairs.

Connie was another colored fag. She (in prison, the kid is usually referred to as "she") was articulate and outspoken, like Pretty Boy, but petite. Connie had a great deal of courage. She would stand up to men twice her size and take a beating—but not back down.

Connie liked to change sexual partners every so often, drawing no distinctions as far as color goes when choosing lovers. But it is not always easy to end a love affair, as Connie discovered more than once.

For a while Connie had been going with a colored football player, then she strayed from the path. Her jocker found out about her cheating, chased her and caught her behind a prison building, where he began choking her. He was so crazed with jealousy that if a buddy had not followed them and intervened Connie would have been strangled.

In prison, rejected lovers may nurse their grievances for a few days in hopes of a reconciliation, or they may take a shiv (a piece of metal sharpened into a knife), slip it under the waist or shirt, and set out for revenge.

"Smiley" took the end of his love affair hard. For a week he tried to bully his kid into returning. One day in the yard he walked up to the kid and asked her if she was coming back. The kid refused. Smiley whipped out a shiv and slashed the kid's cheek and neck and would have ripped out her guts too if he hadn't been restrained by others.

More potentially dangerous than the break-up of a romance is a rivalry over a kid. Like women, I suppose, kids enjoy being fought over. A kid will take up with a second jocker and play each of them against the other. She'll confess to one that she'd like to swing with him alone, only she's afraid of the other one—or that the rival is putting pressure on her and she needs help. Jockers will then strut up to each other with loud threats, or send messages through other convicts, or issue a challenge to meet for a fight-it-out behind some building. Stupidly enough, sometimes they do just this, and a knife-slashing ensues. The kid, from a distance, thrills at the fight for her favor. More good men, I would say, have been maimed or killed in prison because of kids than for all other causes.

"Liz Taylor," a willowy youth with soulful blue eyes and curly black hair, loved to set men at odds over her. She had taken up with Tex, a solid, stable athlete. After a while she began making passes at Eddie, also a regular guy. Liz batted her long black eyelashes, touched her admirers with her creamy skin, and cooed endearingly. Both men wanted her and lost their senses. They never stopped to talk it over, even though worried friends tried to intercede. They honed their shivs, met behind the powerhouse one night, and sliced each other up. Tex died the same night in a hospital. Eddie recovered, received a life sentence, and was sent to another prison. Liz kept to herself for about a month—resentment against her ran high —then sought solace in another liaison.

"Peaches" was another punk who enjoyed provoking a fight between men. She had two knife fights to her discredit, one for each of her terms in prison. I first met her when she had returned to prison for a third time. She was older then, and most of her beauty had faded. Her reputation was known to men who had served with her before, and it quickly spread to the rest of us, and most of us resented the fact that some regular guys bore scars because of Peaches' peccadillos. The participants in the fights were not condemned for being stupid enough to be sucked in. They were regarded merely as unfortunate victims. Peaches continued to receive a number of propositions, but she had lost her beauty and could never again get men hopelessly involved with her.

And nothing is so pitiful as an overaged whore. She slicks back her grey hair, dresses in tight-fitting clothes, and swishes across the yard, her eyelids fluttering. But the crow's-feet around the eyes, the parched and wrinkled face, and the sagging jowls destroy all the allure. Her only associates are other has-beens. They walk around the yard together, lost and bitterly lonely.

* * *

Prison authorities usually try to discourage homosexuality. If they catch the participants in a sex act, they subject them to intense ridicule and humiliation, or haul them off to Mohawk, the punishment block, for 6 months. And the file jackets of both men are stamped "homosexual."

It does little good. Good criminals that they are, lovers frequently employ a watchman to stand guard while they engage in sexual activities. No nook goes unnoticed in the search for suitable trysting places: broom closets, crates, attics, the recess of a shower stall. The prison officials saw off the legs of the steel cots so they're too low for love-making beneath the bed, but the cons will slip wooden blocks or books under the legs, then drape a blanket over the edge of the bed to hide the additions. One couple even snuck under the grandstand during a football game and enjoyed themselves. Once a guard surprised two inmates under a bed in the same cell. At the time, they had their pants on. "What are you doing there?" the guard demanded. "Nothing," one of the cons replied. "Just looking at some magazines."

The guards themselves are none too eager about trying to curb prison homosexuality. Pretty Boy, the kid I spoke of earlier, was even propositioned by two cell-block guards one day. If she would take care of them sexually, they told her, they'd close their eyes whenever she visited other inmates in their cells. Pretty Boy was shaken by the idea of doing business with the enemy, especially since one of the guards was sadistic and completely untrustworthy. The young Negro feared a trap, but also feared the consequences of refusal. Going to the deputy was out of the question: She would be disciplined for maligning the guards. Pretty Boy managed to put off the guards for a while, then begged off because of her impending parole, and gradually the whole thing was forgotten.

* * *

Most convicts, it is true, upon their return to society reassert a heterosexual preference. But the long exposure, and perhaps participation in homosexual practices, leaves scars in the form of blunted sensibilities and guilt feelings.

There *are* ways to cut down on homosexuality in prison. Let wives visit their husbands, girl friends visit their boy friends, for instance. This is permitted at the Mississippi State Penitentiary at Parchman, at least as far as wives are concerned. Wives may visit the prison every Sunday from 1 to 3 P.M., and every third Sunday from 1 to 5 P.M., accompanying their husbands to rooms in a little red house near the main prison building. Columbus B. Hopper, a sociology professor who visited the prison, has been quoted as saying: "Officials and staff members . . . consistently praise the conjugal visit as a highly important factor in reducing homosexuality, boosting inmate morale, and . . . preserving marriages."

The chief objection to conjugal visits is that they clash with our society's mores. Our watchful moral guardians would howl at any proposal to allow conjugal visits at all prisons. Far better to let criminals be degraded by force or persuasion into homosexuality. Better to let sexual tensions accumulate month by month and year by year until in desperation a man is driven to making love to other men.

Still, even conjugal visits are not enough. They do not take into consideration the single prisoner. The ideal solution is outside visits—"furloughs"—for selected prisoners, a plan that is in effect in North Carolina, at Central Prison, and a plan that the former Attorney General Nicholas Katzenbach is said to be interested in. Furloughs for prisoners, according to an article I read, are permitted in Argentina, England, Wales, Canada, Northern Ireland, Scotland, Denmark, Switzerland, Germany, Greece, India, and Sweden. A few countries—the Philippines, Mexico, India, and Pakistan—even allow families of selected prisoners to live with them in open colonies.

But under our present conception of the purpose of a prison, I can foresee no solution to the problem of prison homosexuality. Rehabilitation and punishment cannot coexist, and our society demands punishment. Punishment results in resentment and degradation, loss of respect for oneself and loss of respect for the law. Until prisoners are *treated,* in environments as near normal as possible, instead of being *punished,* in completely abnormal environments, more men are going to be corrupted in prison than are rehabilitated. And prisons will continue to be giant faggot factories.

Situation Wanted: Lawyer, 35, Seeks Position as Janitor

Anonymous

After serving 3 years in state penitentiaries in Pennsylvania for forgery, I faced my approaching parole with a good deal of uneasiness. Though I was only 35 years old, and though I was a graduate of the University of Pittsburgh and the Duquesne Law School, and though before going to prison I had gotten good experience working in a law firm, still I was afraid I wouldn't be able to find a job.

For one thing, it was the spring of 1961, and Pennsylvania was in a severe recession. In Pittsburgh, unemployment hovered around 10%. Also, I had lost track of most of the friends who might have been able to help me. Some I had lost contact with because prison rules limited correspondence to only 10 people. Others I simply didn't want to keep in touch with, out of embarrassment. (The local newspapers had found the case of a lawyer in trouble with the law juicy copy, and coverage of my trial usually made page one of all three local papers.) Besides, prison was—in a way—a pleasant escape from my problems, and the occasional sympathy from friends that reached me permeated my shell and reduced me to tears.

So, with few friends, with few jobs available, and carrying the burden of being an ex-convict, things looked to be pretty rough.

The main rules governing my parole were that I needed a home, a job, and a sponsor—someone who promised to look after me. Also, I had to tell each and every prospective employer that I was an ex-convict.

I had a home—my brother Ted and his wife, Ann, agreed to let me be a nonpaying guest in their small apartment. As for a sponsor, I didn't know anyone. But my sister-in-law, who is something of a card, asked a friendly bookmaker to act as my sponsor. He agreed, and he had such a good line of gab that the parole agent complimented me on getting a man of such high moral caliber. Unfortunately, my job was the same kind of fraud. Ann talked a friend of hers in the used-car business into telling the Parole Board that he would give me a job with his company. Had I actually reported to him for work, though, he would have been flabbergasted.

So, upon my release from prison, I found myself a guest in my brother's home, with $25 to my name, with no one to counsel me, and with no prospects of employment.

Still, it was great to be free, to be able to take a walk when I was in the mood, to go to the refrigerator for a snack whenever I felt like it, and, most of all, to enjoy a measure of privacy unknown in jail. The first few days I was out, I walked all around Oakland, the civic area of Pittsburgh. After the monotony of gray prison walls and barren yards, everything—the buildings, the grass, the streets, the cars, the people—looked beautiful and exciting. Even the sooty smell from the nearby steel mills and the acrid fumes from chemicals were delightful.

My brother and his wife lived in a third-floor apartment consisting of three rooms—a living-room, a kitchen, and a bedroom. I slept on the sofa in the living-room. Both of them went out of their way to make me feel welcome. The dinners were varied, tasty, and plentiful. After the bland fare of prison, each meal was a virtual banquet. The neighbors didn't know anything about me, and friends of Ted and Ann's were told I was from Georgia, just visiting my brother for a while.

But soon the honeymoon was over. My living with them was an inconvenience all around. It inconvenienced me that, before going to bed on the sofa, I had to wait until Ted and Ann went to bed. Later the TV was moved into the bedroom and this helped somewhat, but it was still necessary for them to go through the living-room to reach the kitchen or bathroom, and at night such a trip usually succeeded in waking me up.

Of course, I wasn't exactly a blessing to have around ei-

94

ther. I was always there to witness a flare-up or an argument between my brother and sister-in-law, or to thwart any confidential or loving exchanges. Poor Ann, whenever she wanted a midnight snack, or just wanted to relax without her clothes on, had to don a robe for modesty's sake.

Fortunately, both Ted and Ann had jobs, so I wasn't too much of a financial burden to them. In fact, when I first came to live with them Ted gave me a weekly allowance of $10. Soon this dwindled to $5, and there were occasional weeks when even this wasn't forthcoming. But even when I was flat broke, I hated to ask him for money. Rather than impose, I did without. Whenever I went downtown to look for a job, I walked the 6 miles to save on streetcar fare. I limited my job-seeking trips to town to 2 days a week. I would schedule my first appointment for about 10 A.M., try to finish by 3 P.M., and skip lunch.

Maybe money can't buy happiness, but try living on less than $3 a day. Not just for one day, but day after day and week after week. Sometimes I found myself without even a nickel in my pocket, and if I had been in some kind of trouble I couldn't have made a phone call.

The only shoes I had were a pair of dress shoes and a pair of tennis sneakers. I wore the sneakers as often as I could, and the dress shoes managed to last about a year before the shoestrings broke. For weeks after that I walked around with one shoe held on by a fragment knotted through the two top buttonholes. Then the sole of the left shoe developed a hole. To hide it, whenever I sat down anywhere I would sit with my feet tucked under the chair. And whenever some clod said to me, "You know, you've got a hole in your shoe," I tried to laugh nonchalantly.

I don't seem to remember what happened to the rest of my clothes after I was arrested, but when I was paroled from prison I found I had two suits: the penitentiary suit given to every inmate upon his release, and a sharkskin suit, the crotch of which had been eaten by moths. When I was standing up, the latter suit looked presentable enough, but when I sat down the deterioration became very evident. As for the penitentiary suit, it didn't look too bad, but the style was one that had probably been popular during the Depression.

Dating girls was often an agonizing experience. Some dances didn't cost anything, but on the way home the girl might suggest stopping somewhere for coffee. Mentally I'd add up the change I had in my pocket—25¢ or 30¢. This was enough for coffee and nothing else, not even a tip. While she looked at the menu I'd hold my breath, and try giving her a hint by saying, "Oh, *I* don't want anything to eat." Once a girl did order a hamburger. Later, I swallowed hard and asked as casually as I could, "Say, you don't happen to have a quarter with you?"

* * *

I desperately wanted to find a job. I wanted to get my own apartment, to be independent, to have good clothes to wear and extra money in my pockets. So I made a list of all possible sources of employment, then pursued them one by one.

I visited the Federal building to check on civil-service opportunities, and also checked with the state civil-service office. After scanning the bulletin boards, I chose three or four positions that seemed right, and filled out applications, naturally listing my conviction. I also applied for a position as a social worker with the Department of Welfare, and I passed the test with a high mark. Shortly thereafter, the Federal Government disqualified me for a year from holding any civil-service job. The State Civil Service Board also disqualified me, indefinitely.

I also went to a State Employment Office. As it turned out, the manager and I had graduated from the same high school, and he promised to concentrate on finding a job for me. In the months that followed, I called at the State Employment Office once a week. After the third time, I was referred to an interviewer. He spoke to me a few times, then referred me to another man, and gradually I made the office rounds. Each time I went, the interviewer would study my application, ask about my conviction, and promise to keep on the lookout for a job for me. Nothing ever came of it.

I went to various private employment agencies. At the first place, my interviewer was enthusiastic as we discussed my education and experience. I seemed to have just the qualifications he was looking for. Then, true to the parole code, I told him about my conviction. He stared at me in disbelief. Finally he said, with no trace of conviction in his voice, "I understand how these things can happen, and I appreciate your telling me about it. We don't have any job for you, but I'll certainly get in touch with you if something comes up."

At two other agencies the same thing happened. I decided to forgo visiting the remaining agencies in town, partly because I was getting tired of being humiliated, and partly because the agency registration fee of $1 or $2 represented a week's spending money for me. I never heard from any of the three I did register with.

When I complained to my parole officer, he explained, "It's only fair to the employer that you tell him about your record." "But what about *me?*" I asked. "The only way I can overcome my record is to show what I can do. And if I have to tell about my record, I'll never get a *chance* to prove myself." The parole agent looked at me coolly, and said, "You should have thought about that before you committed a crime." "If I could live my life over," I said, "there are a lot of things I'd do differently. I've got to proceed from the position I'm in right *now.*" He shrugged. "Just make sure you state your record anytime you apply for a job, or you'll find yourself in a barrel of trouble."

In prison I had often heard this subject discussed by the inmates. "I tried for 4 weeks to find a job after my release," one fellow told me. "Every time I mentioned my record, the guy faded away. So I applied at a gas station and didn't tell the manager about my record. I got the job, and did so good he made me night manager. Then one day I see my parole agent drive in. I don't know how he found out I was working there, but he goes into the station and talks with the manager and then takes off again. The manager walks around for an hour or so looking embarrassed, then calls me in. 'Fred,' he says, 'I didn't know you had a police record. You've done a good job, but I'm going to have to let you go. I just couldn't feel easy knowing you were handling my money.' "

This inmate went on to tell me he managed to get another job in a gas station across town. "Two weeks later, I see my parole agent pull into the station. I just walked into the garage, hung my keys on the board, and walked out the back door. I never bothered coming back."

* * *

Actually, I was luckier than most ex-convicts. A Unitarian minister introduced me to the vice-president of a management-consulting firm, and he really did his best to help me, even buying me a new suit and treating me to lunch occasionally. He tried hard to land me a job, but couldn't. Once he told me, "Actually, a job isn't your main problem. You need a lot of internal inspection to develop insight. For a person of your position to do what you did, there's something wrong. Have you considered psychotherapy? You could probably get it through a clinic for a nominal fee." I agreed with him, and told him so as I fingered the two dimes and the streetcar check in my pocket, the extent of my wealth. What I didn't tell him was that when a person is as obssessed as I was with the problem of money, he can't concentrate on psychotherapy.

At this point, I was really desperate. I recalled an incident in the penitentiary. One inmate, Woody, had served 3 years for robbing a grocery store. Two weeks after his release, he went back to the same grocery store, robbed it again, and was immediately identified and sent back to prison with a new sentence. I told him it was a stupid thing to do. He agreed. "I couldn't have fouled up more if I had left a *calling*-card," he said. "But I was out of jail. I didn't have a dime in my pocket. I had nothing to eat. The first thing that popped into my mind was that that store had some *money!*" I laughed at his blunder then, but now I could understand his frame of mind.

I scoured Help Wanted columns every day and answered every ad for which I was even remotely qualified. It was a dreary grind: filling out applications, waiting to be interviewed, and later being told: "Your educational training suits

98

you for a better job than this, and I don't think you'd be satisfied . . .", or "I appreciate your frankness in telling me about your conviction, but. . . ." During the first few months I tried to get an office job or a sales job. I never got close to the former, and as for sales jobs, the only ones open were commission-only types. I didn't have a car, and even if I had one I wouldn't have been able to pay expenses while trying to earn a commission. Eventually I applied for factory work, but even the steel mills were so filled up they were laying people off. I tried writing articles, but couldn't sell any. I applied for a janitor's job at an office building, and couldn't even get that. The most depressing time of my life was returning home on the streetcar after a day spent trying to find a job. Not only was I going back home with the knowledge that another day had been wasted, but I would have the sickening feeling that I might be simply unemployable—there would *never* be a day when I would find a job, never in my entire life.

* * *

I spent one whole year looking for a job. During that time, I must have written about 150 letters to companies in the area —and in my financial situation, the postage costs really hurt. Sometimes the answers were sympathetic, but no jobs ever resulted. One letter I sent out had gone to the owner of a small supply firm. He didn't have a job for me, but he telephoned and invited me to come, as his guest, to a luncheon meeting of the Pittsburgh Experiment.

The Pittsburgh Experiment was the idea of a 33-year-old Episcopalian minister who, as he said, wanted to put Christianity into practice. He got together a group of businessmen—20 or 30—and for a year they had been meeting every Tuesday from noon to 1 o'clock. A prayer opened every meeting, then there was lunch, and either an inspirational talk or an open discussion. Any guest unable to pay his lunch check would leave it on the center of the table, and some other member would pick it up and pay for it.

Most of the guests, like myself, were looking for jobs, though a few were seeking religious or moral support. The

99

members of the group made a valiant effort to obtain employment for us, but because of the recession, the results were almost nil. One alcoholic got a job as a dishwasher in a local hospital, and seemed to be doing well. A few of us got 3 or 4 days' work at heavy cleaning jobs, or lawn-mowing. Nobody I know of received a good job.

Still, the luncheons were fun. They were like a reunion. Often, one-third of the guests were ex-convicts like myself, and many of us knew each other from the penitentiary. After the luncheon, several of us would go out, have a beer, and compare notes. A few were working part-time, and several others were living with girl friends and being supported by them. Some were on welfare. But all of us were struggling to make ends meet. The wealthiest of us was a man drawing $40 a week from unemployment (he had been working as a truck driver, but the firm had had a cutback and he had been furloughed).

As we sat around talking and nursing our beers, hoping someone would be flush enough to treat everybody else to a second round, we became more and more resentful, even after enjoying that free lunch. Here we were, willing to work and able to work, and nobody would give us the chance. One man said: "When I came out of Jackson [a prison in Michigan], I had $25, no family and no home. I got a room, paid a week in advance, had dinner, and had $10 left in my pocket. So I went into a bar and had a few beers, and saw this guy flash a roll of bills. When he left, I followed him. I yoked him, dragged him into an alley beside the joint, grabbed the wallet, and was gone in a few minutes. I got $225, and it was enough to give me support to get started. It's a hell of a strain to have no family and no friends, and to have 25 bucks between you and starvation."

He had gone straight ever since, but I wondered how long he would hold out.

My own way of admitting defeat was to apply for welfare. After a severe cross-examination, I qualified, and within a week I began receiving assistance.

I lived on welfare until my parole expired and I became free to travel, and free to apply for a job without telling my prospective employer of my record. I left Pennsylvania and settled in a place where I wasn't known. Today I'm the treasurer of a small corporation. I bank receipts, check vouchers, and write checks. My salary is adequate and I enjoy the work. To answer the obvious question: No, my employer doesn't know that I am a former convict. I don't like living a lie, and I would like to tell him just to get it off my mind, but my common sense warns me against it.

* * *

Before my release from prison, and later for background in writing this article, I read a number of articles and books about the parole system and the problems of parolees. From them I learned that society is not only suspicious of former convicts, but openly hostile toward them. Most people have the idea that prisoners are given paroles as a favor, but this isn't so. If there were no parole system, and all prisoners served their full sentences, afterwards they could not be supervised in any way—no check could be made to see if they were really going straight, or to see if they could be helped go straight. ". . . parole is not leniency or clemency," says one criminologist. "It is simply good insurance for society. . . . Parole merely transfers the convict from the restraints of prison to the community where he is confronted with another restraint, that of supervision."

Then there are the penalties. In most states, an ex-convict loses the right to vote. In others, he is considered legally dead, or he can no longer serve as a juror or testify as a witness, or he can't run for public office, or he can't make a contract, or he can't take a Federal civil-service examination or a state examination, or he can't even *get married*.

How a state that won't itself hire ex-convicts expects private employers to hire them is perplexing. No wonder that a survey taken of 475 employers some years back showed that 312—or 2 out of 3—would not hire an ex-convict.

As if the ex-convict's desperate struggle for a job were not enough, many jurisdictions impose strict rules on a parolee. Typically, he must be home by a certain time, usually 10

101

o'clock; not visit bars or any place where liquor is sold or drunk; not visit public dances; attend church regularly; not borrow money or valuables; not purchase anything on the installment plan without a parole officer's permission; and not see a girl other than his wife alone in a room.

The New York Times recently quoted the chairman of the State Parole Board as saying: "It may not be quite proper for me to say this, but in many instances we make these parolees lead a hell of a lot better life than we lead ourselves."

Things have worked out pretty well for me, I must admit. Still, I wish many reforms were enacted. Most of all, I wish more states would emulate New York, which is considering a bill to let first-offenders have their records sealed, once a probationary period had been passed. But I also wish that more convicts, while in prison, were taught useful trades. I wish that the civil service were more lenient toward ex-convicts, that parole officers had fewer cases to supervise, and that insurance companies wouldn't be so reluctant to post surety bonds for ex-convicts who have found jobs.

All this is a lot to ask, I know.

In view of the fact that the American crime bill is $27 billion a year, that serious crimes rose 13% in 1964, and that 1 out of 3 parolees and 7 out of every 10 ex-convicts revert to crime, I don't think it's *too* much to ask.

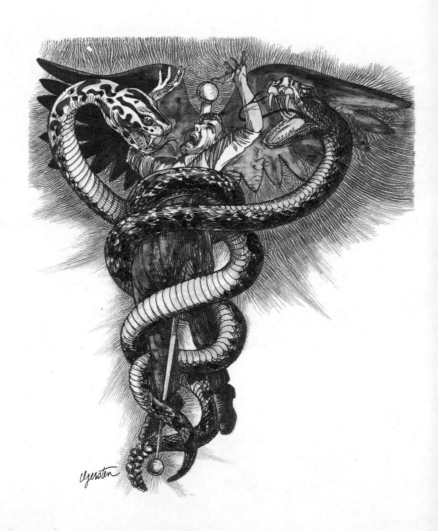

Needed: Medicare for the Chronically Ill

By Robert Reisner

A chronic disease is a disease that lingers. If you fall down a flight of stairs and break a leg, the leg will heal in a few weeks. If you have a severe heart attack, you can count on giving up the ghost within a short time. But if you get a chronic disease like cancer, cerebral palsy, schizophrenia, arthritis, rheumatism, diabetes, multiple sclerosis, tuberculosis, muscular dystrophy, epilepsy, Parkinson's disease, or nephritis, why, you'll live on and on—painfully, and expensively. According to the Bureau of Public Health, 70 million Americans have one or more chronic conditions, not including people who are institutionalized. Of the 70 million, 13.5 million have some limitation on their activity; 3.5 million have trouble getting around alone; 1 million are confined to their homes. These figures are going to jump as people live longer: Chronic disease has an affinity for older people. Of people 75 and over, 55% have a chronic disease, as compared with 40% of the general population. To quote *Health Progress in the United States: 1900-1960*, by Monroe Lerner and Odin W. Anderson, "the survival of a larger proportion of our population to the older ages, when the likelihood of incurring many diseases reaches a maximum, would alone lead to an increased incidence and prevalence of many conditions, especially the chronic diseases."

It's a scary prospect. A man may work hard all his life, and at the age of 50 have amassed a lordly sum to send his kids through college, or to buy a home in Florida to retire to. Then zap! he's got cancer, or a member of his family has schizophre-

105

nia, and along come unending, enormous medical bills. In a few years, the guy's a pauper.

Do chronic diseases really cost that much? Well, let me tell you the story of my life. . . .

At the age of 12, I suddenly began starting down the long hallway of our railroad apartment to the bathroom several times a night. I was also bothered by a great thirst. My father, who was a dentist with a fair knowledge of medicine, told my mother that I should have a blood test, and that I might have diabetes. My mother was quite disturbed at this suggestion, she having a Christian Scientist frame of mind, and I don't think she ever forgave my father when his diagnosis was substantiated by a physician.

Diabetes is caused by the body's inability to break down sugar. The pancreas normally secretes a substance called insulin, which breaks down sugar, but the diabetic's pancreas has gone on a holiday. So if he gets too much sugar in his body, why, he goes into a coma and dies. To prevent this, diabetics regularly get dosed with insulin from animals.

As chronic diseases go, diabetes isn't so bad. It isn't as painful as arthritis or rheumatism, and not as disabling as multiple sclerosis, and not as debilitating as cancer. Like TB, it even has an aura of romance about it—it's the disease of civilized people. But it is also goddam expensive.

When I came down with diabetes 33 years ago, a lot of people must have gone out and celebrated. Take the men who make surgarless foods. I have to pay 20¢ for a sugarless mint that costs 5¢ in the normal confectionary world. Diabetic chocolate bars cost twice as much as regular ones, and diabetic canned goods and diabetic ice cream are also overpriced (even though the ice cream often causes diarrhea). Years ago, I was told that the prices were jacked up because the market was small. Today, however, there are millions of diabetics, and millions more on the way. (Nor do I understand why the "diabetic" foods are usually dangerously high in fat content.) As it is, diabetes ranks eighth among the leading causes of death in this country; soon, it may rank eighth as a major industry.

Doctors also must have rejoiced. Diabetics make wonderful patients. We cannot be cured, and we don't die for quite some time (and when we do, the cause is often something other than diabetes). For the doctor, having a diabetic as a patient is like having money invested in a blue-chip, growth stock. (Kidding aside, in my personal experience, physicians —far from taking satisfaction from the chronically ill—have felt frustrated in not being able to bring about a permanent cure.)

The only people, aside from my parents, who must have wept bitter tears when I came down with diabetes were the folks from the Internal Revenue Service. I haven't been able to help them out much.

You've heard that blind people learn to hear better, and develop a keener sense of touch and smell? Well, one scientist says that when one sense goes, the others suffer, too. And the same holds for people with chronic diseases: They get all sorts of other ailments. Maybe the body is so busy fighting off the main enemy that it's vulnerable to other, less important enemies.

Diabetics, for example, may develop eye trouble—I know, because I've lost the sight of an eye. Diabetics also develop neuropathies: Their extremities become numb. So a diabetic must be cautious about the shoes he wears, and periodically examine his feet for bruises. A few years ago I must have stepped on a nail without realizing it. It took 4 months of hospitalization, and many doctor's visits, to cure the wound. Another time I fell asleep with my leg against a radiator. When I woke up, my leg had third-degree burns. I almost lost it, and it took a year to heal.

These complications from diabetes occur every few years or so, and they require extra money. As for "normal" costs, I have to get a new supply of insulin every 10 days ($2), blood tests two or three times a year ($7), have a regular check-up every 4 or 5 months ($15 a visit), and invest in vitamin supplements (diabetics don't utilize food to the maximum), urine-test equipment, needles, and syringes. The *basic* costs of a diabetic, I would say, run $400 a year.

Those needles present a special problem. A diabetic has

to get them from his doctor via a prescription—he can't just go to a drug store. Once I went to a drug store where I had bought insulin many times, and tried to get a needle. The druggist read the law to me. Irritated, I rolled up my sleeve and showed him my unmarked veins. "Look," I shouted, "I'm *clean,* man. Call a cop and ask him to witness it. I'm not a hophead!" Despite my histrionics, I had to pay for a visit to my doctor.

* * *

Health insurance is no help. Most plans refuse to cover anybody for an illness he had when he first enrolled. But more: Every single policy I have ever had, when I was ill, reneged. When I developed a neuropathy in my feet, for example, Blue Cross refused to give me a penny. The Blue Cross policy didn't cover any complications that came with diabetes. Which meant that it covered *nothing,* as far as I was concerned. What am I likely to get that doesn't stem from my diabetes? Perhaps bubonic plague.

Recently I became a member of the American Federation of Television and Radio Artists. This group offered a limited insurance policy to its members for a few dollars a year. Joyfully, I signed up. Soon after, I entered a Boston hospital for eye surgery—I had retinitis. Coming back to New York on the plane, I was cheered by the thought of the A.F.T.R.A. policy. I didn't expect it to cover the surgery, but hoped it might pay for the medication, and maybe even for a few days in a hospital bed. The policy turned out to be a cruel hoax. It listed a mere eight items it paid for. Like the cost of renting crutches (you can buy them cheaply), the cost of renting a wheelchair (one Catholic charity lends them free of charge), the cost of renting a hospital bed *for home use only,* the cost of blood transfusions *for patients with leukemia* (10 pints only), and so on.

Now, for a diabetic I haven't done badly. I am a jazz buff, and taught jazz history for 8 years at Brooklyn College, and have lectured around the country. I have written 13 books, including *Show Me the Best Parts, Bird: The Legend of Char-*

lie Parker, and *Captions Courageous,* the last of which earned me $20,000. I have sold magazine articles to *Nugget, Playboy, and Esquire,* and my collages and paintings have done quite well. Last year, for example, I earned about $6,000. But I also spent $1,003 on medical bills.

The income-tax people were, naturally, suspicious. I was called down for a hearing. I showed them all my bills. Then one investigator told me: "I knew you were honest. I was just puzzled that you were *alive.*"

I am 45 years old. I have never been married. My parents are dead, and I support no one but myself. I don't have expensive tastes or expensive hobbies. When I eat out, I may spend up to $2 at the Automat, and I am painfully aware that that restaurant is raising its prices. I own two out-of-fashion suits. I live in a 3-room apartment in Greenwich Village, for which I pay $75-a-month rent. I have never taken a vacation, and never left the United States. I am a careful man, and have saved as much as I can. As a result, my bank balance, as of Nov. 1, 1966, was $19.35. All in all, I estimate that over the past 33 years I have easily spent $25,000 paying for my diabetes and its complications.

I have always likened myself to the spider in the story about Robert Bruce: Whenever I put together a little nest egg for a vacation, or perhaps a better apartment, it was eaten up by my medical expenses. And as I grow older, I get ill more often—my other eye, the good one, is threatened. Some time ago, a study was made showing that children who were diabetic are more intelligent than normal children. If I had my way today, instead of diabetes I would choose mental retardation. At least a dumb ditch-digger can earn a decent living.

* * *

The expense is one cross a person with a chronic disease has to bear. But let's not forget about the disease itself.

When I was a child, it was almost fun to be a diabetic, despite my having to get several hypodermic shots a day (slow-working insulins hadn't been perfected then). There was mystery and romance about the needle and the injections. And I got a lot of attention in school: The biology teacher would always ask me for a sample of my urine, then show the class how Benedict's solution reacts to the presence of sugar.

I soon learned that being a diabetic also meant that I had to live life carefully. I had to be careful of what foods I ate, and how much. I had to be careful how active I was—too active and I got insulin reaction; too inactive, and I got sugar reaction. I calculate that in my life I have experienced several hundred reactions, each one different, each producing its own peculiar sense of panic. Little mistakes can have painful consequences.

Bigger mistakes can have even more painful consequences. Once I veered from standard treatment and was put into the hands of an unorthodox healer. This fellow claimed he could cure me by bone manipulations. Naturally, the manipulations necessitated a reduction in my insulin intake. And the treatment seemed to work. Flushed with success, the healer decided to eliminate all my insulin for one day. As a result, I went into a diabetic coma and had to be hospitalized. Since that time, every medical office I enter has to have on the wall, "Doctor of Medicine."

One of my closest brushes with the permanent nod came when I was a student at Brooklyn College. I had met a girl who shared my enthusiasm for old Tin Pan Alley songs. I kept a little notebook filled with titles, and whenever we dated I'd serenade her.

This lovely creature lived at the end of Coney Island. Once we spent a long date together which stretched until 4 in the morning. I bade her farewell on the boardwalk and headed for the subway. The excitement, the walk, and the lack of food for a few hours, of course, had produced a deficiency of sugar in me. I began to feel the weakness, sweat, inner tremors, hunger, and little panicky sensations that spelled insulin shock. I reached for my life-line—a lump of sugar I always carried in my pocket. It wasn't there. I had changed my trousers during the afternoon, and hadn't stuck a piece in the watch pocket. Every store was closed. Not a human being in sight. Was I to pass out and expire just when I had met a girl who knew as many songs as I did?

In my rapidly fogging brain I remembered that I was not too far from the last loop on the Brighton subway line. There was a little all-night eatery there, open for the convenience of subway personnel. After what seemed an eternity I staggered to the counter, ordered a cup of coffee, put three lumps of sugar in it, and within 10 minutes the symptoms of insulin reaction disappeared. The girl married someone else.

Another inconvenience, in addition to occasionally nearly dying, is getting in trouble with the cops. Once, for example, I was lecturing around the country on the history of jazz, and I had brought along a quartet of well-known musicians to underscore my remarks. We entertained at the Berkshire Museum in Massachusetts, and decided to drive back to New York the same night instead of staying over. It was 3 in the morning, and we were cruising through Central Park. A police car came up and we were ordered to stop. The four Negro musicians and I were asked if we had any drugs or marijuana on us. Mustering all the dignity I could, I said, "I am an instructor at Brooklyn College on the subject of jazz music. These gentlemen are musicians, and we are returning from a lecture and concert we gave." The reply: "Get out and place your hands on the sides of the car." They searched the quartet and found them clean. When they came to me, I suddenly remembered that I had a hypodermic needle on me—in case I had stayed over in Massachusetts, I was going to need some insulin. The cops found the works on me, and I could see *promotion* in their eyes. The leader of the quartet looked at me in amazement and said, *"You,* professor!" Then, to his sidemen, "See guys, you never know." I showed the cops my diabetic identification card. They let us go. I never told the cats I was with what was on that card. To this day they think I'm a junkie.

*   *   *

My point is that a diabetic, or anyone with a chronic disease, suffers enough without having to suffer all his life paying huge

111

medical bills. It isn't so bad if you have a chronic disease, or someone close to you has one, and you are very, very rich. Or if you are very, very poor—you can always get state help, despite possible humiliation. But if you are neither very rich nor very poor, you may be wiped out. It's not fair. And that's why I think that this country should provide financial help to the chronically ill, either directly or through government-aided insurance.

This is not a plea for the hypochondriacs, or the girls who want nose jobs. Financial help is a dire necessity for the innocent victim of a cruel and unexplainable tragedy. Chronics often can work up to the end of their lives if their spirits aren't crushed by the double anxieties of physical and financial disasters. Medicare for the chronically ill would induce a frame of mind that allowed for moderate spending, and not just for pinching and hoarding until the day of disaster. It would free the chronic's family from depression, and let them enjoy life a little. It would prevent news articles like the following, which appeared a few months ago:

Mercy Killing—and a Suicide

Houston, Texas—Mrs. May Hyatt, 45, once a vivacious redhead, had been in a deep coma for nearly 6 years, a victim of encephalitis.

She was periodically a patient in a hospital where doctors called her the "sleeping beauty."

Last May, she was placed in a nursing home.

Her husband, Herbert C. Hyatt, 47, buildings manager of the General Services Administration here, drove to the nursing home yesterday and entered her room as he had done many times before.

A supervisor heard two shots and ran into the room. Mrs. Hyatt lay dying on her bed, shot through the left side of her head. Hyatt was sitting on the floor against his wife's bed, a bullet wound in his right temple and a pistol near his hand. He died during surgery.

Police called it a "mercy killing and a suicide."

Two sons, Donald, 17, and Alger, 15, survive.

Mrs. Hyatt, who liked to ride, hunt, and fish with her husband and the two boys, first became ill in October, 1960, when she complained of dizziness and a headache.

By 1964, all her understanding, memory, and consciousness had been permanently erased.

Investigators said the medical bills forced Hyatt to sell the

family home and also consumed a fund put aside for the college education of the two sons.

*   *   *

If everybody who had a chronic disease banded together, we'd be the largest single minority in the country. Our slogan could be, Chronic Power.

An estimated 2.4 million Americans have diabetes. Some 5.6 million are potential diabetics—they will develop the disease sometime in their lives. At least 250,000 new cases are being diagnosed every year.

Multiple sclerosis, a disease of the brain and spinal cord, affects 500,000 in this country. Some of the symptoms: blurred or double vision, tremors, malco-ordination, speech difficulty, partial or complete paralysis. No occupational or racial group is immune. Multiple sclerosis is impartial and unfair.

There are 13 million Americans suffering from some form of arthritis, including 198,000 under the age of 25.

Cerebral palsy is caused by damage to those parts of the brain that control and co-ordinate muscle action. Some 600,-000 children and adults are affected.

Muscular dystrophy, which also debilitates the muscles, has about 200,000 victims. Approximately two-thirds of them are children.

Parkinson's disease, a disorder of the nervous system, is characterized by tremors, rigidity of various muscles, and weakness. A million and a half Americans have this disease.

Some 14.5 million Americans between 18 and 79 have heart disease.

From only this brief survey, which omits many chronic conditions (alcoholism, mental illness, nephritis, cancer, bone diseases, nervous diseases, tuberculosis, etc.), we arrive at about 33 million people with chronic illness. Next year, President Johnson will try to get Medicare coverage for 1 million disabled people under the age of 65. My question is, What of the other millions who have to pay gigantic medical bills? A guaranteed annual wage for all citizens is one way to wipe out

113

poverty. A better way might be Medicare for all the chronically ill: I'm sure that a tremendous percentage of all the poverty in this country is attributable to chronic diseases. One medical expert I've spoken to says that providing Medicare for the four largest groups of the chronically ill—those with heart disease, cancer, cerebral-vascular disorders, and arthritis—would increase the Government's spending on health programs by only a third. And A.P. Merrill, M.D., executive director of St. Barnabas Hospital for Chronic Diseases in New York, has told *Fact:*

It is our considered judgment that the cost of chronic disease care cannot possibly be borne by the individual or his family. It appears that the only long-range solution to the problem is government support. Such support, whether it be on the local, state, or national level, would undoubtedly have to be underwritten through some means of either direct or indirect taxation, such as has been done for Medicare.

Other countries, like England, Australia, and Sweden, make some provision to help people with chronic diseases. But this country does little, banking on foundations and voluntary support. And, considering how fierce the battle for Medicare was, it will likely be many more years before we start extending a helping hand to the chronically ill. Ours is, after all, what the sociologists call a *Gesellschaft* society, where people are impersonal with each other and out for all they can get, and not a *Gemeinschaft* society, where people feel bonded together as allies.

This became very clear to me just a few months ago. I was so down and out, so burdened with medical bills, that for the first time in my life I began thinking of suicide. Now, I have lived in the same house for 12 years. I know and am friendly with almost everyone in the building. One Sunday morning, early, I sat on the stoop with my head in my hands, in utter dejection. A little group of my neighbors came out of the building and, seeing me, asked what was the matter. I told them that I was in terrible trouble. They smiled kindly and said, "We'd love to hear about it and help, but we have to go or we'll be late for church."

Rockefeller's Millions: The Poor People of New York

By Gary A. Youree

Five years ago, soon after my 30th birthday, I arrived in New York City in my 7-year-old Studebaker. I had $11, one suit, and a college diploma. Behind me were 3 years in the Baptist ministry, 3 years of teaching, and 2 years traveling around the South, West, and Midwest doing odd jobs. I was determined that my next job would be one where I could do something meaningful, and when I emerged from the Holland Tunnel into downtown New York City, I was really looking forward to wonderful adventures.

The next day I went to the New York State Employment office. My interviewer there riffled through his card file a couple of times, then asked apologetically, "Interested in social work?"

"I'm *very* much interested," I said, "but I'm probably not qualified. I haven't had many sociology courses."

He shrugged. "All you need is a college degree. *Any* degree."

I told him, enthusiastically, that I was his man. So he wrote me a letter of referral and told me how to get to the personnel office of the Welfare Department. As I left, he said, "This is something to hang onto until you find something better."

And so, after 2 weeks of training, I was assigned to one of New York's 24 Welfare centers, along with a dozen other trainees.

Among other things, I learned that here, in a city of nearly 8 million, the business and cultural center of the world, 500,000 New Yorkers are so poor that they get regular sti-

117

pends from the Welfare Department. Most of those on Welfare —over half—have come from out of town, usually from Puerto Rico or the deep South. They receive, on the average, $70 a month. Eight other states, below New York in per-capita income, spend proportionately more per capita than New York does on Welfare. Yet New York is generally conceded to have the most liberal Welfare laws in the nation. We trainees were given a manual, *Policies Governing the Administration of Public Assistance,* which stated:

The primary duty of the Department of Welfare is the granting of assistance and care to persons found to be in need. . . . The objective is to restore the applicant to a condition of self-support or maintenance by relatives who are legally responsible.

In addition, the Welfare staff must determine exactly who is eligible for relief. And while people are on relief, it was our job to investigate them to make sure they were on the up-and-up. Bleeding-hearts are warned against "exaggerated solicitude" and "overwillingness to do things for the client." Authoritarians are warned: "Equally bad is a punitive attitude which rejects reasonable evidence of need. . . ." The granting of public assistance must be administered "in a sound and humane fashion."

To be honest, in my 3 years as a Welfare investigator and my 1 year in the Welfare office, I didn't see much "exaggerated solicitude." But I saw a great deal of punishment and inhumanity.

I met a supervisor who habitually referred to her clients as "bums." Almost every day I could hear her bellowing on the phone to someone who had the audacity to telephone the office. Another supervisor often expressed the opinion that "They have only themselves to blame for their troubles." I heard an investigator refer to his caseload as "Those lousy bastards."

A lady investigator was interviewing one of her clients. I couldn't hear what he said to her, but everybody heard her scream: "Get out! *Get out or I'll kill you!*" (She has since been promoted to supervisor.)

Typical of how clients are treated is what happened to a worn-out, middle-aged prostitute. After a few minutes, the man interviewing her decided she was not eligible for Welfare. In his record book, he wrote: *Could not satisfactorily explain past management.* In despair the woman cried out, "But what am I going to *do?*" The worker got up and walked away, calling to her over his shoulder: "That's *your* problem."

Prostitutes rarely get Welfare. Single men also are usually passed over, though many apply. Most of the single men are sent to the Municipal Lodging House in the Bowery, where they get meal tickets and are placed in one of the "hotels" there. I have found that most men, in preference to a night in the Municipal Lodging House, would rather go to jail.

I was interviewing Mr. S——, a 40-year-old homosexual. He had never applied for Welfare before. A Broadway stage designer who was unemployed, he had borrowed all he could from his family and friends, then had been evicted from his apartment. He had come to our office, spoken with me, and another worker had sent him to the Municipal Lodging House.

He came back the next day, frantic. "Have you *seen* that place? It's *filthy!* And the 'hotel' they sent me to—it was a flophouse! Bedbugs . . . and those men!"

Two "lush divers" (men who climb over the partitions that separate flophouse beds) had tried to attack him sexually.

"I may be a homosexual," Mr. S—— wailed, "but I'm a *decent* person. My God! How could you people *send* me to such a place?"

Mr. S—— had left the "hotel" and spent the rest of the night in a bus station.

I consulted with my supervisor. She peeked out the door to get a look at him, then decided we could get him a room and money for food because "He doesn't look like a bum."

At other times, I've known single men applying for Welfare to be *rejected* because they didn't look like bums. "Look how *clean* he is. He must be getting help from somebody. Or he's working somewhere."

In short, the decision whether someone is eligible for

Welfare is often made arbitrarily. And even when someone *is* lucky enough to qualify, help may come too late.

Once I was sent out into the field to investigate an emergency case. The family involved was about to be evicted. When I arrived, a marshal had preceded me and all the family's possessions were on the sidewalk. It is, of course, illegal to block the sidewalk, so the Sanitation Department was busy throwing the family's furniture onto the back of a trash truck to be carted to a City depository.

Sitting on a milk crate in their empty apartment I spoke to the family. Their three children ran around excitedly, asking what was happening. My interview took an hour and a half, including time spent calling my office for instructions (nobody seemed to know what to do). Finally I sent the family to the office for hotel placement, giving them carfare out of my own pocket. I don't know whether they ever got their furniture back.

* * *

On the same day, I made another investigation. Mr. H—— was about my age. He had a wife and three small children. Six months before, Mr. H—— had been in a car accident and sustained a back injury, and since then had been unable to work. A lawsuit was in progress, but would take at least 3 years— and his lawyer would get half the award, the hospital and doctors most of the rest. For 6 months the H—— family had been on relief, and they had recently made a complaint.

I was greeted at the door with, "Who the hell are *you?*"

I showed him my identification card.

"*Another* investigator? You're the third in 6 months!"

Mr. H—— went on to tell me that the Department of Welfare was sending him $8 semimonthly. His apartment was almost bare of furniture—he had sold or hocked everything he could. He had also borrowed heavily. With some well-chosen words, Mr. H—— asked me why he was not getting more than $8 every half-month. It took me an hour to convince him and his wife that I was really going to do something about it. They were angry, desperate people, and they were accustomed to better times.

When I got back to the office, I discovered that the H—— family had been the victims of a mix-up. It seems that Mr. H——'s first investigator thought he was getting unemployment insurance of $50 a week, hence the small $16-a-month stipend. But Mr. H—— wasn't getting anything—he had been self-employed, and he was unable to work. So, because of an error, for 6 months Mr. H—— and his family had been needlessly suffering.

*　　*　　*

The worst thing about trying to prove that you need financial help is that you are considered guilty until proven innocent. A man is ineligible until proven eligible—and the burden of proof is on him. As soon as he walks in to apply for Welfare, he is labeled a bum and a liar.

Once I interviewed a family of four in the Welfare office. This was the first time they had applied for Welfare. The father had been employed for 11 years, then his employer went out of business. The man's income had been low, and he had no savings. He brought in all the records that could possibly establish his eligibility. He provided phone numbers, which I called. They were out of food and had come to Welfare as a last resort. Both the man and his wife were embarrassed. Before the interview was over, she was in tears. Very nice people.

I went to my supervisor. I presented her with all the facts. Twice. She could find nothing amiss, except that: "I don't know—it looks too *pat* for me." And she decided that the family would get no emergency cash until an investigator had been in their home. It was a Friday, and the family would have to wait until the following week to get food.

I told them this, and they took it quietly. I had $4 with me, and gave them $2. I felt as bad as they did. They were more "eligible" than anybody else I had ever interviewed.

Maybe the trouble with them was that they were too polite and understanding.

121

On the last day I worked for the Welfare Department, Friday, May 7, 1965, I was interviewing Mr. and Mrs. G——. The Welfare office is, incidentally, about half the size of a gymnasium, and quite as noisy. Row after row of straight-backed chairs were filled with people—about 100 of them—waiting to speak to the investigators. A long line stood at the receptionist's desk. Many of these people had arrived at 9 A.M. and would still be waiting at noon. Some would be there all day.

Mr. and Mrs. G—— had nine children. While I was talking to her, a woman in the crowd suddenly jumped up and yelled: "Give me some money! Give me some goddam money!" The woman started over to the receptionist's desk. Two Welfare patrolmen intercepted her. A call was made upstairs, and her investigator came down to talk with her and calm her down. That was all. But if she had been a man, she would probably have been hauled back into the patrolmen's little room. (Police brutality is not limited to City cops. One of our Welfare patrolmen told me he occasionally raps a client for "getting smart.")

I resumed my interview with Mr. and Mrs. G——. Mrs. G—— had become increasingly hostile during the interview, and I could foresee trouble. She was making me nervous. She answered all the questions with a loud, "I've already been asked that. A hundred times. It's inna record. Don't you people read the record?"

"Mrs. G——, the Department isn't satisfied with all your answers . . ."

"Well, that's all the answers you're gonna get! I've told the truth. Those Puerto Ricans and niggers come in here and lie and they get money. Well, I've told you the truth and I'm gonna get it too!" And so on.

The G—— family had been rejected because of "Inadequate explanation of management." That is, they could not explain how they had managed to live without Welfare in the past—up to 5 years ago. People with bad memories, or people who haven't kept records, are in trouble. "Inadequate explanation" is the most frequent reason for rejection.

Where children are involved, however, Welfare help will always be granted—after a lot of harassment. Mrs. G—— knew this. But the game must be played. It must not appear too easy to get on Welfare.

"Now, Mr. G——," I went on, "what were you doing between March and June of 1963?"

Mr. G——, according to my records, was a diabetic and an alcoholic. He had a history of mental illness. Mrs. G—— had "hypertension," "female troubles," and a history of mental illness. Their 18-year-old son was mentally retarded, suffered from a rheumatic heart, and had a Juvenile Court record. Their 16-year-old daughter was "emotionally disturbed," had a record of "promiscuity," and also had a Juvenile Court record. Four other children were in school, and all had records of high absenteeism. There were three preschool children, one of them mentally retarded.

The G—— family had had no money coming in since Mr. G—— had been fired from his job as a messenger. He had passed out on the street. His boss said he was drunk. Mr. G—— said it was diabetes. Whatever the cause, the result was that the G—— family, right now, had no money, no lights, no food. And their landlord was threatening them with eviction.

I didn't exactly fall in love with the G—— family, but I knew that they needed money. Yes, they were unco-operative, yes, they needed rehabilitation and treatment. But most of all they needed *money*.

I wrote into my case record a strong recommendation that the G—— family get emergency assistance. I went over to talk to my supervisor. "Why aren't the oldest children working?" she asked. "Why isn't Mr. G—— looking for work? Why isn't *Mrs.* G—— looking for work? I think *somebody* in the family is working. They've been managing *up* to now." I argued with her, but authority triumphed. No money for the G—— family until an investigator had visited them.

So I went back to confront Mrs. G——.

"We need money," she snapped. "We haven't eaten since yesterday."

"I'll do the best I can for you."

123

"Just get us some money. That's the best you can do."

"Mrs. G———, I'll send an investigator to your place—on an *urgent* basis. He'll be there within—"

"What about *today?*"

". . . er, and I've been instructed to tell you that either you or your husband will have to look for work, or—"

"Work? I'm sick and I have sick children! My husband's sick! We're gonna get evicted. We don't have lights. We don't have *food.* You're telling me—"

"Now, Mrs. G———," I interrupted, "you won't get anywhere by screaming."

My desk was the center of attention.

"Like hell I won't!" she bellowed. "I won't get nowhere by being *nice!* I'm gonna start a riot! If I don't get money right now, Goddamit, I'm gonna start a *riot!"*

My supervisor called me over. She had decided the G——— family should be given emergency cash for food. And she specifically told me to tell them we were *not* giving them the money because Mrs. G——— had made a scene.

* * *

I do not mean to imply that all of us Welfare employees were heartless and incompetent, or even that we didn't have our own troubles. We had it rough, too.

For one thing, everybody hated us. Not long ago, I overheard two teen-agers walking down my street singing, to the tune of *America,* "Go home relief, go home relief. . . ." In a popularity contest among New York's poor, the Welfare Department would rank even below the Police Department.

As much as anybody, we employees ourselves hated the Welfare Department. We were unappreciated and overworked. Two hours after arriving on the job in May, 1960, I found myself responsible for 60 families—a relatively light caseload. A fellow trainee got 90 and quit the following week.

On my first day, I sat at my desk and spoke to a harassed-looking fellow on my left. "Been here long?" I asked.

124

"Nine years," he answered, apparently glad to be taken away from his work.

"Making a career of it, huh?"

"Naw—just marking time."

When I resigned, he was still there—13 years and still marking time. But of every 100 trainees hired in May, 1964, over 40 had quit by May, 1965.

A job with the Welfare Department does pay $6000 a year, and does offer security. Many people remain because they are not qualified to do anything else. A number have physical or mental problems. Many are middle-aged or older and cannot get other jobs. But for many employees the disadvantages outweigh the advantages. Many staffers, for example, take the test to become a supervisor. Some who pass it refuse the appointment. Being a supervisor is an admission that you're making a career of it.

Even our heartlessness toward our clients was, in a way, understandable. Many of us were only a paycheck away from being a case-number ourselves. Naturally, we didn't want to identify, or be identified, with our clients, so we continually tried to prove that they were different from us—they were lazy, or inept, or bums. *We* would never get so hard up that *we* had to go on Welfare.

The nature of the system also helps explain why Welfare employees often become their clients' enemies. The fact is that Welfare wants fewer clients. That's a sign that the Department is doing its job properly. Besides, if everybody who actually was eligible for Welfare applied for help, chaos would result. There are over 500,000 people on Welfare in New York City now, but there are another million, just as poor, who are not on Welfare. Many of them prefer to remain in extreme poverty rather than lose whatever little dignity they have left. There is a terrible stigma attached to "being on Welfare." In my building, I heard a Puerto Rican teen-ager shout to a friend, "Hey, case-number. . . ." Applicants begin their pleas with, "I wouldn't be here, but—" The Welfare Department, no doubt, finds this stigma helpful. Keeping clients away keeps taxes down, and keeping taxes down keeps the big-time politicos, who rule over the Welfare Department, happy.

* * *

There is no question but that the Department of Welfare, as a rehabilitative institution, is a failure. It dispenses funds on the basis of arbitrary decisions; it denies assistance in cases of genuine need; it has done virtually nothing to make its employees professionals. True, college degrees are required, but my degree in literature didn't help me deal with people's problems. What is needed are intelligent, mature people who want to help others—and to hell with the college degree. Let the frustrated actors and the moonlighting housewives mark time elsewhere. Welfare is a full-time job and demands knowledge and dedication.

The Welfare Department does not do its job in referring clients with mental, legal, or marital problems to other agencies. A majority, I would say, of the people on Welfare have problems other than financial ones. Yet Welfare workers are not even trained to recognize these problems. A man quits his job and can't get another. He comes to Welfare. He has a long history of quitting jobs, always because of "personal conflicts" with his employers or fellow employees. Instead of realizing that this man needs psychiatric help, Welfare punishes him (and his wife and children) for having left his last job by not giving him any money.

Worst of all, the Welfare Department has little compassion. Its prevailing attitudes are arrogance, contempt, and suspicion. It pays no attention to the privacy of the poor, to their need for self-respect, to their elementary human desires. Recently the Citizens Committee for Children of New York condemned the whole Welfare system as "a monster bureaucracy that dehumanizes its clients."

Some rules that Welfare has laid down include: employed men on relief should use only 90 razor blades a year; unemployed men, 50. A 12-year-old should get 20¢ a month for school expenses. A woman should use no more than 48 bobby

126

pins a year. A woman, employed, should buy two lipsticks a year; a woman who is unemployed, one.

Most clients are heavily in debt, but the Department pays no debts other than rent and utilities. It forbids clients to pay other debts out of their Welfare money, even if their furniture is being repossessed. Of course, the Department wouldn't dream of letting a client buy a TV set. Once, at Christmastime, I was interviewing a family of five in their apartment. The mother followed me outside the door and asked half-heartedly, "Uh, Mr. Youree, do you think you could get us a little something extra for toys for the children?" My answer was no: No provision is made in the Welfare budget for luxuries like that.

Yes, the Welfare Department abuses the poor, and so do the government agencies that control the purse-strings. But while I'm on the subject of who's to blame, let me mention

Employers. Many of them pay only the minimum legal wage to their help, counting on Welfare to provide whatever else a destitute family needs. Also, knowing that an employee on Welfare can't quit or he will lose his stipend, employers treat such employees like dirt. The employee becomes a virtual slave. Other employers habitually fire a new man before he becomes eligible to join a union and get a mandatory salary raise—then hire other employees, fire them, and so on.

Landlords. Knowing that the poor are ignorant of the law, and afraid of lawyers and courts, many landlords will neglect making necessary repairs—and evict their tenants whenever they feel like it. Some deliberately jack up the rent for Welfare tenants, hoping that Welfare will cover the increase. If Welfare doesn't, out the family goes.

Retailers. When it comes to finances, the poor are babes in the woods. A widow I had as a client bought an electric iron from a door-to-door salesman representing a large appliance house. She gave him $5 down and a dollar every week for 26 weeks—for an iron she could have bought for $10. Another client, against Welfare rules, bought a portable TV set for $10 down and $5 from each of 53 subsequent Welfare checks. For a $95 TV, all in all she paid $275. (Welfare clients are not

permitted to buy on credit either, but many do rather than ask
—or wait—for a special grant.)

Many grocers pad the bills of people on Welfare. A grocer may keep his bills on pieces of wrapping paper. Later, he adds a new figure to the column, or changes a 3 to an 8. A number of my clients complained to me about this, and I told them to keep their own bills. One lady did. It came to $26. Her grocer's bill came to over $36.

Usually I told my clients to shop at supermarkets, where prices are usually lower and no credit is extended. But even supermarkets in poor areas sometimes charge higher prices for the poor, knowing that the poor don't know better, or don't have the time to shop around. A recent study done by the Citizens Committee for Metropolitan Affairs found that drug stores in poor neighborhoods charge 6% more than drug stores in wealthy neighborhoods. It's damned expensive to be poor.

In short, virtually everyone takes advantage of people in poverty. The poor don't want trouble, they are ignorant of the law, afraid of lawyers and courts, harassed on all sides, and without powerful friends or influence.

* * *

If I were to single out one force that is responsible for stigmatizing the poor, it is our American press, our magazines and newspapers. When a newspaper wants to "crusade," the editor knows he can get into trouble. Sure, the Mayor may summon a patrol car to taxi his daughter to school, the board of education may charge all bidders on school construction a kickback fee, zoning-board members may grant variances in return for certain favors, the planning board may amend its code to accommodate a spendthrift builder, a judge may hold a private hearing for an illustrious citizen, and the police may hush up the fact that a politician in a nearby town was arrested for drunken-driving. But these people, a newspaper editor knows, have money and influence. With the poor, you don't have to worry.

And so a favorite ploy of newspapers is to write about

"Welfare chiselers." Time and again the New York *Daily News* fearlessly exposes these dreadful people.

Yes, there are Welfare chiselers. Some people on Welfare should be working, or are working on the sly, or have money hidden away, or have concealed sources of income. During 1964, the New York Bureau of Resources obtained 113 convictions in fraud cases involving Welfare. Out of 500,000 cases, 113.

Besides, many times I had to sympathize with Welfare clients who cheated. Try to support your wife and three children on $213.45 a month, and you'd probably cheat a little yourself. Or apply for Welfare, endure repeated investigations, and see if you don't feel like chiseling to "get even."

I had several clients who did odd jobs occasionally and didn't report it. If the amount was small or the income irregular, I chose to ignore it. What man is going to clean out a cellar or unload a truck, then march down to the Welfare center and turn over the few dollars he's made? Let him use it to pay off a debt, take his kids to a movie, or anesthetize himself with whiskey for a few hours.

Some of my clients had teen-age children who worked after school, but didn't report it. So let the boy dress up and take his girl out. Why should *he* be penalized because his father isn't a banker? *Other* Welfare Departments across the country recognize the value of incentive, and let their clients keep whatever extra money they've earned.

As for the myth that most people on Welfare don't *want* to work, the fact is that 85% of the adults on relief are elderly, disabled, or mothers of small children. Only 3.6% are theoretically employable. And, according to the Welfare Department itself, many of these cannot get or hold jobs because of "automation, lack of skills, or discrimination."

* * *

Not only do newspapers and magazines love exposing "Welfare chiselers." They also loathe writing about the real problems of the poor. It's depressing reading. It annoys advertisers,

129

who don't like their beautiful, four-color ads facing a photograph of a slum. Besides, magazines want to convince advertisers that their readers are rich enough to buy Bolex cameras and Brooks Brothers suits. And to attract rich readers, you print articles about vacations in Asia and the latest developments in stereo sets—not about the problems of the poor.

Among magazines one exception is *Public Welfare,* published by the American Public Welfare Association. This magazine, in October, 1965, ran some actual case histories of poor people. And if you want to know how the poor really live, here are some of the interviews:

An 8-year-old boy, asked whether he saves any money, answers: "Maybe one of these days I'll be able to save. But if I had money, I would first buy two knives, two guns, and a holster, and then I'd kill the people who robbed my apartment. And then I'd buy a hat and new pants for my father so he could look for a job. And then I'd buy cake, cookies, candy, toys, and furniture so we'd have something to sit on in the living room."

A young mother was pregnant, but didn't want the unemployment office to know—a pregnant woman can't work and will not receive unemployment compensation. She says: "I'd wear a girdle to the unemployment office and as soon as I'd sign the check, I'd run to the ladies' room and take it off and thank God I had another check stacked away. What did I lie for? I'll tell you—to be able to buy my child's crib."

Mr. and Mrs. F—— are explaining some of their dilemmas. Should they complain to the landlord about poor service and risk being evicted—or put up with faulty plumbing and falling plaster? Should they leave the lights burning all night to keep away rats—or keep the lights off to keep the utility bill low, and take a chance with the rats? A child of theirs is sick, but doesn't have adequate clothing. Do they dare take him outside to a clinic? Should the father go to a clinic himself and lose a half-day's pay, or not go at all? Should they send the children to school with shoddy clothing, or keep them home and answer notes from truant officers?

An elderly man is being interviewed: "What can you do if you're not lucky enough in the richest city in the world? We've got to go on Welfare and have the Welfare worker come up and see us and tell us how to live, and then she looks into the icebox at what we have. They want to know what kind of clothes you have, and when they see a telephone they want to know who is paying for it and why the money isn't being used for food. They try every way to get you. They make it hard for you and they don't want to know from nothing. But *they* get a big salary every week.

"But you've got to make the best of it.

"One of these days I'll go to the top of the Brooklyn Bridge, yell 'Here I go,' and then jump off. And you know what? Nobody will know! Nobody will care! Nobody will miss me. Maybe the Welfare will be happy because they wouldn't have to give me money any more.

"Who are you going to fight? City Hall? You've got to have pull, and if you don't have it, it's no good."

Mrs. C—— has three children. When it comes to economizing, she's very clever. Someone gave her family a used TV set, so she decided not to buy a clock—to learn the time, she turns on the TV. Her oldest boy recently was making his first communion. The Welfare Department refused to give her money to buy him a communion suit. So she asked friends for loans of 10¢ and 25¢, and raised $7 for the suit. To quote from the report:

"Being without proper clothes herself, she did not attend the communion. When her son returned home, he was proud of how he looked, and asked permission to visit old friends in the neighborhood. She understood and agreed.

"Many hours later he came back—with over $1 in change. When she pressed him for an explanation, he volunteered that when he arrived at his old haunts, he met the grocery man, who offered him a commission for selling frozen-fruit pies. Of course he agreed.

"And Mrs. C——'s last words for that interview were: 'And can you imagine my little sweet Alex, standing there in his communion suit, selling ices to make some money? What a picture!' She began to laugh. And she laughed and laughed and laughed, and as

131

she looked at me, her cheek bones twitched, her lips trembled, and her tears of laugher dissolved into tears of weeping."

Perhaps if general magazines and newspapers printed interviews like this, the poor might not have to bear, in addition to all their other burdens, the stigma of being on Welfare.

It all boils down to something very simple: the poor need more money. The Welfare Department's own house organ, *The Welfarer,* stated in 1964: "The Welfare budget [set for those on relief] is 25% below the poverty line. . . . The time has come to recognize the inadequate welfare grant as deplorable and in contradiction with the objective of the war on poverty." And until more money is available, the G——s, the H——s, and the S——s, all basically honest people, will beg for money for winter coats and shoes and beds and kitchen chairs, and will continue to "chisel" to buy a TV set or take a trip to the country. A "negative" income tax, a guaranteed annual wage for all Americans, would seem to be the answer.

But the poor need something besides money. They need guidance in consumer practices, they need legal help, they need someone to watch over their interests (like an "ombudsman"—a public officer charged with rectifying injustice), and they need—second only to money—self-respect. Most of the men and women I met had plenty of self-contempt: They didn't need outside condemnation.

* * *

This last point was ingrained in my mind in 1965, just before I left the Welfare Department and took a less-depressing, less-frustrating job with a publishing company.

I had stopped off in a bar on my way home from work. It had been an unusually "normal" day and I needed a drink. The bar was nearly empty, and rather bleak, so I finished my drink quickly and started to leave. Just then a well-dressed young man entered. He recognized me.

"Mr. Youree!"

It took only a second for me to recognize him: It was Mr. H——, the man who had been getting $16 a month because of a bureaucratic mix-up. We shook hands and he offered to buy me a drink. "Never mind that 'Mister,'" he said. "Call me John. What's your first name, anyway?"

Investigators do not encourage clients to call them by their first names. They certainly don't accept drinks from them. Clients aren't even *supposed* to drink. But what the hell? We were two men sitting in a bar.

John paid for our drinks with a $20 bill (approximately one-third of his new semimonthly grant). When he put the change in his wallet, I noticed enough additional twenties to cover his family's basic needs for at least 3 months. The suit he was wearing probably cost another five twenties. What was this guy trying to pull?

"Thanks, John," I said, raising my glass. We drank to each other's health.

He smiled. "Thank *you*, Gary."

We small talked through the drinks while I tried to figure out whether he was testing me. Some clients, when they discover you'll swing along with some minor illegalities, try to see just how much of a swinger you are.

"Have another drink," John said amiably, giving me a friendly slap on the arm.

I told him I had to go home. He smiled. "Well, have one more—I'll drive you home. I bought a car last week." He waited a moment, then grinned. "Don't worry—I'm off Welfare and back in business again. Doing well too!" He rapped the bar sharply and laughed. The bartender refilled our glasses.

As he drove me home, he told me how happy he and his family were since he had gone back to work. And as we neared my neighborhood, he spoke of what a hell of a bad time they had had on Welfare. The first investigator had pulled open bureau drawers, opened closets, boxes, and even looked under the beds. "What was that idiot looking for?"

The second investigator visited him only once, staying about 5 minutes. He had promised everything and delivered nothing.

"I don't know how many times I called him," John said. "He was always 'working on it.' The last time I called, the bastard had resigned."

And I was his next investigator—for 2 months. Then came a reassignment and he had a fourth investigator. Maybe more—he didn't say.

We were turning off the East River Drive. "At least you treated us like other human beings," he said. "And you *did* get the budget straightened out and send us a check for some clothing."

He pulled to a stop in front of my building, shut off the motor, and offered me a cigarette and lit it. "You know, Gary, I realize you people have a tough job—but I wonder how many of you realize how it feels to have somebody come in your home when you're desperate, and treat you like a piece of shit? It's not just the questions you ask—I realize they're necessary. It's the *way* some of you ask them. It's the whole general attitude. . . ." He went on, telling me how his wife used to cry after an investigator had been there, and how so many times his only consolation was a promise he made to himself that he would break open the first investigator's head he saw after he was off Welfare. He hastily assured me that he no longer felt that way. I informed him that I was glad to hear it. We shook hands again and he drove away—reminding me again that his name was John.

* * *

John called me at work the next day.

"I was thinking last night about what I told you, Gary— when I said that at least you treated us like human beings. We were in bad shape when you saw us, worse than anybody will ever know. I take back that 'at least.' If there was anything we needed more than money, it was to be treated with dignity and respect—like human beings."

134

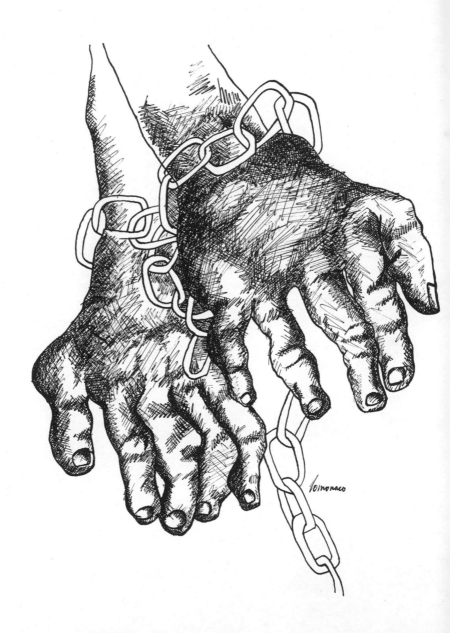

The Psycho Ward:
An Attendant's View

By Frank Leonard

T he grim statistics on mental illness are by now familiar to most people. Half the hospital beds in the country are occupied by mental patients. In 1965, nearly one million Americans spent time in mental hospitals. And the chances are that one out of every 10 people will at some time or another be hospitalized for mental illness—which means there is almost a 50-50 chance that you or someone in your family will spend time in a mental hospital.

Unlike most people, I had a chance to see the reality behind the mental-health statistics—as an attendant at Bellevue Psychiatric Hospital in New York City. I saw first-hand the way America's largest city treats its mentally ill.

I went to work at the hospital after tiring of college and graduate school, where I had spent 7 straight years. Temporarily I wanted something more gritty than academic life, and the idea of a job in a mental hospital intrigued me. I started at Bellevue as an attendant in November, 1960, and stayed until October, 1961, when I was recalled into the Army. After my release in August, 1962, I worked at Bellevue again for a very brief time. In November, 1964, I went back as a volunteer on evenings and week-ends, again for a very brief period.

From my own experience, I cannot say whether Bellevue is better or worse than other public mental hospitals of its kind. Some surveys suggest that other hospitals are probably just as bad, or worse. Most other states, for example, spend less than New York on their mental hospitals, both in absolute terms and per capita. Also, when I met patients at Bellevue who had been in mental hospitals elsewhere, I would sometimes ask their opinion of the worst hospital they had been in. No one ever named Bellevue. Several named Brooklyn State Hospital. One man—a very cantankerous and difficult patient—told me he thought the attendants at Fairfield State Hospital in Connecticut beat him "for the fun of it." He said one attendant there used to tell him when he left the hospital after work, "I'm goin' over your house now and fool around with your wife."

In 1965, a thorough study of one state mental hospital (unidentified) was published by David Kantor and Victor Gelineau of Boston State Hospital (*International Journal of Social Psychiatry*, Autumn 1965). At this hospital,

• the attendants, often just to "offset boredom," made sport of the patients by teasing them, insulting them, and by assigning them impossible tasks to do. "The frequency and severity of degradations varied from patient to patient, but no patient enjoyed complete immunity";

• the attendants did their best to keep the patients from seeing their psychiatrists, and even from seeing members of their own families—by manipulating the visiting hours, for instance (incidentally, the average patient had been in the hospital for *17* years);

• to punish a patient, an attendant might "accidentally" have his name put on a list of people scheduled for shock therapy.

From my own experience, I would say that this hospital sounds even worse than Bellevue. And if other hospitals are even *worse* than Bellevue, this is a terrible comment on the nation's level of patient care.

Bellevue consists of a general hospital and a psychiatric hospital. Unlike other psychiatric hospitals, however, Bellevue Psychiatric does not give long-term care and treatment. It is a "receiving hospital." Every day, 40 to 50 men, women, and children are taken to the Psychiatric Hospital after coming into conflict with the normal routine of the city—for drunkenness, fighting, attempting suicide, behaving strangely, and so forth. They stay for 10 days to 2 weeks. The job of Bellevue psychiatrists is to sift out those who can make it on the outside

—even if they have symptoms of mental illness—from those who can't. Those who can't—about one-third—are sent to state mental hospitals, and they may remain there for a few weeks or for life. The other two-thirds are returned to the streets whence they came.

About 20,000 people from New York City are sent to state mental hospitals every year, and most of them are processed through Bellevue or through Bellevue's counterpart in Brooklyn, Kings County Hospital. Obviously, a patient's first contact with a mental hospital may determine the speed of his recovery. Yet, judging from my experience at Bellevue, which spans, in all, 5 years, I would say that conditions there convey one basic message to the incoming patient: Society does not give a damn about you or your illness.

* * *

Bellevue is so dirty that the health of its patients is endangered. The toilets are filthy, there are not enough for the number of patients who use them, and they have no seats—the patients must sit on the bare porcelain. There is a chronic shortage of clean linen and pajamas. The beds are filthy, and, more often than not, their mattresses are soiled and urine-stained. The wards are drab, monotonous, poorly lit, and poorly furnished —as well as being infested with roaches and mice.

The hospital is also grossly overcrowded. It does not even meet the very minimal standards of the American Psychiatric Association. Although Bellevue Psychiatric was built, in 1933, for 450 patients, a normal census today is 750. This overcrowding would be illegal in any private hospital in the State, but the provisions of the State Mental Hygiene Law don't apply to public mental hospitals.

Bellevue is also understaffed to such an extent that it is dangerous to work there, and dangerous to be a patient there. New York City's Hospital Code makes it a misdemeanor for a private hospital to provide fewer than one registered nurse for each ward in each shift. To meet this requirement, Bellevue would need 57 registered nurses. It has 23. In other words,

139

there are eight registered nurses on each shift to care for 750 patients on 19 wards. The City's Hospital Code, of course, does not apply to public hospitals.

And then there is the brutality. The worst of it is directed at the patients who are the sickest, because they are usually the hardest to control. They are also the least likely to make complaints, and the least likely to be believed if they should complain. A mental patient's testimony is easy to discredit just because he is a mental patient. As a former Bellevue Superintendent once told the newspapers in regard to a brutality case: "Is it regrettable that the statement of a person suffering from a temporary mental illness should gain credence."

The attendants themselves, of course, are unlikely to complain about the brutality. It is one of the tools of their trade, and its use is sometimes a necessity. The proper use of brutality was one of the first things I learned from the other attendants once my formal training period was over. "You go for the throat first," I was told, "then the stomach, and if that doesn't work, you go for the groin." This is the formula for subduing a disturbed and unruly patient.

In "going for the throat," the method is the same as that used by a mugger. One arm goes around the patient's throat and, when pressure is applied, the oxygen supply to the patient's brain is cut off. He then becomes unconscious. And then he can be easily placed in a straitjacket, or tied to his bed and given an injection of a tranquilizer. Care has to be taken in using this method, however, since if a patient stops breathing he will not start again of his own accord. Unless breathing is restored artificially, the patient will die.

Sometimes a patient knows how to prevent an attendant from getting an arm around his throat, especially if he has had any experience in street-fighting. He simply keeps his chin pressed down against his chest. So then the attendant must "go for the stomach." One or two punches there will usually shake the patient up enough so that an arm can be slipped under his chin. Only in the most extreme cases would the attendant have to hit the patient in the groin.

But it would be a mistake to think that brutality is caused

solely by cruel or sadistic attendants. True, there are no educational or experience requirements for attendants and nurses' aides at Bellevue: Practically anyone without a police record can get the job. But I have seen no evidence that the uneducated are more cruel or brutal than the educated.

Some Bellevue doctors, for example, handle patients with the utmost callousness. Their job is not to treat but to diagnose, and this they do as if they were working on an assembly-line. Can the patient make it on the outside, or does he need further hospitalization? This crucial question is decided on the basis of one or two brusque and impersonal interviews. The law requires that two doctors must "certify" that a patient is in need of further hospitalization. At Bellevue, one doctor makes this decision, and a second doctor merely signs the certification form as a matter of routine, usually without having seen the patient.

* * *

To understand the use of brutality at Bellevue—and at similar institutions—one must understand what such hospitals are intended to do, and the role attendants and nurses' aides are expected to play. A man who had worked as an attendant at 49 mental hospitals in all parts of the country summed it up in *Snake Pit Attendant* (1950). "In reality," the anonymous author points out, " 'bug houses' are for the protection of the state rather than for the treatment of the insane." Their main function is to keep the mentally ill off the streets, where they might embarrass or annoy us, or interrupt traffic and commerce. As the Joint Commission on Mental Illness and Health pointed out in *Action for Mental Health* (1961), "More than half the patients in most state hospitals receive no active treatment of any kind designed to improve their mental condition." When an insufficient staff must control large groups of patients, simple and rigid ward routines result, and these in turn naturally lead to callousness and brutality.

This brutality is the price our cities and states agree to pay for inadequate staffs; the arm clamped around the throat of the mental patient and the punch in the stomach are the money-saving substitutes for a sufficient number of nurses and attendants. Year after year, New York City obscures this fact in a clever way. When the yearly budget for Bellevue is drawn up, it includes appropriations for a fully adequate staff. On the other hand, the money appropriated for essential drugs and supplies is far below the amount needed. The City claims to be unable to recruit the number of staff members provided in the budget, and the unused salaries are taken instead to pay for the needed drugs and supplies, thus balancing the budget.

A fellow attendant at Bellevue, whom I will call Albert Diggs, gave me an example of what happens to patients as a result of this deliberate understaffing. One day two brothers, big strapping laborers, were admitted to the disturbed ward after shooting their father. They were very disturbed when they arrived, and insisted they were not going to stay. When they began to pound on the ward door, someone decided they should go into straitjackets. Diggs had seen the muscles bulging under their shirts and knew it would be a tough job to subdue them. There were only four attendants on the ward, including Diggs.

When one of the brothers decided to go into the bathroom, Diggs sent the other three attendants after him with a straitjacket. In a moment, he heard a loud struggle and knew the attendants were having trouble. At that moment, the other brother decided *he* wanted to go to the bathroom, too. Diggs made a quick decision. He slammed the man in the pit of the stomach with his fist. This took the man's breath away long enough to slip him into a straitjacket. Then Diggs went into the bathroom to help the three attendants still struggling with the other brother. In that situation, I believe Diggs made the correct decision. He may have saved himself, the other attendants, and the two patients from injuries more serious than a single punch in the stomach.

But with a sufficient staff such decisions would generally not have to be made. When brutality becomes a necessity, even in a few cases, it comes to be used when it is not absolutely necessary, and even in cases where it is clearly unnecessary. I considered Diggs a good attendant whose competence often

142

prevented serious injuries, and he was capable of real gentleness toward patients, but I once saw him beat a very disturbed patient, who was tied to a bed at the time, simply because the patient called him "a no-good, brutal, sadistic bastard." Another time he beat a patient, also tied to a bed, who was whining that he wanted to die. I have never been able to understand the reason for that beating, but such incidents develop naturally where brutality has been accepted as a natural technique.

A beating that occurred on the children's ward shows again the relationship between brutality and the attempt to keep order with an insufficient staff. On the children's ward, two attendants must control 15 boys who have the natural exuberance of their age plus an emotional disorder. When I arrived on the ward the day of this beating, another attendant, a thin, bitter-looking man in sneakers and dark glasses, had the boys lined up against a wall and was telling them that he expected absolute silence. In his hand he held a long, thin wooden stick, which he kept slapping into the palm of his hand. When he finished his warning, there was a brief silence, then one of the boys giggled.

"Get out here!" the attendant called. A small, chubby 7-year-old came to the center of the room. "Now get down and do the duck-waddle." The boy got down and waddled along for a moment, then lost his balance and fell over. It is a difficult exercise, especially if you are not used to it. "Keep going!" the attendant told him. The boy took a few more steps, then fell over again. The attendant moved in with his stick and began to hit the boy across the back. The boy began to cry but despite his tears the attendant hit him again and again. My first impulse was to seize the attendant's stick and break it. But I was new at the hospital. And it was my first time on the children's ward. In short, I was afraid to act, and so I did nothing.

Later, when I worked regularly on the children's ward, I was often alone with 15 or 20 disturbed children and I found it very hard to keep order. Once several boys literally pulled a bed apart before my eyes. I was often advised by other attendants to hit the children, and finally I began to. I learned how easily one can convince oneself that a cruel practice is necessary and desirable. Eventually I decided to request a transfer from the children's ward rather than continue doing something I considered wrong. It was obvious, though, that the person who took my place—possibly someone with fewer scruples—would be in the same position I had been in.

* * *

Before leaving the subject of brutality, I want to describe one more beating, the cruelest I saw in my time at Bellevue. It occurred on the old men's ward, one of the saddest at the hospital. The "mental" illness these old men suffer from is generally only age, neglect, and the hardening of cerebral arteries—something that will affect most of us if we live long enough. These patients—and those on the old women's ward—are simply the unwanted grandfathers and grandmothers of the City. If New York had a decent and humane nursing-home program, many of these old people would not sit day after day at Bellevue waiting to be shunted off to State mental hospitals.

The night this beating occurred, I had been sent from my usual post on the violent ward to help out on the old men's ward. It was the first time I had worked there. The short, beefy, red-faced woman who worked as night aide on this ward —I will call her Mrs. O'Malley—told me, quite approvingly, that the attendant who usually worked with her took off his belt at bed time and "Boy, do these old fellas *run*" to get into bed.

After supper, men who needed it were cleaned up a little. One man had defecated in his pajamas and Mrs. O'Malley gave him a quick scrubbing. "I hate these shitty old men," she told me as she cleaned him off. I could not entirely blame her. It was unpleasant work and the City indicated how little value it assigned to it by paying her a poverty-level salary. My own take-home pay was $110 every 2 weeks.

After the cleaning up, the old men were packed off to bed. One man in his 80s, whom I will call Nathan Schwartz, had just been admitted that day and was unaccustomed to the ward routine. He didn't know where he was and asked again and again to go home. So inhospitable was the appearance of

144

the ward that he thought he was lost in a subway. (He was not the first old man to make this mistake.) The walls, under a layer of dirt and grime, were a bilious green; loose tiles hung precariously from the ceiling; and the dusty floor instantly blackened the feet of the patients who, in the absence of slippers, walked around in their stockings.

Mrs. O'Malley shoved Nathan Schwartz into bed several times, but each time he got up again and wandered around looking for a way out. Mrs. O'Malley would shove him back into bed a little harder each time she found him up. Finally all the men were in bed but Schwartz. I was in another part of the ward when I heard a cry for help—from Mrs. O'Malley. "Lennie, *help* me!" When I got there, Nathan Schwartz was flailing about with his arms while Mrs. O'Malley was trying to push him down onto his bed again. In the scuffle he had accidentally caught her in the face with one wildly swinging hand, and she began to punch him on his bony chest and flabby stomach. Again and again she hit the old man.

Mrs. O'Malley knew only that she had been hit in the face by a man who was refusing to obey orders. She did not have the slightest doubt that she was right and the old man was wrong. As for Schwartz, he had no idea where he was or why he was being attacked. Under the circumstances, he might well have thought someone was trying to kill him, and his weak and pathetic resistance had a large element of panic and desperation in it. His dark eyes were bright with what must have been pure terror as the blows continued landing on him. I persuaded Mrs. O'Malley that we should tie the old man to his bed—a great act of kindness—and as we began to bind his arms and legs, Mrs. O'Malley asked him, "Why can't you be *nice?*"

* * *

At midnight that night, after my shift was over, I went up to the roof of the hospital, where I could look out over the City, and I thought about the beating I had just seen. I decided people ought to understand the consequences of maintaining a place like Bellevue. If they did not want to do anything about it, that was their business. But I thought they should know the end result: that confused old men, in the last years of their lives, are beaten into their beds for the sake of order, economy, and convenience.

After leaving the hospital to take another job, I began working on a novel about the place. It was accepted for publication as a paperback original by Ballantine Books, and I began to hope that the book would generate a demand for at least some minor reforms. In the meantime I went back to Bellevue and worked as a volunteer on evenings and weekends. Things had not changed in the 2 years since I had left.

Before my novel was published, I sent a copy of the manuscript to the head of the hospital, requesting a meeting to discuss "how best to channel public reaction to the book into constructive channels." A few days later we had our meeting. He handed me back the manuscript with this note attached: "I have not read the manuscript, nor do I have any intention of doing so or of making any comment thereon." He also took the opportunity to inform me that I was fired as a Bellevue volunteer.

A few months later, my book came out under the title *City Psychiatric*. Channeling public reaction turned out to be no problem. There was little if any to channel.

Actually, as I have since learned, to a certain extent publicity about mental hospitals can help. Temporarily. As David Riesman and Donald Horton have written, "the political pressures generated and steered by the exposé may result in an increase of funds and facilities. . . . The resulting adjustments may be regarded as window-dressing designed to take the heat off. . . . Eventually, however, as the furor subsides . . . the institution [reverts] back into the deprived condition and a new cycle of obsolescence mitigated by scandal begins" ("Notes on the Deprived Institution," *Sociological Quarterly,* Winter 1965).

This has been the Bellevue story, too—obsolescence, exposé and possible improvement, obsolescence, and so on.

Bellevue dates back to 1794, but it wasn't until 1825 that a section was added to the hospital for "the pauper insane." From 1820 to 1860, according to *The New York Times,* the

146

hospital was "a vast lodging-house for paupers, lunatics, criminals and diseased depravity in all its loathsome types: no separation, no classification, poor nurses, brutal attendants and inadequate medical supervision." According to the *Times,* "every ward [was] so infested with rats that cases are recorded in which infants were well nigh eaten alive, while the sick mother waged a hopeless battle with armies of vermin." Another *Times* article mentioned the "large number of the deaths caused by carelessness; in fact, only one out of every five who entered the hospital came out alive."

Scandal dogged the hospital into the 20th century. In December, 1900, Louis Hilliard, a patient in Bellevue's "insane pavilion," was strangled to death by three male nurses. After an investigation, the Commissioner of Charities reported: "The nature of the evidence brought to me discloses a shocking condition of affairs. The nature of the abuses in the alcoholic ward and the insane pavilion discloses sheer hardness of heart, a brutality that is shocking, utter disregard for feelings, rough usage, abusive language to the inmates, negligence in nursing, and extreme physical violence."

Sixty years later, as a result of a newspaper exposé, another investigation—headed by Dr. Lawrence C. Kolb—was made of both Bellevue and Kings County Hospitals. The committee's report:

Conditions at the Bellevue and Kings County Hospital Psychiatric services are associated with, produce and maintain a low level of patient care and even threaten health. . . . The overcrowding and uncleanliness establish hazards and provide the background for the potential spread of infectious diseases.

In the United Hospital Fund of New York's *Report on Municipal Hospitals* of 1963–64, Mrs. A. Vittorio Marano says she found at Bellevue ". . . the same urgent and basic problems [that] have been reported by this visitor for the past eight years." The 1964–65 *Report* states that "conditions reported by the psychiatrists and social workers who were on Dr. Kolb's Committee in 1961 have *NOT* been corrected."

* * *

Why are America's mental institutions so abominable? One reason is that victims of mental institutions are usually poor, inarticulate, and unorganized. Another reason is that the public at large just doesn't like to think about mental illness. "Many studies," say Riesman and Horton, "indicate that, even today, the great majority of Americans consider mental illness something slightly shameful, [and] view psychiatrists with a combination of fascination, malice and ignorance. . . ." Jules Henry, writing in *Trans-Action* (May, 1964), carries this point further: "We lose interest in what we hate to think about. . . . This hatred helps to make possible the incompetence in prisons, mental hospitals, old folks' homes, and the other igloos in which society's castoffs are walled off. . . . Public *lack of interest* in whether a job is done well or poorly ultimately means incompetence." Which is why, in this country, "one of the most important centers of general incompetence . . . is the public mental hospital."

Another basic reason for the shame of our mental hospitals has to do with our society itself: its traditional neglect of the public sector of the economy and its traditional concern with the private, luxury economy. To quote Riesman and Horton: "The nonprofit institutions—government agencies, schools and colleges, hospitals, social service agencies, libraries, and so on—have traditionally operated barely above and sometimes under the subsistence line of poverty; . . . the private sector has always been able to condescend to the public sector, and to attack its alleged wastefulness and nonproductiveness."

There are powerful forces fighting to see that the interests of big business and the military are looked out for; and these same powerful forces are among those fighting against higher spending for nonprofit institutions in our society like schools and public hospitals.

Riesman and Horton go on to say: "We do not intend this . . . as a counsel of despair and do-nothing—any more than we would recommend to a housewife that she stop cleaning because dirt will gather again.

"But we do feel that, in addition to reformist steps to improve each deprived institution, the relation between these institutions and a luxury economy . . . cannot be handled through what passes for a free market, but requires a vision of society in which individuals are not persuaded by all the agencies of mass communication and public opinion to produce and consume by the standards of the luxury economy, while underneath this, supporting it and being starved and shamed by it, the deprived economy suffers a long . . . depression."

* * *

The contrast between American public mental hospitals and those in some European countries is scandalous. According to *Psychiatric Care in Europe and America,* published in 1961 by the American Psychiatric Association,

The most significant difference apparent to one familiar with American medical hospitals is the greater respect for the patient as an individual which we noted in nearly all psychiatric institutions in Europe.
   Wards are generally small, not overcrowded, and are attractive places in which to live. Because they are viewed as temporary homes, they are comfortably furnished with appropriate upholstered chairs, not heavy-duty types or benches. There are rugs, draperies, framed pictures, and flowers. Coffee tables, room dividers with fragile bric-a-brac, and potted plants are widely used. There are birds in cages, fish in an aquarium, pet cats, and, in several institutions, even small zoos.

The difference between the hospitals in Europe and those in the United States is simply the difference between a society that cares as much about schools, housing, and the general welfare as it does about cars, cosmetics, and bombs.

149

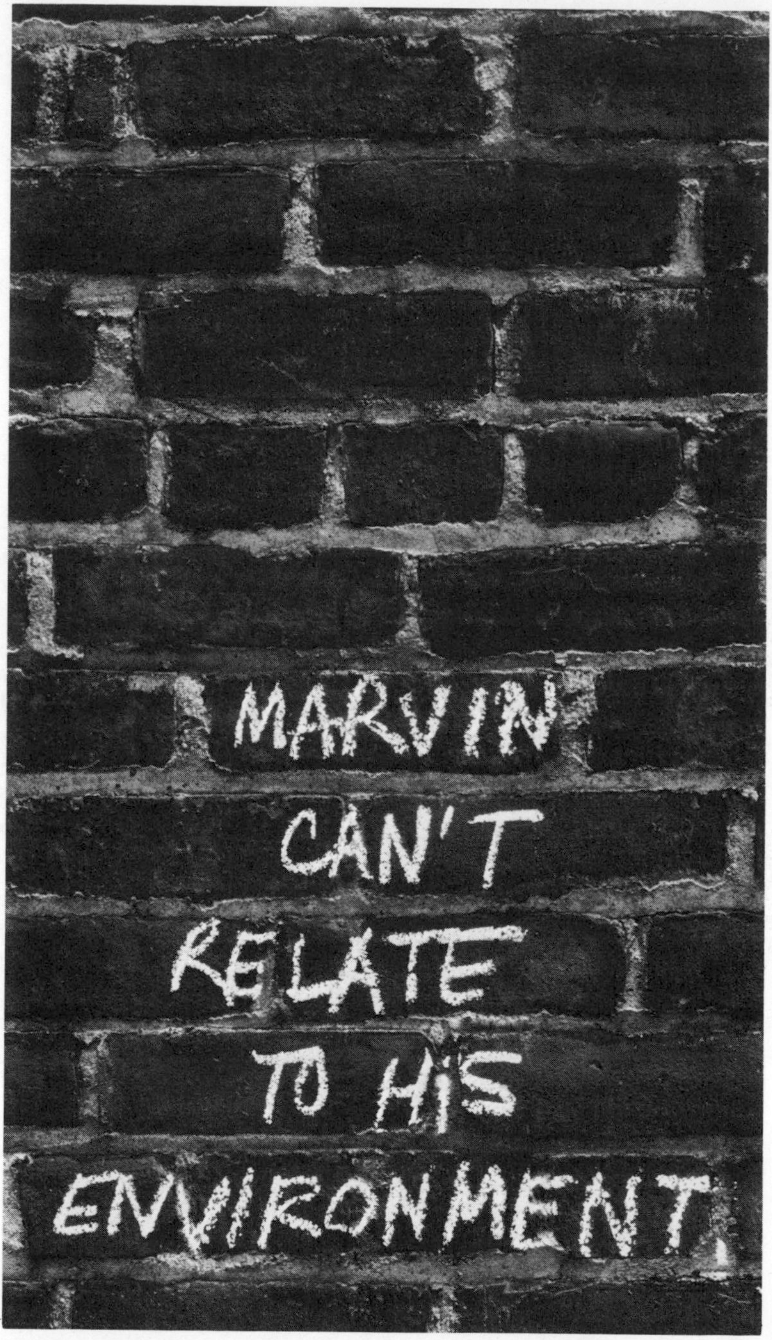
MARVIN
CAN'T
RELATE
TO HIS
ENVIRONMENT.

The Golden Age of Graffiti

By Warren Boroson

G raffiti—scrawls on walls, sidewalks, books, etc., from the Italian word for "scratching"—have suddenly begun undergoing a glorious rebirth. Once despised and sneered at by all save students of psychopathology, today graffiti are being searched out and scrutinized by journalists, politicians, sociologists, and even by ordinary men and women who happen to appreciate wit and whimsy.

Irrefutable evidence of this new fascination with graffiti is the way newspapers and magazines have been quoting them as expressions of popular opinion. To illustrate anti-American sentiment in Santo Domingo, for example, *Life* ran a photo of a wall bearing the graffito **Fuera Yanks de Vietnam.** The Left Wing *Minority of One* has published a letter from a Frenchman who saw, in Paris, graffiti like **U.S. = S.S.** and **Americans = Assassins.** The Right Wing *America* has reported that when Warsaw was plastered with posters announcing Polish-Soviet Friendship Week, someone scribbled beneath one of them, "Okay—but not one second longer."

This rebirth of the political graffito has a number of possible parents. In poverty-stricken areas, the man lying in the street has few literary outlets for his hotblooded polemics, and hence uses chalk and the nearest wall to express his discontent. Graffiti of this type include **Yanqui Go Home** (in South America, *passim*) and **I Hate Mr. Skins** (in Watts, discovered by Mr. Joseph Alsop on the back of a bench after the first riot).

In totalitarian countries, the graffito is the last, all-but-ineradicable medium of free speech. For even if 1984 does come to pass, in the dead of night a malcontent can always slip out and scrawl on a sidewalk, **Down With Big Brother.** No wonder dictators seem to have an irrational aversion to graffiti. At the Potsdam Conference after World War II, someone scribbled the sassy graffito **Kilroy Was Here** in one of the guarded toilets assigned to the Big Four. As psychiatrist Martin Grotjahn writes in *Beyond Laughter,*

The story has it that Stalin was quite upset and the meeting came to a temporary standstill when he found that Kilroy had been in the dictator's bathroom and had left his signature there. The search for Kilroy was called off after complicated translation, interpretation, and explanation. Stalin either misunderstood the joke of Kilroy or, in a deeper analytic sense, he understood the spirit of rebellion all too well and disapproved of it.

As for nontotalitarian but overdeveloped countries like America, the trouble is that our newspapers and magazines have little available space after all the ads have been shoveled in; most of the contents are staff-written anyway; and even the letters-to-the-editor columns are finely screened. On the other hand, it's no problem at all for someone to visit the nearest subway station and scrawl **If You Liked Hitler, You'll Love Buckley,** sans censors and sans editors.

* * *

Not all modern graffiti are political, though. Many are genuinely funny. Evidence comes, once again, from our magazines and newspapers. For a number of years now, the upper-class *New Yorker* has been amused by what it considers lower-class whimsy, and has regularly published graffiti like **Mrs. Moynihan Eats Watercress.** *Esquire* recently recorded this incident: A man and his wife, leaving a theater where they had seen and suffered through *The Loved One,* paused to read the notices: " '. . . a daring comedy'—Cue; 'Ferocious fun'—Telegram." Unable to restrain himself, the man walked over to a marble column and scribbled, " '. . . a real bomb, believe me'—Jacob Miller." A graffito has even been chosen *The New York Times*'s Quotation of the Day. After Yale University produced the Vinland Map, which suggested that Columbus had not

152

really discovered America, a *Times* reporter found the following scrawled on a wall in the Italian section of Boston: **Leif Ericson Is a Fink.**

Most likely, it is the Sexual Revolution that is responsible for the resurgence of witty graffiti. Now that four-letter words are losing their shock value, and homosexuals can make assignations through night clubs, and movies and magazines have enlightened many people about the finer details of human anatomy, the deviates have largely ceased writing obscenities on subway walls and have gone on to expressing sentiments like **Bomb Hanoi** and **Be a Man, Join the Klan.** This, by Gresham's Law, has left the field open to the wits, and the result is that some of the cleverest writing in America today can be found scrawled on walls. (The selection of graffiti that follows this article should prove this beyond cavil.) Not since the days of ancient Pompeii (see *The Common People of Pompeii, A Study of the Graffiti* by Helen H. Tanzer) have the graffiti-writers enjoyed such a Golden Age. Comic Jackie Vernon boasts that he used to write Rx on Christian Science Reading Room windows, and draw Stars of David on Volkswagens. Poet Allen Ginsberg was temporarily expelled from Columbia for one of his earlier graffito-writings. Playwright Edward Albee got the title for a play from a graffito he once saw: **Who's Afraid of Virginia Woolf?**

It remains to be said that the future promises much more of the same. As totalitarianism increases, we can expect to see ever more political graffiti. And as the Sexual Revolution inches ahead, we can look forward to a profusion of witty graffiti. Clearly, the handwriting is on the wall.

Reported by *Drum* Magazine, seen on a subway poster:
My Mother Made Me a Homosexual
(*below*)
Great! Would she make one for me?

Al Dort, West Side IND Station:
Jesus Saves!
Moses Invests!

David Forsberg, San Francisco's North Beach:
> **Alice B. Toklas Loves Gertrude Stein**
> **Release Oscar Wilde**

Herb Caen, on a wall:
> **Support Mental Health like Crazy!**

Boroson, on 86th St. Lexington Avenue subway station:

Brotherhood

Frank Farrell, Greenwich Village pavement:
> **Marvin Can't Relate to His Environment**

Joan Mathews, Canal St. subway:
> **Atomic War Now**

Jeffrey Page, Greenwich Village subway:
> **DeSapio Lives!**

Support Mental Health or I'll Kill You

Mary Poppins Is a Junkie

Hugh Heffner Is a Virgin

John Wilcock, on a subway poster saying "Did You Make New York Dirty Today?":
> **New York Makes ME Dirty Every Day**

John Scanlon, men's room, Greenwich Village:
> **Judge Crater, Call Your Office Immediately**

Wilcock, *Métro* in Paris:
> **God Is Retrogressive and Hostile**

New Yorker, Flushing subway:
> **Peace Is a Cool Scene**

M.S. Stoddart, Washington Heights station:
New York Is a Summer Vegetable

Ron Nordell, on Harvard Square wall:
Hugh Is a Dirty Neoclassicist

Anonymous, men's room in Hollywood:
I'm 10½ Inches Long and 3 Inches Wide
(*below*)
How Intriguing! And How Big Is Your Penis?

New Yorker, on a fence along with graffiti like "Joe loves Betty":
Sue Wilson and Nobody As Yet

New Yorker, IRT subway station:
Chicken Little was Right

Robert Thomsen, Chinatown (the Chinese are taught to always be respectful):
Wong Is a Very Naughty Boy

Boroson, on subway poster stating, "I got my job through *The New York Times*":
So Did Castro

Mrs. Nat Norflett, Buenos Aires!
Yankee Go Home
(*below*)
by Pan-American

Robert Sylvester, Greenwich Village sidewalk:
John Feels Insecure About Mary

George Monteiro, grammar-school book:
The Lord Giveth and the Lord Taketh Away;
Indian-Giver Be the Name of the Lord.

Thomsen, in Greenwich Village at Christmas time, on a men's room wall:
A Merry Christmas
to All Our Readers

155

Robert Reisner, from a forthcoming book of graffiti found in men's rooms:

I've Got What Every Woman Wants
(*below*)
You Must Be in the Fur Coat Business

Take a Viet Cong to Lunch This Week

James Baldwin Eats Watermelon

Leda Loves Swans

God Is Alive and Living in Argentina

(after a string of obscenities)
This Is Why We May Be Second to the Moon

Merry Syphilis and a Happy Gonorrhea

**Occupancy By More Than 401 Persons is
Dangerous, Unlawful, and Somewhat Unsanitary**

**Now Being Organized: The Greenwich
Village Heterosexual Club**

(at the posh Four Seasons restaurant)
Screw Home Cooking
**Millard Fillmore Was the First President Born
in the 19th Century**
(*below*)
Who Was Millard Fillmore?
(*below*)
Millard Fillmore Was a Dirty Commie Rat

George Metesky* Is Alive and in the White House

Keep Vietnam Out of U.S. Politics

Love Thy Neighbor, But Don't Get Caught

(*on an empty towel machine*)
Pray for Towel

Socrates Drinks Hemlock

* The "Mad Bomber."

156

We Need Another Oswald

Billy Graham Is the Religious Editor of Time

Legalize Pot!
(*below*)
Legalize Outlaws!
(*below*)
Legalize Me!
(*below*)
End Legalization!

Harvey Saltzman, on a wall:
Down With Graffiti!
(*below*)
Kill all Italians!

(Mrs.) Agnes Lazzeri, subway:
King Kong Died for Your Sons

John B.L. Goodwin, Santa Fe, New Mexico:
**Please Someone Help Me Overcome This Mad Infatuation
I Have for Sabu**

Bernard Carr, Cheshire, England:
John, not Jesus

Cosby M. Newsom, Norwalk, Calif.:
For Sale, Cheap: Beer Bar in Watts Called Whitey's

The New York Times, at Columbia University:
God Is Dead: Nietzsche
(*below*)
Nietzsche Is Dead: God

Mike Nichols, on wall of a building:
I Love Grils

(Next day, this was crossed out and in its place was written:)
I Love Girls

(Third day, new handwriting:)
WHAT ABOUT US GRILS?

157

TIME: The Weekly Fiction Magazine

Ralph Ingersoll
former publisher of Time

Time's technique for handling news is so simple that it seems to have eluded several generations of critics—and yet it is almost solely responsible for (A) *Time*'s monumental commercial success and (B) *Time*'s equally monumental failure in the fields of ethics, integrity, and responsibility.

The problem Henry R. Luce* and the late Briton Hadden tackled when they set out to invent their new kind of weekly news magazine was how to condense a week's news—on all fronts: national, international, cultural, and business—into a package of words that could be read cover to cover in a couple of hours.

It was the same problem that the then-great *Literary Digest* had successfully solved by clipping the week's output of newspapers and magazines for their gist. Controversial matters, such as political news, were handled by snipping quotes from both sides. But Luce and Hadden felt that this approach had limitations—both as to the quantity of news it could handle and its readability. After all, the *Digest* technique was self-limited; it confined its editors to the material to be digested —and most public utterances are on the dull side to begin with.

Luce and Hadden's solution was brilliant. Instead of digesting the news, they would rewrite it into short articles, each having its own literary form: a beginning, a middle, and an end, though not of course necessarily in that sequence. Thus they wrote their own literary license for a new kind of news

* Henry Robinson Luce has died since the writing of this article.

writing that was not news writing at all but good old-fashioned, time (small t)-tested fiction writing.

It would, of course, be fiction that used real people and real facts as material, but for readability's sake the fiction form was the important ingredient. Only by the fiction writer's art could the secondhand news that *Time* proposed to package and sell be made inviting enough to attract the readers Luce and Hadden hoped to get. It was Hadden, probably, who stepped up the voltage even higher by the studied use of bizarre adjectives, chosen and inserted for their shock value alone: *snaggle-toothed, bumble-footed,* and like *Time*isms.

The irritant quality of what came to be called *Time*-style was originally a calculated addition—and a vital necessity to two very young men trying to get a then-indifferent public to pay them mind (and buy their little magazine). But the use of dramatic narrative for the presentation of "news" was inherent and germane to the whole idea.

In this writer's opinion, it remains the basic reason for *Time*'s success. It does indeed make "news" more readable. You can be esoteric about it if you like: It makes it possible for the reader to escape the realities to which responsible journalism is confined; to live in dreamland forever. Or you can simply feel that the advantage (to the *Time* writer over the responsible journalist) of being able to dramatize at will is so obvious that it merits no more than a shrug as comment.

Less obvious, but just as real, is the equally inescapable truth that, once one has committed oneself to writing news as if it were fiction, one has opened a Pandora's box of evil temptations.

I believe that *in the beginning* the magazine's romantic young writers and editors did try, and try hard, to keep their fictions in touch with their facts. I believe, in fact, that they still do, but for other reasons now. Originally they meant no harm, saw themselves as dedicated to dispelling the ignorance of their elders, took for granted their responsibility. Now I believe no such things about what they and their successors have become. The only hold that reality has on them now is the necessity to

160

remain plausible, to fool enough of the people—with their claptrap about responsible journalism—to get by. *Time*'s staff has long been both intelligent and sophisticated. Only the juveniles amongst them have any lingering illusions about their essential dishonesty or the basic corruption of the business they are engaged in: taking hard-earned facts and weaving them into snares for the ignorant—for their personal and corporate profit.

What makes the contemporary *Time* truly sinister is that its corporate profit has been *so* great that it has been able to build up the largest and, probably, the most efficient news-gathering organization ever created by man—all to the purpose not of telling more truth to a world in sorry need of same, but of making grist for its mill of plausibility. It is as if our greatest scholars were dedicated not to revealing truth but to distorting it for their personal profit and for the gratification of whatever whims might move them.

It is also an essential part of *Time*'s technique to insulate its public from its raw material—by means of group editing and anonymous writing. This phase of *Time*'s corruption is probably the most commented on by *Time*'s perennial critics. But to me it seems no more than an enraging insult added to a mortal injury.

The mortal injury is the poison inherent in *Time*'s technique of mislabeling fiction as news. The bittersweet coating is its plausibility. The way to tell a successful lie is to include enough truth in it to make it believable—and *Time* is the most successful liar of our times. Hitler overdid his act; Mao simply hasn't learned *Time*'s secret of including enough reality to be plausible.

Elizabeth, New Jersey

Sloan Wilson
author

Any enemy of *Time* is a friend of mine. I'll try to sort out my personal prejudices in telling you of my relationship over the years with this magazine.

161

In 1947 I had the title of assistant to the director of special projects at *Time* and *Life*. The funny title meant that I helped Roy Larsen, who was then president of the whole corporation, write speeches and form a well-intentioned project for the benefit of the public schools. I quit *Time,* to work for the school commission that we formed and to write books. My association with Roy Larsen was in general happy.

My second relationship with this curious corporation has been as a journalist. I have written three articles for *Life,* one of which was published under the pen name of John William Sperry because Roy Larsen was afraid that my opinions of teacher education would be attributed to his school commission, which I am very much afraid turned out to have no opinions at all after spending a great deal of money. Now as a writer I won't work for *Life* anymore because, although they pay a lot, they dishonor me. They change what I write without requesting my permission and they often insert their own horrible sentences under my by-line. Their editors also have the curious feeling that they are totally superior to writers. It has been my experience that I can work better with good editors than I can work alone. I love talking an article over and a good editor can often show me how to sharpen my work. But the editors at *Life* are different. I don't think they know it and I feel sorry for them but they form the same kind of sick relationship with writers that sick men form with sick call-girls. They do not know the meaning of love.

Time and *Life* would say that the reason I am hostile to them is that they have been hostile to all my books. The book-review section of *Time* has devoted several columns over the years to the task of explaining that I am a venal idiot. It does not become a writer to protest bad notices and I must be careful here to stick to facts. I am a human being who has written five novels which have been translated into many languages and which have been bought by millions of people who do not ask for their money back. I am a human being who works alone, except for my good wife, and although I have made a great deal of money I have no business sense and because of taxes and lawyers I cheerfully live in a two-room apartment. I am getting old enough and wise enough not to quiver when *Time* magazine ridicules me but their hostility confuses my children. When I labor to write a book I do not think they have to like the book, but I don't think they should write me up as though I had just mugged somebody in Times Square. I know they are jealous of my ability to survive as an independent writer and I know that though they probably don't realize it they are catering to the tastes of other jealous people who like to see other writers destroyed, but I do wish that Mr. Luce with all his money would send all his people to psychiatrists and get help in the proper way.

I am speaking not only from indignation at the way this corporation has treated me, but with a deep anger at the way they have treated many writers, including James Gould Cozzens, a good man whom they held up to public ridicule. They have not discovered the elementary truth about themselves, that they make their magazine important by decrying people most people think are good and by praising people that most people have never heard about.

It becomes me at the age of 43 to try to speak the truth, not only to vent just anger. *Time* and *Life* in the balance provide a lot of entertainment and a lot of education for a lot of people. Although they hurt me I am in the balance glad that they are there, creating in their big corporate way just as I create in my little individual one but I'm sorry that this great animal of *Time* and *Life* is so hostile. The good people of the world should not spend so much time at each other's throats.

New York, New York

Bertrand Russell
philosopher

I consider *Time* to be scurrilous and I know, with respect to my own work, utterly shameless in its willingness to distort. I cannot give you specific instances, because I have long ago discontinued attending to it. However, I do recall the remark of Zachariah Chafee upon being given an award by the Luce publications. He said: "I note that I have been attended by the Luce publications. You know the ones I mean; the one for those who cannot read and the other for those who cannot think."

Penrhyndeudraeth, Merioneth, Wales

Mary McCarthy
author

I'm writing this in a hurry and don't have time to look up mistakes, if any, in the early *Time* pieces involving me.

But about the most recent, the review of *The Group*, Sept. 6, 1963, I can cite the following. "20 years in the writing"—actually 11. The book was begun, and this has several times been printed, during the fall of the Stevenson campaign, 1952. Priss, according to *Time* "destined for social work," was an economist who worked for the consumer division of N.R.A., then for the League of Women Shoppers. It was Dottie who planned to work for a Boston settlement house. Kay's husband has no "sexual shortcomings" that I'm aware of, unless that means infidelity. The white dress is "off white" in the book. The "Vassar clublady" (*Time*), Helena's mother, never went to college; this point is underscored in the book. And the quote from her is wrong: "the first American war casualty" (me) is turned into "the first casualty in America's war against fascism."

More serious is the falsification in *Time,* July 4, 1960: "Western literature is the mirror on the ceiling of the whorehouse." This sounds as if it came from East Berlin. What I said was that writing about mass culture for a mass audience was the mirror on the ceiling of the whorehouse. I wrote a letter of protest and correction which was printed some weeks later, perhaps at the end of July. *Time* cut the paragraph from my letter which asked why their reporter did not consult the transcript of the Congress and commented *"Time* heard Miss McCarthy." I always thought I should have sued them for this, since the transcript did exist and there were dozens of witnesses to bear me out, but I was living in Europe at the time and it all seemed too complicated. Incidentally I did not "moan" but laughed.

Paris, France

John McClellan
United States Senator (Arkansas)

I regard *Time* as prejudiced and unfair in its reporting.

Washington, D.C.

David Merrick
theatrical producer

As far as I'm concerned there is not a single word of truth in *Time* magazine.

New York, New York

Leonard Rowe
attorney and educator

I'm an avid reader of *Time,* but don't for a minute think I've been buffaloed by Henry R. Luce's personal editorials masquerading as news. My interest is purely professional.

As a teacher of semantics and propaganda analysis, I find *Time* indispensable as a sort of laboratory manual and clinical exhibit for my classes. Granted there are any number of books on propaganda; but the general contents too often suffer from academic dryrot.

Before I discovered the usefulness of *Time,* I used to invent hypothetical examples based on recent news and current topics to explain to my students such classic propaganda devices as false identification of the writer with the reader, the "bandwagon appeal," the *ad hominem* argument, the "black-and-white" interpretation of complex issues, distortion by lifting text out of context, distortion by the calculated omission of relevant facts, and distortion by sly juxtaposition.

Then, on Feb. 23, 1959, the *New Republic* published a journalistic *tour de force,* Ben H. Bagdikian's exposé and analysis of *Time*'s chronic slantings: "TIME-Study: Accuracy in a Weekly Newsmagazine."

In the course of but seven blistering pages, this article made me throw my own examples to the wind and use *Time* as Exhibit A to illustrate the shabby tricks used to subordinate facts to the prejudices, predilections, and antipathies of *Time*'s publisher, Henry R. Luce.

At the same time I discovered another excellent study made by *UAW Ammunition* (official publication of the United Automobile, Aircraft and Agricultural Implement Workers of America) in its issue of December, 1956, entitled "How *Time, Life* and *Newsweek* Covered the Campaign."

The argument and conclusion of the U.A.W.'s study:

The sanctimonious Mr. Luce, publisher of <u>Time</u> and <u>Life</u>, most especially is guilty of hypocrisy . . . his magazines are masterpieces of bias.

They snigger rather than laugh. They rarely strike but they often stab. They are mean-spirited and vindictive. They are unctuous and patronizing.

. . . If students and teachers continue to read these periodicals, we hope they will read them for what they are—unofficial organs of the Republican Party and spokesman for a big-business point of view.

Thenceforth, instead of racking my brain to contrive examples of slanted, manipulated, and masturbated news, I merely read *Time* every week, particularly the first 10 to 12 pages of national politics and foreign news, where the man-handling is always at its blatant and flagrant worst.

Behold how *Time* prepares the reader to accept with due reverence the platitudes of the Republican candidate, Dwight D. Eisenhower (*Time,* June 18, 1956):

Head bare under a hot sun, Ike welcomed his youthful guests, admonished them to search for truth and apply it, reminded them that political parties must be dedicated not to the seizure of power but to ideals.

As for a Democratic candidate, *Time* prepares its readers to give the rascal the contempt he deserves (*Time,* Sept. 17, 1956). The dog-house treatment of Sen. Estes Kefauver begins by labeling him the "Professional Common Man." This, of course, means that he is strictly a phony. *Time* quotes an unidentified friend (and what a beautiful example of smearing by unattributed quotation: *Time*'s contribution to slanted journalism—the one-man cross-section!) as saying of the Democratic Senator that "he is the type of fellow who, if he was out campaigning and came across a farmer pitching manure, would take off his coat, grab another pitchfork and start to work." Then *Time* delivers the knockout punch: "This week, pitchfork in hand, Vice-Presidential Nominee Kefauver was all set to start work on the key part of his Democratic campaign job. . . ." A beautiful illustration of brainwashing the reader by subliminal impressions. Pitchfork. Pitching manure. Pitchfork in hand. And now the reader, both on the conscious and on the unconscious level, gets the impression, believes, feels in his very bones, that this phony, Kefauver, posing as a yokel, wasn't really campaigning: He was slinging horse manure at the voters.

Time continues the assassination: "Kefauver's poor-mouthed Southern drawl . . . a penchant for Wilsonian liberalism . . . fuzzily expressed . . . his enormous, ever-present briefcase, stuffed with all the items that long campaign experience has taught him he needs: an extra shirt (he perspires heavily) . . ."

Subliminal impression: Republicans are clean and immaculate, always freshly bathed, smelling of expensive after-shave lotions. But this Kefauver guy—like most Democrats—stinks of horse manure and sweat and B.O.

Now, let's see how *Time* treats another political personage, depending upon whether he is consorting with blessed Republicans or with accursed Democrats:

Time, Aug. 12, 1946, on the character of George E. Allen under a Democratic administration.

Last week . . . the President [Truman] eased his croniest crony, George E. Allen, into the Board of Directors of the Reconstruction Finance Corporation.

And, some 7 months earlier, *Time*'s issue of Jan. 28, 1946, this less-than-glowing tribute was paid Mr. Allen:

167

George is all the more remarkable because, to the naked eye, he is a clown.

But in the theology and metaphysics of *Time*—particularly since Sen. Joe McCarthy of hallowed memory revived the concept of Guilt by Association—there is Innocence by Association, especially if that association be with Holy Republicans. And so, in *Time* of Dec. 14, 1954, George E. Allen, erstwhile "clown" and "croniest crony" of stinking Democrats, is now beatified:

Last week . . . the President [Eisenhower] chatted quietly with . . . golfing companion George E. Allen, Washington lawyer and friend of Presidents.

Time's abuse of Adlai Stevenson when he ran against Mr. Eisenhower in 1952 is legendary. Before the campaign, Stevenson was described by *Time* as Illinois' "good Governor" who was "dedicated to the . . . dynamic proposition that the U.S. is not a static pattern but 'an experiment—among other things—in good government." After Stevenson became a candidate, however, *Time* scoffed at his record as Governor and said, "He never so much as slapped the wrist of the Cook County Democratic Organization, the most corrupt and powerful of existing big-city machines."

Sen. Joseph Clark of Pennsylvania has charged that *Time* deliberately prints unflattering photographs of those it does not favor. He has said that such a picture of himself, with his mouth wide open, appeared in *Time* of March 16, 1959, in connection with an article on his budget proposals. "Balanced Budget—Liberal Democrat Style," the story was labeled, and *Time* stated that "nowhere did Clark suggest where costs could be cut." Clark said on the floor of the Senate that this was an outright lie, and that *Time* had chosen to ignore his suggestions for economies. Senator Clark has inserted a huge collection of *Time*'s inaccuracies into the *Congressional Record,* along with perhaps the most insightful statement that has ever been made about *Time*'s inaccuracies:

If Time magazine were selling apple-sauce instead of a weekly publication, it would not be able to call itself, as it does, "The Weekly Newsmagazine," because the Federal Food, Drug, and

Cosmetic Act of 1938 requires that all such goods be labeled truthfully.

Cincinnati, Ohio

P. G. Wodehouse
author

Time is about the most inaccurate magazine in existence. They will write just about anything to be picturesque and amusing.

For instance, during the German occupation of France, when I was living in Le Touquet, they did a short squib on my internment by the Germans. They had me "throwing a cocktail party in the jolly old pine woods at Le Touquet" as the German army was sweeping toward Paris. According to *Time,* all of us "revelers" were ceremoniously arrested and carted off— still in jolly good humor. Can you imagine the bastards inventing an idiotic story like that? . . . Apparently everyone believed the story because it has been picked up time and again. It did me a lot of harm 20 years ago, and is still repeated often. It is embedded in the world's folklore—thanks to the inventiveness of one of *Time*'s editors.

Remsenburg, New York

Rockwell Kent
artist and author

Time is too strongly inclined to the ultra-right to be trustworthy in the forming of fair judgment in current political events. I feel its style of writing to be objectionable and inclined to value smartness above truth.

No, I don't like *Time,* and just one year ago declined a friend's generous proffer of a subscription.

Ausable Forks, New York

Burgess Meredith
actor

I have been aware of inaccuracies in *Time* for longer than I care to remember.

Pomona, New York

Eugene Burdick
author and educator

My disenchantment with *Time* started back in 1950. At that time I was at Oxford University and wrote a satirical piece on Oxford for the literary magazine. *Time,* by careful paraphrasing and omission, gave the impression that I was charging that Oxford was full of homosexuals, miserable food, and sad lectures.

Later, *Time* reviewed and praised my book *Fail-Safe* and in several subsequent issues quoted it, apparently with approval. Then quite obviously someone high up the ladder decided to give the book a blast. So the special section "Opinion" was introduced and a wild swinging attack was made on the book. We wrote a long letter pointing out that, despite the information that *Time* had, they had deliberately misread the thesis of the book. They had really written an editorial in their news columns and a poor one at that. It purported, however, to be based upon "inside dope" from the Air Force. My personal view is that Henry Luce is very sensitive to anything which might lead to disarmament. It is an honorable and, perhaps, a viable view. But it should not be pursued with dishonest tactics. We also pointed out that the Strategic Air Command itself thinks that war by accident is possible and has a special group which studies precisely that possibility. Also, Secretary McNamara will not associate himself with those who believe that war by accident is impossible. In any case, *Time*'s arguments were vapid in the extreme.

In the end they cut our letter to pieces without the courtesy of putting in the traditional three dots which indicates that they have made an excision.

I might add that by pure accident I ran across somebody at *Time* who worked on the original story on us and our book. He reported that the article was written by direct orders from "up there" and that although most of the staff objected there was nothing they could do. This writer was sympathetic with the book but had a job to protect.

Berkeley, Calif.

P. A. Sorokin
sociologist

On the basis of my irregular reading of *Time* Magazine, I believe you would have no difficulty to collect a multitude of such misinformations which can be found in any copy of this magazine.

Winchester, Mass.

John Osborne
playwright

Delighted to hear you're doing a piece on *Time*. It is such a vicious, dehumanizing institution and needs all the bricks it can get. The coverage of things from here is often appalling, not only for the indecent bias but its treacherous inaccuracy. I have twice started litigation against them.

London, England

Jeannine Ouimet
private secretary to Princess Grace of Monaco

Her Serene Highness Princess Grace has asked me to let you know that she has often been the victim of *Time*'s inaccuracies and slanting.

Monaco

Igor Stravinsky
composer

Every music column I have read in *Time* has been distorted and inaccurate.

Hollywood, Calif.

Marshall McLuhan
professor, University of Toronto

The overwhelming fact about *Time* is its style. It has often been said that nobody could tell the truth in *Time* style.

Toronto, Canada

Vincent Price
actor

My feeling and the feeling of many others is that *Time*'s style and derogatory attitude is not only dated but a terrible bore.

Los Angeles, Calif.

Brownlee Haydon
writer

After a sheltered life as an editor of *Business Week,* where I was free to call my shots as I saw them, I made a pass at *Life*.

Even then, in the late '40s, the *Time/Life/Fortune* clan was known for its venality and inaccuracy. I was interviewed at *Life* by Ed Thompson. . . . I will never forget telling him (innocently) about my respect for the writer's integrity, only to have him reply, "Well, say you're covering a labor story. If we don't like the way you play it we ask you to try again. If it doesn't come out right—or, let's say you refuse, for instance. Well, you may wind up in some other department. No, I don't think you'd really be happy writing for *Life*."

This was as forthright a statement as one might ask of the *Life* philosophy—write as we think it should be, or go somewhere else.

Pacific Palisades, Calif.

Irwin Shaw
author

Long ago, a bright young man came out of Yale determined to establish a magazine nastier than any other magazine of the day. Unhappily for us all, he succeeded beyond his wildest dreams. The bright young man was Henry Luce, of course, and the magazine was *Time*.

A few years after it first hit the stands, a friend of mine described it in terms that are still valid for today. *"Time,"* he said, "seems well-informed on any given subject, as long as you know nothing whatever about that subject yourself. . . ."

I have hit only one critic in my life. He wasn't even an American, but a small Frenchman who had given a book of mine a very good review. I didn't hit him because of the review but because of his drunken and objectionable behavior at a party. I was ashamed of myself, as I should have been, and made a resolve to keep my hands in my pockets in the presence of critics from then on.

Still, it takes a stern exercise of self-discipline for me to keep my hands in my pockets as I pass the *Time* building. While, through the years, if *Time*'s circulation figures are not falsified, the magazine must have done me a great deal of harm, I have not as yet publicly struck back. First of all, the question of whom to strike at is a complicated one. Understandably, anonymity is the rule on *Time*. (If I wrote like that I would hesitate to sign my work, too.) And it is difficult to know if one man has done the deed or a regiment, since anywhere from one to a thousand people may have worked on each offense, and identifying them would need the resources of the FBI.

Of course, one could always hold the boss responsible, which at least would cut the possible opposition down to one. I suppose I could have copied the example of Hemingway, who once invited two British critics to Cuba, at his expense, for a duel, which unfortunately never took place. But I am a peaceful man and I couldn't imagine sending seconds to present my compliments to Mr. Luce and asking him to meet me at dawn in front of the fountain in Rockefeller Plaza. Failing a *mano a mano,* there remained the possibility of the use of terror, by now an almost respectable aspect of modern society. One could always place small bombs at strategic points in the lobby or on the worst floors of the *Time* and *Life* building and hope for the best. But the organization is too big. Rid yourself of 20 hired scolds and 40 substitutes are panting to replace them, from the graduating classes of our better colleges.

Naturally, while this is the first time I have ever written anything about the Luce Empire, I have not kept my opinions about it to myself. On certain occasions I have said, in the presence of witnesses, some of them undoubtedly hostile, that

Time's treatment of me at almost every opportunity makes me wonder if a false report hadn't reached headquarters that I had once, inadvertently, slept with the wife of one of the editors. And I have said to acquaintances of mine, some of them employees of *Time* and *Life,* that the members of the organization you meet elsewhere or who are sent to interview you by the main office are invariably charming young ladies or soft-spoken and friendly young men who swear that they only intend to be objective, fair, and friendly. While in most cases I am sure that's what their reports are like, a sea change occurs once the pages are back in the office and whatever the charming young ladies or the soft-spoken young men have written is changed into *merde* for publication. I have even speculated, in their presence, on the magic construction of the machine which accomplishes this transformation and expressed my admiration for the machine's cleverness and the reliability of its performance.

I do not pretend that I am the only student of the magazine who has discovered the existence of this machine. The real sufferers are the people who work or who have worked in outlying districts for *Time,* like the war correspondent, now famous, who was threatened with death by a sergeant of the First Division in Algiers because of a piece in the magazine which contained derogatory remarks about the Division. The correspondent escaped with his life by persuading the sergeant that the piece as written was exactly opposite in tone and intention and that the Machine in New York had done its work, unbeknownst to the correspondent. Since I have known the correspondent for many years and have never heard him lie, this explanation satisfied me, as it did the sergeant and his large, belligerent friends.

Just after the war I heard a story very much like this from a *Time* correspondent who sent back a report from Prague, and only recently two of Luce's men in Saigon resigned publicly on the same grounds. In fact, all the Luce men I ever knew and admired either resigned or were fired for similar reasons. These included John Hersey, Jack Belden, Theodore White, William Walton, T. S. Matthews, and Charles Christian Wertenbaker, who were responsible among them for a high proportion of the best reporting in *Time* and *Life* from the various fronts during the war. In fact, for a few years after the war I found that as a useful rule of thumb, resignation—either forced or voluntary—divided the admirable men in the Luce organization from what I shall call, out of politeness, the others. And it cannot just be coincidence that all the many books written by members of the staff of the magazine about *Time* are approximately as cordial in tone as the memoirs of the survivors of Stalingrad on the subject of the German Army.

My first introduction into what can be loosely described as the *Time* process came a long time ago, in 1936 to be exact, when my name was first mentioned in the magazine's columns. This was on the occasion of the production of my first play. I no longer remember whether the review was a good one or a bad one, but I do remember that in describing me the critic called me a third-rate football player. Since I played football for Brooklyn College, a team that was not known for the size of the crowds that attended its games, the chances of the reviewer's having followed my career closely enough to judge me in relation to Red Grange or Cliff Battles or Ernie Nevers were remote. So the estimate must have been made on pure guesswork, tinged with premature bile. My estimate of myself as a football player was that I was a second-rate back on a fourth-rate team, which is not the same thing at all. It is only now, when the coach of the New York Giants, Allie Sherman, who played on a later Brooklyn team, has made our mutual Alma Mater illustrious, that I have felt free to give my considered opinion on the subject.

Later, personal considerations kept me from a public judgment on the magazine such as the one I am making now, although my opinion of it has never changed. Through the years I have noted that *Time* is run on what might be called The Theory of Instantaneously Reversible Infallibility. That is, what is propounded with great skill and energy and conviction on one Friday as an eternal Truth is neither denied nor explained the following Friday when a diametrically opposed eternal Truth is propounded, with equal vigor and conviction. . . .

The personal considerations mentioned above have to do with Mrs. Luce, who was a playwright herself in the Thirties, and who invited me down to the Luce plantation in the Carolinas for a week. I accepted with pleasure, as I admired her then, as I do now, for her beauty, brains, and ambition. At the end of the week, as we said our good-byes, she told me I was free to come there whenever I wished, on condition that I never write about the place. This struck me as a little odd, since even at that early stage in my career I had been a guest in other houses without being sworn to secrecy upon my departure. But I was young, candid, and agreeable at this period, and ready to humor a lady's whims, so I made the promise freely.

Up to now, I have kept this promise. But promises, like copyrights and international agreements between unfriendly powers, must run out eventually. I have been rummaging through my memories of the visit, and have recalled that there was nothing particularly damaging in what I saw or heard except, perhaps, for the treatment accorded Mr. Luce by the people who worked on the plantation. They thought he was absurd and their relations with him were based on covert contempt. Whatever his talents may be in other fields, Mr. Luce can hardly be called a sportsman. . . . Guests were quietly taken aside and told not to gallop any of the horses, as the grooms didn't want the idea to get around among the brutes that it might be fun to move the editor of *Time* magazine at more than four miles an hour. Except for one frisky roan gelding, the message had gotten through to all the other horses. The gelding, I was told, was to be sold as soon as possible. My manners as a guest were not as polished at the age of 24 as they are now, and I mischievously insisted upon riding the gelding. I had exhilarating gallops all over the countryside while Mrs. Luce confided to a friend that she was sure the horse would come home without me.

Besides this ungracious exuberance, I outraged the principles of hospitality (again I plead youth and ignorance) by going on ahead one day and making the gelding prance up to

the top of a little knoll, where I sat stiffly, like a general review-
ing troops, my arm outstretched in the Fascist salute as Mr.
Luce and entourage came upon the scene on their sedate nags.
This would be a bad joke at any time but it was especially
foolish at that period, when Luce, avid for power, was trying
various political garments on for size and was not averse to a
little preliminary flirting with the Far Right. . . .

The last time I saw Mr. and Mrs. Luce together was in a
restaurant in Rome quite a few years ago, some weeks after a
novel of mine had been published and had been given the
usual bath by *Time*'s reviewer. I discussed the review with the
Luces, in civilized terms. It had received, along with a generous dose of harsh reviews, many good ones. It was climbing
steadily on the best-seller list, and success, except in the case of
neurotics, appreciably sweetens the character and diminishes
the desire for vengeance. Still, I told the Luces that I thought
the notice vindictive. Mrs. Luce, who on ordinary matters is a
strikingly well-informed woman, said that she had heard that I
had dragged this particular novel from the bottom of my
trunk, where I had put it before I wrote my plays, my two
previous novels, and my books of short stories. Since she had
at her disposal one of the most widespread networks of information in the world, this bit of news must have come, freshly
fabricated, from the home office, although the novel in question had taken me four years to write and I had given it to my
publishers, with a huge sigh of relief, the day I finished it some
4 months before. I offered this bit of literary chronology to the
handsome couple and asked Mr. Luce to try to find out how
this particular rumor had started. He made a note in a little
book and said I would hear from him. Seven years or so later, I
am still waiting to hear from him.

Through the years the provocations continued. I have a
feeling that there must be a file in the imposing building on
50th Street of a list of names, under the heading *To Be Provoked at Every Opportunity,* and that my name is well up on
the list. Still, until this year I never indulged in any communication with the magazine, since I had the feeling that letters on
the subject would be a little like writing letters of complaint

about the weather. But in April, 1963, in an article that had nothing to do with me but which was about Sam Spiegel, the producer of *On the Waterfront, Bridge on the River Kwai,* and *Lawrence of Arabia,* there was an error of fact that demanded retraction. In the article, Mr. Spiegel was depicted as a very difficult and demanding man to work with, a reputation of which he is justifiably proud. To illustrate this point, the writers of the article composed the following anecdote:

The story goes that when Writer Irwin Shaw was working on Waterfront, his wife awoke one morning at 3 o'clock to find her husband in the bathroom, shaving. What was he doing? "I'm going out to kill Sam Spiegel," he said. (Time, April 19, 1963)

I have never worked with, or for, or on, Sam Spiegel, so after reading the article I sent off the following cable:

Editor Time Magazine
I do hope the reporter who discovered that I write under the nom de plume of Budd Schulberg is handsomely rewarded for his Time-Style accuracy.

Irwin Shaw

For some weeks I received no reply from *Time* and saw no correction in its pages. I did receive some letters from friends and even from strangers telling me how well they thought I had written certain scenes in *On the Waterfront.* I sent gracious thank-you notes in return. Finally, I received a letter from the magazine, which is here reproduced in full:

Dear Mr. Shaw:
Time's apologies for substituting your name for Budd Schulberg's in referring to the author of On the Waterfront (April 19 Time). We obviously did not check carefully enough in this instance. Thank you for wiring to correct us.

Cordially yours,
Marylois Purdy
For the Editors

Mr. Irwin Shaw
2 Bis Square Lamartine
Paris, France
MP: for

Not to be outdone in manners, I promptly replied to Miss Purdy:

May 16, 1963

Dear Miss Purdy (For the Editors),

I'm afraid that Time just can't get anything straight about me. Although Klosters, where I live, must have been printed at the top of the cable I sent to Time your letter was sent to an old address of mine in Paris, at least two years out of date.

Still, a letter sent to the wrong address is better than no letter at all. I know you must be very busy but I wonder if you could take the time to write me again (Chalet Mia, Klosters, Switzerland) and let me know in what issue of Time my cable was published. From your letter I have an uneasy feeling that the information that I am not Budd Schulberg and that I never said I was going to kill Sam Spiegel is being kept as a cozy secret between you (for the editors) and me, as a non-Budd Schulberg.

Yours truly,

By now I was enjoying this exchange. Miss Purdy's communications, I felt, would add a welcome fillip to the usual collection of bills, complaints about my dog biting other dogs, and unwanted manuscripts that the scrupulous Swiss Post Office deposits daily at my door. Unhappily, Miss Purdy fell silent after her one outburst of eloquence. Perhaps, as is the custom on *Time,* she had been promoted to the religious page or the department of medicine and was too busy writing pieces proving the existence of the Devil or describing new cures for leprosy which make those sections of *Time* so interesting to the general reader.

After a decent interval I realized that Miss Purdy was out of my life for good, like so many other friends of my youth, and I reached the reluctant conclusion that the moment had come for me to write my first letter to Mr. Henry Luce, a literary exercise I had hoped to be able to avoid in my lifetime. *That* letter follows.

Dear Mr. Luce,

In the last few weeks there has been an exchange of cables and letters between me and Time on the subject of a mistake in the article on Sam Spiegel in the April 19th issue of your magazine. In the article, I was named as the author of On the Waterfront, which I regret I didn't write, and as the hero of a foolish little anecdote

179

which obviously never could have happened. I'm enclosing copies of the two letters and the cable. None of it is of much importance and I won't pretend that I mean to rush over to New York to horse-whip Miss Purdy, who obviously is the _Time_ delegate-at-large to handle complaints for the editors who are too busy getting out the next issue to bother with errors in the last one. I don't know what your attitude is in matters like this, but I do know that Harold Ross, who was the only editor of a magazine I have ever known well, would have been exasperated by this kind of sloppy journalism.

The reference to Harold Ross was, of course, not acci-dental. Mr. Luce, like everybody else on _Time,_ knows what the editors and contributors to the _New Yorker_ have always thought about the bias and inaccuracy of _Time_'s reporting and the tortured, smart-alecky, teacher's-pet style of the writing in its pages. They also know that most of the _Time_ staff only work for _Time_ because they can't get jobs on the _New Yorker._ But Mr. Luce, with the century-tested serenity of the China in which he was born, held his peace. The letter I had thought to prod out of him with this calculated slur to his vanity never was written, any more than the promised letter from Rome. . . .

Just where and when this vendetta started is hard to say. Perhaps I should not have galloped the roan gelding, or I should have fallen off, as predicted by Mrs. Luce. Perhaps I should not have given the Fascist salute to Mr. Luce as he trotted nervously into the field below me on his nag. Perhaps the fact that I live in Europe, which seems to make the people on _Time_ regard me as a latter-day Benedict Arnold, is excruci-atingly painful to the rank and file of the _Time_ organization, who probably would like to live there themselves. Actually, I spend more time in the United States than most of their foreign correspondents, a piece of information that I can conceive to be of no interest to anybody but myself. Perhaps they believe the beguiling fables my agent spreads about the huge amounts of money I earn, which I wish I could believe, too, but must seem galling to writers who have to go to an office every day at a fixed salary and write what they are told to write. Perhaps they are swayed by the common misconception that I do not have to pay taxes in the United States, a misconception that the Internal Revenue Service unfortunately does not share. Perhaps it is just the hatred of the tame animal for the animal who lives in a state of nature (a writer who must write to order, in this case, to be considered tame as compared with a writer who writes to nobody's order but his own). Perhaps it is a hangover from my political opinions of the 1930s, when I was for the Spanish loyalists and opposed, too early, to the Nazis. If I had only been a Communist and recanted publicly, I might not have aroused such wrath, and even if, on literary grounds, the people on *Time* had disliked my work, their dislike would have been expressed in rational terms. Perhaps, somewhere, somebody overheard me expressing a doubt about the divinity of Chiang Kai-shek, an icon that has long hung, prominently displayed, in the *Time* office. Perhaps I should have allowed myself to be converted to Catholicism or publicly approved of Senator McCarthy. Perhaps I should have written for *Sports Illustrated* (I did, once, but only on Swiss food). In retrospect, the possibilities of a *rapprochement* with Luce and his employees seem endless, but alas, it is all too late now. . . .

Klosters, Switzerland

The Great Smokescreen

By Arthur E. Rowse

Writing about lung cancer in *Cosmopolitan* magazine a few years ago, Gordon and Kenneth Boggs reported: "Now that the furor has died down and experts have had time to examine the supposedly damning statistics, the cigarette seems to be all but exonerated." Besides, "filters have removed much of the sting from the general condemnation."

What do Gordon and Kenneth Boggs say today? Not a word. They can't.

The article was originally submitted to *Cosmopolitan* by two writers who said nothing whatsoever about cigarettes being "all but exonerated" and about any protection afforded by filters. The editors asked the writers to insert a few sentences to that effect; they refused. The editors themselves added the sentences. Onto the article they put the by-line "By Gordon and Kenneth Boggs," who do not exist. Two pages away from the article when it appeared was an advertisement: "Viceroy gives you that *Real Tobacco Taste* you miss in every other filter brand!"

Cosmopolitan's performance was flagrantly dishonest; the performance of most other American magazines, newspapers, and TV stations with regard to the lung-cancer story has been only dishonest. For the most part our fearless free press remained stonily silent—until Emancipation Day, Jan. 11, 1963.

Suddenly, because of the government's official report condemning cigarette smoking as harmful to health, the massive media ended their 25 years of shilly-shallying and admitted that the subject was news. TV networks that rarely allowed their documentaries to probe into controversies closer than Angola and Afghanistan broke out with a rash of half-hour and 1-hour programs; newspapers that used to relegate items about lung cancer to the space between truss ads began blossoming with eight-column banners on the front page. The news media, it seems, had been infected with lung candor.

Even doctors, including those who smoke Camels "more than any other cigarette," admit that the government's report offered not a bit of new evidence. The 10 panelists themselves, chosen by the Public Health Service, just reviewed old studies. Then why did the press suddenly decide the jig was up and stop filtering the bad news?

In the first place, the fact that a government-sponsored panel had affirmed all the horrible things that others had documented was news in itself—and the "jury" had the *imprimatur* of the tobacco industry itself. Second, no study of the smoking-lung cancer link had received so much advance build-up. Third, cigarette sales had shown they could recover no matter how bad the news. And finally, in numbers there is safety. Most newspapers and TV stations with cigarette advertising would hesitate before initiating any study of the smoking problem on their own. But when it seems likely that every other newspaper and TV station will also be offending the tobacco interests, there is nothing to fear. The American Tobacco Company may not need the Podunk *Tribune* to advertise in, but it does need *all* of the nation's Podunk *Tribunes*.

A more pressing question is why the mass media saw fit to ostracize lung-cancer news in the first place. And the answer is that, while newspapers are in business to inform the public, sometimes informing the public can be bad for business. More and more it is getting to be true that he who pays the paper calls the tune. The history of how the news media covered—an apt word—news about the link between cancer and cigarettes is an object lesson in the inherent limitations of American journalism.

* * *

184

Our story opens in 1938. That was when Dr. Raymond Pearl of Johns Hopkins University presented statistical "life tables" based on his studies of 6813 men. The results, he said, proved "that smoking is associated with a definite impairment of longevity." *Time* called the report "enough to scare the life out of tobacco manufacturers and make tobacco users' flesh creep," but few other publications were willing to scare anyone. The shortage of publicity about Dr. Pearl's report led George Seldes and Harold Ickes to accuse New York City papers of having suppressed the story. Of eight papers, only two, the *Times* and *World-Telegram,* ran anything in their editions of record. This was at a time when full-page cigarette ads were just beginning to bring full-bodied pleasure to publishers (contemporary slogans included, "Not a cough in the carload"; contemporary jokes included, "It's not the cough that carries you off; it's the coffin they carry you off in").

Since many smokers could not then, and cannot now, tell any difference in taste between brands, advertising became essential in the fight for sales. Tobacco became what *Business Week* called "the classic case, studied in every business school in the country, of how a mass-production industry is built on advertising." With few exceptions, brand sales have run almost parallel with ad spending.

When the first mass of scientific studies linking smoking with mortality were made—between 1948 and 1953—many editors thought twice about publicizing them. The temporary drop of sales in 1953 and 1954 indicates that often the editors' consciences won out. But in the great majority of cases the newspaper coverage was sporadic, brief, and variable. The greatest public impact can be attributed to Roy Norr's article "Cancer by the Carton," in the December, 1952, *Reader's Digest,* a reprint from the *Christian Herald*. Probably the next most powerful blow came from *Life*'s issue of Dec. 13, 1953. Here, for the first time, smokers were shown photographs of how Dr. Evarts A. Graham of Washington University, using cigarette tars, induced skin cancer in mice. These articles, along with accumulated ash from other stories, were enough to

185

depress sales. Up to this point, radio and TV coverage was next to nothing.

Alarmed by what they called "loose talk," the leading tobacco companies accepted a proposal of Hill & Knowlton, their public-relations voice, to strike back. In January, 1954, they formed the Tobacco Industry Research Committee to conduct "independent" research and to "communicate authoritative factual information." Henceforward, nearly every news item containing harsh ingredients was made milder by simultaneous T.I.R.C. statements dismissing the new evidence as inconclusive—often before there was even time to review the facts. Tobacco spokesmen capitalized on the misconception—common even among newspapermen—that objectivity means giving every side of a controversy equal publicity, regardless of relative newsworthiness. Naturally, tobacco interests deserved space for comment, but their repetitious rebuttals soon lost all possible newsworthiness and took up space that could have gone toward fuller descriptions of new findings.

* * *

Of the hundreds of studies examined in the government report, only two received anything like front-page treatment when they first became news. Both studies were made by the American Cancer Society. The preliminary findings, released in June, 1954, showed that, of 187,000 men age 50 to 70, cigarette smokers had a death rate from heart attacks and coronary diseases 50% higher than nonsmokers. Deaths from lung cancer were 5 to 16 times greater. This was by far the most conclusive evidence to date, dwarfing previous studies in size and in the contrast between the health of smokers and nonsmokers. Surely it was of the greatest concern to people in general and to the 65 million smokers in particular. It was released almost 10 years before the Surgeon General's report. Why didn't it have a similar impact? The *Times* gave the story a two-column picture and headline on page one. *But of 19 major newspapers across the country, fully 13 decided that the story just was not front-page news.*

By this time, however, enough information had seeped

186

through printed media to give most people a whiff of the health issue. A Gallup poll found that 90% of its national sample had heard something about cigarettes and lung cancer. But what their knowledge amounted to was a big question. How many thought they were being protected by "exclusive micronite" and "selectrate" filters? How many realized the weight of the evidence already in?

Questions like these were soon buried under an avalanche of competing claims of low tar and nicotine content. The "tar derby" was set off, ironically, by tobacoo's most consistent critics, *Consumer Reports* and *Reader's Digest,* with their detailed laboratory analyses of cigarette brands. (Why the *Digest* should add cigarettes to its hate-list of taxes, Democrats, foreigners, sex, atheists, Indians, negligence lawyers, and intelligence is an interesting question. The best explanation is that publisher DeWitt Wallace is a pleasure-hating Puritan, which is why the *Digest* was against smoking back in the '20s, before a really sound case had been made by the prosecution. True to form, the *Digest* recently ran an article extolling the "safety" of American automobiles in the same issue with 20 full-page, color ads for various cars, at $55,675 a page.) As a result of the tar derby, filter cigarettes jumped from 10% of total sales in 1954 to 40% in 3 years, and mentholated brands rose from less than 1% to more than 7%. And this meant more profits, too, because the tobacco companies could use inferior tobacco in filter cigarettes without anyone's tasting the difference.

Then, in June, 1957, came the final report of the Cancer Society, showing an even greater incidence of illness among smokers than the first report did. It got the best coverage any such story received before 1964. Ten of the same 19 major papers placed the story on page one.

The next month was the newsiest of all until January, 1963. Rep. John A. Blatnik (D., Minn.), having heard that filters don't filter, began hearings to find out why. He invited top authorities, including representatives of tobacco companies, to testify. The tobacco men refused, but saw to it that their views were expressed by Clarence Cook Little, chairman of the T.I.R.C., plus a few other pro-tobacco spokesmen. Their consistent demurrer: more research is needed before drawing conclusions. As one ad man said after hearing how smoke causes lung cancer in mice, "It proves that mice shouldn't smoke."

Coincidentally, 3 days before the first of Blatnik's hearings, U.S. Surgeon General Leroy E. Burney announced that government scientists had confirmed the presence of benzpyrene in cigarettes—benzpyrene is a suspected carcinogen. A check of 26 large papers with 42% of all morning circulation showed that *only nine printed anything about Dr. Burney's announcement.*

The same shabby press coverage characterized the Blatnik hearings. Both sides took turns at the microphone opening day, allowing editors to print both viewpoints and thus have less timidity about printing anything anti-tobacco at all. To lighten their worries even more, wire dispatches, for no good reason, led off with Little's pro-tobacco views. Of the eight news breaks of major importance on the cigarette-cancer controversy in this 2-week period, the first day's hearing got the most play. Two of the 26 papers used it on page one, and only three ignored it altogether.

Far more significant testimony came at the second hearing—from Dr. Ernest L. Wynder of the Sloan-Kettering Institute for Cancer Research. Dr. Wynder reported on clinical tests he had made which showed that filter-tip cigarettes often carried residues more harmful than those of nonfilter cigarettes. Although this was little-known except to readers of the *Digest* and *Consumer Reports, only 12 of the 26 papers printed anything about it. None used it on page one.*

Dr. John R. Heller, director of the government's National Cancer Institute, went even further at the next session: "We don't believe any filter can selectively filter out the component or components in the tars that are responsible for lung cancer." Here was news even to *Digest readers, yet 16 of the 26 papers ignored it completely.*

The next day, newspapers got a chance to give their readers detailed analyses of the tar and nicotine content of individual brands. But half the papers omitted all wire dispatches, and only three revealed any of the brand differences that would have been of tremendous interest to smokers.

During the eight days of key developments, including two final hearings and an interview in which Heller said that lung cancer killed more people annually than automobiles, not one newspaper reported all events.

The *Boston Globe* and the Boston *Daily Record* printed only one of the stories.

The *Des Moines Register* and the Pittsburgh *Post-Gazette* used only two stories.

The *Philadelphia Inquirer* and the Charlotte *Observer* used only three stories.

Papers with the best performance—six stories—were the *New York Herald Tribune*, Minneapolis *Tribune, San Francisco Chronicle*, Denver *Post*, Louisville *Courier-Journal*, Miami *Herald, The Houston Post*, and *The New York Times*.

Of the 208 possible newspaper stories (26 papers for 8 days), *only 57% saw print, and only 4% made the front page*. This is not to imply that all the stories deserved page one. Newsworthiness is a relative thing, complicated by local factors, competing events, and available space. But as the commercials tell us, "It's what's up front that counts."

* * *

If newspapers were shamefully remiss about publishing news the public needed to know, TV was worse. By 1957, more than half the $150 million advertising budget of tobacco companies was being spent on TV commercials. People like Arthur Godfrey gave folksy assurances that smoking was one of the greatest pleasures and health elixirs known to man. "You hear stuff all the time," purred Arthur, "about 'cigarettes are harmful to you,' this and that and the other thing." Then, holding up a picture, he went on: "Here's an ad. You've seen it. If you smoke, it will make you feel better, really. 'Nose, throat and accessory organs not adversely affected by smoking Chesterfields.' " He proceeded to cite a study by what he called a "competent medical specialist" substantiating these claims.

189

Now amiable Arthur, after a lung-cancer operation, smokes small cigars. In replying to a question recently on why he himself had changed from cigarettes to cigars, he said, "You don't have to inhale them."

* * *

It would be unfair to blame advertising pressure alone for the scarcity of news about the cancer–cigarette link-up. The mass media generally tend to undervalue the public interest in consumer news, and to be unaware of the need to catch up with important items later if they are missed first time round. But advertising pressure deserves *most* of the blame. The news blackout on the cigarette–cancer story was not the result of an ugly, open conspiracy—it was more subtle than that. Here are two scenes, the first real, the second imaginary:

• At a story conference of one of the nation's leading magazines, a new staff member suggests an article on "How to Stop Smoking." The managing editor replies testily, "Yeah, we'll run it next to the L&M ad." The other staff members exchange superior smiles; the new staff member smiles apologetically. Next suggestion.

• A city editor examines a wire-service dispatch dealing with the danger of cigarettes. If the dispatch were printed, he knows, his publisher might be quietly annoyed, his advertising director might be quietly furious, and he himself might quietly never become managing editor. Ads bring in three times more money than subscribers' pennies. Perhaps barely conscious of his reasoning, the city editor throws aside the wire-service dispatch and uses something innocuous to fill the hole on page two. And not a word has been exchanged between advertiser, publisher, advertising director, and city editor.

A comparison of the various news media through 1963 shows a clear correlation between ads and lack of news. The two magazines that have penetrated the deepest, the *Digest* and *Consumer Reports,* get no tobacco revenue—whereas the *Digest* refuses such ads, *C.R.* accepts no ads at all. The small-circulation, intellectual magazines, like *New Republic,* the *Nation,* and *Harper*'s, also have no worries about withdrawal of cigarette advertising. Among the big weeklies, *Time* and *Newsweek* have done a conscientious job. *Life,* with all its cigarette ads, has occasionally treated the subject with complete frankness. So has the *New Yorker.* Of the other big slicks, however, few have done anything. The "crusading" *Saturday Evening Post* has never yet dared offend its big tobacco customers. *Look* has covered its journalistic eyes. And so, for the most part, have the big women's journals, despite little or no cigarette advertising.

Radio and TV, partly because of the nature of the beast, did not have room between commercials for more than a glance at the lung-cancer story. There is little time in 3½-minute news capsule for much news about anything, much less about lung cancer, and especially if the show is sponsored by Camels. The best means of telling such a story on TV is, of course, documentaries. Replying to a query late in 1962, ABC reported it had done no documentaries on the subject and did not contemplate any. NBC, which calls itself "the largest single source of news, entertainment and information in the free world," also had done none and planned none. Until 1963, the only network to give the lung-cancer story more than a shrug was CBS, but even its efforts were paltry.

* * *

Radio and TV, since they seldom present editorials, can be excused for not warning people directly about the dangers of cigarette smoking. Not so newspapers and magazines. And not only were there scarcely any editorials anywhere until 1963, but the few there were harped on the refrain that more evidence was needed—which was just what the tobacco industry wanted. CIGGIES ASSAILED AGAIN—HO HUM. That was the headline over an editorial in the New York *Daily News* during the filter hearings. "Sure," snarled the subway slangster, "the *News* takes cigarette advertising and likes it, and so what?" Ya wanna fight? Two years later, America's best-selling paper again demonstrated its sense of responsibility by adding that "until the scientists make up their minds one way or another, we don't see why Americans shouldn't go on calmly smoking

191

as many cigarettes as they damn please." This courageous stand did not earn a Pulitzer Prize for the paper that *Time* lists as one of the nation's best, but it did bring an accolade from a prominent tobacco publicist for "a fine editorial stand" and "an excellent service to readers." Other newspapers that have been praised by industry spokesmen for editorial excellence along these lines have been the *Detroit Free Press* and the Louisville *Courier-Journal*.

Of the newspapers that did take a public-minded editorial stand, none was more outspoken than the *Washington Post,* which long before 1966 argued that warnings should be printed on cigarette packages. The *Times* has also spoken strongly, though less frequently. One of the frankest statements from a newspaper in a tobacco area came from the Charlotte *Observer:* "The problem can be licked if all the people who have a stake in it would quit beating around the bush and admit the cancer problem exists."

The threat that cigarette companies would withdraw advertising if a news medium played too rough was a very real threat. An advertiser is free to advertise where he wants to, and why should he help a newspaper or magazine that knocks his product? True, there are no known cases where a tobacco firm withdrew advertising because of pique over editorial policies. Perhaps the unspoken threat proved effective enough, and perhaps the tobacco men were afraid of starting a public controversy. Then too, as a general rule, the small-circulation, financially insecure newspapers and magazines cannot afford to offend advertisers, while the big-circulation, prosperous ones can—because they will survive any such withdrawal of advertising and because the advertisers may need them as much as they need the advertisers. Yet though circulation is a good clue to financial health, it is not infallible. Some media with large readerships can be financially and morally insecure too—like *Cosmopolitan.*

The tobacco firms have occasionally shown how concerned they are about who prints what. In 1957, the American Tobacco Company asked its ad agency, Batten, Barton, Durstine & Osborn, to stop handling the *Reader's Digest* account.

The *Digest* was spending $1.3 million a year; American Tobacco was spending $22 million. The request was granted. Two years later, Bantob Products of Long Island, makers of a tobaccoless (and probably tasteless) cigarette, began a $15 million antitrust suit against the Big Five cigarette companies. Bantob claimed that the companies had blackjacked papers, radio, and TV into refusing Bantob ads, and quoted *Tobacco Leaf,* a trade publication, as saying, "The most effective weapon against invaders [of this kind] is economic pressure, and we believe that it should be used in whatever legal manner the industry deems necessary for its own preservation." Also in 1959, the makers of Aquafilter, a cigarette holder and filter, voiced the same complaint. These suits apparently worked, at least to the easing of this kind of pressure. But the important point is that newspaper and magazine editors and publishers knew beyond doubt that the tobacco companies were sensitive about what was being printed and were not averse to using their big stick.

* * *

The problem presented by the way the mass media ignored the cigarette–lung cancer story is an old one: Advertising often influences editorial columns, and sometimes it can even undermine the basic function of the press, which is to keep the public informed. Short of getting rid of advertising altogether, by having the government, private foundations, or universities subsidize all or some mass media, the only solution is that eternal cliché, eternal vigilance. For there are other areas, right now, where the public is not being kept sufficiently informed. Alcoholism, for instance. Currently it is America's No. 3 health problem, coming right after heart disease and cancer, and the ranks of alcoholics are steadily being joined by women and even by teen-agers. Yet do newspapers that take liquor ads print enough news about alcoholism? What about the mass magazines—has their choice of articles reflected the importance of alcoholism in America? Will *McCall's,* which has run a Schenley ad urging homemakers to serve liqueur *"always, with any meal,"* ever print an article about America's 750,000 women alcoholics? Will it take another U.S. Public Health Service report to make Americans sufficiently aware of the dangers they risk by drinking?

Still another area where the mass media can be counted on to suppress information is excessive coffee-drinking. Dr. Oglesby Paul and his colleagues at the University of Illinois recently made a long-term study of 2000 male employees at the Western Electric company in Chicago. They found that men who drank more than five cups of coffee a day ran a greater risk of having heart disease. Another study made by Dr. D. R. Huene, a Naval Reserve flight surgeon, showed that excessive coffee-drinking causes irregular heartbeats.

Commenting on these studies, a spokesman for the Coffee Brewing Industry has said, "More evidence is needed to prove any association between coffee drinking and heart disease, if any association does, in fact, exist."

To quote George Santayana, "Those who cannot remember the past are condemned to repeat it."

The Free Press: An Obit

By J. David Stern

A s the only newspaper, we don't want to tread on anyone's toes."

Harry T. Saylor, managing editor of a newspaper I owned, the Camden (New Jersey) *Courier,* dropped this remark at our first editorial conference after the *Courier* had become a monopoly newspaper. I had just bought out its only competitor, the Camden *Post-Telegram.* The year was 1926.

Harry's words annoyed me. I had not foreseen this side-effect of becoming a monopoly publisher.

"You mean we're to have no editorial policies?" I asked.

"Sure we can have editorials," Harry reassured me. "But less noisy ones. Why chance making any readers or advertisers angry?"

That hurried meeting was a turning point in my career. Crowded into my small office on the third floor of the ramshackle Courier Building were the key men who had been with me in a hectic 6-year newspaper war, an old-fashioned free-for-all. A variegated crew, they were all excited and elated over our victory. The *Courier* had defeated the reputedly impregnable Baird machine, which had controlled South Jersey for 25 years. Now we could enjoy the rewards of monopoly: more profits and less work.

But Saylor's advice took the tang out of my triumph. Would dull routine replace the stimulation of competition? I could not see then that the American press was trading its political power for profit and that the editorial page was deteriorating into a vermiform appendix, to which publishers paid little attention and the public even less. I did not know that the proud rooster atop the NEWS weather vane—in the newspaper trade symbol—would turn into a capon.

Just before it sold out, the *Post-Telegram* had bellowed across its front page. DAVE STERN IS A DIRTY DOG. The *Courier* did not refute the charge, but I enjoyed the last laugh. The night the headline appeared, I met David Baird Jr., publisher of the *Post-Telegram*, at a public dinner. I shouted across the room, "Dave, you know what a dirty dog does to a *Post!*" In those days of personal journalism, such exchanges between publishers were not unusual.

Now all contention was over. My capon newspaper waxed fat with higher earnings than anticipated, while my job as publisher grew tiresome. So I went hunting for trouble and found it. In 1928, I bought the Philadelphia *Record,* bottom of the heap of six keenly competing dailies and five Sundays. In 1933 I took on the New York *Evening Post,* low sheet on the totem pole of nine struggling for survival. I was pursuing the youthful dream that had lured me into journalism: that newspapers fought for causes, molded public opinion, determined government policies.

It was a vanishing dream. That type of newspaper is fast becoming extinct in these United States. It has been replaced by today's monopoly newspaper, which serves a smooth mixture of many comic strips and syndicated features, with innocuous local news and a minimum of wire stories, as regularly and impersonally as other local monopolies supply gas.

The creeping blight of monopoly has engulfed the American press. Less than 10% of our dailies are competitive. One publisher rules the roost in 1417 of the 1485 cities where daily newspapers are published. Of the 1760 or so English language dailies in the United States, only about 150 are in competition, and many of these 150 are losing money. Their publishers face the alternative of suspension or merging with their competitor. At the present rate of consolidations, by 1970 competition will be reduced to a score of newspapers in our ten largest cities.

In 1912, when I bought my first newspaper, the New Brunswick (N.J.) *Times,* there were 19 cities in New Jersey

198

with two or more competing dailies. Now monopoly newspapers serve all but two of these towns. Soaring costs are one cause of monopoly. Another is the growing importance of advertising in attracting readers. Half a century ago, retail advertising was drab. It was illustrated, if at all, with poor stock cuts, usually supplied by the newspaper. Food stores seldom advertised. As for national advertising, descriptions of patent medicines—often objectionable—predominated. But as advertising developed bulk and attractiveness it became a main reason why people bought newspapers. No longer does the man select a newspaper for its editorials and news. His wife chooses the daily for its advertising. Women want the most complete catalogue of bargains and latest fashions.

In 1940, American dailies averaged 24.15 pages a day, of which 10.4 were advertising, 13.75 news and features. Recent figures were 37.5 pages a day, 23.11 advertising, 14.39 news and features. Advertising had increased 122%, news and features 5%. Capons put on fat faster than sinew.

The average reader cannot spare time to wade through all the ads in an oversize paper of 64 pages or more. It would be better for reader and advertiser, as well as for the publisher, if he charged more for advertising and limited the size of his paper. But such a policy would give his competition an advantage, and the slogan of newspaperdom these days is "Starve the opposition, make for monopoly."

* * *

As if monopoly newspapers were not enough of a threat, 560 American dailies, with 40% of the national circulation, are owned by chains—like Hearst and Scripps-Howard. Because chain managements vary so widely it is difficult to generalize about them. Some chains maintain tight supervision of editorial policies. On the other hand, one of the most successful chain operators (Sam Newhouse) boasts that he pays no attention to news and editorial departments, only to the balance sheets of his many newspapers. But the consequences of chain operation are usually much the same as those of monopoly. The hired manager hesitates to start a controversy that might get him in bad with the absentee owner. Most chain newspapers are robbed of initiative and enterprise.

Newspapermen blame the trend to monopoly and chain ownership on increasing competition from television, radio, and magazines. In 30 years the newspapers' share of the advertising dollar has dropped from two-thirds to one-third. Whatever the causes, this change from a competitive to a monopoly press is unhealthy, sinister. It is making a travesty of our vaunted freedom of the press. Because once established, a monopoly paper is impregnable.

What if the monopoly publisher is intensely partisan, unfair, and unscrupulous? What if he opposes all public improvements and retards municipal development—or, just as bad, urges too many bond issues and bankrupts the town? Can public-spirited citizens establish another newspaper? Legally, yes. Practically, no.

When I say a monopoly newspaper is impregnable I speak from experience. The citizens of Camden never tried to break my monopoly. But, because of a newspaper war across the river, the *Philadelphia Inquirer* twice attempted it—putting out South Jersey editions. Both times they spent a lot of money but got nowhere. Camden merchants refused to advertise in the South Jersey *Inquirer*. Both Republican and Democratic officeholders tipped our city desk to news ahead of the intruder. It was the natural instinct of officials to keep in the good graces of the monopoly publisher.

Several times I was approached by disgruntled citizens of monopoly cities who offered to put up capital if I would establish a rival daily. While I never revealed the names of these citizens, I did tip off the threatened publisher to watch his step. We monopolists stand by one another. Recently, New England monopoly newspapers banded together to help a fellow monopolist, the Haverhill (Massachusetts) *Gazette*, drive out an intruder. In the course of litigation that grew out of this battle, the court found that "Haverhill is a one-paper area . . . what might be termed a natural monopoly . . . a city of that size [45,000] cannot support two good daily newspapers under present-day conditions." So now newspaper monopoly has the sanction of the law. To say that the judge was practically right, legally wrong, is to raise a fundamental philosophical question.

A newspaper monopoly is protected by other things besides the high cost of competition. Even if they are furious at a publisher, the community's men of money are reluctant to invest in a second newspaper—the bank, the factory, the store are vulnerable to attack by the established newspaper. They hesitate to stick their necks out in open revolt. Then too, merchants generally are against a second newspaper. Even if they are paying high rates to the monopolist, they figure it would cost more to advertise in two newspapers.

Control of the circulation system gives the monopoly newspaper a stranglehold. By its domination of newsstands, newsboys, and suburban agents, it can retard, if not prevent, the distribution of an intruder. When I sold the Springfield (Illinois) *News-Record* in 1919 I received a most attractive offer to take over the Kansas City (Missouri) *Journal,* which was withering under competition with the Kansas City *Star.* I was confident I could save the *Journal* until I looked into the circulation situation. The *Star* had such complete control I turned down the offer. Eventually the *Journal* died. When it was too late, the U.S. Department of Justice stepped in and convicted the *Star* of unfair competitive practices. A fine was paid, but the *Star* still holds its monopoly in a city of half a million.

Syndicated comic strips and features give the monopoly another advantage. Would newspaper readers welcome a change of entertainment in a new daily? They certainly would not. Their appetite for features is similar to that of children for bedtime stories. My children wanted the same tales repeated over and over without change of a word. We grown-up children crave the soothing repetition of the familiar rather than the stimulus of the new.

The high value publishers place on features in retaining or increasing circulation is illustrated by two incidents.

• In deference to the government's request to conserve newsprint during World War II, publishers of the four Philadelphia dailies met once a month to devise ways and means to reduce paper consumption. After polite greetings we sat around a table in silence. No one wanted to risk an opening remark. A poker game of strangers, holding their cards close to their vests, was a talkfest in comparison. After discussing such trivia as free papers to police and fire stations, we would adjourn with nothing accomplished. Once I ventured a suggestion: "All of us are running two pages of comics. Why not cut to one and save 3000 tons of newsprint?" Dead silence was the only answer. After a few minutes one publisher looked at his watch and said, "I've got a golf date." The meeting broke up and the embarrassing subject was never mentioned again. During the greatest war in history all four newspapers had cut news space to the bone, but none of my competitors dared to deprive his readers of their accustomed escape "literature."

• When the Philadelphia *Evening Ledger* suspended publication in 1945, King Features Syndicate offered the *Ledger*'s features—Walter Winchell's column and three comic strips— to the highest bidder. The *Ledger* had been paying $250 a week. I bid $600, the *Bulletin* $650, and the *Inquirer* placed a value of $52,000 a year on attracting Winchell fans. For half that amount it could have hired a top-flight feature writer. But the present tendency is to buy packaged features like brand-name goods in a supermarket.

* * *

The lone newspaper is not only secure; it is also profitable. Monopoly has lifted it from little to big business in its community and has correspondingly raised the status of the publisher. As owner of the *Courier* I associated with neighboring merchants, rarely met the heads of big industries. After I became a monopolist, and my gross soared well over a million a year, I drifted into the company of factory owners, bankers, and utility tycoons. Instead of a quick lunch at the nearest grill, where I knocked elbows with the butcher and the baker, I was taking time out for a leisurely midday meal at the country club with the "gentry." Their company was pleasant but dull. They were so intent on their jobs they had little time for other interests. Every public question was weighed and measured by its immediate effect on each man's enterprise. "New water system?

How much will it add to my taxes?" They were as shut off from the world as wives in a harem. Secretaries substituted for eunuchs to guard their bosses from outside contacts. Occupied with technical reports and trade literature, they had little time for outside reading. I have a reporter's hunch that when Krupp and Thyssen were giving Hitler millions of marks they were too busy to read *Mein Kampf.*

Once I was invited to lunch with General W.W. Atterbury, president of the Pennsylvania Railroad, and a half-dozen other executives. Hothouse strawberries from the Atterbury "farm" were served for dessert.

"General, if you can grow strawberries like these you ought to give up railroading for farming," one guest remarked.

"Fine advice," Atterbury replied. "All I make as a railroader I lose as a farmer. These berries cost me a dollar apiece."

"You must be for the McNary-Haugen bill," I said, referring to a controversial farm-relief bill twice passed by Congress and twice vetoed by President Coolidge.

"Perhaps I would be if I understood it," Atterbury said. "Can you explain how it works?"

"As head of the biggest grain-mover in America you know more about the bill than I do." I backed off. I thought he wanted to get me into an argument about the many editorials I had written in favor of the plan.

"Perhaps I should, but honestly I don't," Atterbury persisted. "And I don't think my associates are any better informed. Please give us a briefing."

"The General is trying to pull my leg," I said, turning to a neighbor. These top officials could not be ignorant of major legislation that so directly affected their railroad. Finally I was persuaded to give a short explanation. It was an hour before they ran out of questions.

Even an altruist like Eldridge R. Johnson, founder of the Victor Talking Machine Company, eventually became blinded by the big-money smog. Just after I bought the Philadelphia *Record* he complimented me on my campaign to clean up the Delaware River so that the people would not have to drink chlorinated sewage. "The pollution is terrible," Johnson said. "It's ruined the paint on my new yacht."

Most monopoly publishers are suffocating in this plutocratic atmosphere. They travel with big businessmen, think like big businessmen, and talk like big businessmen. They may call themselves independent and claim to be impartial, but when the chips are down on any crucial issue, nearly all of them will be found in the big-business camp.

If newspaper publishers had not been so detached from their readers they would not have been so bitter and extreme in their denunciation of the New Deal in 1936. On the New Deal side were but a handful of metropolitan papers, the *St. Louis Post-Dispatch,* the Louisville *Courier-Journal,* and my newspapers, the *New York Post* and the Philadelphia *Record.* Through a virulent verbal barrage by 90% of the press, the voters marched to the polls to give President Roosevelt the largest majority in history. That election marked the end of American newspapers as a major force in national politics.

Loss of influence is not the saddest catastrophe. Even worse, our newspapers are growing dull, and dullness to a newspaper is what loss of beauty is to a woman. By misconduct a beautiful woman may forfeit social standing, but wrinkles and fat mark the final tragedy. Few newspapers can withstand monopoly's enervating effect. Lack of competition lowers morale from editor to cub reporter. Much of newspaper work is routine. The same stories have a way of recurring. A common repeater is the recluse found dead in his room or shack. Rarely does such a tragedy prove newsworthy. But competitive reporters will dig for the one chance in ten of a story—the deceased was once a person of note or a miser who lived in penury to accumulate a fortune. The lone reporter for a monopoly newspaper accepts the police report. A buddy of the department, his tendency is not to discover additional facts that might embarrass his friends. This difference between competitive and monopoly reporting applies to stories of greater public importance. The capon is a lethargic and lazy bird.

Is dullness slowing the growth of our newspapers? Our population is increasing at the rate of 1.85% a year, newspaper circulation at the rate of less than 1%. Annual net paid daily circulation in this country is 60 million—333 per thousand population; in Great Britain it is 573 per thousand; in Sweden, 464 per thousand. Newspapers blame their arrested growth on radio, television, and neighborhood weeklies in metropolitan areas. Equally important is the lack of incentive for a monopoly newspaper to increase its readership. A 5-cent monopoly newspaper, averaging 32 pages per edition, loses money on circulation, makes its profit from advertising. To justify higher advertising rates it must show a 10,000 increase in circulation. But this will cost $50,000 for promotion, plus high delivery expense to suburban areas. While making this drive for new readers, net profits will be reduced. A similar local monopoly situation kept farmers from obtaining electricity until President Roosevelt, in 1935, initiated rural electrification, financed by the government. Local electric monopolies did not want to cut present profits for future growth. The capon is an unambitious bird.

* * *

In a nation dedicated to free enterprise and a free press, the monopoly newspaper is a perplexing paradox that breaches both these fundamental principles. Where technology has made monopoly necessary, it is either government-owned (water system, post office) or government-regulated (telephone, electricity, gas). But in the field where monopoly is most obnoxious, the press, it is unregulated.

The Department of Justice has brought a few actions against monopolistic press practices. I have already mentioned the suit against the Kansas City *Star*—where the government locked the barn door after the horse was stolen. In *United States v. Associated Press,* 1945, the Supreme Court ruled, 5 to 4, that the First Amendment's freedom of the press does not include freedom to keep others from publishing newspapers. The A.P. was ordered to discontinue exclusive memberships and sell its service to all newspapers that wanted it. In 1955 the government won a district-court conviction against the New Orleans *Times-Picayune* for monopolistic practices in restraint of trade. In another 5-to-4 decision the Supreme Court reversed the lower court's ruling on the ground that the government had not shown damage to the *Times-Picayune*'s competitor, the *Item,* of which my son Tom (David Stern III) was publisher. During this litigation the *Item* had been barely breaking even. In the recession of 1958, the *Item* began to lose money. Tom sold to the *Times-Picayune,* and another great city became "blessed" with a newspaper monopoly. As A.J. Liebling's *Wayward Press* explained it, the *Times-Picayune* backed Tom "into a corner and shoved $3.5 million into his navel."

Uncle Sam is not to blame for the economic developments that have produced a monopoly press. His legal eagles are shackled not only by the First Amendment but also by the court ruling that a losing newspaper cannot be prevented from selling out to its competitor. If two publishers want to merge, it is not too difficult for one of them to go into the red.

But for the shameful extension of local communication monopolies, blame does rest on the government—and on President Franklin D. Roosevelt's first administration in particular.

"How do you feel about newspapers owning radio stations?" the President asked me in 1934, when the importance of this new medium was beginning to be recognized.

"It's against the public interest," was my answer. "Especially in one-newspaper cities."

"That's the way I'm thinking," Roosevelt said. "And that's what I'm going to tell the F.C.C., but your fellow publishers are bringing a lot of pressure to get into the radio game."

As soon as I reached my home in New York that evening, Tom, then publisher of my Camden papers, had me on the phone. "Dad, I made a great deal with Mayor Brunner to buy the municipal radio station for $10,000. The city is losing $25,000 a year. We'll make $50,000."

"Tom, we can't."

"Why not?"

"A few hours ago I told President Roosevelt he should not permit the sole publisher in a town to own a radio station."

Tom was fit to be tied. "Within the year they'll be dishing out radio franchises to newspapers," he predicted. He was so right. When I confronted the President with his shift in policy, he was frank: "I've more important fish to fry on the Hill." At the time I did not blame him for his expediency. I knew how publishers were putting the heat on their Senators and Congressmen, who, in turn, were ganging up on the White House to grant radio licenses. A score of newspaper-owned radio stations seemed a small price to pay for New Deal legislation. Thus died the obviously sound policy against newspaper-radio (and later television) monopolies. Between my first and second conversations with the President, Camden sold its radio station. It was not until 1946 that I acquired a radio subsidiary.

The general public probably is unaware of it, but Cowles Magazines and Broadcasting, Inc. owns not only *Look* magazine but three newspapers and two radio-TV stations. Time, Inc. owns not only *Time, Life,* and other magazines but also six radio-TV stations. Today more than 750 radio and television stations are owned by newspapers. In 76 cities a monopoly daily owns the only radio station.

Railroads must not control paralleling bus or truck lines. Steamship companies may not have interests in airlines. Suppliers of electricity and gas must be kept competitive. But, all hail consistency, the monopolistic combine of printing and broadcasting news is sanctioned.

* * *

The fat's in the fire. This unhealthy piling of monopoly on monopoly will never be corrected. Legislation to compel newspapers to divest themselves of radio and television subsidiaries has as much chance of success as a law making them pay the cost of second-class mail. Politicians are gun-shy of publishers, who are allergic to regulation. Any act that even remotely affects the newspaper business is denounced as an invasion of that holy of holies, freedom of the press. So many newspapers are being run from the business offices that the owners cannot see the distinction between the two functions of publishing.

I had plenty of warning that the role of the newspaper was changing and that the daily journal of opinion was becoming obsolete. Adolph S. Ochs, the able publisher of *The New York Times,* kept cautioning me not to be so controversial and abrasive: "Take sides and you make more enemies than friends." In his early days E.W. Scripps, the newspaper genius who founded the Scripps-Howard chain and the globe-encircling United Press International, wrote: "A good newspaper comforts the afflicted and afflicts the comfortable." But in old age he warned fellow publishers never to support a candidate who had any chance of winning an election, lest the newspaper be saddled with responsibility for the man when he took office.

Perhaps I am merely expressing the nostalgia of a retired publisher for the glamorous days of old when Greeley and Pulitzer never hesitated to call a spade a goddam shovel. The press of yesteryear was far from perfect. Partisanship was often distorting, crude, and cruel. From the earliest days of the republic, its record is unsavory. One newspaper rejoiced at the death of our first President. Abraham Lincoln was called an ape and a gorilla.

Granted our old-fashioned partisan press smelled to high heaven, it was the stimulating stench of human emotion. It roused the nation to brave deeds and great accomplishment.

Today most newspapers—especially monopoly and chain newspapers—follow Saylor's formula and avoid treading on toes. But there never was a worthwhile reform that did not bruise someone's toes. Propose stopping stream pollution and the chemical plant threatens to close, which will throw a thousand employees out of work. Demand that school teachers be paid as much as truck drivers and overtaxed home owners cry out in anguish. When the monopoly newspaper cannot avoid such a controversy it tries to be impartial.

"Impartial" is a tricky word. It is humanly impossible to be completely objective in thinking and writing. The publisher can be sure a dispute is being handled fairly only when both sides complain that he is unfair.

A letter from a student at the Columbia School of Journalism posed a question: "Does the *New York Post* permit editorial policy to influence its news reporting?" Saylor, by that time editor of all my newspapers, wrote our answer. I liked it so well I used it as an editorial. An excerpt:

A proposed constitutional amendment comes up for consideration at Albany. The Post headlines "Child Labor Amendment up for Vote." The Herald Tribune headlines "Youth Control Amendment up for Vote." Both papers are reporting the news. Or are they? The theory that news columns are reserved solely for facts, and editorial columns held sacred for opinion, is one of the hoariest pieces of bunk ever peddled to a class in journalism. We think it good for our readers to know the facts of life. We do our best to print both sides. But we are only human. So, thank God, are our competitors.

Child Labor or Youth Control Amendment? It is such conflict in news and editorials that stimulates public interest and thinking. Two points of view give perspective on public problems. This insight is denied communities served by monopoly newspapers. The spirited arguments of yesteryear have been replaced by polite conversation that avoids subjects that might give offense. "I can take anything but an evening of polite conversation," my friend Arthur Garfield Hays used to say.

The monopoly newspaper's tact and restraint generate apathy, which reveals itself in the small percentage of citizens who take the trouble to go to the polls. Our nation's voting record is much below that of other democracies. How little grit the capon has in its gizzard.

* * *

Today, looking back at the age of 76, I tend to see two sides to most questions. With old age comes double vision and the frustration of recognizing more than one solution to a quadratic equation. For 35 years, as publisher of seven dailies, I was so busy telling my readers what to think that *I* had no time to think. As a fighting liberal I wrote thousands of editorials, always on the side of the angels. Now, in retirement, I have time to think.

I look back and laugh at the strong medicine I peddled and in which I had such complete confidence. And yet I realize that more important than the failure of cure-alls is the faith that renews itself after each disappointment. We may laugh at the perplexed and pretentious little animal who talks big, but we must admire his courage and persistence.

The danger to man is not that his formulas fail to cure, but that he give up trying new ones, that he sink into complacent acceptance of the status quo. There lies the peril of monopoly newspapers. The competitive newspapers may have sold some bad medicine, but they did whip up interest, did make their readers care about public issues. The monopoly newspaper, by treading on no one's toes, is offering soothing syrup as the cure for mankind's bellyache.

Muzak: Chewing Gum for the Mind

By Raymond Mount Jr.

Revolting," says *The New York Times* music critic Harold Schonberg. "It gives me indigestion," complains jazz musician Dizzy Gillespie. "Horrible stuff," artist Ben Shahn calls it. "Pallid pap" is the way musicologist Helmut Blume characterizes it. "Hostile to human values," grumbles social philosopher Lewis Mumford.

They're all talking about that infernally incessant music you hear nowadays in restaurants, elevators, bus terminals, factories, funeral parlors, hospitals, libraries, dentists' offices, Turkish baths, beauty parlors, gas stations, zoos, jails, banks, and in at least one brothel (in Stuttgart, Germany). It really can't be called *music,* yet it isn't quite bad enough to be called *noise,* but so far no one has come up with the perfect compromise name. (Leading contenders are "background music," "piped-in music," and "police-state music," followed by such neologisms as "Pavlovian music," "moronmusic," and—my own personal favorite—"pablumusic.") Whatever it's called, just about anyone who has any vestige of taste left agrees that nothing so disastrous has hit the music world since the first singing commercial, for something called "Tasty Yeast," in 1924.

What's wrong with pablumusic—to settle on a name for it—is twofold.

First of all, it's impossible to turn it off. You're a captive audience, just like that accursed little girl who had rings on her fingers and bells on her toes and had music wherever she went. Russell Baker, the *Times'* columnist, even thinks that "The chief objection to such music is that, good or bad, it abridges the priceless human right not to be entertained."

Actually, the chief objection to pablumusic would appear to be something else—namely, that it's awful. You never hear Bach or Basie, only the fluffiest popular tunes, abridged never to exceed 3 minutes and rearranged never to lapse into a minor key or get rousingly loud or romantically soft. You're left with soggy rhythms, an absence of soloists, and a flood of fudgy violins. There's nothing wrong with *Stardust,* of course, but what the pablumusic-makers do is take a lovely song like *Stardust,* pummel it, chew it, mangle it, mash it, whack it, stomp on it, flail it, and strain it—until what remains is as insipid as warm beer, as flat as the Texas landscape, and as painfully boring as *Lady Chatterley's Lover* without the sexy passages. It's Walt Disney music, *Reader's Digest* music, lowest common-denominator music, chewing gum for the mind, music without soul or body or flavor or teeth—in short, pablumusic. Not surprisingly, the principal peddler of pablumusic, the Muzak Corporation, is run by the Wrather Corporation, which also owns the *Lassie* TV show and a slice of Disneyland.

Muzak is a hotshot outfit, all right, coming up fast. It began life in 1934, really got going after World War II, and right now is in its greatest glory. Today Muzak's pablumusic is heard by 60 million people in 20 countries; 20 of America's 25 biggest corporations have their offices wired for Muzak; and every year, 30,000 companies pay $15 million to be supplied with Muzak's telephone wires.

Of course, with all that money coming in, Muzak can pay PR men to think up all sorts of excuses and alibis. Thus the typical Muzak spokesman insists that music with any sort of bite would interfere with a listener's concentration, which is why poor *Stardust* has to be made into mush. As for the squawks from discriminating people who loathe listening to this godawful slop, Melvin Cohen, Muzak's boy-genius of a research manager, sneeringly dubs them a "vocal minority," going on to say that "negative responses come from no more than 3 to 5% of the population: elderly spinsters, just-plain-contrary people, individualists who won't accept any music

214

that others have chosen for them, and folks who think that, because they know something about music, they know about Muzak."

Melvin Cohen, after all, knows best.

* * *

Now, there's no getting away from it. A lot of people *like* pablumusic. But a lot of people like the New York *Daily News,* too—2 million of them—yet that doesn't mean that *The New York Times* readers should be compelled to read the *News,* which is clearly what Melvin Cohen, boy-genius, thinks. Nor are the critics of Muzak such a sorry lot after all. Among them are English novelist J.B. Priestley, who boasts he has had Muzak "turned off in some of the best places" all over the world, and who warns that "This constant drip of sugary stuff is very bad for the ear, and I'm certain that all this soothing does the mind no good." Another critic is the aforementioned Helmut Blume, dean of the faculty and director of the Conservatorium of Music at McGill University in Toronto, who has been quoted as saying: "It is pallid pap that will cause all of our musical teeth to fall out."

In fact, I think I myself must have the world's largest collection of complaints about Muzak. A few years ago, I placed a tiny ad in the *Saturday Review:*

HOW CAN WE STOP loudspeaker-piped music? Exchange ideas. Box ———.

I wasn't exactly inundated by replies, but I did receive quite a number of them.

One man wrote in: "I am in great sympathy with your cause. We have it in our office and it is a most disturbing irritant. I have complained about it to no avail and have probably been classified with those who feel 'the air conditioner is too cold.'

"Perhaps an organized campaign to appeal to the companies who provide this (dis)service would help. . . . Or perhaps ASCAP should demand higher royalties proportional to the number of persons within earshot and it would be priced out of existence."

A 21-year-old woman from Connecticut wrote to me pessimistically: "How can you fight it? Airlines will tell you it's for the nervous passengers; restaurants will say it's cheaper than hiring an orchestra (it also *sounds* a lot cheaper, if you ask me)."

A young folksinger wrote in: "Most background music is *bad* music. It is what I call anti-music. It lowers our appreciation of *real* music when it comes along."

From Tangier, Morocco: "Even so far afield from so-called 'civilization' we have heard of this thing. We are unaware of methods to combat this menace."

An Indiana woman wrote me: "The decibel count is rising geometrically, and I am more than concerned—I am scared. Fortunately, I work in a library. Whenever I go grocery shopping, I carry ear plugs, and use them. Frequently I'm asked, 'Don't you like music?' My answer, now, is 'No,' though earlier in life I did some more than average amount of singing, band, and piano work."

A man who lives in Chicago suggested that businessmen thoughtful enough to ban Muzak might advertise: "PEACE AND QUIET. NO ANNOYING BACKGROUND MUSIC." For restaurant sufferers, he suggests a new kind of diners' club, called Diners Against Music Noise (DAMN).

Alan Swallow, the poetry publisher, wrote me: "Background music is like the 'family' magazine: it must seek out the lowest common denominator of taste. But with the magazine, or comparable book, we can take it or leave it. Background music is thus more insidious to individual taste and development, since it can't be 'taken or left' at one's will."

Lewis Mumford wrote: "I regret I have no time to elaborate on my conviction that the invasion of privacy, the increase of meaningless noise, and the destruction of positive taste brought about by background music are all hostile to human values."

Mrs. Vladimir Nabokov, writing on behalf of her novelist-husband from Montreux, Switzerland, said:

"My husband asks me to convey to you *his* reply to your

questionnaire regarding his attitude to enforced music in public places. Here it is:

'I am opposed to all background music in public and every kind of music forced upon the public or played outside of concert halls.

'I find those enforced moronic melodies an abominably offensive imposition with police state undertones. Soviet citizens on trains, in stores, etc. are permanently enclosed in a prison of music. I cannot say how violently I am opposed to the brainsoftening and conditioning which result from exposure to "background" music inflicted on the individual.

'An uninterrupted exposure to public music is bound to be damaging to the majority of people even if many of them think they like it, or are apathetic to it.

'I am convinced that the forcing of mass musical tastes on the individual everywhere he goes in civilized surroundings will have unfortunate consequences for the world.' "

* * *

By telephoning people at random, the *Fact* Magazine staff obtained a number of provocative comments about pablumusic, too, among them this statement from folksinger and actor Theodore Bikel:

"I really can't stomach background music. It's, you know, lowest-common-denominator type music. It pleases no one in trying to please everyone. I don't even like music to be used that way. I have too much regard for music to relegate it to a background of any kind."

From radio commentator Barry Gray:

"I don't mind the idea of having music everywhere, but Muzak music irritates me. I think that the choices that are made are awful, and they use the worst orchestrations. It's Mickey Mouse music.

"Many, many times I've been in a restaurant and been irritated enough to ask them to lower the canned music. I prefer to hear the sound of people conversing to hearing that tinny music."

From Harold Schonberg, *The New York Times'* music critic: "One word—revolting. I don't have to explain anything more, do I? Revolting—it's a terrible practice."

From artist Ben Shahn: "Oh, *that* horrible stuff. Yes, well that's what I think about it.

"I think that the most horrible experience I've had with it was at the Kennedy Airport in New York. Our airplane was delayed and we had to stay there until the next morning. This damn music went on all night. All night. We were doomed.

"Another terrible experience I had was during Christmas week. I was up in the '50s, at Saks Fifth Avenue in New York —carols and St. Patrick's and all the electronic stuff—and I thought, you know, I thought I would suddenly go *mad*. I had to have the cab drive me away.

"I don't like any of it, wherever they have it. It's so damn mechanical."

Lawyer Melvin Belli suggests fighting fire with fire: "We're never going to put Muzak in our office because we've done much better putting our *own* in. We've got a good hi-fi set that cost us about $400, with a couple of speakers, and we have enough records to run for about 5 hours. It's installed on the receptionist's desk, and we can put anything we want on. And it's even cheaper than Muzak.

"I've got nothing against Muzak music. Everybody to his own horse's tail and cat's gut. In other words, some people like violins, some like cellos. But I do think there is too goddamned much of this uniformity. And I wouldn't want to listen to someone else's choice of music any more than I'd like the Flying Chicken Restaurant to bring fried chicken to my office— the way *they* like it instead of the way I like it.

"What really worries me, though, is whether Muzak says anything subliminally. Who knows whether in its higher ranges, at a pitch we can't hear consciously, they're saying, 'Buy Muzak, buy Muzak!'?"

From composer Meredith Willson:

"I think there is too much music around on the American scene, considerably too much. Circumstances are such that if one isn't careful one would be hearing music 24 hours a day, because it's *there,* you know, and with piped-in music, of course, you don't have the option to turn it off.

"I do quite a lot of flying in various parts of the country, and it's very disquieting to get on a plane and be a prisoner to completely inferior music, sitting there just waiting for it to go off. Rather than suffer through that again, I'd be for passing a law against any piped-in music.

"But then, oversaturation with *anything* is wrong, whether it's the repetitive idiocies and the meaningless and amateurish words of rock and roll songs or it's a Beethoven symphony cycle. Whoever perpetrates such a thing should be locked up."

Folksinger Tom Paxton: "Not only is it an intrusion on privacy, but as music it's conceived by idiots and designed to pacify morons. I think that what you ought to do is to get—anonymously—some advice from an engineer on how the average citizen can sabotage the damn things. That would be very helpful. We need direct action."

Dizzy Gillespie: "It gives me indigestion. It's like an assembly line. You just grab a bunch of things and you play it. If you make mistakes, it don't make any difference."

Folksinger Pete Seeger replied in a letter:

"I'm glad you are doing an article on the endless, mindless 'music' piped in these days to restaurants, waiting rooms, even elevators, etc. I have no expert comments to make, except that I don't like it, and have many times walked out of a restaurant and gone far out of my way to find one without it. I have found it effective to offer to bribe a waitress or airline stewardess to turn it off, or at least lower the volume. They have yet to take the bribe, but at least they recognize I am serious.

"If a citizen wishes to hear constant background music throughout his or her life, he should carry a transistor radio and earphone. I know that some people do like it, and miss it when they don't have it. But they don't have a right to inflict it on others.

"A friend of mine wants to invent a laser-gun which can put an offending loudspeaker out-of-action, but I urged him that non-violent methods, though seemingly slower, will in the long run be better.

"I suppose I wouldn't mind this 'music' so much if they played my own favorite music. But this would not be fair to others, since my own favorite music is certainly not that of most people. Come to think of it there is no music which is really the favorite of most people. We are a nation of minorities, thank God.

"On reflection, I think I would mind piped-in music even if they played my favorite banjo pickers and blues singers. Because then my train of thought would be continually derailed.

"No, piped-in music is an invasion of privacy. If we can't get rid of it completely, let's at least set up zoning laws to restrict it."

* * *

Actually, since pablumusic infests private places and not places owned by the public, there is nothing our lawyers and legislators can do. So, until someone comes up with a simple way of sabotaging the Muzak apparatus, our best recourse is to try to convince the people who buy Muzak that they're out of their blinking minds.

Action like this isn't always fruitless. Tom Prideaux, a senior editor at *Life,* circulated a petition in the Time-Life Building in New York against Muzak in the elevators, and as a result the thing was taken out. So petitions can certainly be helpful.

So are letters to editors. So are boycotts. Before going to any new restaurant, telephone first to find out if Muzak is served, and if it is, ask the man if he can recommend some other restaurant. Boycott supermarkets and hotels and airlines that have Muzak, too, since, after all, you're indirectly paying for the pablumusic. Places that *don't* subscribe will in all likelihood have lower prices. Always ask, when subjected to Muzak, if it can be turned off. Form an anti-Muzak club in your hometown. Get a rubber stamp printed that says MUZAK IS A FORM OF AIR POLLUTION. Send copies of this article to your friends, to your employer, to your friends' employers.

Spread disagreeable stories about the company, like the one about the woman who became hysterical aboard an airliner when Muzak played *For All We Know*, the first line of which goes, "For all we know, we may never meet again. . . ." And about the experience of Carroll Carroll, who, writing in the *Saturday Review* of Oct. 21, 1961, told of hearing *Stormy Weather* and *Would You Like To Take a Walk?* While aboard a plane, and, on arriving at the airport, heard *It's Good To Be Alive*.

* * *

If all of us who love good music at the appropriate time and in the appropriate place do our bit, maybe, *maybe,* we can eventually drive the Muzak men into a more reputable line of work and start enjoying a new Golden Age of golden silence.

Don't procrastinate. Melvin Cohen, after all, gurgles ecstatically about new markets. "Every new phenomenon must be served," he says. "Trading stamps mean Muzak in redemption centers. Increasing longevity means Muzak in sanatoriums and rest homes. Emancipation of women means Muzak in billiard parlors, which have a growing female clientele. More leisure time means more Muzak in bowling alleys, race tracks, and swimming pools."

Melvin Cohen must be stopped.

The time for a massive counterattack is *now*.

The Great Insurance Swindle

By Onofrio Bruni

The men who run America's insurance companies have successfuly spread the myth that the coverage they sell is the great bulwark of the nation, a consolation in time of tragedy, the orphan's friend, the widow's solace. As a result, most Americans regard life insurance with the reverence due motherhood and the flag; as another result, most Americans are pitifully unaware that the life-insurance business has degenerated into a fast-buck flimflam.

The president of the Hartford Life Underwriters Association himself has pointed out that "it appears that life-insurance companies are interested in only two things: making money and keeping the government out of the life-insurance business." In fact, the main trouble with the whole life-insurance business, to put it in a nutshell, is that it's immune to U.S. Government regulation.

Back in 1945, the powerful lobby of the life-insurance industry induced Congress to exempt the industry from Federal supervision in any state that had regulations of its own. Control of the industry is thus split 50 ways by 50 states. Imagine the confusion if there were no Securities Exchange Commission to oversee the stock market, or no Federal banking agencies to keep an eye on the thousands of banks around the country. Yet the life-insurance industry is as vital to the national economy in its way as the banks or the stock market. Life insurance directly affects 90% of American citizens and indirectly affects the whole populace.

With no national referee to worry about, many insurance

companies have even gone about making puppets out of the appointed state insurance officials. According to insurance-expert Norman F. Dacey, in some states the companies actually dictate the appointment of the very commissioners supposed to regulate them. Often a commissioner is a retired insurance-company official drawing a monthly pension check from the very company he is presumed to be regulating. In other states, notably New York, the commissioners and deputy commissioners frequently resign their jobs to take lifetime posts with one of the companies they were supposed to be overseeing. Recently all of the state insurance commissioners got together for an official meeting in Las Vegas. The *National Underwriter,* a leading trade publication, later deplored the fact that the convention transacted so little business, and observed sourly that the dice tables seemed to have a greater attraction for the commissioners than the committee rooms.

Under such circumstances, it is no surprise that many state insurance commissions are hopelessly inept—to take the most charitable view. The Attorney General of South Dakota recently described the insurance department of his own State as "a mess." The insurance commissioner of Colorado recently resigned under fire because he had been involved in transactions of questionable propriety. The insurance commissioner of Ohio and several of his aides were recently required to repay Ohio insurance companies money they had been given for an excursion to Arizona. And the chairman of an Oregon insurance committee had to have police protection when his life and his wife's life were threatened because he *refused* a $25,000 bribe.

Summing up the situation, Robert Dechert, general counsel for Penn Mutual, has said that "the present disorderly conflict in the insurance laws of the 50 states might be called a national scandal. . . . Scandal is a strong word, but in my opinion it is justified." And *Probe,* a newsletter circulated within the life-insurance industry, in its New Year issue prayed that the future might produce "state insurance commissioners with knowledge, integrity, and courage." The prayer has been unanswered.

What has gone wrong with the life-insurance industry? The answer, basically, is not complicated at all. The original aim of life insurance was to enable a man's family to carry on if he died. It was as simple as that, and it worked. But the businessmen who ran the life-insurance companies felt that they could sell more policies if they changed their pitch—if they ballyhooed insurance as a magic cure-all for every financial trouble, as not just "life" insurance but as "living" insurance. Not only would a policy take care of a man's family if he died, but it would also pay his mortgage, educate his children, act as a handy savings account, and enable him to retire at 65.

Because they supposedly were offering more than just death protection, the life-insurance companies were able to convince people that they should pay higher premiums. For example, one of the industry's main selling points has been that an insurance policy is also a savings account. But the truth of the matter is that an insurance policy is just about the worst kind of savings account anybody could have. Here's why.

Month after month, year after year, the policyholder pays his premiums. He can make use of the money accumulated in two ways. First, he can die. If he does, the company uses his "savings account" to help pay the death claim. If he had $600 in "cash value" in his $1000 policy, the company takes the $600, adds $400 of its own money, and pays it out to his beneficiary. In other words, the policyholder in this case furnished 60% of his *own* death benefits. The more the policyholder pays into the account, the more he builds up his "savings" and the less the company has to pay out of its own funds when he dies. As Norman Dacey puts it, "The greater part of the insurance premium you pay each year goes not to buy protection but to build the savings account. There is little incentive for you to build the savings account, though, for a dollar added to it adds nothing to your estate—it simply reduces the company's risk by another dollar."

But suppose the policyholder wants to draw on his insurance savings while he is still alive. It is then that he finds he is getting a very bad deal indeed. He will discover that his account has been accumulating interest at only 2½%, whereas any sav-

225

ings bank would have paid him 4%, 5%, or more. If the policyholder later wants to pay back the money he borrowed from his account, he will find that the company will charge him 5% interest! Dead or alive, he loses.

To put the insurance scandal into the proper perspective, let us examine some figures for 1960, the latest year for which detailed information is available. At the start of the year, $369.3 billion of life insurance was in force in the United States. This amounted to 200 million policies. During the year, 21 million more policies were sold, with a face value of more than $63 billion.

It might seem from *these* statistics that we Americans had succeeded in providing financial security for ourselves and our families. But here are the remaining figures: In 1960, 1.7 million policies were settled as death claims. In the same year, 16.7 million such policies were allowed to terminate by lapse or surrender by the policyholders. For every policy paid as a death claim, 9.7 policies were lapsed at substantial losses to the policyholder. In other words, for every person who made money on his life insurance by dying, nine people lost money on it by living.

These 16.7 million lapsed or surrendered policies were worth $30.2 billion. Of the policies terminated by lapse or surrender, 30% were canceled with some benefit to the policyholder, and it's estimated that the loss to these individuals totaled more than $1 billion. The remaining 70% of the policies were canceled with no benefit whatsoever to the policyholders. These individuals may have lost as much as $2 billion. One conscientious insurance man, Michael H. Levy, president of Standard Security Life, has warned: "The huge lapse rate is outstanding proof of bad service to the public. Every one of us must face up to our responsibility in this crime against those who have been trusting us."

The reader may be wondering why so many people lost so much money by letting their policies lapse. It might seem that the fault lay with the people, not with the companies. But the truth of the matter is that the life-insurance industry has cajoled and frightened millions of Americans into buying more insurance than they can possibly afford. An apt term has come into common usage to describe this state: *insurance-poor*. Millions of families who have been oversold on insurance have found they cannot keep up the payments, and the result is disaster for them—and a windfall for the companies.

In 1960, a year that death benefits totaled $3.4 billion, the life-insurance industry of this country paid $3.7 billion for sales commissions and other expenses. In the case of 31 of the 38 leading companies, sales commissions alone exceeded death benefits. In 1960, fully 22.5% of the industry's total premium income went for commissions and other expenses.

What this means, obviously, is that America's insurance companies—for prestige and for advertising—are far more eager to get *new* customers than they are in providing more benefits to old customers—by reducing the premiums, for instance. "I get the impression," says Joseph B. MacLean, retired vice-president of New York Life, "that volume is the No. 1 interest and objective in many companies, and that the interests of the policyholders are secondary."

Many of the most respected men in the insurance business have been horrified by this supersalesmanship. William C. Smerling, Connecticut Mutual's New York manager, recently told a meeting of insurance agents: "I do not think that the evils of the past were anywhere near what they have been these last 7 or 8 years. . . . The thing that is most regrettable is the fact that the public, which has relied upon our ability, has been the victim of these evils. . . . The life-insurance public was ravaged, was raped and, in my opinion, was defrauded through misleading representations, enabling new commissions to reach an all-time high, with a total disregard for the owners of life-insurance contracts who have made possible our successful existence in this business." And Norman Dacey says bluntly: "I estimate that at least 90% of the life-insurance policies in force in this country are sold through fraud and misrepresentation."

The wild scramble for new business in life insurance has

led the companies to raise commissions to astounding heights in order to encourage their salesmen to sell harder and faster. For every $100 a company now adds in new policies, it often has to pay out from $135 to $200 in commissions and other expenses. This is the truth, although it sounds impossible. How is it done? How do the insurance companies turn the trick? By stealing the difference from other policyholders.

* * *

Life-insurance companies naturally invest the premiums they receive into various business ventures. Some of the profits from these enterprises are used to pay claims, or to give dividends to stockholders. But the great bulk of the funds is "banked" in a special account called "surplus," which the companies set up long ago to protect policyholders in case of some financial disaster to the business.

These surplus funds are now being looted to pay salesmen's commissions and other first-year costs. The companies dare do this because the more they tap from the surplus funds to use in spurring their salesmen, the more new policies they will get. And many of the new policyholders will default. This means, of course, that they will never have to be paid off from out of the surplus fund. *Probe* has justifiably wondered whether a prospective policyholder might ask himself, "If, to attract me, the company is willing to take from the present policyholders surplus money it cannot hope to replace through earnings on my business—what may it not be willing to do to *me* later on?"

* * *

Another source of tremendous profits to the life-insurance industry is the fact that it bases its premiums upon antiquated mortality tables. A mortality table is a statistical record of the death rate in the past. Putting it very simply, if the tables showed that men died at an average age of 48, the company would make sure that the premiums paid by a man during a life-span of that length would be appropriate to his death bene-

228

fits. If the average age of death was 56, the premium naturally would be lower, since the average policyholder would have 8 more years of payments to build up his account.

Obviously, it would be to a company's advantage if it used a mortality table that had people dying at an earlier age than actually was the case. The company could set a high premium to build up death benefits. When a person lived past the supposed date of his demise, he would keep right on paying premiums—which would be pure profit for the company.

This is perfectly clear and perfectly outrageous, and it is precisely what the insurance industry has been able to do. With minor exceptions, policies issued before 1948 have premiums computed upon the *American Experience Table of Mortality,* which reflects the death rate in this country *between 1843 and 1857.* Needless to say, people died much, much earlier in those days. Policies issued between 1948 and the present are based upon the *Commissioners Standard Ordinary Table of 1941,* which reflects the death rate between 1931 and 1941 (before even penicillin, first of the "wonder" drugs, was on the market). Now the 1958 *Table* is being introduced. Allegedly, it is based upon the death rate between 1950 and 1954, but as Norman Dacey points out, it is rigged: For example, the table assumes the death of 2.03 persons out of every 1000 in the 28-year-old age-bracket, while the truth is that only one person in that bracket died.

Because of these scandalously outdated tables, the insurance industry takes in far more money than it needs to pay death benefits. For every 48.9 claims it pays, the industry collects enough to pay 100. Many Americans have always wondered how the National Service Life Insurance (the so-called G.I. insurance) could pay such huge dividends year after year. The answer is that the insurance is based on that pre-Civil War mortality table. The Veterans' Administration has no need to "hide" the profits that result from the use of this antiquated table, and therefore returns them to the policyholder in the form of dividends. Insurance companies do not.

Is it any wonder then that the stocks of many life-insurance companies have skyrocketed in recent years? Here is what $10,000, invested in the stocks of some representative insurance companies in 1950, would be worth today:

Businessman Assurance Life	$ 382,500
California-West. States Life	143,130
Gulf Life	232,650
Liberty National Life	283,000
Northwestern National Life	233,240
Philadelphia	500,000
Republic National Life	1,300,000
U.S. Life	505,800
West Coast Life	300,440

Insurance firms like these are in business to earn money for their stockholders, and they make no bones about it. But there is another kind of insurance firm known as the mutual company—one of the greatest frauds in American business. A mutual company has no stockholders. Theoretically, it is controlled by its policyholders and, theoretically, it is in business to make life insurance available at cost. In practice, both of these theories are flouted.

"The fact is that in many mutual companies the directors and officers, in effect, control the company," states Joseph MacLean, an elder statesman of the industry. "The officers of mutual companies, although in theory accountable to the policyholders, are not really so."

Then too, mutual firms tell their policyholders that they are distributing the profits of the company to them in the form of "dividends." The use of the term "dividend" in this fashion should be prohibited by statute.

Mutual life-insurance companies charge premiums that are 15% to 25% higher than those charged by stock-issuing life-insurance companies. They use the money to pay generous salaries and high commissions. At the end of the year, they refund a portion of the overcharge—and give the policyholder the idea that he has received a dividend!

The policyholder is the only one who is fooled. If the dividend really *were* a share of the company's profits, it would be taxable as income. But the Internal Revenue Service goes to the extent of exempting such dividends from the income tax.

* * *

The mutual and stock-insurance companies are part of an industry so vast and wealthy that even the experts have difficulty grasping their true scope. Let me cite some figures to show what I mean. From 1940 until 1960, the industry took in $260.7 billion. It paid out the following sums:

Living benefits	**$51.6 billion**
Death benefits	**38.1**
Expenses	**39.1**
Taxes	**6.9**
Added to reserves	**71.2**

These figures add up to $206.9 billion. On this basis, the industry made profits of $53.8 billion over a 20-year period. Putting it another way, for every dollar the life-insurance industry paid out between 1940 and 1960, it took in $2.90. The average policyholder might have gotten a better return if he had taken his money out to the race track.

The scandal of the insurance industry has been known for years. The late Estes Kefauver initiated an investigation of the life-insurance industry when he headed the Senate Antitrust and Monopoly Subcommittee. Sen. Thomas J. Dodd of Connecticut was named to head an insurance subcommittee. When a whole year passed without his having taken any action, he was removed as chairman. Shortly thereafter, Senator Kefauver died and was replaced as chairman of his Subcommittee by Sen. Philip H. Hart of Michigan. Senator Dodd promptly returned to the insurance-subcommittee post. The insurance investigation came to an abrupt halt and has stagnated ever since. Senator Dodd is a resident of Hartford, the so-called "insurance capital" of the nation. It is patently ridiculous to assign him to investigate his own friends in the insurance industry in Hartford, upon whose substantial campaign contributions, incidentally, he depends.

Senator Hart's wife was an organizer, director, and still is an important stockholder in a life-insurance company. The market price of her holdings has tripled. The Senator therefore has a vested interest in a continuation of the unconscionable profits that have resulted from the industry's exploitation of the public.

While he was still a Senator, Hubert Humphrey wrote Norman Dacey, president of the National Estate Planning Council of Bridgeport, Connecticut, author of *How to Avoid Probate,* and a man long interested in insurance reform, that Senator Hart had acknowledged to him that he was in possession of the facts about the life-insurance abuses—yet Hart did nothing. Under Senator Kefauver, the Senate Antitrust and Monopoly Subcommittee asked Mr. Dacey for a copy of a brilliant, comprehensive exposé he had prepared on the industry. Under Senator Dodd, the insurance subcommittee has ignored Mr. Dacey's book.

The time is long overdue for a full-scale Federal investigation of the insurance industry. The most recent drive for an investigation began 3 years ago when the late John F. Kennedy appointed a committee of distinguished citizens "to review legislation and administrative practices relating to the operation of financial intermediaries" and "to consider what changes, if any, in government policy toward private financial institutions could contribute to economic stability, growth and efficiency." This "Committee on Financial Institutions" consisted of Douglas Dillon, then Secretary of the Treasury; Orville L. Freeman, Secretary of Agriculture; Kermit Gordon, then director of the Bureau of the Budget; Joseph P. McMurray, then chairman of the Federal Home Loan Bank Board; James J. Saxon, Comptroller of the Currency; Walter W. Heller, then chairman of the Council of Economic Advisors and chairman of the new committee; Robert F. Kennedy, then Attorney General; Anthony J. Celebrezze, former Secretary of Health, Education and Welfare; William Martin Jr., chairman of the Board of Governors of the Federal Reserve System; Robert C. Weaver, Administrator of the Housing and Home Finance Agency; and Erle Cocke Sr., alternate director of the International Bank for Reconstruction and Development.

In its report delivered to the President on April 9, 1963, the Committee on Financial Institutions declared: "In part because the Federal Government has no supervisory responsibilities over insurance companies, existing knowledge and experience in the Government provide less foundation for judgment on this question [of the adequacy of existing regulation] than on most of the other issues within the Committee's terms of reference. The Committee has neither the time nor the resources to undertake an intensive study of the life-insurance industry and its regulation. It has had indications, however, of particular cases of unduly lax supervision. . . . There are inherent difficulties in regulation by individual States of companies that operate in many States. Furthermore, the setting of national standards may more properly be a function of the Federal Government."

While the members of the committee did not agree completely on all aspects of the final report, one conclusion of theirs was unanimous: "In view of the apparently lax supervision in some States, the inherent difficulties in State regulation of companies that operate across State lines, and the limited applicability of the antitrust laws, the Congress might wish to conduct a study of life-insurance practices and regulations so as to determine whether Federal regulation is desirable."

* * *

If President Johnson's dream of a Great Society is to be realized, it can be built only upon a foundation of individual financial security for all Americans. A study by the University of Kansas has shown that only a minority of our citizens are financially independent at the age of 65, and of that minority, only 7% acknowledge that they owe their financial independence to life insurance. For every individual who is secure through life insurance, eight others have found security in another, better way. And for the insecurity that plagues the majority of our people over 65, the principal blame may be laid at the door of the life-insurance industry.

Ideally, President Johnson will take it upon himself to launch an investigation, after which a Federal life-insurance law can be enacted, a law that will be administered by a Federal insurance commission not unlike the Securities and Exchange Commission. I share the general distaste for bureaucracy, but the S.E.C. has added immeasurably to the financial security of American investors.

Meanwhile, the insurance companies themselves had better hurry up and do a little self-criticism. As Harold Franklin, president of the Association for Advanced Underwriting, has warned: "I caution against the delusion that we are above reproach. If an important segment of our industry does not awaken to the responsibility owed the stockholders, we're going to deserve the restrictions which will be imposed by new Federal legislation. An industry which considers itself above reproach and underestimates the force of public opinion is riding for a fall. We need some honest revaluation and self-policing of abuses against the policyholder. It may be too late for the answer if we wait until the public raises the questions."

Suzi, What's a Nice Girl Like You Doing in Jail?

By Martin Cohen

What happened to Suzi should happen to Bill Buckley, Luci Johnson Nugent, Soupy Sales, Ronald Reagan, and Ann-Margret but should never have happened to Suzanne Williams, especially not her. Suzi is a nice girl and a very good girl.

In July of 1966, Suzi, 17 years old, a high honor student, Girl Scout counselor, winner of a Daughters of the American Revolution Award for good citizenship, a girl who doesn't drink, smoke, use narcotics, or swear, a deeply religious white Anglo-Saxon Protestant whose lineage goes back to colonial days, was charged with criminal contempt for refusing to rise when a judge entered a court and then, shades of Charles Dickens, was imprisoned with junkies, adulterers, drunks, and thieves.

Suzi was first sentenced to 30 days by Judge George E. Kinmonth, a husky, handsome Circuit Judge in Connecticut, and at the conclusion of that term, sentenced to 60 more days by Judge Luke Stapleton, a mature man, and also the father of a teen-aged daughter. Both Judges are courageous men. It takes courage to publicly kick an infant in the belly. An infant is exactly the way the law describes a minor.

Actually, Suzi was lucky. She could be spending the remainder of her life in jail without ever being arraigned or ever having the benefit of an attorney, a legal guardian, or a trial by jury. Suzanne Williams was a victim of "contempt power," once described in the courts as "perhaps nearest akin to despotic power of any power existing under our form of government."

Simply, criminal contempt is defined as any action that interferes with the processes of justice or any action that is construed as disrespect for the court. The definition is so vague that a lot of people get construed.

Contempt could be calling the judge "a dirty bastard," as many people do, but it could also be tobacco breath or wagging a grimy fingernail under his honor's nose. Whether you are in court for double-parking or littering the streets, the result is instant anarchy. Without trials or counsel, the offender may be sentenced to 6 days, 6 months, or longer, and dragged posthaste off to jail.

Is it fair?

Supreme Court Justice Hugo Black once wrote, "When the responsibilities of law-maker, prosecutor, judge, jury, and disciplinarian are thrust upon a judge, he is obviously incapable of holding the scales of justice perfectly fair and true and reflecting impartiality on the guilt or innocence of the accused. He truly becomes the judge of his own cause."

What most of us don't know is that "contempt power" is peculiar to Anglo-American courts alone. In his book *The Contempt Power,* Ronald L. Goldfarb, a member of the Department of Justice, takes the view that contempt was conceived not for a democratic country, but in early England for and by kings. It is archaic and willful. The contempt power's victims have included Prince Hal, who became Henry V; Gen. Andrew Jackson, who became the fifth President of the United States; former Gov. George Wallace, who hopes to become the 37th President; and Suzanne Williams, who is too young to have become anything but a high-school graduate.

There have been thousands of contempt-power victims and there will be thousands more. One may be this writer, for the power is so broad and despotic that Judges Kinmonth or Stapelton may decide this article is contemptuous of their action in the case of Suzanne Williams. Without any review or warning, they may summarily pronounce a jail sentence. But this is doubtful. These are honorable men, and judges are well-educated in freedom of speech, the First and Fifth Amendments, and due process of law. Furthermore, Judges Kinmonth

238

and Stapleton live not in Mississippi but in New England, the cradle of democracy.

To this writer, as he drove to Suzi's home in Massachusetts, it seemed very unlikely that Suzi's long imprisonment was merely for refusing to rise in court. Obviously there had to be something about the girl to make a judge go off the deep end.

Was she guilty of an unspeakable crime, not fit to print? Or a Communist?

Was she a big mouth who made a bad scene?

Or an obscene gesture?

Was she merely homely? To some men an ugly girl is offensive.

Suzi, what was a nice girl like you doing in jail?

* * *

Suzi lives in the beautiful, small mountains near Amherst, Massachusetts. Her home is an old, handsome frame house, originally built in 1776. The house on the top of the hill commands a wonderful view of a deep meadow that drops into a river. Beyond the river are steep, fast-rising hills, wooded and wild.

For the most part of 2 days Suzi and I talked across the dining-room table or in her father's study, a long, quiet room with homemade desks and tables and raw-wooded shelves with hundreds of books. Suzi's father, Schafer Williams, M.A., S.T.B., Ph.D., is a student of Medieval and canon law, presently a visiting professor at the University of New Mexico. Jean Clark Williams, Suzi's mother, is an intelligent, educated, reasoning woman, relaxed with her children. Suzi has a younger brother and sister in public schools. Her older sister and brother are in college. Suzi may go to college when and if she wishes. The Williams, however, are not wealthy, nor even well-to-do, but certainly Suzi is not to be numbered among the underprivileged.

Is Suzi pretty?

Do you care?

Well, Judge Stapleton cared. He found her a "very attractive young woman." He was wrong, as judges rarely are. She's not a woman. She's a "teen"—but not a twitchy, teen-aged sexpot in a tight miniskirt. During my visit she wore loose blue jeans and a heavy, warm shirt. She is probably shapely, but with her indifference to clothes, who would know?

I did see her face. She has an olive complexion, dark brown hair and eyes. Her eyes are a striking exception to the New England countryside. They are almond-shaped with prominent epicanthic folds. The eyes derive from her father and his Welsh ancestry. The family makes the joke that somewhere in the past a seagoing Williams sailed into the Orient. The fact is that Suzi's eyes are exotically beautiful and you could look at them by the hour but for the fact that she wears strong glasses.

Suzi's appearance in a Connecticut courtroom had its origin several years ago when she became close with members of the Society of Friends.

Enter Suzi, talking.

"Although my father is an ordained Presbyterian minister, he has not attempted to influence his children one way or another. His attitude is that we should inquire about religion and decide for ourselves.

"I call myself a non-Christian Quaker because I'm not really a member. Although I believe Jesus of Nazareth was a great teacher, I don't believe he was divine, so I can't classify myself as a Christian. But I consider myself extremely religious.

"I believe with the Friends that there is an inner light they call 'that of God in every man.' It is kind of a humanistic philosophy, and I'm convinced that the important thing in the world is people and my relation to them.

"I wholly endorsed the Friends' testimony against war and I began to educate myself in current affairs and read the literature of the Committee for Non-Violent Action, which is opposed to war and violence of any kind."

That's the way Suzi talks.

In the spring of her senior year Suzi decided that being morally opposed to war wasn't enough and she went to the

Boston Army Base to participate in a peace demonstration. Suzi was arrested for "sauntering and trespassing," then chose to spend 20 days in the Charles Street Jail rather than pay a $20 fine.

Suzi so impressed Boston C.N.V.A. members that one young man was moved to write Mrs. Williams, "Suzi is very steadfast in her beliefs and unfeigning in courage. I'll be 20 years old next week and wish that I had half her courage."

Suzi was somewhat of a celebrity or a fink, depending on one's political views, but when she returned to Amherst she was welcomed home without much fanfare. Her older brother had spent 15 months in the Deep South engaged in the civil-rights movement. Her mother is secretary of Amherst's Human Relations Council. Her father, a life-long liberal Democrat, was active in labor movements during the '30s and has continued to strongly identify himself with human causes. Suzi says, "I have been raised to feel responsible for the welfare of every man."

Suzi, a consistent A and B student, had no problem in making up her studies when she got out of jail. When she decided not to apply to a college, she annoyed her parents and teachers, particularly her language teachers because Suzi excelled in Latin, French, and Greek.

Suzi says, "Languages are fun but not a goal in themselves. I just didn't want to go into college without any goal."

* * *

As you can see, when Suzi begins talking she doesn't quite sound like a perfect American teen-ager. She doesn't identify with the Pepsi Generation and the chances of her graduating to LSD and all that other fun-stuff are rather slim. She has this eccentric strong sense of obligation to other people.

About war Suzi says, "I was violent as a kid. I fought with my older brother. After a while I stopped fighting back and when he hit me I said, 'So what does that prove?' and he stopped hitting me. So what does a war prove, and another big war will be suicidal for the world. Today I believe in total non-violence. Pacifism is religious to me and I believe pacifism is

241

extremely practical. People have called me a Communist but that can't be true because Communists are violent and I oppose all violence."

Suzi shows no emotion when she argues. She really doesn't argue. She was never concerned whether or not I agreed with her. She has no wiles, feels no need to touch a hand or sleeve. She is direct and quietly self-confident. One of her former teachers told me that the only word she could think of to describe Suzi was "stolid." But "stolid" is wrong and so are "cool," "serene," and "placid."

The teacher explained, "It's perplexing. Suzi is very sincere and gets involved and identifies strongly, yet doesn't seem to be emotional. She's quite different from any other teen-ager I've known."

Suzi told me, "I try to make decisions on a moral and logical basis rather than on emotions. I try to push myself around emotions. Then, as Shakespeare said, 'Above all to thine own self be true and it must pass, as day unto night, that you cannot be false to any other man.' I believe that if I do what is right for me that I can have a more true relationship with others."

Suzi left a few marks on Amherst Regional High School. Once the school bulletin-board was embellished with such patriotic slogans as "My country, right or wrong." Suzi went to the principal and had a little talk. Another board was put on the wall where Suzi could post information on civil rights and Vietnam, to cite instances when she thought her country was wrong.

In her senior year she aroused some strong feelings among her classmates. Seniors were offered "privilege" passes, which meant they could go wherever they pleased during a study period so long as they signed a pledge that they would obey every school rule all of the time. Suzi was the only senior who refused to sign, because it was against her principles (although she was a model of good behavior).

Teachers remember her as the kind of student who was interested in what she was doing rather than the grade or credit she would get out of it. She appeared to be a disciplined, steady student if not a brilliant one. Her Latin teacher told me, "When Suzi took her Latin College Board she scored 798, and 800 is tops. I was surprised. I hadn't realized she was really that good. She was a slow worker, careful and deliberate."

In the course of telling her story to me, Suzi said over and over that she spent her time in jail re-examining her position on contempt power. This is not child's talk.

Once I worked for an editor who asked me if I liked the person I'd interviewed for him. It was, curiously, a question that hadn't occurred to me. It's a good question to ask about Suzi.

I found that I could like her goodness, her concern for humanity, and her dedication to principle and morality.

However, Suzi, as a person, is an island, an institution unto herself, neither to be liked nor disliked. She asks for no sympathy. She hopes to make you understand her viewpoint but if you don't she remains patient and courteous. She is never patronizing. In her home, in the courtroom and jail, she remained dignified and composed.

Little wonder she scared hell out of those two judges in Connecticut.

* * *

"Hey, hey, LBJ, how many kids did you kill today?"

That's a slogan of some peace-advocates. A little revolting but effective. It is not a sign carried by the Committee for Non-Violent Action. C.N.V.A. signs read, "How Did You Tell Your Child About War?" and "The Weapons of War Must Be Abolished Before They Abolish Us." The man who wrote those last two has no future on Madison Avenue.

The nature of C.N.V.A. demonstrations is a let-down for anyone looking for action. C.N.V.A. people are serious, philosophical, dedicated, and even poetic. Their instruments are vigils, fasts, nonco-operation, and an occasional act of civil disobedience. The act of civil disobedience, however, is always carefully planned to make certain it will cause no injury to anyone but a member of the C.N.V.A.

They practice, and they preach, nonviolence. Only a few

days before Suzi's imprisonment, a dozen fun-happy, beer-sopped patriots attacked a C.N.V.A. headquarters. The merry gentlemen broke windows, smashed furniture, pawed the women. Finally, when one tried to make out with a 13-year-old girl, the child's father threatened to defend her. He didn't. The constable and Tonto arrived in the nick of time.

The C.N.V.A.'s principles were as important in this adventure as they have been to Suzi. In court, she speaks of non-co-operation rather than of contempt. She says, "If someone asks you to steal or do something immoral, you will not co-operate. To assist in my punishment for taking a stand against war is wrong, so I nonco-operate. To be told I must pay respect to a court whose actions I consider wrong requires my nonco-operation."

Nonco-operation is a curious word. It merely sounds negative. It is actually the affirmative action of a strong conscience. In the end it is confrontation. The instruments of the C.N.V.A. are deceptively negative. The C.N.V.A.'s success is actually computed in the violence inflicted on C.N.V.A. members, whether the aggressors be high-school boys attacking vigilers on Boston Common or judges throwing a minor into the subjective violence of prison. Some people call the C.N.V.A.'s instruments "philosophic anarchy."

You think I'm making this up. Well, Gandhi is one of the great inspirations to Suzi and the C.N.V.A. Yet Gandhi's nonviolence, his vigils and his fasts, resulted in his assassination and blood baths that, historically, rate among the worst.

Suzi is no fool. She knows most of this but she is young enough to believe in communication. She believes you can talk people into wanting a nonnapalm world. She talks to police, prostitutes, shipyard workers, and judges about pacifism and nonviolence. And on July 21, 1966, she got about her work early.

* * *

Geographically, the scene is New London and Groton, twin cities in Connecticut separated by the Thames River. Suzi arrived in Groton about 6 A.M. dressed in a freshly laundered

244

cotton dress because the C.N.V.A. does not want demonstrators looking like beatniks. It was a nice turquoise-colored dress but an old one, because there was a possibility of a riot and then the dress would be ruined.

At 6:30 A.M. Suzi and her friends were outside the gates of the General Dynamics Electric Boat shipyard. For an hour she passed out leaflets to men coming off the night shift. There were no incidents.

After breakfast Suzi returned to the shipyard to begin a vigil (a stand in mourning), for this was an important day in naval history—the launching of the Will Rogers Polaris submarine. Among the honored guests were Mrs. Hubert H. Humphrey, the Governor of Oklahoma, the Secretary of the Navy, and Will Rogers Jr.

The submarine's launching marked the culmination of 10 years' work. It is quite a fish. Its nuclear reactor gives the Will Rogers an almost limitless cruising range, and it can unleash missiles from under the surface of the ocean to targets more than 2880 miles away. It is a fantastic achievement. It made Suzanne and her friends sick to their stomachs. Suzi tells me, "It can kill 60 million people." Maybe she meant only 6 million.

By 11 A.M. a hundred men, women, and children were standing in vigil. Some held anti-war signs and some passed out leaflets. Shortly after 11, Suzi took part in the planned civil disobedience for which she had volunteered. She tried to enter the main gate to distribute leaflets. A guard stopped her and asked if she had an invitation. Suzi told him that she hadn't, made no pretense about why she was there, and was turned back. Suzi then sat on the curb. When the police asked her to move, she nonco-operated and went limp. The police dragged her and other demonstrators to a bus.

A little bit of hell was to break loose after Suzi left the scene. Shipyard workers threw beer cans, rocks, lighted cigarettes, and cherry bombs at the demonstrators. Several demonstrators took a beating. Well, it was a mob scene. A man who had to clean up the rubble said, "It gives you an idea of what it was like during the Watts riot." He was only guessing, but the day rates among the most successful of C.N.V.A.'s ventures.

Suzi in the meantime had been hauled to the old courthouse in New London and then dragged up three flights of wooden stairs into the courtroom. Her dress was torn, her ankle bruised and hurting, but Suzi explained to the police who were dragging her that she had nothing against them as persons or policemen and apologized for the inconvenience she was causing them. That's Suzi.

She told me, "You mustn't say in the article that I went to jail. I was *taken*. I wasn't going to help them put me in jail or assist in any way when I thought what I did was right."

The C.N.V.A. does not order its members to participate in any activity. You take your choice: send cash, stand in quiet vigils, pass leaflets, stay home and fast, or enter into civil disobedience.

Some members who had been civilly disobedient were dragged into the courtroom, and others co-operated by walking. The arrests were made for "breach of peace," "trespassing," and, for those who had to be dragged, "resisting arrest."

Suzi had been dropped onto a bench. She found the courtroom a little disarming, because it looked like the inside of a small church, sombre with pews and a pulpit. Of the ten demonstrators arrested, Suzi alone had decided not to co-operate in the court.

Suzi had no idea of what the judge would do when she refused to stand. She knew of demonstrators who had been so nonco-operative that they had been brought into court in wheelchairs, but the judge in that case had ignored it and gone on with the arraignment. Suzi had personally demonstrated with a group at the Sikorsky Helicopter Plant at Hartford, Connecticut. In that case the judge had complimented the demonstrators for being well-behaved and then dismissed the case.

Suzi found Judge Kinmonth a good-looking young man, but he was curt and quick about the charges. She had hoped to communicate with him and suddenly realized this might not be possible.

Her name was called. Suzi refused to stand. When she

246

was called again, Suzi said, "I'm sorry, sir, I don't think I should co-operate."

Judge Kinmonth appeared startled, then said, "This is a court of law and it demands respect. It's not my province to ask what your reasons are."

Suzi said, "I don't in good conscience feel that I can co-operate with this court."

The judge sentenced her to 30 days and she was lugged out of court. No one asked if she wanted an attorney, a trial, or a Band-Aid. In the opinion of a former Connecticut District Attorney, Suzi, as a minor, should have had a legal guardian appointed, and her case should have been sent to juvenile court. So what? Judge Kinmonth probably had something more important on his mind.

Suzi was feeling a little frustrated because she hadn't prepared a better speech to establish communication with the judge.

Suzi told me, "I wasn't frightened and I had no resentment toward the judge. Resentment is a kind of anger that is a block, something which is not entirely grown-up. I thought his sentence was ridiculous, pointless, unspeakable. I didn't stand up. This is worth 30 days. But he was in a hurry, you know. He did have ten cases to dispose of and so he had to move along quickly."

The late Felix Frankfurter was critical of the contempt power. He once noted that "the power . . . is not unappealing even to high-minded judges bent upon the quick dispatch of business."

April fool! I don't know whether or not Judge Kinmonth is a high-minded judge. I don't care. The story is about the abuse of the contempt power. Kinmonth is just one of the many thousands of judicial minnows who had the weapon at his disposal.

* * *

Montville State Jail is a great comfort to the more progressive citizens of Connecticut. It looks like a modern elementary school. The costly landscaping includes trees and a garden, a pond, and an honest-to-God babbling brook. If you have to spend the summer in jail for some trivial reason like being too poor to get up a court fine, or even refusing to rise before the judge, this place appears to have status.

The innards of the jail are disappointing. No sauna bath. No murals. No Muzak. Not even a cheap Picasso print. The female inmates call their living-quarters a "cage," but prison authorities know it is a dormitory. Suzi's dormitory contained about seven cots, a couple of toilets, and a washbasin. The dormitory was surrounded by bars. Between the bars and walls was a corridor where prison officers and tourists could saunter and view the inmates.

Suzi recalls, "It was a clean jail except you'd get a funny feeling when people walked around the cage looking at you. I don't think I could ever enjoy visiting a zoo again."

Upon entering the jail Suzi was issued a pair of slippers, pajamas, two pink smocks, bras, and baggy, cotton panties. Suzi had decided to co-operate in jail. "I didn't feel right to ask them to lug me around when it was the fault of the courts that I was there."

The first couple of days Suzi mainly caught up on her sleep and felt more refreshed than she had in weeks. After that she recalls, "It was a drag, a crashing bore."

Besides three meals a day ("The food was pretty good") and cleaning up the cell in the morning, the remainder of the day was prisoner's choice. Every evening there were 3 hours of television: Ed Sullivan, "Peyton Place," "Hullaballoo," "Batman," "The Girl from U.N.C.L.E." All of the educational and rehabilitation programming was planned from a copy of *TV Guide*.

Suzi was allowed to write two letters a week, although some were censored. Some of the books sent to her were confiscated. A Greek Bible, the writings of Thoreau and Gandhi were passed on, but a college catalogue and a blank notebook were withheld. That makes sense.

On August 6, Suzi began a 4-day fast, which ran from Hiroshima Day to Nagasaki Day. She explains, "The fast had nothing to do with being in jail. I was expressing my personal sorrow for the people killed by the bombs. I felt particularly bad because President Johnson's daughter was celebrating her wedding and I thought that was in bad taste, like thumbing your nose at humanity, so I had to do something."

Most of the time in jail Suzi spent re-examining her position on contempt—had she been right to refuse to stand, and would she refuse to stand again? You must remember Suzi still hadn't been arraigned in court on the charges of "trespassing," "etc."

Suzi told me, "Many times I would say to myself, 'Okay, Williams, what are you doing here and do you really believe these things and if not, what *do* you believe?' I'd throw out my position and start from scratch."

Suzi goes on, "I can't deny that my action in court had something to do with my actions at the shipyard. It's part of the same personal conscience, the same brain, the same body. But I don't hold the concept of justice in contempt. I didn't hold the judge as a person in contempt. But I don't like what the courts do to people. They are discriminatory. A man who is well-off is fined $40 or 20 days in jail. He can pay it. To a poor person, that $40 is impossible to raise so he goes to jail.

"And courts mete out punishment to young men who refuse to co-operate with the draft when they consider the draft to be an unjust and immoral law. That's political coercion.

"And jails are destructive to people. They have no corrective effect. They are a waste of taxpayers' money."

Suzi had a long, long time to study and assess the value of jails to society. This comes from her mental record:

Janet was an alcoholic in for drinking. Suzi notes, "Yet all doctors agree that alcoholism is a disease, not a crime."

Mary, 19, was in for the flimflam game, a variation of the con racket. Suzi: "Mary and I got to be good friends and she told me when she got out she'd just do the same thing in a different state."

Carol, 16, a high-school drop-out, had gone to a party. The police broke in and arrested everyone for receiving stolen goods. The boys had stolen the beer. Suzi: "The court set Carol's bail at $300. Her mother couldn't get a bail bond.

Carol maintained she hadn't known the boys had stolen the beer and, when she got to court, the case was thrown out. But here was a child who had spent 2 weeks in jail for nothing."

Dorothy, 39, was convicted of possessing heroin. Her sentence was 90 days and $1000. Suzi: "Dorothy's parents washed their hands of her, so she has to work out the fine at $3 a day."

Barbara, 25, was a pathological liar, in jail for either child neglect or adultery, or both. Suzi: "By sitting in jail she wasn't helping either herself or her kids."

It's enough to make a person sigh but not Suzi. She says, without emotion, "None of these cases inclined me toward more respect for the court."

But Suzi, herself, wasn't in for television rehabilitation. What can you teach a disciplined student about learning? What can you teach a D.A.R. medal-winner about good citizenship? What can you teach a Quaker about responsibility?

Well, Suzi, you know, when the judge says stand up, baby, stand, Suzi, stand.

*   *   *

Suzi wasn't going to stand but she was going to communicate with the next judge. After all, she had no trouble talking to the girls in that dormitory. They understood. She explained to them that the Quakers had refused to doff their hats to English kings and had gone to jail before they escaped to America. Not standing up for a judge's robe was the same thing.

The girls understood about conscience. Come on now, if an adulteress, a junkie, a thief, and an alcoholic can understand about conscience, then why not a judge? Of course, Judge Kinmonth didn't have time to talk it over, but the next time it would be different.

Suzi knew a different judge would be in court for her next appearance. She would use the word "sir," as she had always done when talking to adult males, and then explain to him why she couldn't rise for his robes. At best he might suspend sentence on the other charges in view of her having served 30 days. At the worst—but Suzi doesn't think bad about people.

250

She says, "People are good. It's just that sometimes they are shackled by precedent and procedure."

* * *

On Aug. 19, 1966, Suzi had served 30 days. That morning the matron called Suzi to put on her dress. It was to be a long, hot, and memorable day in Connecticut.

Suzi walked to the police car outside the jail. She was in the custody of a policeman and a policewoman. Once Suzi got into the sedan, she explained to them that she would be noncooperating and what it meant. She knew it would be hard on them to move her from the car to the court. She told them that there was nothing personal involved between her and the police. She apologized in advance for the physical effort it would cost them to move her.

At the Groton Courthouse, the policeman very gallantly carried her into a cell to await her turn in court. It was a small victory in communications. From that point on, everything went downhill.

She sat in the cell during lunch, not particularly concerned about the meal that wasn't offered to her. When the police, the judge, and the others returned from the noon recess, Suzi was dragged into court below the judge's dais, where she was dropped on the floor. The police had taken away Suzi's glasses and she is very near-sighted. But even so she could see that Judge Luke Stapleton was a kindly-looking man, perhaps in his late 50s, his hair white and wavy in front.

Judge Stapleton looked down into Suzi's naked, exotic eyes and appeared to be in no rush to dispose of her case. He questioned Suzi and they talked amiably for some 5 minutes.

He asked Suzi about her background, her education, and why her mother wasn't present. Suzi answered, "My parents believe I've made my decision in good conscience and don't want to influence me by their presence."

When Judge Stapleton asked about her disrespect for the court, Suzi explained at length that she was not putting down the concepts of justice but that she could not enter into a false relationship, such as rising for the judge's robes, because she

251

didn't think a judge deserves any more or less respect than any other human being.

She also pointed out that her attitude was not aimed at Judge Stapleton as an individual in the court but for the many injustices perpetrated by the court system. She covered all the points she had thought out so carefully in jail.

Judge Stapleton plucked at his robe as he remonstrated with her for not respecting the court and then asked her if she would abolish the entire court system.

"No," Suzi replied, "but I would change many things."

The judge was obviously puzzled, as Henry Luce would have been, and murmured, "Only 17 years old."

Then in a clear, strong voice Judge Stapleton went on, "We've been operating this way for a long time before you came along and apparently we've been doing very well. You are in contempt for not standing."

Suzi said, "I appreciate your concern, sir, but I'm hoping you can dissociate yourself from the formality of structure and look at me as a human being."

Judge Stapleton said, "I see you as a human being and find you an attractive young woman."

Suzi blushed as a woman would never have done.

Judge Stapleton pounded the gavel and sentenced her to 60 days and concluded, "I'm sure my successor will keep meting it out until you conform. You just cannot come in here and tell the court how to operate."

Suzi was dragged back to the same dormitory. She still hadn't been arraigned for "trespassing" and the rest of it. The girls in the dorm told Suzi she was on a merry-go-round.

* * *

"**Dear** Mrs. Williams,

"You must be proud to be the mother of this cheap tramp of a daughter???

"Every decent mother in Amherst hates the sound of her name in this decent town.

"Please, you and that stinking family of yours move into the ocean and at the bottom is the best place for all cowardly bastards like your family."

Unsigned, of course.

Now, that letter may be misleading. The chief industry of Amherst is education, with Amherst College and the University of Massachusetts being the major corporations, so most of the citizens have a good grasp of syntax. And Amherst is really a fairly liberal town. But the letter brings up a question that many people were asking.

How could nice parents like Dr. and Mrs. Williams let their daughter rot in jail? Generally, it just isn't the thing to do. Not in this generation anyway.

Mrs. Williams is a pacifist but believes in working politically for peace. She agrees with all of Suzi's criticisms of the courts but thinks Suzi was in error in not rising. She said all this publicly and added, "I may not agree with all that Suzi does but I'm proud of her for standing by what she believes."

While Dr. Williams is opposed to the Vietnam war, he is not a pacifist. But like his wife he, too, respects conscience and a moral viewpoint.

To her parents, friends, and many innocent bystanders, Suzi's second sentence of 60 days was a shock. And on the same day she received the sentence, Suzi began a ten-day fast. There was deep concern for her health. Friends phoned the jail and were told that Suzi was getting a daily medical examination.

The Williams's family physician wrote to the Montville Jail asking for a letter from the hospital physician describing Suzi's health.

Professor Williams, from Albuquerque, wrote a letter published in the Hartford *Courant* that said, in part, "Suzanne is now on a fast. She will fast for ten days on water. My reports show inadequate medical supervision of inmates."

Actually, a physician dropped by the jail on the fifth day of Suzi's fast and cursorily took her heart beat, pulse, and blood pressure. He came back again 3 days after she had ended her ten-day fast. Not being a student of Gandhi, the physician didn't know that ill-effects, problems with the heart or kidney, usually appear on the seventh or eighth day of a fast. Or maybe he just doesn't like to make house calls.

Luckily, Suzi's health held up. She actually had less discomfort during the long fast than during her Hiroshima vigil.

However, a few people began thinking that perhaps Suzi's sentence had been a little too severe for a minor. Dr. Williams pulled no punches in his published letter: "Suzanne is not looking for mercy, only justice. She is a political prisoner and is being treated more harshly than are prisoners of war under the provisions of the Geneva convention."

However, Dr. Williams wrote in a personal letter to Suzi, "As procedures go in the sovereign state of Connecticut I expect you will die in jail for not conforming with their procedures. That is your decision. But I would prefer that you die in jail than compromise what you consider to be the correct course of action."

Dr. Williams also noted, "I've not studied the history of law for thirty years for nothing. It has taught me that many people have died at the hands of governments just because the law and courts were a generation or two behind the current acceptable standards. In Connecticut in 1776, a man's house and cattle and land were protected by law. In 1778, many were victims of theft of their lands because their lands were stolen by patriots, and courts of Connecticut upheld the thievery because these were patriots with a capital P. And so it's the old story, with liberty and justice for some."

Both Dr. and Mrs. Williams wrote the Honorable John Dempsey, Governor of Connecticut. Mrs. Williams, in a lengthy, intelligent letter, discussed the entire case. She stated emphatically that she would not ask Suzi to stand up in court, but added, "Yet it seems incredible to me that an adolescent idealist should be made to serve ninety days in jail for breach of protocol!"

Governor Dempsey is a noted man. He is listed in an encyclopedia under the head of "RED-LETTER DATES IN CONNECTICUT . . . 1961, John N. Dempsey, an Irish immigrant, became governor."

The Governor wrote a seemingly sympathetic letter to Mrs. Williams. However, he noted that the constitutional separation of powers gave him no authority over the judicial branch.

Is contempt power so sacrosanct that a Governor can't grant a pardon?

Suzi herself held no more contempt or resentment toward Judge Stapleton than she held toward Judge Kinmonth. It was her feeling that both men were victims of an archaic system. She hadn't lost faith in Judge Stapleton's being a reasonable, humane man and she wrote him a long letter detailing her own deep interest in justice for all, and stating that she was not contemptuous of him. He answered by telegram saying that any time she wanted to come into court and co-operate, he would purge her of contempt and then try her on the other charges. Impasse.

* * *

However, public opinion was raising its lovely head. People were bombarding newspapers, judges, and the Governors of Connecticut and Massachusetts expressing their concern about Suzi and the course of Connecticut justice. Preachers discussed the subject on Sundays. Pacifists held night and day vigils and fasts in front of the jail. C.N.V.A. members staged a 3-day and 2-night protest walk from Boston to Montville.

This public arousal was the only important thing that happened, because meanwhile back at that nice ranch-style jail Suzi Williams hadn't changed her mind one bitty whit. She was bored and she was trapped but, by God, she remained so cool and sweet-tempered that the jail administrator took it upon himself to write a letter to Mrs. Williams telling her how pleasant it was to have Suzi around.

Suzi was no mean tactician. She let it be known that she would refuse to rise when she returned to court on October 17 and, furthermore, during those last ten days she would go on another fast. Her plans were published in newspapers.

Early in September, Suzi was visited by a Connecticut lawyer as an interested friend. He explained that in some areas he was in agreement with her. He had a son in Mississippi during the long hot summer of 1964. He was anguished about the Vietnam war. However, he thought Suzi should apologize to the court. Suzi thought he was kind, and interested in her, and she discussed the case with him. But she didn't change her mind.

While it was the consensus of many adults that Suzi should apologize, no one publicly supported the harsh sentences of Judges Kinmonth and Stapleton. No person of any importance tried to justify the 90-day sentence given to a minor whose disrespect could only be based on the matter of not standing in court.

It is this writer's guess, and the reader may dispute it, that what evolved was a face-saving operation to preclude another confrontation with that nice little girl from Amherst.

Suzi knew nothing about it. On September 25 she wrote her sister, "I'm going to get a lawyer and fight the constitutionality of the powers of judges to give contempt sentences without any of the usual safeguards."

Three days later, a lawyer for the American Civil Liberties Union appeared at the jail. He and Suzi talked for 2 hours. Suzi recalls, "He agreed that I shouldn't be in jail. He was interested in the facts that I had no counsel and no guardian. I don't think he agreed with my acts in court, but I made it clear that I would not change my course."

The lawyer said he would ask for modification papers. Then they spent a long time drafting a statement for Suzi to sign because she again told the attorney, "I will not apologize."

Her statement read, "I would like to apply for a reduction of my sentence to time served. My actions in court were not intended to indicate disrespect for justice. To me, the achieving of justice is one of the highest aspirations of man and those who wear the robes of justice, the symbol of such aspirations, are entitled to the decent respect of mankind. I am sorry that my actions in court were taken for disrespect. They were not so intended."

Ambiguous? Compromising? Read it over. You decide.

Suzi went back to the cage. For the sixty-eighth day she had lunch with the girls and then played gin rummy. At 4:40 that afternoon, a matron called Suzi and, without explanation, told her to change into her long-suffering street dress. Suzi

256

walked to the door. The A.C.L.U. attorney was waiting, but there were no police.

"You mean I'm free?" Suzi asked.

He nodded.

"It'll take a few minutes to get used to," Suzi said.

She was completely free. Judge Stapleton had also persuaded the prosecutor to nolle the charges against her.

A direct confrontation with Suzi Williams had been avoided.

Late that night Suzi was at home in Amherst and the next day she was out with a bunch of kids looking at a Canadian moose that had wandered into a farmer's pasture.

The following day Suzi wasn't so pleased. The newspapers in reporting her release from jail said that she had apologized to the court for not standing. Suzi says, "If that were true I would have walked into the court on my own two feet to apologize."

Alfred M. Bingham of Norwich, one of the attorneys who had interceded for Suzi and prepared the legal spadework, told the Hartford *Courant*, "I felt she was well-intentioned but foolish, and that her discourtesy did not justify such a severe sentence."

Bingham noted that he was also concerned about Suzi's lack of legal representation, and felt the courts are lagging behind in contempt matters.

"When a girl of this young age protests as a matter of conscience, she could be referred to juvenile court," Bingham continued. "Instead, she was treated as a common criminal."

* * *

The story of Suzi Williams and contempt power is unique. Suzi makes it so. She is well above the average person in spirit and discipline and intelligence.

A noted authority on law, James T. Brennan, who also happens to be a member of the Connecticut bar, writes about the average person caught up in the drama and emotion of contempt, ". . . the mixture of fear and hate and disbelief in the eyes of the husband who is adjudged in contempt of court for failure to comply with an unrealistically high alimony order . . . the little old Polish man speaking only broken English who is cast into a jail by a judge after he has failed to comply with a court order to convey his property . . . the screaming man being dragged to a cell by two sheriffs because he failed to put out his cigarette before he walked through the courtroom door."

It's not likely that the judiciary will move toward reform. Men are not inclined to diminish personal power. But every story should have a moral, just like in the *Reader's Digest*. And perhaps the moral here is that the next time Dean Martin or Batman or your neighbor asks you to write letters, write. Power to fight contempt or any other injustice is in the hands of the people.

As for Suzi, she may go to college next fall. Everyone thinks she should, especially the justices of the New England courts. Among recent reports on Suzi, one from *The New York Times* notes that Suzanne Williams was at the Boston Federal Court when David A. Reed, a former Harvard student, was sentenced to 3 years in prison for refusing to report for induction into the armed services.

Suzanne Williams then ran to the courtroom and sat down.

"You had no right to sentence Reed to prison," Miss Williams told the judge. "I will continue to sit here in protest."

How Louella Mae Burns Just Missed Becoming a Famous Writer

By Robert Byrne

The Famous Writers School, advertisements for which appear regularly in the *Saturday Review, Ramparts, Harper's,* and other magazines, has been quite a success since it started 6 years ago. Today it has about 20,000 mail-order students, who may pay up to $625 for the privilege, and an annual gross income in the millions. The Famous Writers themselves, according to *Business Week,* receive about $4400 a year for their services: (1) occasionally traveling to Westport, Connecticut, to consult with the school's instructors, and (2) permitting the use of their names for publicity—Bennett Cerf, Faith Baldwin, Bergen Evans, Bruce Catton, Mignon G. Eberhart, John Caples, J.D. Ratcliff, Mark Wiseman, Max Shulman, Rudolf Flesch, Red Smith, and Rod Serling.

It was in the *Saturday Review* that my wife and I saw an advertisement for the Famous Writers School 2 years ago. My wife happens to be a concert pianist and I happen to be the editor of a trade journal, and though both of us have literary ambitions, we were really not seriously interested in enrolling in the Famous Writers School. But seeing that advertisement gave my wife a mischievous idea.

To us, there was something terribly sad in seeing established writers permit the use of their names in such a rankly commercial manner. Besides, the school's promotional campaign seemed intent on spreading the notion that practically anybody, with hard work and a good correspondence course, can join the exciting world of the highly-paid professional writer. The one proviso the school made was that would-be writers have talent. Thus, according to the *Saturday Review* ad, the school weeded out the talentless from the talented by means of its Aptitude Test.

That test was what gave my wife her idea. She proposed to send for it and fill it out with outrageously silly answers.

I haughtily informed her that she was wasting her time, and that any organization represented by such respectable people would never encourage incompetents. But wives can be stubborn and she went ahead anyway.

And so my wife created a potential Famous Writer. Her name was Louella Mae Burns, and she was 62 years old and a widow. Mrs. Burns, using our address in San Francisco, promptly wrote away for the Aptitude Test.

The test arrived on March 4, along with a letter that stated: "If we fail to find that you have writing ability worth developing, we'll tell you quite frankly." The test itself was all of 8 pages long. It began with a section entitled YOUR PERSONAL BACKGROUND. Mrs. Burns—in longhand—answered all the questions, revealing that she had been a housewife for 42 years, had never been to college, had three children, had been interested in writing for 6 months, and read the *Reader's Digest*. Her favorite authors were Kathleen Norris, Margaret Mitchell, and William Shakespeare. The last question was, What do you hope to achieve as a writer? Mrs. Burns's reply:

I would like to share some of my really interesting experiences that I've had quite a lot of and I think with changing some names of people and places that I could write a really interesting novel or book or maybe some short stories. I think this would be a richly rewarding experience for me and fill some of the lonely hours that I find weigh heavy some days ever since dear Fred departed this world.

The Aptitude Test was divided into six sections. The first listed five sentences, all of which contained long-winded phrases that the student was supposed to condense. Example: "It isn't difficult *to add more length to* your novel." The right answer, of course, is *to lengthen*. Alas, Mrs. Burns's answer was *to add length to.* For *as soon as,* she substituted *soon as*—instead of *when.* For *so as to,* she substituted *so to*—instead of

262

to. For *prepare an outline that covers,* she substituted *prepare an outline for*—instead of *outline.*

Section Two listed five famous characters. After each name were six adjectives, and the student was asked to choose the three that were appropriate. For example, after "Sherlock Holmes" the adjectives "daring," "deductive," and "urbane" should have been checked. Mrs. Burns checked "daring," "deductive," and "corpulent." She also thought that Scarlett O'Hara was "aloof" and TV cowboy Matt Dillon was "cruel."

Next, a vocabulary test. Five words were listed, then easy multiple-choice definitions. Mrs. Burns thought that *parch* meant *dissect, interpose* meant *change,* and *vestige* meant *payment.*

Section 4 involved choosing which of two paragraphs was better written. There was a 50-50 chance, and Mrs. Burns guessed correctly.

Next came the challenge of supplying words for the blanks in a paragraph of fiction. Here is the paragraph:

It was a———evening in late spring and the apartment windows were open to the———sounds of the city's roar; but the girl standing in the———of the living room and nervously twisting a plain gold band around her———finger, heard only———sounds. One was the———throb of the automatic elevator in the corridor outside and the other was the———chime of the mantel clock as its———marked 7:30.

Mrs. Burns came up with these words: *gorgeous, fascinating, middle, delicate, some, heart, bell,* and *chimes.*

The final section of the test was its heart: "In not more than 150 words, tell of an experience you have had at some time in your life." This stopped my wife for a few days. If her contribution were too ridiculous, her fraud would be all too clear. If it weren't fairly ridiculous, nothing would be proved. In fact, she took so much time that, finally, a friendly note of encouragement arrived from Westport. Properly stimulated, my wife penned the following essay:

I think I can truthfully say to the best of my knowledge that the following is truly the most arresting experience I have ever under-

gone. My husband, Fred, and I, had only been married but a short time and one beautiful cloudless day in springtime we went a-strolling down Central Avenue in East Orange, New Jersey. All of a sudden there was no longer just Fred and I but a whole flock of people who started merging along the sidewalk. Fred and I did think this was a little funny, but then the day was so gorgeous with fluffy white clouds splattering the sky that we thought well everybody is just out enjoying the gorgeous day as we were. When out of the blue came a honking and cars and motorcycles and policemen. It was really something! Everybody started shouting and waving and we finally essayed to see the reason of all this. In a sleek black limousine we saw real close Mr. Calvin Coolidge, the President Himself! He was smiling and waving and then he looked right at us, at Fred and I, at which point he smiled again. I just stood there so awed and dumbstruck that it was like a dream. It was truly an unforgettable experience and one which I shall surely long remember.

* * *

After the completed test was mailed off, my wife and I waited eagerly for its return. And not long after, the test—scored and commented upon—came back.

The grade on the first section (eliminating superfluous words) was D. The second section's grade was C (apparently Matt Dillon *is* "cruel" and not "kindly," and my wife got that right). The third section (vocabulary) was graded D.

The fourth section, choosing the better of two paragraphs, was marked A, and the grader apparently couldn't contain his elation: "Good work, Mrs. Burns," he had scribbled.

Section 5—supplying key words—earned Mrs. Burns a C- and this comment: "Your words *do* have consistency in feeling & meaning but the girl would be more likely to hear irritating sounds in her nervous state."

Section 6—the essay on Calvin Coolidge—was marked C-. Wrote the grader: "You have an interesting story here, but wish you had written in an easier less stilted manner."

Well, had Mrs. Burns passed or failed? To us, it seemed obvious that she should not be encouraged to embark on a long, rather costly writing course in order to be a professional free-lance writer. The Famous Writers School owed it to her to inform her that, unfortunately, the school was overbooked for the season and all seasons to come.

*   *   *

On the last page of the Aptitude Test, Mrs. Burns was given an over-all grade of C+ and informed that she qualified for the Famous Writers School. According to the school's chart, C was "above average." A D would have been "fair." And a few days later, on April 15, the following letter arrived from Donald T. Clark, registrar of the Famous Writers School:

Dear Mrs. Burns:
 One of my pleasantest duties is to write to aspiring writers who have scored well on our Aptitude Test. Congratulations! . . . You couldn't consider breaking into writing at a better time than today. . . .

Of course, I don't mean to suggest that there is anything wrong with offering a course of writing by mail, or even to suggest that the instruction given at the Famous Writers School may not be the best thing of its kind ever concocted. But I do think it is clear that the school is willing to accept feebly-qualified applicants, and to cajole them into enrolling with descriptions of the luxurious lives led by a group of the best-paid writers in the country. And I think that this is the cruelest kind of huckstering—the kind that feeds on day-dreams and loneliness. The Twelve Famous Money Makers ought to be ashamed of themselves.

Why 7 out of 10 Cops
Will Use the 3rd Degree

By Thomas R. Brooks

A re all cops brutal? My daughter doesn't think so; she thinks the policeman who waves her across the street every morning on the way to school is "the nicest man."

Stanley Slater, a 30-year-old consultant for a Federal agency in New York City, once thought the police were decent, too. An active citizen of his Bronx community, Slater even used to pass out "Your Friend—the Policeman" leaflets for the Police Department. Then, one Sunday evening in June of 1964, Slater took his mother out for a drive, along with a friend of his, Miss Noreen Colby, a 25-year-old business representative for the New York Telephone Company. On the 181st Street Bridge, crossing from Manhattan into the Bronx, Slater got into an argument with a man who had been driving erratically. As Slater drove away, he noticed in his rear-view mirror that the other driver was tailing him. So Slater stopped his car at a police-call box to summon help.

Just then, the other drive pulled his car up alongside, jumped out, and punched Slater in the face. He grabbed the phone from Slater's hand and yanked it off its moorings. Then he proceeded to pummel Slater, knocking him over a 2-foot fence. Miss Colby rushed to Slater's side; the assailant slugged her with the phone, so hard she had a brain concussion and suffered from double vision for about a year.

A crowd gathered. Slater's assailant thereupon pulled out a shield and identified himself—Patrolman George Goldsand, attached to the West 100th Street Station. Goldsand ordered Slater, his mother, and Miss Colby to go with him to a nearby precinct house. Slater's party and a dozen or so witnesses were questioned over a 6-hour period. Then they were suddenly ordered to leave.

"I was told I was very lucky," Slater said. "They told me that 99% of the time when a man is brought in by a police officer, he's charged. I asked for Goldsand's arrest and they told me to go home."

But Slater didn't let the matter rest. He complained to the Bronx District Attorney, who sent the case to a grand jury. The jury voted "no bill." (It's a rare grand jury that hands down an indictment against a cop on charges of brutality.)

Slater and Miss Colby then filed a complaint with the Police Department's own Civilian Complaint Review Board. Soon, Slater began getting threatening phone calls in the middle of the night. Throughout 3 months of off-again-on-again hearings, however, Slater and his witnesses persisted. Unlike many victims of police brutality, Slater had no charges pending against him, so he could proceed without the possibility of police retaliation that way. Finally, Goldsand was found guilty of several infractions of departmental rules, of erratic driving, and of simple assault. His punishment: a month's pay.

"I never thought these brutality charges were true," Slater said afterwards. "Now I know differently."

Thousands of other people are in the same boat. Indeed, it sometimes seems that we are in the midst of a police-brutality epidemic. According to the FBI, in fiscal 1963 it received 1376 allegations of police brutality; fiscal 1964 brought 1592 complaints; and in fiscal 1965 there were 1787 complaints. In the 2½-year period ending in June, 1960, there were only 1328 allegations of police brutality. Negroes, who constitute 10% of the population, accounted for 35% of all these complaints; as the Commission on Civil Rights says, "The statistics suggest that Negroes feel the brunt of official brutality proportionately more than any other group in American society." In terms of region, the Commission on Civil Rights states that

. . . approximately two out of every three complaints over the last few years . . . originated in the 17 Southern States and the District of Columbia (1961 Report, Book 5, "Justice").

The American Civil Liberties Union, on the other hand, points out that right now controversies over alleged police brutality are exploding in the Northern states too, in cities like New York, Newark, Seattle, Detroit, Los Angeles, Chicago, Springfield (Mass.), Baltimore, Boston, Buffalo, Rochester, Denver, and Cleveland.

Not all allegations of police brutality are valid, of course. "Police brutality!" has become the habitual plaint of every two-bit thug caught heisting somebody's handbag. Still, there is absolutely no gainsaying the fact that many policemen do use force, unnecessarily, and often.

Criminologists say so. According to Paul W. Tappan, for example, formerly professor of sociology and law at Washington Square College, New York University, and formerly chairman of the U.S. Board of Parole:

. . . Where suspects are more stubborn or their inquisitors more brutal, various forms of violence may be employed, beatings with the fist or rubber hose being most common, perhaps. Other more esoteric and effective measures are used, however, such as the water cure [i.e., pouring water down a victim's nostrils until he nearly strangles], probing the teeth with dull dentist's drills, kicking and squeezing the testicles, repeatedly striking the Adam's apple, and pounding with soft objects (e.g., sand or oranges in cloth bags.) (Crime, Justice, and Correction, Paul W. Tappan, 1960)

Other weapons used by the police on their victims have included electric cattle prods (in Bogalusa, Louisiana, and elsewhere), the parking light of an automobile (*The New York Times,* 9/21/54), blackjacks, pistols, ropes, whips, chains, sections of tires, boxing gloves, and an electric chair, used with reduced current (*Times,* 11/23/29).

And even the police say so. Ex-Deputy Police Commissioner Richard Dougherty of New York City once wrote, "It is hardly news that suspects of serious crimes often get 'worked over' in the back rooms of station houses" (quoted in *Time* 8/16/65). A policeman told sociologist William A. Westley, who questioned him about police violence,

Sometimes you have to get a little rough with them, see? The way I figure it is, if you can get a clue that a man is a pro and if he won't

co-operate, tell you what you want to know, it's justified to rough him up a little, up to a point. You know how it is. You feel that the end justifies the means.

A final witness is James F. Johnson, former state trooper, Secret Service agent, security officer, and private investigator, who has written:

I have noted a fearful thing; when a new member comes into the department whose natural instincts are opposed to brutality, and he finally takes the first step and employs the third degree and gets a confession, from then on he thinks it's the only way to handle prisoners. He becomes a subscriber to planned brutality (New York World-Telegram & The Sun, 3/10/53).

* * *

Certain policemen do use violence, then. There is no doubt about it. But basic questions remain. These questions are:

• Do enough policemen use unnecessary force, or *would* enough of them use it, to justify our doing something about it—or do just an insignificant number of cops condone violence?

• Do cops use violence on just the dregs of society—degenerates and Mafia-type hoods—or do they also pick on wholesome middle-class people too, like you and me?

• Finally, is violence an ingrained characteristic of cops, or is it something that can be halted with a rap on the knuckles and a few disapproving clucks and *tsk! tsks!* from a police chief?

The answers to two of these questions are found in what is probably the most important document ever written about police violence, a document that would settle many arguments if it became better known. I refer to an article entitled "Violence and the Police," written by William A. Westley, originally published in the *American Journal of Sociology* and reprinted in *Readings in Criminology and Penology,* edited by David Dressler, in 1964.

Dr. Westley, a sociologist at McGill University in Montreal, visited an industrial city in the United States—not identified—of some 150,000 inhabitants. He accompanied the cops

270

there in walking the beat and cruising in squad cars; he observed raids and actual interrogations. He also had extensive interviews with 73 of the cops, over half of the men in the department, men from all ranks—veterans and tyros, Negroes and whites, Catholics, Protestants, and Jews, traffic cops and cops who patrolled a beat. He asked all of them just one question: "When do you think a policeman is justified in roughing a man up?"

Now, a policeman is justified in using violence when it is impossible to avoid—in self-defense, to give one example. Seventeen of the cops, 23%, gave this as their answer: "when impossible to avoid."

But 77% admitted that they would use force even when it was not necessary.

* * *

The largest number—27, or 37%—admitted they would use force if someone showed "disrespect for the police." Here is what a few of them told Dr. Westley:

For example, if you stop a guy for routine questioning, say a wise guy, and he starts talking back to you and telling you you are no good and that sort of thing. You know you can take a man in on a disorderly-conduct charge, but you can practically never make it stick. So what you do in a case like that is to egg the guy on until he makes a remark where you can justifiably slap him, and then, if he fights back, you can call it resisting arrest.

You gotta get rough when a man's language becomes very bad, when he's trying to make a fool of you in front of everybody else.

If a fellow called a policeman a dirty name, a slap in the mouth would be a good thing, especially if it was out in the public where calling a policeman a bad name would look bad for the police. There was the incident of the fellow I picked up. I was on the beat, and I was taking him down to the station. There were people following us. He kept saying that I wasn't in the army. Well, he kept going on like that, and I finally had to bust him one. I had to do it. The people would have thought I was afraid otherwise.

One reason why so many Negroes are the victims of police brutality is that they can unconsciously show "disrespect for the police," simply by making economic gains. No one is more anti-Negro than the man on the same or a lower economic level, for he fears being identified with the outcast, "inferior" Negro.

A case in point: Mr. and Mrs. James Brazier of Dawson, Georgia, Negroes, bought a new Chevrolet in 1956. In November, 1957, Brazier was arrested for speeding and taken to jail. According to Brazier.

When I first entered the door of the jail, Y——— hit me on the back of the head and knocked me down and said, "You smart son-of-a-bitch, I been waiting to get my hands on you for a long time." I said, "Why you want me for?" Y——— said, "You is a nigger who is buying new cars and we can't hardly live. I'll get you yet."

The next year, Brazier made the mistake of buying another new Chevrolet. On Sunday, April 20, 1958—so says Mrs. Brazier—a gang of Dawson cops ran over to Brazier's car and dragged him out. Y——— began beating Brazier with a blackjack, saying, "You smart son-of-a-bitch, I told you I would get you." Then he kicked Brazier twice in the groin, slammed the car door on his legs, and threw a hatful of sand into his bloody face. That night, in jail, Brazier was given a working-over by Officers Y——— and X———. He died a few days later from brain damage and a fractured skull. The *1961 Commission on Civil Rights Report* states, "Not long after Brazier died, police officer 'Y' was promoted to chief of the Dawson Police Department."

Fourteen cops—19%—admitted that they would use force "to obtain information"; 6 cops—8%—said they would use force "to make an arrest." After all, a "good pinch" results in good newspaper publicity and in possible promotions. Various policemen told Dr. Westley:

One time Joe and I found three guys in a car, and we found they had a gun between the seats. We wanted to find out who owned that gun before the dicks arrived so that we could make a good pinch. They told us.

There's a case I remember of four Negroes who held up a filling station. We got a description of them and picked them up. Then we took them down to the station and really worked them over. I

guess that everybody that came into the station that night had a hand in it, and they were in pretty bad shape. Do you think that sounds cruel? Well, do you know what we got out of it? We broke a big case in ————. There was a mob of 20 guys, burglars and stick-up men, and 18 of them are in the pen now.

If it's a big case and there's a lot of pressure on you and they tell you you can't go home until the case is finished, then naturally you're going to lose patience.

* * *

Five of the cops interviewed in Dr. Westley's study—7%— said they would use force "for the hardened criminal"; two of them—3%—admitted they would use force "when you know the man is guilty." Thus, veteran police reporter Emanuel H. Lavine, in his book *The Third Degree,** tells of a reception organized by the police for seven members of the so-called Aspirin Mob. This 1920s gang, which included such luminaries as William ("Dummy") Taylor, John ("Buzzer") Tracey, John ("Pinochle") Raffone, and James ("Pat the Burglar") Dougherty, was arrested and charged with stealing a truckload of aspirins worth $92,000. As Lavine tells it,

An entertainment committee was formed of all the handball players [i.e., athletes] in the building. As the [Aspirin Mob] began to filter in, led by various groups of detectives, they received a very warm welcome. . . . Everything the police could lay their hands on to inflict punishment or torture was used. The detectives beat the thieves until they themselves were muscle-bound. One of the men shoved his face under a piping hot radiator to save it from being crushed.

The willingness of the police to assume the role of avenger is never clearer than in a cop killing. Recently, a rookie patrolman, Robert H. Kuhn of Baltimore, was killed by David Cooper, a convicted burglar and narcotics pusher. What happened next was succinctly reported in a U.P.I. dispatch: "Moments after the young policeman died, two patrolmen swinging nightsticks subdued the gunman in a furious street fight. Still cursing the police, Cooper died at a hospital!"

* An expression, dating back to 1900, borrowed from the difficult tests used in Freemasonry for candidates for Master Mason.

In another cop killing, the first double murder of New York policemen in 35 years, the police tortured a witness, Richard Melville (described by the New York Court of Appeals as a "small-time criminal"), by touching lighted cigarettes to his testicles (*Times,* 3/12/65).

Finally, 2 cops—3%—told Dr. Westley that they would use force against sex criminals. A rookie patrolman said:

They [veteran cops] feel it is okay to rough a man up in the case of sex crimes. One of the older men advised me that if the courts didn't punish a man, we should. He told me about a sex crime, the story about it, and then said that the law says the policeman has the right to use the amount of force necessary to make an arrest and that in that kind of crime you can use just a little more force. They feel, definitely, for example, in extreme cases like rape, that if a man was guilty he ought to be punished even if you couldn't get any evidence on him. My feeling is that all the men on the force feel that way, at least from what they have told me.

Another cop told Dr. Westley:

Now, in my own case, when I catch a guy like that [a homosexual] I just pick him up and take him into the woods and beat him until he can't crawl. I've had 17 cases like that in the last couple of years. I tell the guy that if I catch him doing that again, I'll take him out to those woods and I'll shoot him. I tell him that I carry a second gun on me just in case I find guys like him, and that I'll plant it in his hand and say that he tried to kill me and that no jury will convict me.

I myself happen to have a friend, an occasional homosexual, who recently was solicited by a stranger and invited up to a hotel room. It turned out that the room was reserved by the police as a place for the entrapment of sex offenders. But instead of arresting my unwary friend for his "crime," the plainclothesman and an associate beat him up. They beat him so badly he had to be taken out of the hotel by the back stairs on a stretcher. To justify the beating, the police charged him with assault, disorderly conduct, and resisting arrest. My friend was tempted to counter with a complaint of police brutality, but the prospect of a sentence—or having a sexual offense entered on his record—restrained him. He wisely entered a guilty plea on

the disorderly-conduct charge and received a 30-day suspended sentence.

Dr. Westley's over-all findings are summarized in the
graph below.

**Bases for the Use of Force Named
by 73 Policemen**

Type of Response	Frequency	Percentage
A. Disrespect for police	27	37
B. When impossible to avoid	17	23
C. To obtain information	14	19
D. To make an arrest	6	8
E. For the hardened criminal	5	7
F. When you know the man is guilty	2	3
G. For sex criminals	2	3

How reliable is the finding that 77% of the police will use
unnecessary force? Dr. Westley himself thinks the figure is too
low. To quote him, ". . . both the police chief and the community had been severely critical of the use of violence by the
men, and the respondents had a tendency to be very cautious
with the interviewer, whom many of them never fully trusted."
And since anybody trying to duplicate Professor Westley's experiment nowadays would never get the frank—or nearly
frank—replies *he* received, it would appear that Professor
Westley's report will be, for a long time to come, the last word
on the subject.

Two other men queried by the *Fact* staff lent a degree of
support to Dr. Westley's findings. Said Eason Monroe, executive director of the American Civil Liberties Union in Los Angeles: "Well, I'm not surprised at the 77% figure. Our experience here, and particularly during the Watts incident, leads me
to believe, on the basis of fairly conclusive evidence, that the
police here pretty regularly go further than they need with
Negro arrestees, Mexican arrestees, and so forth. And that in
the Watts incident they went very considerably beyond what
was required even by that event. I do think that 77% is a little
high. I would put the figure closer to 50%, which is bad
enough."

James Forman, executive secretary of the Student Nonviolent Coordinating Committee (SNCC), told *Fact:* "Well, 77% seems about right to me."

* * *

Our first question, then, seems to have been answered. Violence is *not* a device used only by a few scattered sadists, but a weapon used by the great majority of all policemen.

A few readers, however, may side with the police, arguing that there is some justification for beating up known criminals, or for torturing someone to obtain information. Indeed, a study conducted some years back showed considerable public support for at least the milder forms of the third degree ("Approval and Disapproval of Specific Third Degree Practices," *Journal of Criminal Law and Criminology,* November-December, 1937). It is for those readers who are inclined to approve certain third-degree tactics on certain people that the following story is provided:

Some time ago, a New York patrolman was killed by a gangster named Peter Heslin during a hold-up. At the same time, Heslin accidentally shot himself in the groin. The police trailed Heslin to his tenement. To quote Emanuel Lavine, author of *The Third Degree,*

The police entered the flat and there in bed was Heslin . . . badly wounded and bleeding profusely. . . . Heslin, who was attired only in his undershirt, was dragged from the bed and into the hallway, despite the screaming protestations of his wife. . . . The wounded man was kicked, dragged, and poked with night-sticks until he was . . . at the head of the stairs. Once there, a few well-directed kicks and blows sent him hurtling down the steps to the second floor.

From the rear to the front of the stairway he received the same treatment. After being kicked and stepped on and moved along by blows from night-sticks, some athletically inclined cop picked him up like a sack of potatoes and tossed him half way down the stairs. He rolled down the balance of the stairs and lay there in a huddled mass.

He was quickly but not gently unscrambled and knocked to the lower hallway, dragged the full length of the distance by his legs, and dumped on the sidewalk. . . .

[An ambulance stopped, but the police sent it away.]

Due to the gathering crowd . . . , the prisoner had had a sort of respite from his mauling, except for an occasional short but heavy kick from one of the cops.

The stretcher carried by the patrol wagon was opened and placed on the sidewalk. Heslin was picked up by the arms and legs and thrown on the stretcher, which in turn was picked up and thrown upside down in the wagon.

He was carried on the stretcher to the rear room of the police station. . . . When the stretcher-bearers reached a designated place they raised the stretcher as high as they could and "accidentally" upset it by dropping one side. Heslin fell to the floor with a thud. . . .

In a few minutes he asked for a drink. He was becoming slightly delirious from the bullet wound and treatment. . . . The men on reserve . . . came down and one of them said, "Sure, buddy, I'll take care of you." He walked over to the corner and slowly picked up a cuspidor, which was filled with the outgoing and incoming platoons' expectorations and their rejected cigar and cigarette butts. Deliberately, he poured the contents over Heslin's face. The cuspidor itself he left on the man's head. This brought some guffaws from the reserves. . . .

After a few minutes, a detective walked over to the bulletin board on which the men on reserve hang their night-sticks and . . . picked out the largest and heaviest in the group. . . . He walked over to Heslin and with all the power in his body struck a blow at the point of entry of the bullet just below the groin. The force of the blow opened the wound afresh, and the blood spurted up like a miniature fountain. . . .

One young cop carefully gathered as much dirt and dust as he could find on the floor, crevices, and walls, and deliberately rubbed it into four different wound openings, hoping, as he expressed himself, that the son-of-a-bitch would die of an infection.

Another youthful member of the force . . . walked over and said: "I'm going to spoil a perfectly good cigar on you." With that remark he slowly poked the lighted end of the half-burned cigar against the pit of Heslin's stomach and twisted it about there until it was entirely extinguished. The groans of pain were met with ugly epithets from the men, most of whom would walk over and take a poke at him at intervals of a few seconds. Others on the side lines took deliberate aim and flipped lighted cigarettes on the exposed parts of his body. . . .

Even Pete Heslin, cop-murderer, deserved better than that.

277

Another point to be made about police brutality is that, like censorship, it's impossible to draw a line. As the veteran policeman James F. Johnson has said,

The average citizen who says, "It served the bum right" forgets the officer who resorts to brutality doesn't always confine his activities to the guilty. . . . If a cop gets into the habit of beating up bums he'll soon be beating up everyone who crosses his path. It is a deadly narcotic-type habit.

Testimony before the Seattle City Council in 1965 on the desirability of a civilian-review board proved how police violence, ostensibly confined to the criminal classes, spills over to touch others.

Kenneth Spencer, then a graduate student in electronics at the University of Washington and a citizen of Jamaica, testified that he was stopped by two Seattle policemen while walking home late at night. He was knocked to the ground, handcuffed, and tossed into a patrol car. The two cops then proceeded to slap him around and cuss him out. He was beaten with a flashlight. Then the policemen took him in and charged him with "being abroad at night." His case was dismissed in court.

Richard Hoidal, a spastic involved in a minor traffic accident, testified that he was placed in the back seat of a patrol car and punched. Every time he protested, the cop tightened up the handcuffs another notch. The doctor who examined him the day of arrest and the next day after his release from jail reported, "Examination at that time revealed injuries which I feel could only come from being beaten and could not have occurred due to the type of automobile accident which he reported."

Maximilian Contraras, a University of Washington student from the Dominican Republic, testified that when he was arrested on a minor traffic charge, he was handcuffed so tightly that both wrists became so swollen and tender that he could not type for 3 days.

The final question was, Is violence an ingrained characteristic of cops, or simply a habit that can be easily broken?

The fact is that for the police, violence is often an irresistible temptation—employing it, they can make arrests, obtain information, keep certain offenders "clean." To quote Dr. Westley again, ". . . from experience in the pursuit of their legally prescribed duties, the police develop a justification for the use of violence. They come to see it as good, as useful, and as their own."

But more: The policeman, because of his very role, is liable to become fond of violence. Dr. Westley states:

The policeman finds his most pressing problems in his relationship to the public. His is a service occupation, but of an incongruous kind, since he must discipline those whom he serves. He is regarded as corrupt and inefficient by, and meets with hostility and criticism from, the public. . . . Since policemen are low in the occupational prestige scale, subject to continuous criticism, and in constant contact with this criticizing and evaluating public, they are profoundly involved in justifying their work and its tactics to the public and to themselves. . . . [The policeman] regards the public as his enemy, feels his occupation to be in conflict with the community, and regards himself as a pariah. The experience and the feeling give rise to . . . an attempt to coerce respect from the public, and a belief that almost any means are legitimate in completing an important arrest. . . .

Violence, for the policeman, is thus not only a way of fulfilling his duties; it is also a way he can discharge his antagonism against the public, and prove himself superior and privileged. A Detroit patrolman named Frank Foucault recently told the Associated Press, "I have the power of life and death. In 10 seconds, I can kill someone or let him live, and I don't have a jury or anybody there to say yes or no."

Dr. Westley's over-all conclusions are:

(a) the police accept and morally justify their illegal use of violence; (b) such acceptance and justification arise through their occupational experience; and (c) its use is functionally related to the collective, occupational, as well as legal, ends of the police.

* * *

Clearly, something must be done. We need, of course, better salaries for policemen, higher recruiting standards, more intensified professional training. And we need more effective ways of dissuading policemen from using unnecessary violence and more effective ways of disciplining those who do—namely, by the establishment of civilian-review boards to act on charges of police brutality. Philadelphia and Rochester, New York, already have such boards, and their value is demonstrated by the few cases brought before them: The cops have been watching their step. New York City's civilian-review board, before it was defeated in an election, also had done excellent work.

Naturally, the police—from J. Edgar Hoover on down—are foursquare against the idea of civilian-review boards and they are preparing to fight the plan up and down the line. Despite all the evidence, despite all the documented cases of police brutality, despite the admissions of police themselves and despite the expert opinions of criminologists and sociologists, the attitude of the police has remained unchanged. As Inspector Paul H. Ashenhurst of the Dallas (Texas) Police Department has scornfully written, "There is a dirty phrase 'police brutality.' This term denotes something which is almost entirely nonexistent today."

Help Wanted: Honest, Intelligent People to Run Employment Agencies

By Malcolm Margolin

I n February, 1966, my wife and I moved to New York City and immediately set about looking for jobs. Our carefully written résumés announced that we were both 25-year-old college graduates, and had been working in the Caribbean for the past 2 years. Irene wanted a job as a psychological research assistant, while I myself was (typically) undecided about what I wanted to do.

We turned to the Help Wanted section of the Sunday *New York Times*. It was as dazzling as an Oriental bazaar. Some 300 employment agencies had spread their wares over 50 pages, and with such enticing catchwords as "Hi pay," "Exclusive agent for A-1 company on the go," "Real opportunity," and "Generations of expert guidance."

The two of us plunged in.

In the dreary weeks that followed, my wife and I became very well acquainted with dozens of Manhattan employment agencies. But that was all. The minute we began to sift through the merchandise, the Oriental bazaar proved itself a mirage. With sickening regularity, "Exciting creative work for Hi $" turned into clerical jobs paying hardly more than the minimum wage. But "Grab what you can," we were told. "The labor market is in bad shape." "February is a terrible month to be out of work." "The stock market is shaky." We heard so many bleak forecasts that we even began to doubt the fact that 1966 had been a year of unprecedented economic expansion and opportunity.

We had almost exhausted our patience, our résumés, and

our money when I happened to apply to an employment agency that specialized in the publishing field. The agency itself offered me a job as an interviewer and "reader." (A reader studies the job-openings reported by employers and, before placing an ad, searches through the agency's files for qualified applicants.) The woman who owned and managed the agency seemed congenial. The pay was decent. I certainly needed work. So I accepted. And for the next few months, I partook in a racket that the economist John Clarke once ranked second only to patent medicines as "best able to thrive on the marketing of false pretenses."

After I quit, I spent 2 months looking into the whole employment-agency situation to find out whether my own experience was unusual. I read close to 100 articles, pamphlets, and books, wrote about two dozen letters requesting information from authorities, traveled to the State capital to acquaint myself with the State laws and legislators, studied relevant court cases, and interviewed many people connected with the personnel field.

In response to one of my letters, Nelson M. Bortz, director of the U.S. Bureau of Labor Statistics, suggested that I examine the Senate hearings held in 1962 on the role of employment agencies in the District of Columbia. Sen. Wayne Morse had presided, and these hearings had attracted witnesses from all over the country. The minutes of the proceedings are available to the public (S. 3259, Hearings and Report, 87th Congress). Because of the thoroughness of the inquiry, and the objectivity and integrity of the investigators, I have drawn heavily on its findings. All this research—as well as my own experience—has led me to a single conclusion: Today's private employment agencies are hopelessly inefficient and corrupt, and hurtful not only to job hunters but to employers as well.

* * *

There are over 5000 private employment agencies currently operating in the United States, and they are thriving. Their number has been increasing at the astonishing rate of 15% a

284

year. In other words, within a month after you have read this article, 60 new employment agencies will have arisen.

Today's employment agencies deal primarily with the salaried positions—90% of their placements are on the white-collar level. Yet these agencies are responsible for distributing millions of jobs every year. In California alone, the private agencies reported 500,000 job placements in one year, which suggests the extraordinary grasp the job brokers have on the labor market.

Along with their enormous power, employment agencies have attained an almost impenetrable aura of dignity and prestige. Their owners proudly assume such status-oozing titles as "personnel consultant," "employment counselor," and "vocational guidance expert." This veneer of respectability, however, hides a multitude of outrageous abuses.

Racial and religious discrimination is only one of these abuses. Discrimination is practiced by virtually all private employment agencies—unashamedly, and as in all their dealings, profitably. Mrs. Shirley Siegel, assistant attorney-general in charge of the New York State Civil Rights Bureau, has hunted down such famed job brokers as Office Temporaries, a giant that maintains an active file of almost 10,000 names of men and women experienced in typing, stenography, bookkeeping, and other office skills. When Mrs. Siegel subpoenaed the company's records, she found that Negroes were designated by the code NFU—Not For Us. Employers' cards bore notations like "No NFU's," "Christian girls only," and "No orientals" (Civil Rights Bureau, 3rd Annual Report, 1962). Another noted agency, Lynhall Placement Associates, used the code POK— Persons of Color (Civil Rights Bureau, 4th Annual Report, 1963).

When Mrs. Siegel began prosecuting the employment agencies did change. They adopted more subtle codes. The Prestige Personnel Agency distinguished colored applicants by the number 8, or just by underlining the applicant's signature (Civil Rights Bureau, 4th Annual Report, 1963). The agency for which I worked was small enough to avoid the risks of coding. The manager would simply scrutinize the application of any non-white until she had implanted his name in her memory, and could be certain never to accidentally recommend him for a job.

An employee at another agency has described still another popular system whereby Negroes and Puerto Ricans are shunted aside: All of them are automatically classified as "beginners," and are handled by the agency's "beginner specialist," who offers them only the most menial, underpaying, futureless jobs.

Mr. Burdette Hockaday of Hockaday Employment Services was frank enough to admit (to Wayne Morse's committee) the unquestioning compliance of employment agencies to the prejudices of their clients. "It is not unusual," stated Mr. Hockaday, "for us to have employers request white and Negro workers for the same job at different salaries, paying the white worker $10 or $15 more a week."

Why does an agency even bother to refer Negroes to low-paying jobs when it can collect only a similarly low percentage of their salaries? Mr. Hockaday explains: "Many jobs available to Negroes are of a temporary nature. Because they pay unusually low salaries, the Negro finds himself constantly in the position of having to better his financial position. . . . In far too many instances, the job is beneath his qualifications."

In sum, the Negro earns less, and thus pays a lower fee for each placement. But he will end up having to return to the agency again and again, only to be referred to other low-paying temporary jobs. Employment agencies thrive on return business.

Employment agencies have actually prospered under the various state and Federal laws forbidding discrimination. More employers than ever have turned to these middlemen to continue their prejudiced hiring practices. Naturally, the employers assume that the agencies will weed out non-whites and save them from the trauma of having a qualified Negro show up for the job of sales manager or receptionist.

The refusal of the ordinary job broker to deal with Negroes has been a windfall to certain other agencies, such as

Richard Clarke Associates of New York. Richard Clarke and his subsidiary, Hallmark Agency, specialize in Negro executive and secretarial help. Employers under government pressure can now go to such agencies for their showcase Negroes, while consulting other agencies for the rest of their help. Ironically, complaints against Hallmark have been lodged because of Mr. Clarke's alleged refusal to deal with whites. But, after all, one can imagine the chagrin of an employer who has meticulously selected a niche for a Negro, only to have a qualified WASP apply.

The typical employment agency does *not* merely cater to the prejudices of industry. In attempting to create a reputation for itself of handling only "safe" personnel, an employment agency usually originates more bigotry than any company it deals with. I rarely heard anyone telephone in with a frankly prejudiced job-order while I was working as an interviewer. But we would never have dreamed of recommending any non-white. As it was often explained to me, "We must always show our clients that we deal only with the highest-type applicant."

We are all well aware of the tragic consequences of the employment agencies' bigotry. They are a major link in the chain that keeps 33 out of every 100 college-educated Negro men tied to some kind of laboring or semi-skilled occupation. Employment agencies are also partly responsible for the fact that the average professional or technical worker who has completed college and who is not white earns less than a white worker, in the same occupation, who has completed only the eighth grade (Northrup & Bloom, *Economics of Labor Relations*, 1966).

* * *

Employment agencies go far beyond the ordinary forms of discrimination, though. They also exhibit a fascinating variety of petty bigotries whereby they further define what constitutes the "highest type" applicant.

The manager of the employment agency for which I worked spent several hours teaching me the dozens of criteria to judge our applicants by. She called them the "fine points." I will pass on only those standards I have found are shared by many other employment agencies.

After an interviewer has ascertained that the applicant is not a Negro, Jew, Latin-American, etc., he shrewdly analyzes the appearance of the job hunter. On our forms, the code for "appearance" was the letter A, next to which any deviations from normality were carefully inscribed. Male applicants, for example, were expected to be dressed in a conservative suit, with a white shirt and a conservative tie. We would examine shoes, too, to make sure that the supplicant was not offending our sensibilities by wearing loafers. Anyone overweight or underweight, in need of a haircut, or afflicted with acne was immediately eliminated. Nor could we recommend anyone who gave a "bad impression" by seeming awkward, depressed, or nervous.

For our female applicants, a fairly stylish dress, nylons, lipstick, and a good figure were *de rigeur*. An attractive girl, unless she wore no lipstick or her hair fell below her shoulders, was always acceptable. Many employers would undoubtedly have preferred a woman who worked like an ox, even if she looked like one, to some of the prima donnas we finally recommended, but that never influenced our judgment. We knew what the "highest type" applicant looked like, and we would never endanger our reputation by sending over the other kind.

Next, we would take it upon ourselves to judge the sexual acceptability of our applicants. One of the symbols we used was the letter F. For Fag. Anyone with an overly polite deportment, a weak handshake, a slight lisp, tight trousers, an overcultivated voice, or unusual mannerisms was eliminated— no one, it was thought, could be "that way" and be normal. Our manager was especially gifted in ferreting out faggotty characteristics. A dubious case never slipped by her. Whenever she spotted one, a special gleam would brighten her eyes, and with almost childish glee she would recite the death knell: "We could never recommend *that type* of person to *our* type of clients."

Particularly pathetic were those applicants who thought

that, just because they were willing to part with close to a month's salary, they were entitled to considerate advice and personalized help. One lady in her mid-30s was about to be referred for a job when, in a misguided moment of confidence, she confessed that she had once received treatment for emotional problems. She was quickly ushered out of the office, and the inscription appeared on the application: "Nervous breakdown. Cannot recommend."

Older applicants were automatically cast aside. "Too old" was sufficient reason. But sometimes the interviewer allowed himself the luxury of philosophizing. Thus one of our "vocational guidance experts" once expressed this delicate sentiment: "Imagine that old fart looking for work!"

We also sloughed off anyone with unusual qualifications, a foreign accent, or any other "oddities." On the application form, for instance, was a space for information on language proficiency. Those who wrote "A reading knowledge of French (with a dictionary)" were normal and acceptable. But those who could read, write, and speak several European tongues were strange. There was, obviously, something wrong with them.

In some ways, these inane criteria (which a great many employment agencies abide by) are more threatening to the civil liberties of the individual than either racial or religious discrimination. Each of these petty bigotries effectively denies the basic (although increasingly theoretical) right of every American to develop his own personality and to be unique.

Even the lucky individual who is bland and conformist enough to satisfy all of an employment agency's silly criteria is not yet assured of a referral. He must now pass the acid test. He must demonstrate proper humility. Job-hunting is normally an ego-deflating task in itself, but employment-agency interviewers seem determined to make it even more painful, perhaps believing that a person who has lost his self-esteem entirely becomes ready and willing to take almost any opening that comes along. For now the interviewer sits back in his chair, purses his lips, and demands: "What makes you feel you have managerial potential?" or, "Just how much do you think you're *really* worth?" or the classic, "What are your long-range goals?" Finally, the few who have met all of the interviewer's parochial standards and who, by politely answering his arrogant questions, have expressed the proper amount of respect for his importance, can go on to the next step. They have now qualified for the privilege of being fleeced out of a few hundred dollars.

* * *

There is a very good reason why employment agencies judge their victims by such narrow and outdated standards. The sad truth is that, despite their importance, their prosperity, and their prestige, few of the practitioners of the fine art of employment counseling have any of the skills or experience that would qualify them for their own jobs. Incompetence is endemic to the employment-agency field. Anyone with a few dollars to pay a bonding company, a telephone, a desk, and two chairs can become an employment agent. In all but a couple of the states, entry into this lucrative business is open to all, qualified or not.

One result of this permissive situation is the absence of professional people working for employment agencies. The owners of the agencies tend to regard any knowledgeable employee as a future competitor. Thus, Annette Tatelman, of the Annette Tatelman Employment Services in Washington, D.C., has complained about instances where interviewers and clerks, "thinking they have learned something, go out to open employment businesses of their own." To avoid future competition from their own employees, agencies tend to hire the lowest possible grade of help. Mrs. Tatelman sums them up as "untrained and incompetent, many of them young girls with no office or business experience [who] assist in making actual placements."

Another indication of the quality of employment-agency personnel can be gleaned from a report of the Wage and Hour Division of the Department of Labor: It cites numerous instances of agency employees' being paid below the minimum

290

wage of $1.25 an hour. And these unskilled, underpaid clerks are the "vocational counselors" upon whose judgment so many applicants hang their careers.

Although many of today's smarter agencies are distressed by their own lack of professionalism, few have done the obvious: hire capable, trained personnel. Instead, they cover their bare walls and barren identities with "degrees"—like the Certified Employment Consultant designation, and the Recommended Employment Counselor certificate. The C.E.C.s and the R.E.C.s, as they are affectionately called in the trade, are awarded by the American Institute of Employment Counseling. An impressive name.

Mrs. Ann Palmer Haynes, owner of a Washington employment agency, told Wayne Morse's committee about her experience with these degrees. One day she received a direct-mail circular offering her the honor of competing for her C.E.C. She tried to telephone the American Institute of Employment Counseling, only to discover that it had no phone. Further investigation revealed that the organization was not even licensed to do business in Washington.

Mrs. Haynes finally tracked down the elusive Institute by getting in touch with the manager of the building whose address was listed on the Institute's return envelope. All mail for the American Institute of Employment, she learned, was being turned over to a local company, the Graebner Employment Agency. "This type of thing is most misleading," concluded Mrs. Haynes. "What qualifications does the Graebner Employment Agency have to bestow initials of any kind on anyone?" Yet hundreds of status-hungry job brokers have acquired these "degrees," and although I would hate to be a spoilsport, I suspect that Mr. Graebner's sheepskin is a bit less valuable than a college education.

* * *

The incompetence of agency managers and employees is neither a recent nor a passing phenomenon. Few of today's older, more established employment agencies have histories they can be proud of. Many of the agencies founded before 1920 started in a saloon, where the "job boss" specialized in sending immigrants off, for a fee, to nonexistent jobs in far-distant cities. Hundreds of other agencies were spawned during the depression by people whose only qualification for this field was the fact that they themselves were unemployed. One agency was launched by a young man who, according to a muckraking pamphlet published in 1930, *Employment Agencies Officially Exposed,* was "incapable of holding down any job except day work. He could do cutting lawns and cleaning up around places very well." He borrowed $25 and became the manager of his own agency.

His initiative was not unusual. The Connecticut Department of Labor once investigated 32 of its private agencies at random. It found that a majority of the agency managers had never graduated from high school, while six had never gone beyond elementary school. Only one manager was a college graduate. More than half of the proprietors had never had any experience whatsoever that would help them in running an employment agency. Four had never held *any* other position before. Three had been domestic servants, four had done clerical work, while others had been nurses, governesses, and dressmakers. And although the field was dominated by the fairer sex, the report found that two-thirds of these agencies were engaged in criminal malpractices.

Incompetence, bigotry, and narrow-mindedness are three typical failings of the typical employment agency. Now we come to another—disregard for the applicant's welfare.

Many cynical employers, for example, give the same job order to several agencies at the same time. The result is a free-for-all. Each agency, hoping to fill the post, sends over as many applicants as it can. It wasn't unusual for us to wish five or six different applicants the best of luck, telling each that we were firmly in his corner, and send them all off to the same company for the same job. Where particularly attractive positions were up for grabs, 30 or more applicants from one agency would have to fight it out with scores of applicants from each of the competing agencies. The employer now had an enormous pool of job hunters to scrutinize, without having spent a nickel for advertising.

On the whole, our agency was better than some. At least we respected the right of the applicant to a certain amount of privacy. Some female job hunters applying at another agency found that, after giving out their names, addresses, phone numbers, and personal information, they were pestered by non-businesslike phone calls from the interviewer or his friends.

But, like the other agencies, we were reluctant to spend much time with any applicant. A job hunter who wants to take a week or so to consider a position, or who wants to look over many openings before choosing one, is swiftly ditched. He is called a "shopper," and is shunted aside in favor of the "live ones." The manager of my agency once explained, "Watch out for guys who walk slowly. Don't waste your time. Anyone who walks slowly will take forever to make up his mind."

Those prudent applicants who want to deliberate over their future careers are the very individuals most likely to become permanent and loyal employees of the company they finally choose. Yet they regularly lose out to the "live ones" who make hasty decisions. Actually, those who snap up the first job offered to them are, from the agency's point of view, preferable. The chances are that they will soon be back looking for another job, and will leave their old positions vacant for the agency to refill.

* * *

Another example of how employment agencies typically treat their clients is their habit of advertising enticing jobs that don't exist. Every job hunter must have run into this situation: He is waiting at the door when the agency opens, so he will have the first chance at an attractive position advertised the previous night. After filling out a lengthy application form, he is told: "The job you want is already filled. We are working on other openings, and we'll contact you if something else turns up."

This fraud is so widespread that at least 40 states have enacted laws prohibiting agencies from placing false ads. The laws have proved unenforceable. Advertising nonexistent jobs is too valuable a tool for the agencies to give up. Not only does it bring in many new clients, but it also is the wedge they use to force their way into new markets.

Take the employment agent who wants to foist his services upon some part of the publishing industry, although he is new to that business. First, he advertises positions for writers, editors, copy editors, researchers, proofreaders, and production people. Since these positions exist only in his imagination, he can promise whopping salaries, fringe benefits, and guaranteed opportunities for advancement. Sometimes he gives his own address and interviews all the suckers who show up. Sometimes he places the ad with only a box number for the applicant to send his résumé to. The agent answers none of the letters he gets, as anyone who has answered these blind ads is well aware.

Once the agent has a thick inventory of names, he combs trade journals devoted to the publishing industry for Help Wanted ads placed directly by the hiring companies. He then calls the employer and shows him the piles of résumés of "people he represents." Of course, all these job hunters will fork over the placement fee. So the employer can meet these qualified, ambitious people without any obligation. Few companies resist this sales pitch.

As for other cases of fraud and deceit practiced by employment agencies, it is impossible to compile a complete catalogue: Job brokers who specialize in one type of personnel—like temporary help, teachers, domestics, top executives—have developed their own peculiar ways of exploiting their part of the labor market. But a list of the most common swindles would include:

Exorbitant fees. More than half the states have passed laws setting the maximum fees an agency can charge—usually no more than 60% of the first month's salary. Despite these laws, agencies may find ways of extorting more. Sometimes they add illegal surcharges for "special services," such as "counseling" or "advice on preparing a résumé." Often they calculate the worth of a company's fringe benefits and consider that as part of the applicant's wages. Another ploy is used in those states where there is a sliding scale of fees: The agency upgrades the applicant's job classification. Thus, if a state allows an agency to charge more for placing someone in a skilled position, a "freight handler" will be designated as a "skilled worker" if his job so much as includes reading labels on packages.

Registration fees. Some agencies charge fees to all who apply, whether or not the applicant ever gets a job offer. These fees may range from $2 to $5, supposedly to help the agency cover expenses incurred in the applicant's behalf. Unfortunately, agencies that levy this charge often concentrate on attracting job seekers, while all but ignoring the other part of their business—finding people jobs. The U. S. Bureau of Labor has urged that all registration fees be outlawed.

Fee splitting. Prohibited in at least 32 states, fee-splitting works like this: An employment agency makes a deal with an employer that he keep an applicant on his payroll only until the agency's fee is paid in full. The new worker is then fired, the placement fee is divided between the agency and the employer, and a new worker is sent over. This way, a job broker can collect up to a dozen times for filling the same job.

Inducing employers to fire employees. After placing applicants and collecting their money, some agencies then try to have them fired—so as to place someone else "more qualified," and thus extort a *second* fee.

Failure to return the fee. More than half the states have laws requiring employment agencies to return most of the placement fee if an employee loses his job within a specified time. This is meant to discourage fee-splitting, to stop agencies from trying to get their applicants fired, and to keep them from lying about their applicants' qualifications. Yet comparatively few applicants whose jobs don't work out ever see their money again, unless they actually go out and hire a lawyer. Applicants, naturally, are afraid to antagonize any agencies that might eventually get jobs for them.

Referring applicants to fraudulent companies. One employment agency, for example, recruited workers for a contractor who arranged to clean factories, office buildings, and warehouses. The contractor would work his victims like horses for a few weeks, then disappear, neglecting to pay his workers for their labor. The agency, of course, was getting a kickback from the contractor (*AFL-CIO News,* 6/8/63).

* * *

Yes, employment agencies exploit their applicants. But they exploit the employer as well.

It used to amuse me no end to hear the owner of some company painstakingly describe exactly the type of employee he was looking for. If such employers think that the employment agent on the other end of the line is listening, they are deluded. The need for a high turnover prevents an agency's giving much personal attention to any client's request. An occasional employer does complain that the applicants the agency is sending over are hardly what he had in mind, but he is immediately enlightened about the "labor shortage" and how "impossible it is to find good help nowadays." The truth of the matter is that many an employment agency is interested only in filling jobs and collecting money. Whether the applicant is qualified for the job is of minor moment.

Industry pays high for the job brokers' lack of scruples. It would probably surprise many employers to find out how many of the workers, sent by employment agencies, plan to stay only a few months. They would be even more surprised to learn that the agency probably knew about a worker's real plans, and may actually have encouraged him to make a job change. A large number of jobs are sold as "something to hang on to until a better opportunity comes along."

How do the agencies get away with all this? One reason: Agencies are virtually immune to public criticism. The press, energetically pandering for patronage of its classified pages, showers them with favorable publicity. A typical article repeats the success story of Snelling and Snelling, which has opened 230 offices since 1956 and for the past 2 years has been selling franchises at the rate of about one a week. These bits of free advertising, of course, fail to mention the complaints of the N.A.A.C.P. against Snelling and Snelling, or any of the other less savory aspects of the agency racket in general.

For example, 87 bills have been introduced in the New York State legislature since 1960 to cope with the employment-agency abuses. No newspaper has given a single one of these bills adequate coverage. Even those readers who have carefully digested "All the News That's Fit to Print" have been left ignorant about 84 of these bills. *The New York Times*'s neglect of 96% of the news is typical. After all, one New York agency alone—the Fanning Personnel Agency—spends over $65,000 a year on classified ads.

The *Times* goes a step further. It also distributes a slick, 65-page booklet sketching the agencies that advertise in the *Times,* bestowing fulsome praise on the "Highly trained specialists who are in constant touch with the employment market." Employment agencies have responded appreciatively to this kindly regard for their welfare and profit. The *Times* runs more employment ads than all other New York papers combined.

*   *   *

The unpublicized flurry of activity within the New York legislature is characteristic of the shotgun approach the various states use to deal with agency malpractices. Law is heaped upon law in the hope that maybe one more regulation will do the trick. But the lumbering legislative process never seems to catch up with the variety of abuses invented by the private agencies.

Besides finding ingenious ways of bypassing laws, job brokers have developed a chameleon-like trait of changing color with each new regulation. Employment agencies somehow change into "executive recruiters," which claim exemption from the law. The "vocational counselor" evades the statutes by not dealing with specific job openings. The temporary-employee agencies, like Manpower and the Kelly Girls, set themselves up as employers that contract out labor, and are thus able to retain up to 30% of their workers' wages.

It isn't easy for legislatures to pass any laws, anyway. The employment agencies have formed a powerful lobby, the National Employment Association, to "protect" their interests. Dale Hughes is the leading spokesman for these "employment agency folk all over America," as he calls the members of the N.E.A. He solemnly denounces "the mongrelization of the private employment agencies" by state regulation. "Any regulation," he lectures, "is objectionable to clear-thinking Americans."

The N.E.A.'s campaign to educate "clear-thinking Americans" runs into a lot of money. In one year alone, the N.E.A. set about raising $163,000 for its war chest, and 3 months later it appealed for another $75,000. And the N.E.A. uses its enormous wealth with great skill.

Take the way it tried to manipulate Senator Morse's hearings. These hearings were brought about largely because of the statements of William J. Mawhinney of the Washington, D.C., Better Business Bureau, who demanded stricter legislation to stem the flood of complaints pouring into his office. Called to the witness stand, Mr. Mawhinney said he was no longer connected with the Better Business Bureau. He also denied he had ever made the statements attributed to him. And he opined that the current laws were adequate. Senator Morse was perplexed. But further questioning elicited the fact that Mr. Mawhinney was now an employee of one of the Washington employment agencies being investigated.

The Washington employment agencies also raised a special fund. They imported witnesses from all over the country. Their lawyers pleaded for more time to study the situation. But Wayne Morse held firm. His report to the Senate urged strict regulation of the employment-agency business. The bill was introduced in 1962. It has been reintroduced for the past 4 years. Each time, the N.E.A., the U. S. Chamber of Commerce, and the other big-business lobbies have seen to its defeat.

The individual states have been taking their lumps, too. For over a hundred years, they have been wrestling with employment-agency abuses. In 1915, the State of Washington, by public referendum, outlawed all employment agencies. The Supreme Court, however, declared that the vote was an unconstitutional restraint on free trade. More recently, Montana enacted a law setting the maximum placement fee at $3. But, as Mr. Hughes of the N.E.A. frankly admitted to Wayne Morse's committee, these regulations "are openly and notoriously violated with the tacit approval of the state licensing bureau."

Since the individual states have been unable to handle employment agencies effectively, Federal regulations are clearly called for. The fact that employment agencies are a multi-million-dollar industry that operates across state lines and even national boundaries makes Federal control a necessity. Certainly enough authorities are agreed that employment-agency fraud and deceit must be ended. Justice Louis Brandeis once stated that "the evils of private agencies are inherent and ineradicable, so long as they are permitted to charge fees to workers seeking employment." Justice Harlan F. Stone noted that "The business is subject to grave abuses, involving frauds and impositions upon a peculiarly helpless class, among which the exaction of exorbitant fees is perhaps the least offensive." Mrs. Frances Perkins, former Secretary of Labor, has written that "the business is one which lends itself easily to abuses and to perpetuation of fraud and extortion." In 1953, President Truman urged Congress to curb the "unscrupulous agencies [that] disrupt the labor supply and exploit the workers by charging excessive fees, referring workers to nonexistent jobs, and misrepresenting the nature of the work." And Senator Wayne Morse has eloquently stated that "No private business in this country has the right to exploit the weak."

* * *

Strong Federal action is still far off. In the meantime, many people would be better advised *never* to consult any private employment agency, *anytime*. They should go directly to employers. And then they should go to one of the best bargains the government has to offer—the state employment agencies, which are under the direction of the U. S. Employment Service. The state agencies are eager to find suitable work for anyone, no matter what his occupation or salary level, and whether he is unemployed or just looking for a more satisfying job than the one he has.

Furthermore, the Employment Service has now instituted a "professional placement bureau" for highly skilled applicants. These bureaus are manned by employment counselors who are college graduates and who have been intensively trained by the government. The interviewers freely use the statistics of the Bureau of Standards, and are well up on labor trends and the general employment situation. In addition, the professional placement bureau actively solicits job-orders for both the unskilled worker and for top executives. Any job hunter, or employer, who does not use the services of a professional placement bureau is throwing his money away.

That is how my wife got her job. No one at the professional placement bureau told her about the catastrophic condition of the economy; no one insisted that the job she wanted was not to be had in all of New York; no one even tried to sell her on the idea of looking into "this lovely position we have for a bright young woman as a trainee-clerk." Instead, she was referred to an interviewer at the agency who knew something about her field, psychology. First he found her a temporary job with a research project, a job no private agency would bother with, since it lasted for only a month. When this job was up, my wife called the State agency again. By this time, her interviewer there had found a permanent job for her, doing precisely the kind of work she wanted to do. The total cost to her: $0.00.

The moral is self-evident.

The Misleading Advertisements of Bayer Aspirin

By Louis Lasagna, M.D.

Over 3 years ago, TV viewers first began learning of a scientific study that purported to show that no pain-killer could surpass Bayer aspirin in efficacy and safety. The study had been sponsored by the government; the TV ads were sponsored, not surprisingly, by Sterling Drug Inc., makers of Bayer aspirin. The public's response to these ads, it is safe to say, has pleased the Bayer people no end. The company's annual report, for example, mentions the government's study, and also proudly refers to "a notable performance by Bayer Aspirin in the United States, where consumers gave our No. 1 product an impressive vote of confidence in the form of the largest dollar sales gain for any year in our history."

The story behind these events reads like a plot for the Theater of the Absurd. It begins in the late 1950s, when the Federal Trade Commission became concerned over the way pain-killers were advertised. Once upon a time ads for aspirin-type analgesics were moderately restrained. Bayer had a large corner of the market. Empirin, another tremendous seller, didn't even advertise to the lay public. Then St. Joseph's aspirin suddenly took over a good portion of the aspirin market for children. But the battle began in earnest when Bufferin arrived on the scene.

Bufferin rode to popularity because its advertising claimed it worked faster, and with less irritation to the stomach, than did "unbuffered" brands of aspirin. Though no one had ever shown in a clinical study that either claim was true, the new product had tremendous sales. In fact, the Bayer people began underwriting their own studies, and every study concluded that "buffering" was a worthless gimmick. Bayer's scientists periodically checked the composition of Bufferin tablets, and found, oddly enough, that the percentage of ingredients changed from time to time, without rhyme or reason. Still, none of the recipes seemed capable of neutralizing much stomach acid. (Alka-Seltzer is the only aspirin preparation that does.) Yet Bufferin continued its hold on a large part of the market. TV advertising of the most blatant sort also brought success to two other products, Anacin and Excedrin.

At this point, the Federal Trade Commission started building its case against the widespread advertising excesses. At first blush, the job seemed easy. Since each drug manufacturer was claiming that *his* brand was better and safer than any other, most of the drug makers had to be lying. (As one F.T.C. attorney cheerfully put it, "It seems to me that at worst I can lose only *one* of the indictments.")

Alas, things are not always what they seem. It would not be enough if the manufacturers could not substantiate their claims; the F.T.C. would have to prove that the claims were actually *false*. Accordingly, F.T.C. officials began asking reputable clinical investigators to check out the claims made for the various drug products.

At this point, my colleagues and I at the Johns Hopkins Univerity School of Medicine got into the act. In 1960, the F.T.C. asked us to study the pain-killing efficacy and side-action drawbacks of several aspirin-type remedies. Our first reaction, to be frank, was less than enthusiastic. It seemed likely that the drugs were so similar that we would detect no differences at all—hence the prospect did not exactly overwhelm us with curiosity. Besides, the scientific value of such an experiment seemed small. On the other hand the F.T.C. lawyers convinced us that the only way they could halt advertising abuses in this field was for independent investigators like us to reach just such a conclusion—that no significant differences between the preparations in question could be detected. So, as a public service, we finally agreed to perform such a study.

Within a year the study was completed. We found that Bayer aspirin, Bufferin, St. Joseph's aspirin, Anacin, and Excedrin were equally effective as pain relievers. We also found that after they took Bayer, Bufferin, or St. Joseph's our patients suffered upset stomachs no more often than they did after taking ordinary milk-sugar tablets. Excedrin, however, produced more upset stomachs. So, it seemed, did Anacin.

It was not until 1962 that the F.T.C. granted us permission to publish our findings. A paper was submitted to the *Journal of the American Medical Association* and accepted.

Then, around Christmastime of 1962, things exploded. The Bayer people wanted to purchase thousands of reprints of the *J.A.M.A.* article. Fortunately, very large orders for *J.A.M.A.* reprints go to the editor's office in Chicago for approval. This resulted, in turn, in my being contacted for permission. I refused.

Next came a visit from Dr. Theodore Klumpp, the president of Sterling Drug, makers of Bayer aspirin. In the pharmaceutical industry Dr. Klumpp enjoys the reputation of being a statesman. He has had long experience in the field and he once served as medical director of the Food and Drug Administration.

Our chat was most amiable. Dr. Klumpp argued that the reprints would be mailed to physicians only, and without further comment. Why not set the record straight with the doctors of America? I explained that it was our group's policy never to allow our scientific communications to be used for commercial gain by anyone. Dr. Klumpp said that he couldn't see things my way, but he would respect my decision. I thought the matter closed.

To my great shock, suddenly there began a cyclonic nationwide campaign of Bayer advertising, based on our paper, which included full-page ads in 188 newspapers in 98 cities, as well as numerous radio and television spots. At the end of the newspaper ads was an invitation to write in to the advertisers for free reprints of our paper.

The ads themselves claimed that a "government-sponsored medical team had compared Bayer with four other popular pain relievers and reported in the highly authoritative *Journal of the American Medical Association* that the higher priced combination-of-ingredients pain relievers upset the stomach with significantly greater frequency than any of the other products tested, while Bayer Aspirin brought relief that is as fast, as strong, and as gentle to the stomach as you can get."

My only consolation was that the Glenbrook Laboratories, the division of Sterling Drug responsible for the ad, would be embarrassed by its inability to fill requests for reprints. The *J.A.M.A.* had refused to furnish any, and making photocopies of the article would have infringed the copyright laws. I reckoned without proper appreciation for the ingenuity of today's businessman. Glenbrook proceeded to buy up issues of the December 29 issue of the *J.A.M.A.* and tear out those pages containing our article—the *J.A.M.A.* had sold Glenbrook 2500 of the 3300 extra copies.

On learning what had happened, I complained to the manufacturers. A Glenbrook vice-president named McGuigan blithely replied: "I am pleased to inform you that our supply is exhausted."

Bristol-Myers, makers of Bufferin and Excedrin, felt called upon to get into the picture after Sterling wrote a "Dear Doctor" letter to physicians calling our study to their attention. Bristol-Myers questioned the wisdom of generalizing from one patient population to the entire universe, and could not refrain from pointing out that the Bayer ads had elicited an F.T.C. complaint "in almost record time."

And so they had. There was hell to pay at the F.T.C. when the news broke. The study *and* the government were now being used for profit by one of the companies whose ads had *started the* whole F.T.C. crackdown!

The story since then has been one of total failure to stop Bayer's advertising campaign. Apparently the general feeling is that since most advertisements are inaccurate, and since Bayer's ads are not the worst offenders, why single them out for special punishment? The government's first request for a temporary injunction was denied by the New York Southern

District Court. The United States Court of Appeals considered the case carefully, and concurred.

The learned judges demolished the government's case by analyzing the ad as if their own skepticism were typical of what most people would think—even though the F.T.C. works on the basis that the ad must be read in terms of its impact upon the most ignorant and foolish of readers.

Perhaps the judges were correct in assuming that no reader would interpret the ads as implying governmental or A.M.A. endorsement of the findings (although I find that an incredible assumption). But one can take issue with their conclusions in terms of their own guidelines. Their opinion contrasted the Bayer case with a case in 1950 when some Old Gold cigarette ads were thrown out as misleading: "Although the statements made by Old Gold were at best literally true, they were used in the advertisement to convey an impression diametrically opposed to that intended by the writer" of an article about cigarette smoking.

As a writer of the aspirin article in question, I feel qualified to comment on this aspect. There are at least three claims or implications in the ad that rub me the wrong way. The first is that our study shows that the pain relief from Bayer aspirin is "as fast as you can get." *One can certainly get faster and better pain relief from a shot of morphine.* The second is that Bayer aspirin is as "gentle to your stomach as a sugar pill." My colleagues and I specifically stated, in a letter published in the *J.A.M.A.* on March 23, 1963, that we (along with almost all doctors) firmly believe that *any brand of aspirin can cause gastric irritation and bleeding.* Further, there are analgesics that are certainly *less* irritating to the stomach than aspirin. The third statement is that the 15-minute pain-relief performance by Bayer aspirin was better than that of the other products. We had specifically stated in our article that the slight edge in pain relief held by Bayer was *not significantly different from that of the other products.*

* * *

What is the upshot of all this? From my own standpoint, it has meant a great deal of time wasted trying to straighten things out, and considerable embarrassment over the unexpected use to which our study has been put. (Waggish colleagues still sidle up and ask how much I get from Bayer for each ad they run.) I have also become reluctant to participate in other "public service" experiments of this type.

From the consumer's standpoint, the fact is that no one can go very wrong buying Bayer aspirin. The Bayer people unquestionably make a fine brand of aspirin. And Bayer aspirin is cheaper than most of the widely selling drugs competing against it, although it is not the cheapest aspirin you can buy (and the cheapest aspirin in all likelihood works as well as Bayer).

In sum, no one was really seriously harmed by what the Bayer aspirin people did, neither we scientists at Johns Hopkins nor the general public. It is depressing, however, to learn that one of our most respected and powerful drug companies will stretch truth to boost sales of its product, and its "penalty" for so doing will be "the largest dollar sales gain" in its history.

The Bellicose Mr. Belli

By Warren Boroson

"**My** best recommendation," says lawyer Melvin M. Belli, "is my enemies." He has a good point. For over 30 years Melvin Belli has been mercilessly skinning the fat-cats and scalping the big-wigs of American society, and his enemies as a result are as formidable as they come—the most regal of economic royalists and the most princely of princes of the blood. Belli's powerful enemies have been instrumental in foisting upon the general public a picture of him as a court jester, a publicity-mad pettifogger, but the plain truth is that Melvin Belli is one of the very few genuine people's lawyers practicing today and the one living lawyer most fit to wear the mantle once worn by the great Clarence Darrow.

Belli's lust for strife is so insatiable that he almost makes Ivan the Terrible seem as timid as President Eisenhower. Just recently, for example, a new name was added to his drop-dead list: the former U.S. Attorney General, Robert F. Kennedy, brother of the man killed by the man killed by the man Belli defended. "Bobby Kennedy," Belli says with aplomb, "is the most vicious, evil son-of-a-bitch in American politics today. He's been bad ever since college. He's a hypocrite—why, he's no more concerned with getting civil rights for Negroes than the head of the American Communist Party. If he thought it'd win him votes, he'd see to it that all Negroes had to be whitewashed before they could enter an all-white school. Sure he wants to be President, but what he *really* wants is to become head of the universe. The *Pope* isn't safe with that little bastard around."

Belli and Bobby have never met—their only contact has

311

been a series of three letters Belli wrote to the then Attorney General about gambler Mickey Cohen, one of Belli's clients. All went unanswered. "Hell, I wouldn't write that many times to the Archbishop of Canterbury," says Belli. "He's arrogant, rude, and even ignorant of the law. He's the moneyed Little Lord Fauntleroy of government. Every newspaperman knows what he is, and even Johnson can't stand him, but everybody is too scared of the son-of-a-bitch. I suppose *I* can expect a knock on the door some night for what *I've* just said.

"The little tyrant ran roughshod over Hoffa, and there are a lot of things Hoffa's done I don't like, but there are some I do—he's done a great deal for unionism, he's built a cohesive organization, improved conditions, made the Teamsters a power. If Hoffa has done wrong, the law will take care of him —he doesn't have to be persecuted. It just shows that Kennedy doesn't respect our democratic processes.

"Bobby's different from his brother, all right. Jack bought the Presidency, there's no denying that, but he could have lived it down. Others have. I met him in San Francisco during the campaign and I was very impressed. Another year and he could have made a magnificent President."

Bobby Kennedy isn't the only person who knows better than to expect a Christmas card from Melvin Belli this year. Belli (the name is pronounced "Bell-eye," but he doesn't correct anyone who says "Belly") also speaks bitterly of Richard Nixon, coming right out and calling him dishonest for pulling strings for industrialist Howard Hughes back in the '50s after Hughes had loaned Nixon's family $205,000. And when I asked him what he thought about capital punishment, Belli shot back, "I'm against it because it doesn't do a damn thing to deter crime, only a brutalized community allows it, and we have no right to make that ultimate judgment. Why, when you listen to the creeps who want capital punishment you get the feeling they want to pull the switch themselves. Now that I think of it, though, the *main* reason I'm against it . . . is that Dick Nixon is wholeheartedly for it."

* * *

312

Belli particularly relishes mixing it up with someone bigger than he is. Take his running feud with that lawyers' social club, the American Bar Association. For years he's been twitting the insurance-company lawyers, John Birchers, and segregationists who run that organization (fittingly enough, his own membership plaque hangs on his bathroom wall, upside down). And when a few of the A.B.A. kingpins started thinking of drumming him out of the ranks (ostensibly because of his outburst after the Ruby-trial verdict but actually because, embittered by his abuse, for years and years they've been salivating for his scalp), and when it might have been smart if Belli cooled it a bit, suddenly he began shouting from the rooftops everything he knows and loathes about the A.B.A. "Over the years I've been at war with the few 'leaders' of the American Bar Association," he says, "because they want the American lawyer to be a conforming, second-rank professional—a sort of athletic supporter to insurance companies and big business. I want the American lawyer to be a leader.

"The American lawyer has lost all his individuality, and with his individuality his sense of *individual* conscience, ethics, and courage. He's joined a big firm and now he too has become big business. The individual lawyer, who to me was first and foremost a trial lawyer, has become the corporation lawyer, the tax lawyer, the accountant lawyer. He's becoming a ledger jockey for corporations seeking to evade payment of taxes.

"In the old days it was to the lawyer, the individual lawyer, that the community looked for leadership. When there was a Red Cross drive, a swimming pool to be built, an emergency to be met, it was the lawyer who gave leadership—not a banker or an insurance man or a businessman, as now. The lawyer was something *special* in his community. He stood for integrity as well as individuality, and he stood for imagination and courage as well as freedom of speech.

"What's happened to him? He's succumbed to American Bar Association-itis. American Bar Association presidents on the social circuit—after the *filet mignon* and the *petits fours*—usually have an inspiring subject for their talks: *The Defense of Unpopular Causes.* Yet these same men approve the abolition of law-school courses that would actually *teach* the student lawyer how to try an unpopular cause. A.B.A. presidents talk eloquently about the lawyer's duty to represent his unfortunate brother—until it comes time to represent these poor devils, the defendant in a child-rape case, a Negro in the South, a Communist anywhere in America, a *live* Oswald. Then there's the mad scramble back to the corporation desks, accompanied by, 'Sure he's entitled to the best defense, but *you* defend him—I can't afford to.'

"It's been my bitter complaint against the American Bar Association that, since its beginnings, it has not spoken for the *individual,* the grass-roots American lawyer. Instead, it's spoken for the corporate cash register, the Right Wing conservative, the status quo, the fat few, those who have against those who have not. It has spoken against the old child-labor amendment, and until very recently it spoke against *every* forward piece of legislation in Congress. Proponents of the return to 'McKinley's America' had but to call upon the American Bar Association whenever they needed a voice against progressive legislation. The American Bar Association is a rich man's club, run by insurance companies and by insurance companies' lawyers; it does not represent the individual practitioner, and it does not stand for the cause of justice. It has an ignominious history of fat-catism, Jim Crowism, and McKinley-ism."

* * *

If Belli is somewhat pained when he thinks of the modern American lawyer, he positively retches when he thinks of the modern American doctor. (The dislike is more than mutual: The name Belli is for most physicians synonymous with malpractice suits. Belli has tried more malpractice suits against doctors and hospitals than any other lawyer alive, and more successfully, too.) What irritates Belli no end is the medical men's conspiracy to protect their buddies whenever one of them commits a botch. "It's a notorious fact that you can't get

314

one doctor to testify against another. I don't care *how* flagrant the case is. Good old Dr. Joe may have come into the operating room dead drunk, carrying a rusty knife and wearing an old pair of overalls, but as long as good old Dr. Joe is a member in good standing, no doctor will testify against him. You can force a doctor to take the stand as a witness, but all you can get out of him is something like, 'Old Joe *did* have an untoward result in this case, but such things do happen often, and old Joe can scarcely be held to account.'

"The medical profession insists on setting itself apart, it tries to make itself immune from retaliation for careless and even criminal acts. If you ever actually *get* a doctor to take the stand and testify against another doctor, he'll be ostracized for life."

Another squabble that has noisily dragged on down through the years is *Melvin M. Belli v. the Old Holy Grail Insurance Company*. In a typical year, Belli successfully sues insurance companies for over a million dollars—they're the defendants in 9 out of every 10 cases he tries. As a personal-injury lawyer, Belli has, more than anyone else, led the way in getting American judges and juries to give reasonable awards to people injured, physically or emotionally, because of someone else's negligence—those struck down by drunken drivers, those who discover a week after an appendectomy that the M.D. left a sponge in their insides, those who sit down in theater seats (an actual case) onto which the previous occupant has defecated, those taken ill at cocktail parties when they discover (another actual case) that the "new" dress they are wearing smells of embalming fluid—because at the last moment it was wrenched off a corpse and returned to the store. Belli's brilliant court techniques, relying heavily on "demonstrative evidence" (the exhibition of artificial arms, prosthetic hands, skeletons, huge photographs of the plaintiff after some hideous injury), have been gratefully and profitably imitated by personal-injury lawyers throughout the land. And if all this weren't enough, Belli—on his own time—has given many, many helpful lectures to personal-injury lawyers, written books to guide them, and was even the moving spirit behind the formation of the National Association of Claimants' Counsel of America, a lively bunch of lawyers who exchange tips on how to get insurance companies to fork over. In brief, Belli is to insurance companies what—well, what Belli is to the American medical profession.

Having dealt the insurance people a few staggering blows to the midsection, Melvin Belli is now concentrating on roundhouse rights to the head. "The trouble with insurance-company executives," he says, "is that they forget that the money they have is money they're holding in *trust*. They forget that the money is the public's money, given to them by you and by me, to protect anyone that you or I happen to injure. You and I, God knows, don't want to shortchange cripples. But the insurance companies stupidly think of that money as *theirs,* and they'll be damned if they'll give it up without a fight. Did you ever to try to *collect* some money from a big insurance company?

"And do you know how much a stock-insurance company takes out of your premium dollar? Half of it. Only *half* of your dollar goes to pay for property damage and personal injuries. All the rest is eaten up by salesmen, agents, brokers in commissions, excessive administrative expenses, distributions to surplus, and payment of dividends."

Insurance-company adjusters are as bad as their bosses, Belli goes on, and sometimes even cruddier. Because they're underpaid, it galls them no end to give someone else what *they* regard as a whopping fortune. "They'll call on the plaintiff as he lies on his bed of pain, slip him the glad handshake, a cigar, a box of Band-Aids to put on his fractured pelvis, and 29 cents in stamps, and get him to sign a release waiving all further claims. The poor dumb plaintiff doesn't know what the hell's coming off. Or they make *ether* settlements. In an ether settlement, the adjuster waits until the poor bastard is just regaining consciousness, and *then* shoves the release and pen at him. (It's only illegal if you get him to sign while he's *still* unconscious.)"

* * *

For his latest blood-feud Belli has once again pitted himself against a tough customer—Dallas, Texas. According to a sociologist who served some time there recently, Dallas is run by an upper-crust that calls itself the Citizens' Council, a happy little oligarchy that knows everything it wants is right because it has the money and the power to prove it. Other recent visitors report that typical denizens of Dallas are mean-minded, mean-spirited yahoos, so poisonously ignorant and parochial that they begin frothing at the mouth when someone uses a word they don't know (like the psychological term "fugue-state," which so perturbed Ruby's prosecutor, Henry Wade), or when they meet up with someone who isn't quite convinced that Barry Goldwater is the brightest guy around or who has doubts that the Golden Age will be ushered in as soon as Earl Warren is impeached. As for the typical Dallasite's chest-thumping patriotism, the general impression seems to be that he'd vote for Fidel Castro for President if it would make him some fast dough. Dallas is the place where judges read comic books while court is in session, where jurors go to sleep while experts testify, where the prosecutor refers to a defendant as "the Jew boy" and cutely insinuates that the defendant's lawyer is a Red because, to quote Mr. Wade, "He writ a book about Roosha" (*Belli Looks at Life and Law in Russia,* by Melvin M. Belli). Maybe it was only a trick of fate that Oswald killed Kennedy there, but no other city in America would have been so appropriate. A year before the assassination, writer John Bainbridge in *The Super-Americans* called Dallas "the murder capital of the world."

Belli, having had his own dose of Dallas, fired away with a few of his trusty bellistic missiles. He told the Ruby-trial jury, "Thank you for a verdict of bigotry and injustice"—on national TV yet. He has publicly berated the city's "dictatorial" Citizens' Council and its "publicity-conscious" prosecutors, maintained that his client was "railroaded," pointed out that the trial Judge, Joe Brantley Brown, is locally known as "Necessity" Brown,* and summed up his impressions of the biggest city in the greatest state in the union this way: "Dallas is a city

---

* "Necessity knows no law"—Publilius Syrus.

317

of hate and shame, a rich, oligarchical, festering sore." Somehow the parlor Fascists who run Dallas (and most of Texas), the men who hired a public-relations man to protect Judge Brown, who let everyone know, apparently successfully, that they wanted Ruby convicted, and who through the plutocratic right-winger H. L. Hunt offered Belli $100,000 *not* to defend Ruby, didn't cotton much to such loose talk. Ever since the trial, the beady eyes of Texas have been upon Melvin Belli. "After I got back to San Francisco," he says, "I found that my insurance policies had been canceled, a book publisher had reneged on bringing out my *Black Date: Dallas,* my mortgages were called, my name withdrawn from official lists of lawyers, my credit was frozen, TV shows and lectures canceled. I'm not paranoiac, but it's those bastards in Texas who were behind it. You can't imagine the strength and power of that wicked city of Dallas—they're really vicious down there." Despite his vast experience with vendettas, Belli was genuinely awed by the swiftness and the authority with which the Dallas multimillionaires had retaliated, and also by all the hate mail he suddenly began getting from down there (a rather tame one began, "Dear Rectum"). He was, of course, about as intimidated as a bull someone has whacked across the head with a dandelion. As soon as he found the time, he sat down in his San Francisco office, erected a new motto on his bulletin board (DELENDA EST DALLAS!!!), and began furiously and joyously completing *Black Date: Dallas.* "Those stinking bastards," he promises, "won't know what the hell hit 'em."

* * *

Melvin Mouron Belli, now age 57, first gave the world a hint of his penchant for pugnacity when, as a lad of 17 growing up in Sonora, California, he sued his high-school principal. It was a remarkable thing to do, but Belli came from remarkable stock: Most of his male relatives were doctors, and his grandmother was the first lady pharmacist in the history of California. The *casus belli,* as far as the principal was concerned, was as follows: Belli had been named valedictorian at Stockton High School, but the night before he was to deliver his address he came down with an attack of drunkenness, and the after-effects were such that he was prevented from even putting in an appearance the next day. The principal, horrified when he heard the story, decided to withhold Belli's diploma. The young man visited a friendly judge for advice, slapped the principal with a half-dozen writs, replevins, and bench warrants, won his diploma, and realized he had been called.

Probably one would have to probe deeper to discover the origins of Belli's bellicosity and his sympathy for the underdog, but that will have to wait for the autobiography he's writing. In any case, he went from high school to the University of California at Berkeley and thence to law school at California's Boalt Hall. Even in those days he was quite a wheeler-dealer: One way he supported himself (his father, an investor, had gone broke) was by writing away for free samples of soap, shaving cream, and so on, then selling them to his fraternity brothers. Belli got his LL.D. in 1933 and began working for the government. His assignment: snooping on the Okies. He posed as a bum, got arrested dozens of times throughout the West Coast, and learned what he never learned in law school —that kangaroo courts still exist in these United States.

Gradually Belli built up a thriving law practice in L.A. and Frisco, and he did it simply because of the shrewd, painstaking, colorful way he conducted, and won, his cases. He has always scorned the "Boston Blackstonian in a Brooks Brothers suit" type of lawyer, and his own courtroom tactics are dramatic, surpriseful, imaginative, and occasionally a trifle hammy. His tactics have led the press, with wearying regularity, to characterize him as "flashy" and "flamboyant," two words he has come to loathe. "Reporters," says Belli, somewhat aggrieved, "visit me on week-ends at home, when I'm wearing a flaming red sports shirt and cowboy boots, then go back and say I'm bizarre and flamboyant. Well, I've never gone to court dressed like that, and whatever colorful things I've done in court have been for dramatic interest, to bring in adequate awards for my clients. I've got as much respect for the dignity of the courtroom as anyone practicing."

Another source of annoyance is that many articles about

him, even the admiring ones, make his court trials resemble scenes from the early Marx Brothers movies. This is certainly unfortunate, but perhaps unavoidable. One of his first cases, for instance, involved a man named Avilez, also known as the Black-Gloved Rapist, an unpleasant fellow sentenced to 400 years in jail. Belli, handling Avilez's appeal, was astonished by what his new client told him. "Why, he says the women would scream when he started and get angry when he stopped. Some of them would actually *assist* him in the act, then scream and call the cops and carry on like mad. Shocking!" Belli's spirited defense got the Black-Gloved Rapist's sentence reduced to 200 years.

Then there was the young fellow who, because his physician carelessly diagnosed cancer of the penis as a harmless old wart, had to be castrated. Belli gave the jury a vivid, unforgettable picture of the man's deprivation, pointing out that the plaintiff was 27 years old, had a life expectancy of 65, and, according to Dr. Kinsey, could have been expected to make use of his missing organ some 5929 times before giving up the ghost. "Ah, ladies and gentlemen of the jury," Belli sighed, "what value can we place on this? Can we place an arbitrary value upon a loss so devastating? Can we say that he should be awarded one dollar per occasion, or five dollars, or . . . ?" His point, made in an unusual way, was unusually effective, for the jury came across with $100,000.

* * *

In another case, now a legend, Belli was representing a woman who had tragically lost a leg. For a few days he brought into court a long, narrow package, about the size of—a leg. It was wrapped, ominously enough, in butchers' paper. After he had milked the situation for all the suspense it had, Belli began unwrapping the package—slowly, and with evident distaste. To everyone's relief it turned out to be only an artificial limb. But the jury was properly shaken, and had gotten a taste of what a horrible, *real* thing the accident was. Award: $100,000.

Another time, representing a circus fat man who became

paralyzed after an auto accident, Belli felt it would help his case if he hauled the fellow before the jury. Trouble was, he weighed 682 pounds (he was so huge that even X-rays couldn't totally penetrate him). "The logistics," says Belli, "were like landing in Okinawa." No ambulance was large enough, so the fat man was hoisted onto a moving van. At the courthouse, another hang-up: The elevator itself was too small. Belli was stumped. Then he had a bright idea: He rented a crane. "We got the crane boom going," he recalls, "the fellow was on the bed, and they had just given the signal to raise him up when the insurance adjuster raced over and said, 'Here's your goddam $10,000, now lemme go home. . . .' "

In another unusual case, Belli brought suit against a San Francisco undertaker. It seems that Belli's client was a young man who doted upon his mother, and when the old lady died at 99, her son determined that her body would be preserved like the mummies of old. So he persuaded an embalmer to do a whiz-bang job on her and paid him lots of money. The embalmer, a rascal if there ever was one, did a quick $39.50 job and pocketed the difference.

Later on, Belli's client began visiting his mother at the mausoleum. "I would go out to the mausoleum with my wife just to see how things were going," he said, "and we would sit around for a while and then go home."

After a few months the man got suspicious. "She was up in a niche in the wall, and I noticed a lot of ants and things crawling up the wall, so I got a-hold of the man in charge of the mausoleum and I said, 'What's going on here? Is everything all right with mother?' and the guy said, 'Sure, it's nothing, the ants come here because they're attracted by the flowers. I'll just spray them.' "

Another couple of months went by. Belli's client got increasingly upset. "I kept seeing more and more ants, so one Sunday I said to my wife, 'Let's get mother down from the niche and take a look.' "

The court record reads as follows:

Belli: And so then what? You got the coffin down out of the niche. Did you open it?

321

Client: Yes. The man from the mausoleum was there. You only need a screwdriver.
Belli: What did the man say?
Client: He kept telling us not to look, that we must be crazy.
Belli: But you opened it anyway?
Client: Yes.
Belli: And you looked?
Client: Yes.
Belli: And what did you see?

The cavernous courtroom was absolutely quiet. No one breathed. The face of the man in the witness-box became distorted with horror, and he let out a shriek so blood-curdling that the judge turned white, Belli himself leaped back, and everyone else in the courtroom shuddered violently. It was minutes before the trial could be resumed, and when it was all over, Belli's client was $10,900 richer.

Even outside of the courtroom Belli manages to be the life of the party. In 1957, for example, he introduced Professor O'Brien of the Harvard Law School to an American Bar Association convention in Miami. Dr. O'Brien spoke on the pitfalls of tax evasion, giving a salty if curious speech that ended with the line, "All I gotta say is, youse guys better pay your taxes." Professor O'Brien was later unmasked as gambler Mickey Cohen, just out of the pen after serving a few years for tax evasion. Needless to say, the A.B.A., like Queen Victoria, was not amused.

Partly because Belli goes in for shenanigans of this sort, to many people he doesn't project the knight-on-a-white-horse image that, say, Edward Bennett Williams does. Williams would never dream of palming Mickey Cohen off as a professor of law, any more than he would, as a lark, lead a delegation of tittering ladies into Errol Flynn's bedroom to gaze upon the actor sleeping in the nude (Belli did, in Paris, and almost lost Flynn's friendship). But Belli, as a human being, is as full of surprises as his courtroom tactics. A man who loves the Good Life, crêpes suzette, homburgs, and Silver Cloud Rolls-Royces, he has spent his career defending the poor and the helpless. ("Bankers," he explains modestly, "seldom get hit by trucks.") A man in a profession notoriously sedate and stiff-necked, he is a hard-core Democrat, a man so impulsive he hardly lets a day go by without firing off a poison-pen letter to someone or other, a man breezily accustomed to delivering such slanderous asides as, "————'s such a lousy lawyer he couldn't get an Archbishop off for overparking on Christmas Eve." He may be a prankster and even the S. Hurok of the legal profession, but Belli is also one of the great lawyers of our time. He has written no fewer than 29 lawbooks, including *Modern Trials and Modern Damages* (in six volumes), *So That's the Law, The Adequate Reward and Demonstrative Evidence, Trial and Tort Trends, Life and Law in Japan, Tort and Trial Yearbook, Criminal and Medical Yearbook,* and *Modern Trials,* this last a work universally accepted as a modern legal classic. In his 30 years before the bar, he has lectured to medical societies, law schools, and groups of lawyers in 45 states. His knowledge of medicine is extraordinary, even in this day of forensic medicine, and frequently he is called in just to shake the testimony of some medical specialist (physicians on the witness stand will argue with him, "Yes, doctor, but on the other hand . . ."). During his long career Belli has defended such people as Caryl Chessman, Ferdinand Demara ("The Great Impostor"), Errol Flynn, Ann Jeffreys, Maureen Connolly, Mickey Cohen, and Mae West, and a while back he won a whopping $924,393 for the widow and child of pianist William Kapell, killed in an air crash in 1953. Before the Ruby trial (and this will surprise many people) Belli had defended over *100* other murderers. More than 100 times he has gotten awards of over $100,000 for clients injured negligently, a record no other lawyer even approaches. His most historic case was a personal-injury suit he handled back in 1947. Representing the family of a fireman turned into a vegetable when his fire engine was rammed by a truck, Belli went all out to show that the fire engine's siren must have been audible to the offending truck-driver, putting 29 witnesses who had heard the siren on the stand and pinpointing their exact whereabouts on a huge aerial map. Up to then, typical awards in such cases were $20,000 or so. Melvin Belli was the man who brought in the utterly flabbergasting figure of $225,000. That case was one of the most important in the annals of American law, and by comparison it makes the trial of Jack Ruby piddling and inconsequential.

*   *   *

Melvin Belli has made many enemies and aroused lots of envy, but there is no denying that he ranks with Mike Fallon, Clarence Darrow, and Sam Leibowitz as one of the very greatest of American trial lawyers. Judge Theresa Merkle of the San Francisco Superior Court has said of him, "He is the best trial lawyer I have ever seen," and others who have gone on the record in appreciation of his ability and his achievements include William Prosser, former dean of the University of California Law School, the late Roscoe Pound of the Harvard Law School, Judge Michael A. Musmanno of the Pennsylvania Supreme Court, and last, and least, Judge Joe Brantley Brown of Dallas, who has been quoted as saying, "This is the most brilliant lawyer that ever came into my courtroom."

*   *   *

For people living on the Coast, this rehearsal of Belli's background is probably somewhat familiar. There Melvin Belli is a celebrity. Everyone knows about his three marriages and two divorces, everyone knows he keeps a skeleton in his office named Elmer, everyone knows that it was he who said, apropos of his efforts to get a divorce for Barbara Hutton and Prince Troubetzkoy, "It's practically settled—only a few million dollars is keeping them from being apart." Back East, though, hardly anyone had even heard of him before the Ruby trial. In fact, today the first question any Easterner asks him is, "Did Oswald really kill Kennedy?" The first question a West Coaster asks is, "Where's your next trial? I want to be there."

As an Easterner, I questioned him almost exclusively about the Ruby trial when I first saw him in New York. He was staying at the Americana Hotel, and I had telephoned him for an interview. It was 2 in the afternoon when I could see him, but he was still in his pajamas, the remains of a lavish breakfast—the kind you see in Doris Day-Rock Hudson movies—

lying on the table, and on a nearby bureau, stuffed with papers, a red-velvet briefcase. Once he had leafed through an issue of *Fact* he agreed to co-operate with a story, though when I eagerly pointed out that this article would give him national publicity, he gave me a scornful look and boomed, "I've had far too *much* national publicity already." Diplomatically, he added, "Actually, most of the press has been fair, very fair." I called to his attention the snide things *Time* had said. "Yes, well the *editors* of *Time* were fair, but their bastard in Dallas hated me. And I hated him."

In person Belli is not the overweight owl he appears to be in his photographs. He is, in fact, quite tall, as graceful and as athletically built as a first-baseman, and extraordinarily handsome. His speaking voice is magnificent, as delightful to listen to as the late Leonard Warren's singing (which it resembles), and he radiates charm, confidence, and happiness in being alive. Female jurors, I recalled, have occasionally complained to judges after a trial that Belli had "hypnotized" them into siding with his client.

We agreed to continue our chat the following day, at John F. Kennedy Airport, before he took off for San Francisco, and overnight I boned up on his background and prepared a list of questions. The next day he arrived at the airport a few minutes after I did, and I watched as the porters carried out his red-velvet luggage, covertly glancing at the name-tags. Belli and I spent about half an hour together, I jogging after him scrawling down everything he said, he striding along buying papers, checking the schedules, and ogling the airline stewardesses.

My first question was, "Would you have defended Oswald?" "Of course I would have, otherwise I would have had to hand in my shingle. I'm to hire to *anyone*."

Why did he take on Ruby as a client? "I was eager to take on the Ruby case because I believed then, and I know now, that Jack Ruby is a sick man, and I thought I could do something for him, for psychiatry, for law, for tolerance. The Rubys promised me a fee of $100,000, but the only thing I came out of that trial with was a stack of bills the Rubys left, their checks marked 'insufficient funds,' and the knowledge that our good common law can still be raped in some American cities. I didn't receive one cent in fees from them, and I don't suppose I'll ask for anything now, though I will submit a brief for the appeal. They can throw it in the wastebasket if they want to. Of course I don't blame them for getting another lawyer—I couldn't stay in Dallas after the trial, or anywhere in Texas. But I would do today exactly what I did then."

I questioned him about Ruby's future, and about the first trial. "Ruby very early gave signs of being psychotic, and anyone who wanted to see it could have. There's no question now —he's deteriorated. He's tried to insert his finger in a light-bulb socket, he's tried to bash his head against a wall. Everyone knew his conviction would be reversed on appeal, automatically, and they're all embarrassed as hell down there—they'd all like to shove it under the rug. Dallas is worse as a hate city now than it was at the time of Kennedy's assassination.

* * *

When I asked the old question "Did Oswald do it alone?" Belli looked at me with alarm, and began, "The fact that *you,* an intelligent man—" I hastily cut in that yes, *I* thought Oswald was alone, but an amazing number of otherwise-rational people seem to have doubts. *"Of course* Oswald did it alone," Belli resumed. "My investigating staff is better than the Attorney General's, and I know as much about the assassination as any man alive. Oswald was just a crazy man. He didn't know Ruby and Ruby didn't know him. I know why these rumors spread. It was because the Dallas police and the D.A. wouldn't quash them. I tried, and without prejudice to my case or the state's case, to get the D.A. to announce during the trial that there was no truth to these rumors. But the prosecution felt they could get some prejudicial benefit by encouraging these rumors—it made Ruby look like a monster instead of just the sick man he is. So these rumors, which hurt us immeasurably abroad, continued. They hurt us because it was made to appear that our law-enforcement agencies, local and national, the F.B.I., could not or *would* not report the 'plot' in all its particulars. There was even a rumor that President Lyndon Johnson, a Texan, assisted in having Kennedy done away with to succeed his office!"

Well, I asked, was there anything about the Ruby trial that "won't come out in our lifetimes"? "No, no, a thousand times no!" he roared. "That was a horse's ass thing for Justice Warren to say." He did add, nonetheless, that there *was* something most people don't know, namely, that the night before the shooting a Dallas policeman and his girl friend spoke to Ruby, trying to get him to approve of the idea of having Oswald lynched. "They picked on Ruby because they knew what a weak-minded guy he was. The cop and his girl just disappeared, and I could never locate them, so I didn't mention them at the trial."

My next question dealt with the proposal—supported by Prof. Sheldon Glueck of the Harvard Law School and psychiatrist Philip Q. Roche of the Pennsylvania School of Medicine, among others—that, when the question of sanity is raised in a criminal case, the jury should merely find the defendant guilty or innocent, and then a panel of behavioral scientists should decide the prisoner's fate. "I'm definitely against it," Belli said. "If the district attorney isn't bigoted and the judge is fair and honest, we'll get justice. The layman is as good as the scientist in deciding what should be done—I've seen too many psychiatrists who thought they could turn gorillas into human beings. The fact is, we have the best courts and the best juries in the world. We don't need new laws—our common law takes care of open occupancy, of integration, and so on. What we need are good judges, good D.A.s, and good lawyers. No other country in the world, I believe, not even England, has a better or fairer legal system than the United States has."

The current Supreme Court, Belli thinks, is the best in the country and the most humanitarian in American history. "Warren is no great shakes as a lawyer, or even as a judge, but he's a tremendous administrator. He has integrity and ability. The current Court has become the greatest decision-maker we've ever had. For good or for bad, it's become a second legislature in Washington. I say that not in criticism, but just as something in the nature of things."

It was 11:45 and Belli's plane was ready to take off. I got in one final question: "What's your next case?" "Oh, let's see, there's Ferdinand Demara, the 'Great Impostor' . . . Oh, by the way, did you know I once sued the San Francisco Giants? I went to Candle Stick Park one night, just to relax, and it was cold as the inside of an iceberg. They'd advertised radiant heating, but there wasn't any. So I brought suit. *Someone* had to stop them from trying to get away with things like that." That was all the time there was, so we shook hands and he rushed off to his plane, cheerfully waving good-bye.

* * *

Two days later, while I was continuing my research, I happened to run across a short item in the sports pages: "Melvin M. Belli, the flamboyant attorney, yesterday was awarded $1,597 after bringing suit against the San Francisco Giants. . . ." What really startled me, though, was the headline over the story. It was so appropriate, it seemed almost uncanny:

**Belli Victor
Over Giants**

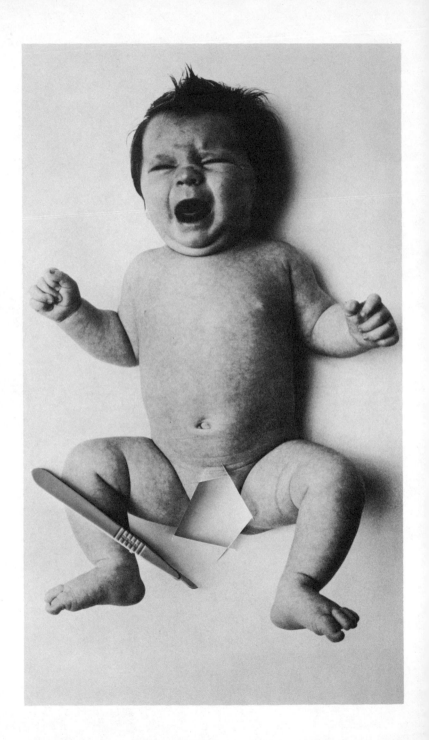

The Unkindest Cut of All

By John M. Foley, M.D.

O n July 20, 1964, the *Medical Tribune* published a letter from a Baltimore physician who called for the compulsory circumcision of all men seeking to get married. Indeed, he went on to demand Federal legislation requiring the circumcision of *every* male infant within the first 8 days of life.

Now, just why anyone would want circumcision made compulsory may seem puzzling. After all, circumcision is already a routine operation in this country. What need for legislation when 98% of all newborn boys, before leaving hospitals, are circumcised? When *Sexology* Magazine can maintain that circumcision has become a "status symbol," and when a physician can lament that "one has to lop it off along with the Joneses"? When just about everyone, including physicians who should know better, has bought the myth that circumcision in some mysterious way prevents certain forms of cancer?

One answer, of course, is that if circumcision were made compulsory, the circumciser would be protected whenever he happens to cripple or kill the little boy he operates on—a "complication" that is not so very uncommon. Another answer, I think, must be sought in the darker regions of the human mind, because circumcision is simply an unmitigated fraud. It is nothing but wanton and unnecessary mutilation. The annual 2 million assembly-line circumcisions in this country are a monument to the gullibility and stupidity of the American public.

For 60 years, a powerful and articulate minority in our

profession has tried to enforce a taboo against any objective discussion of the merits or demerits of circumcision. Over in Great Britain the climate of opinion is decidedly against routine circumcision, but here the operation has become a sacrament: To question its value has become all but unthinkable. The medical literature is virtually closed except to those who drool over the operation's alleged advantages.

Still, once in a while dissident voices manage to be heard. William Keith C. Morgan, M.D., of the University of Maryland School of Medicine has written in the *Journal of the American Medical Association* that "98 times out of 100 there is no valid indication for this mutilation other than religion. . . . Why is the operation of circumcision practiced? One might as well attempt to explain the rites of voodoo!" Peter Van Zante, M.D., of Iowa writes in the *Medical Tribune*: "Circumcision of a helpless child is a crime." Elsewhere he has said: "Circumcision is cruel and mutilating and actually should be outlawed." In 1920, a British physician named G.S. Thompson, who had once circumcised himself, later concluded that circumcision was nothing more nor less than "a barbarous and unnecessary mutilation" (*British Medical Journal*, 1920).

At this point, the reader may do well to examine his own conscience. If he has been circumcised, either ritually or surgically, and is chagrined that anyone would dare question the advisability of circumcising every single male infant, let him read no further. He has about as much chance of being objective as he has of growing himself a new foreskin.

* * *

Efforts to justify circumcision have been made since the very beginnings of history. The desire to mutilate came first; the "reasons" came later, and run the gamut from spiritual through cultural, esthetic, and finally medical.

This process of rationalization has culminated in the supposed relationship between the husband's foreskin and cancer of the genitals—one of the greatest hoaxes in the history of medicine. The theory is that the uncircumcised penis, because

332

it may generate a waxy substance called smegma, can produce cancer of the penis and cancer of the cervix (neck of the womb).

The only evidence in support of this theory is that Jewish men and Jewish women rarely get cancer of their sexual organs.

But granting that genital cancer is rare among Jews, circumcision is almost certainly not the reason. As Dr. Van Zante has observed, Jews in general seem to be more resistant to certain diseases than gentiles and to have a greater longevity: Genetic and cultural factors are probably at work. Thus, Paul Sherlock, M.D., of the Cornell University Medical College is convinced that ulcerative colitis and regional enteritis are *more* common among Jews because these diseases have a genetic basis (*Medical Tribune,* 3/9/66).

That the lower incidence of penile and cervical cancer in Jews is genetic or cultural seems perfectly clear when one examines the incidence of genital cancer in other ethnic groups.

In Finland, fewer than one man in a thousand is circumcised, yet the incidence of penile cancer in Finnish men is less than in Americans. Finnish women also have less cancer of the cervix than American women.

In Java, the Moslems are ritually circumcised, yet Java has one of the highest incidences of cancer of the penis in the world.

In Ethiopia, Coptic women have a high incidence of cervical cancer, although 90% of Coptic men are circumcised in infancy.

In India, the Parsees are not circumcised. Yet the Parsees have one of the lowest incidences of penile and cervical cancer in the world.

Further evidence that circumcision is not linked with cancer comes from tests of human smegma. In 1942, the National Cancer Institute conducted careful experiments and found that smegma had no carcinogenic effect whatsoever. This test was duplicated in 1963 on a more extensive scale by Dr. D.G. Reddy and others, with the same conclusions. Negative results have also been obtained in a number of other experiments ("Circumcision in Infancy," Charles Weiss, M.D., *Clinical Pediatrics*, 1964). In addition, if smegma *were* carcinogenic, the use of a contraceptive sheath would lower the incidence of cervical cancer in women. Studies have shown that it doesn't (*Journal of the American Medical Women's Association*, 1962).

Finally, control groups of circumcised and uncircumcised gentiles have been studied, and cervical cancer has not been correlated with the presence or absence of the foreskin in male sexual partners (*American Journal of Obstetrics and Gynecology*, 1958).

Yet even if circumcision and penile cancer *were* connected, this might not be justification enough to warrant circumcision. As Dr. Morgan points out, "this is an uncommon form of cancer and generally has a fairly good prognosis. Appendicitis causes many more deaths every year in the United States than does cancer of the penis, but nobody yet recommends routine appendectomy." Dr. Van Zante gives a more graphic analogy: "Why not amputate all female breasts to avoid mammary cancer?"

Well, does circumcision at least prevent venereal disease? Thirty years ago, routine circumcision was being urged for just this reason. Today, our circumcised teen-agers have the highest V.D. rates in history. Dr. Morgan adds: "Any U.S. or British physician with experience in North Africa or the Levant [where circumcision is common] knows that the Middle East has a venereal disease rate which is second to none."

Does circumcision prevent phimosis, the constriction of the foreskin? The answer is yes, but the fact is that true phimosis, as every physician knows, is extremely rare.

Does circumcision lead to a more hygienic penis? The answer, again, is yes. Except that the ears also collect dirt. Should they also be lopped off? "Soap and water," writes Dr. Morgan, "work wonders with the body's other orifices and appendages, and there would seem to be no reason to doubt their efficacy with respect to the foreskin." And while it is true that genital cancer may someday be linked with lack of cleanliness, Dr. Van Zante points out: "The male should be taught cleanliness, and if he follows this, I doubt that the noncircumcised male will contribute any greater percentage of penile and cervical cancer than the circumcised male."

Dr. Morgan's conclusion is the only conclusion possible: "There are a variety of reasons advanced in favor of circumcision, most of which are unconvincing when critically examined."

* * *

Since circumcision has practically nothing to recommend it, an important question is: Why has it become a routine operation? A few physicians go so far as to suggest that money may have something to do with it. Dr. Van Zante asks rhetorically: "Don't you think that the doctor delivering the baby thinks more about the $10 or $15 surgical fee he'll get than the possible after-effects?"

My own view is: Circumcision provides a convenient and socially acceptable outlet for the perverted component of the circumciser's libido. I have had personal experience with the psychopathology that underlies the wish to circumcise. The pitiful wails of the suffering infant are all too often the background for lewd and obscene commentary by the obstetrician to his audience of nurses. Several years ago I saw an infant born with multiple deformities. He could not live more than a few months at most, but to add to his miseries, this unfortunate bit of humanity had to undergo a thorough circumcision.

I have seen two medical students fight over the privilege of doing circumcisions on the newborn, although these same students showed neither interest in nor aptitude for opening boils or doing other surgical tasks.

In 1951, I witnessed an autopsy on an infant who had died from an infected circumcision—a death rendered even more tragic because the mother had tried to persuade the obstetrician to spare her infant this ordeal.

Dr. Alexander Schaffer, a noted pediatrician, tells with horror of a case in which an infant was being delivered as a frank breech (buttocks first). Before delivering the baby, and just as the penis came into view, the obstetrician seized it and circumcised it. That obstetrician, I would say, may be capable. He may be an all-round fine fellow. But sexually I say he is a monster. And I say that one of the reasons why circumcision is so common in this country stems from the sadism of the crypto-pervert.

My viewpoint is not very novel, though, for psychiatrists have long been agreed that circumcision is basically a punitive act. According to Dr. Karl Menninger, for instance, the original and basic purpose of circumcision was to serve as a symbol of castration, and the practice was initiated by fathers—to punish their sons for whatever incestuous feelings they might have for their mothers.

Another explanation for the prevalence of circumcision: latent female antagonism toward the penis. To quote Dr. Morgan: "Perhaps not the least of the reasons why American mothers seem to endorse the operation with such enthusiasm is the fact that it is one way an intensely matriarchal society can permanently influence the physical characteristics of its males." I myself do not doubt that among the biggest boosters of circumcision are neurotic females, whose unhappy sex lives prompt them to injure a man where he feels it most.

One could go further and consider the obstetrician: Perhaps the same stimulus that drove him into the traditionally feminine role of midwife is also responsible for his attack upon the penis. However, in all fairness, it should be pointed out that these male midwives know very little about the penis and, of all physicians, are surely the least competent to decide about circumcision. Besides, the obstetrician rarely sees the hemorrhage, the infection, and the deformities that sometimes result from his handiwork—these are the lot of the emergency-room staff, the pediatrician, the urologist, and the plastic surgeon.

Others who can be counted on the side of the circumcisers are:

A. Certain Christian clergymen, who are quick to point out that Jesus Christ submitted to circumcision. (They are not so quick to point out that Jesus also submitted to crucifixion.) The Roman Catholic Church solemnly celebrates the Feast of the Circumcision on January 1.

B. Homosexuals, who—according to psychiatrists—are in dire fear of being castrated. No doubt it pleases them when others, instead of themselves, submit to an operation that is similar.

C. Anti-Semitic Jews, ashamed of their mark and eager to make it universal.

D. All men, including physicians, who have already been circumcised. To paraphrase an expression, they suffer from "foreskin envy." Cut off a man's tonsils and it does not affect his feelings toward his neighbor's tonsils, but cut off his foreskin and his neighbor's foreskin becomes the object of envy and hatred. The circumcised have always behaved as if their circumcision were a stigma of inferiority. Jew, Moor, and Turk forced circumcision on servants, slaves, and whole nations of conquered people.

Because the motivations of the foreskin-phobes are so irrational, these people are hard to combat. The introduction of routine circumcision as a "medical" measure at the turn of the century aroused vigorous opposition within the profession. Dr. Warren Stone Bickham, an eminent surgeon, declared that circumcision was a disgrace and a discredit to the surgeon responsible. Nonetheless by 1920 the opposition had dwindled, and the fanatical circumcisers were in possession of the field. The opponents of circumcision failed because they did not understand the motives of the circumcisers and therefore could not grapple with them.

* * *

So far, I have considered the "medical benefits" of circumcision and explored the possible motives of those who favor circumcision. Now I want to consider the harmful consequences of the operation.

The circumcision of a newborn boy is a spectacle so appalling and revolting in its cruelty that, on their first encounter with the ordeal, many robust medical students faint. The infant is tied down securely to a circumcision board, with his genitals exposed. Next, the entire foreskin and much of the penile skin is pulled through a clamp, and as the clamp's screw is tightened, the skin is crushed off. As much as 80% of the total penile skin is removed. In this country anesthetics are rarely used. The infant struggles and screams, and often vomits and defecates, before lapsing into unconsciousness.

As a result of circumcision, some infants die. Countless thousands are doomed to become sexual cripples. In 1958, a 4-year-old boy underwent surgery for an undescended testicle. The surgeon, noticing that the child still had his foreskin, just couldn't pass up this tidbit. The circumcision failed to heal, and 5 days later the penis sloughed off. The parents sued for $150,000 and settled for $80,000. In a similar case last year, the parents asked for $4,500,000. These are two cases that have come to public attention only because of lawsuits. In England and Wales, however, it is known that an average of 16 children died annually from 1942 to 1947 as a direct result of circumcision.

Dr. Van Zante has this to say: "Proponents of circumcision do not mention any of the ill-effects of circumcision. Duf and Ware state, 'Major losses of penile skin are fairly common as a complication of circumcision.' The child may get a meatal ulcer. The sensitive, exposed glans [the head of the penis] sometimes becomes infected with diaper rash. . . . Occasionally a babe, especially of hemophiliac parents, bleeds to death."

Dr. Weiss mentions these other possible complications: sepsis, eczema of the glans and meatus, meatal stenosis, surgical adhesions, interference with nutrition, edema of local tissues, seepage of blood with resulting anemia, and injuries of the glans or scrotal skin.

Dr. John Van Duyn of Georgia, a plastic surgeon, has complained that often circumcisions are performed by young interns, and after they perform a few circumcisions, they are left unsupervised. "Unless the operator is competent and care is exercised," he writes, "there is always the possibility of damage from poor technique."

Dr. Van Duyn goes on: "A short time ago, I was called upon to split-graft the penis of a newborn where too much skin had been inadvertently removed, and in reporting this case

338

found that this error had occurred in a number of other instances.

"In another case, involving the incorrect use of a circumcision clamp in an infant, the glans was found gangrenous on removal of the clamp and was subsequently lost.

"There is also the distinct danger from hemorrhage, especially if the baby is placed in a prone position and supervision is minimal. In a near fatality from this cause, of which I have firsthand knowledge . . . a growing puddle of blood beneath the baby was not discovered for a considerable time."

* * *

Another hazard of circumcision is the possible diminution of sexual pleasure. Only the circumcised refer to the foreskin as a "useless appendage." The intact penis is an instrument admirably suited for its natural purpose—which is *not* simply to serve as a waterspout.

During a boy's growth, the foreskin protects the sensitive glans. Normally the surface of the glans is composed of a smooth, glistening membrane only a few cells in thickness. The surface cells are alive, and naked nerve-endings are distributed among these cells. After circumcision, when the glans is exposed to soiled diapers and rough clothing, this membrane becomes 10 times thicker, and the free nerve-endings disappear. The surface becomes covered with an adherent layer of dead cells, rough, dry, and insensitive.

For the mature man, the foreskin provides a covering during erection, when the organ increases in bulk from six to eight times. In coitus, it rolls back to expose the sensitive glans. And especially when the vagina is snug, this elastic covering promotes sexual satisfaction: It enables the penis to penetrate smoothly and without friction.

A number of students have confirmed that the uncircumcised man has a sexual advantage over the circumcised. For instance, Martin L. Edwards Sr., M.D., a Texas physician, writes: "I have counselled with many married men who are circumcised, and this alone has been a great drawback between man and wife."

On the other hand, Dr. William H. Masters and Virginia E. Johnson, in their recent book *Human Sexual Response,* call it a "phallic fallacy" to believe that the man who is circumcised is at a sexual disadvantage. But a close reading of their book makes their conclusion seem erroneous.

To begin with, they maintain that it is a widespread belief that the uncircumcised man has better ejaculatory control than the man who is circumcised—because his glans is *less* sensitive than the circumcised man's. Medical opinion, actually, is just the opposite: The man with his original foreskin has a glans that is *particularly* sensitive.

In their book they also state: "A limited number of the male study-subject population was exposed to a brief clinical experiment designed to prove the false premise of excessive sensitivity of the circumcised glans." Experiments on 35 men in each category demonstrated no "clinically significant difference" in sensitivity of the glans.

Let me suggest that when an experiment "is designed to prove the false premise" of some belief or other, even if it uses a "limited" number of subjects in a "brief" experiment, its outcome is really not in doubt.

Aside from its lack of objectivity, the basic fault of the experiment Dr. Masters and Mrs. Johnson describe is that no mention is made of when the circumcised men were circumcised. The fact is that if circumcision is delayed until adult life, degenerative changes are minimal. The glans does not suffer such a profound loss of sensitivity, and the penis gets a "tailored fit."

But even if there is no sexual advantage to having one's original foreskin, and even were complications not so numerous, there would still be other dangers attendant upon circumcision—psychological dangers.

The reason that anesthetics are rarely used on infants undergoing circumcision is that—in addition to the possible danger—it has been taken for granted that infants are not sensitive to pain. Recent experiments, and contemporary opinion, however, flatly contradict this.

Charles Weiss, M.D., of the Albert Einstein Medical Center in Philadelphia, states: "Experimental psychologists and physiologists who employed the techniques of pin-pricking or applied medical electric shock to different parts of the body have demonstrated that sensitivity in neonates increases sharply within the first four days of life."

A Leipzig pediatrician, Prof. A. Peiper, states: "I have not the slightest doubt that a newborn infant is definitely sensitive to pain."

A London physician, A.W. Wilkinson, M.D., states: "I do not think there is any doubt that infants in the first week of life are sensitive to pain because, when inadequately anesthetized, they respond very sharply to an incision with a knife."

Since infants apparently do feel the pain of circumcision, no wonder that a number of psychiatrists—including Freud—have held that circumcision must leave severe scars on the personality. Recently Dr. René A. Spitz observed: "I find it difficult to believe that circumcision, as practiced in our hospitals, would not represent stress and shock of some kind. Nobody who has witnessed the way these infants are operated on without anesthesia, the infant screaming in manifest pain, can reasonably deny that such treatment is likely to leave traces of some kind on the personality. This is one of the cruelties the medical profession thoughtlessly inflicts on infants, just because these cannot tell what they suffer."

One possible result of circumcision is impotence: Impotence seems to be frequent in circumcised men, but rare among the uncircumcised. Problem-masturbation is also as common among the circumcised as it is rare among the uncircumcised—the exposed glans explains it.

Then too, homosexuality also seems to be related to circumcision. First to report this was Melitta Schmideberg (*Psychoanalytic Review,* 1948), who treated two patients, homosexuals, who had been circumcised. In one of them, "The resentment and fear of his mother associated with circumcision was an important factor in the development of his homosexuality." More recently, a study was made of admissions to a large Naval hospital. Of all admissions, 32% had been circumcised. Of all admissions with the diagnosis of "overt homosexuality,"

100% had been circumcised. Before he died, Dr. Alfred Kinsey intended to investigate the relationship between circumcision and homosexuality.

Unfortunately, one cannot be sure about all the possible psychological illnesses that can be traced back to circumcision. As Dr. Spitz has observed, "Characteristically, no research seems ever to have been done on developmental and personality differences between a group of circumcised and one of uncircumcised infants."

* * *

Finally, in addition to the physical and psychological harm done by circumcision, there is the societal harm.

It is a truism in psychoanalytic literature that circumcision is a major cause of anti-Semitism.

Circumcision, in the unconscious, is confused with castration. Thus, in *Man Against Himself,* Dr. Menninger writes: "I could cite many illustrations from psychiatric practice to show how, in the unconscious, circumcision and castration are equated. Because the fear of cutting in connection with the genitals is so widespread, and apparently so basic in the formation of character, any surgery in connection with the genitals is apt to be associated with strong emotional feeling which psychoanalysts, on the basis of their daily experiences with the language of the unconscious, ascribe to the 'castration threat,' i.e., the fear that the genitals are to be irremediably injured."

How do the Jews fit in? To impressionable Christian children, circumcision is considered mutilation of the genitals—and Jews are identified with the practice. Freud himself thought that the castration complex was "the deepest unconscious root of anti-Semitism; for even in the nursery little boys hear that a Jew has something cut off his penis."

Not surprisingly, in-depth interviews with antisemites have revealed that many of them have a deep fear of being castrated. Some 100 anti-Semitic students studied by Else Frenkel-Brunswik and R. Nevitt Sanford (*Anti-Semitism: A Social Disease,* 1946) betrayed "unconscious inferiority feelings centering mainly about the castration complex." To them, the

Jews, the symbol of the circumciser-castrator, automatically became an object of hate and fear. Dr. Nathan W. Ackerman, in *Anti-Semitism and Emotional Disorder* (1950), cites a patient who told him: "I can't understand why so many gentiles are circumcised. That's what the Jews did to America. Their mission is to circumcise every single Christian in the country." Asked by a *Fact* staffer if he had been circumcised, Nazi leader George Lincoln Rockwell became upset: "I won't answer any such degrading question as that." Rockwell evinced his ready confusion of circumcision and castration by adding: "As far as the Jews are concerned, it isn't thorough enough. They should cut about 5 inches more off."

Many psychiatrists, Jews among them, are therefore eager that Jews give up the practice of circumcision. C.G. Schoenfeld, writing in the *Psychoanalytic Review* (1966), acknowledges that because circumcision is "a fundamental tenet of Judaism . . . Jews can hardly be expected to renounce circumcision readily—or indeed at all." But he goes on:

Nevertheless, the tenets of religions do change (consider, for example, the results of the recent Ecumenical Council of the Catholic Church). Hence, it is conceivable that knowing that circumcision helps to engender anti-Semitism will have an effect upon Jews, and as a result, upon Judaism especially if Jews also familiarize themselves with certain anthropological and psychoanalytic studies and discoveries regarding circumcision.

For one thing, Jews ought to be aware that circumcision, far from being a uniquely Jewish custom, was once a common practice in ancient Egypt . . . and, in addition, that circumcision is to this very day a common practice among many of the world's primitive peoples.

* * *

To recapitulate: Circumcision has few if any medical benefits. Any link between circumcision and the prevention of genital cancer is at best unproved. Circumcision is not only unnecessary but barbaric. It can cripple children, both physically and mentally, for their whole lives. And as for the motives behind circumcision, psychiatrists are agreed that they are irrational and punitive.

What can be done?

One possible course is to wait until the physicians in this country become well-informed on the subject. However, a fascinating survey conducted a few years ago (*American Journal of Diseases of Children*, 1963) of 126 physicians in Ohio revealed that 69% favored routine circumcision, 20% opposed it, and 11% were of the opinion that circumcision was not a "medical" decision and should rest with the parents.

The men who conducted the survey—Robert A. Shaw and W.O. Robertson, M.D.—were quick to point out that none of the reasons given were firmly established, and many were imaginary. "The results," they concluded, "cast reasonable doubt on the belief that the decision—'pro' or 'con'—is reached in any scientific manner."

The authors also were skeptical that the medical men will, in the near future, make themselves better informed on the subject. "One would hope," they write, "the situation might change in the next century—but do not bet on it!"

Another survey the authors conducted was of parents who let their children be circumcised. What were their reasons? I quote a few: "Thought it was a *mandatory* hospital procedure"; "Because it 'looks better' "; "Thought all males were circumcised"; " 'Everyone in our family is circumcised' "; " 'I thought it was a law' "; and " 'The doctor just did it.' "

Still, at the present time I think that it is parents who are our best hope. It is they who can campaign for a more open discussion of the problem. It is they who can prevent their sons from being circumcised. And it is, therefore, to parents that I appeal:

Let us be honest and fair enough to let our sons grow up to decide for themselves if they want to exchange their foreskins for the very dubious advantages of circumcision.

And I would like to remind parents of that perceptive remark of the great historian Henry Thomas Buckle: "Every great reform which has been effected has consisted, not in doing something new, but in undoing something old."

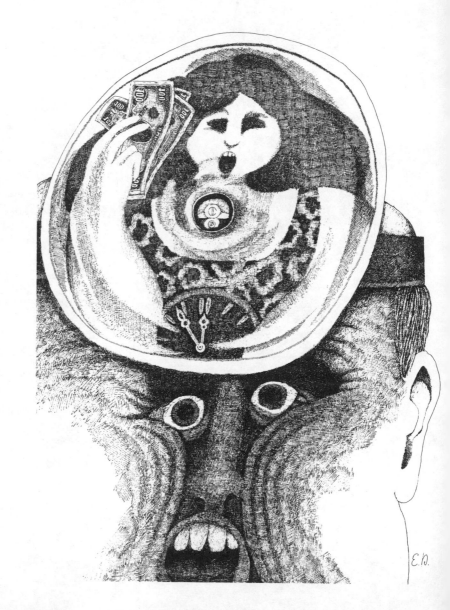

How a Middle-Class American Housewife Goes About Getting an Abortion

By Francesca Milano

I t takes an experienced doctor about half an hour to perform an abortion. The amount of pain involved varies
from patient to patient, but the operation is roughly
equivalent, in my experience, to a bad half-hour in a dentist's
chair. For the woman who, for whatever reasons, dreads the
alternative to abortion, the operation—in capable hands—is
thus really not so bad after all. The nightmare, the horror, is
finding a doctor.

I am a New York housewife with three children. Last
winter I found myself expecting an unwanted fourth. My husband and I decided that the least unpleasant way out of our
dilemma would be for me to have an abortion. Our decision
was made when I was only a few weeks pregnant, so during the
first part of our search for a doctor we managed to avoid the
panic of fighting against the calendar. Plenty of time, we felt,
to find someone safe, and perhaps someone whose fee would
not be exorbitant. There was no possibility of my leaving the
country: We don't have that kind of money.

Our first problem was deciding where to begin looking,
whom to ask. My obstetrician was out of the question. I knew
his opinion in advance: immovably opposed to abortion on almost any grounds. So we went through a list of our friends,
bypassing those who seemed too innocent of these matters on
the one hand, and too sordidly experienced on the other. For
we wanted something more than any abortionist. There were
three conditions: we must find a qualified doctor, an M.D.; he
must perform the operation nowhere but in his office; and he
himself must perform the operation from beginning to end.

We also tried to avoid asking those friends who might be inclined to talk too freely. After all, I intended to participate in a criminal act. But at no time did I have any feelings of guilt: My main emotion was anger at the United States for *making* what I was trying to do a criminal act.

Well, at last we asked three people for information and from them we got seven names and seven telephone numbers. One emerged as the most promising. A friend knew of several women who had been to him and all were satisfied; he met our three conditions; his price was only $300; and, for a wonder, he was almost casual about that fee—"Pay me when you can," he reportedly told one girl. This man was the first I tried. And tried, and tried. Never an answer. The phone number was listed in the Manhattan directory, and I tried it at all hours of the day and evening and for nearly 2 weeks. Never an answer. Later I learned that there had been no answer for over a year. The second doctor was, according to his nurse, ill and unavailable for a month. The third was on Lenox Avenue, and while I had not the slightest objection to a doctor who was Negro, it was not a good year, it seemed to me, for a white person to walk alone in Harlem.

The fourth man was also "ill." (There seems to be a high incidence of illness among these doctors.) The fifth was not a doctor at all. We were told he was a man who, in response to a phone call in what amounted to code, "would come out to the house and discuss the price of the furniture." The sixth was a doctor who, for only the cost of an office call, would—in response to the woman's calculatedly pathetic "I'm *afraid* I'm pregnant, doctor"—induce an abortion. But from that point she would be on her own: Another doctor would have to finish the operation. I came close to going to this man when time suddenly became important and all our other avenues turned into dead ends. In the meantime, there was the seventh name.

* * *

This was the legendary Dr. Smith (that is not his real name) of Benson, Pennsylvania (which is not where he lives). We had

348

heard of him and probably almost everyone in our position has heard of him: An elderly man who, so the story goes, once had a daughter die in the hands of an abortionist and who thereafter devoted his life to helping girls out of their trouble for a relatively nominal fee. It used to be $50 or $60. Now, we were told, it was $100. Dr. Smith had, during the course of a long life, served a prison term or two, but now he was apparently free and operating again. We knew he had a high medical reputation and that he ran what amounted to an abortion clinic, with nurses and anaesthetics and the most up-to-date medical techniques.

One could not make an appointment by telephoning this doctor. Our contact told us the procedure: "What you do is take the bus there. It's a very small town—just a few stores, a motel, a gas station. You just show up there and appear in his office. It's easy enough to find. Everybody in town knows him. You have to stay overnight. He gives you a shot the first day and operates on the second. I know definitely he was working 2 weeks ago." "But isn't there an address?" I asked. "No, but you don't need one. Just ask a cop."

A few days later when we found our way to Benson we asked, instead, the proprietor of a gas station. The town was not so small as I'd expected, but it was hard to find because some route numbers had been changed since our road map was printed. When we finally drove into the depressing little Appalachian town—all those hill towns seem determinedly ugly—it was nearly 3 in the afternoon and I was afraid we'd be too late for Dr. Smith's office hours by the time we found him. But the gas-station man gave us copious instructions and 5 minutes later we walked down a long, narrow hallway to Dr. Smith's small waiting-room. The only light in it came from a dirty little window and a fluorescent desk lamp directed downward on old *Newsweeks* and *Looks* and, surprisingly, a collection of pamphlets by the prophets of the Far Right. A formidable coatrack and about six chairs completed the furnishings. One of the chairs was occupied by a young and pretty girl who wore an engagement ring with the stone turned underneath her

349

finger. She was reading an article about Liz and Dick with every appearance of attention, and occasionally she smoked a cigarette with a good deal of calm self-possession.

For nearly three-quarters of an hour the three of us sat in a row, turning unseen pages, shifting restlessly, smoking and listening intently to the muffled voices that came sporadically from behind the door leading to the doctor's office. Eventually the door opened and a small thin man in a surgical coat, a man too young to be Dr. Smith, came out and told us in a regretful voice that we were out of luck. The doctor was not in, was ill, would not be available for 2 weeks or so, and anyway was booked for a month or two to come. But if we would wait, the young man said, he would give us some names. We waited.

In a few minutes he returned with two slips of paper, one of which he handed to the girl, the other to me. These men, he said, were "both good medicals." On my slip was the name and telephone number of a Baltimore doctor. The girl's slip—I saw it later—bore the name and number of a New York doctor. The names were incomplete, reading merely "Dr. Vincent" and "Dr. Charles." (These names are fictitious, but those given to us could similarly have been either first or last names.) "Just say you were referred by Dr. Smith," we were told. He again assured us that both were "good medicals," and the three of us filed down the long hallway again.

The girl, it turned out, was from New York too. She had come to Benson alone on the bus and accepted our offer of a lift back. On the way, she told us that she had gone to Benson a few days before and had visited Dr. Smith's office. At that time she too had been given the Baltimore number, and had called it. "But the doctor," she said, "just kept repeating the price—$500. He said it about six times and it unnerved me. Not just the amount—that's awful enough. I don't know where I could get that much. But that was all he would say—he just sounded so terribly eager for the money." So she had returned to Dr. Smith's office to get a different telephone number. I agreed that a pretense, at least, of altruism would be welcome in the circumstances, and added, "Maybe the New York number will be different."

350

I tried it the next morning, and got an answering-service girl. She took my name and number. That was early, around 10 A.M. Not until 6:30 that evening, after I'd given up hope, was the call returned. The voice was a woman's, briskly efficient, with a very faint Southern accent. The first thing she said was, "Who referred you to Dr. Charles?" "Dr. Smith," I answered, "In Benson." "Oh, yes. That's all right. We have to be very careful, you understand." "Yes, of course."

"Now then," she continued, "the doctor can take you tomorrow at either 1, 2, or 3 o'clock. The fee is $500, and you will have to come to Philadelphia." The next day was a Thursday, and we had made arrangements for that evening that could not be canceled without some awkwardness. Also, I still had hopes of reaching the $300-fee doctor. And I was dismayed at the prospect of leaving town again. Finally, my interlocutor, despite her briskness, did not inspire confidence. I was becoming slightly bitter over the fact that the disciples of the humanitarian Dr. Smith seemed to be five times as interested in money as he was. So I hedged a little: "I'm afraid that's too short notice, I can't make it tomorrow." "In that case, the next available time would be Monday evening at 8. Now. How will you be arriving in Philadelphia? By train or bus?" "Oh . . . bus, I suppose." "Then you will take a Greyhound bus to the terminal at 17th and Market, go up two flights on the escalator, and wait at the Market Street entrance to the terminal. What color coat will you be wearing?"

This efficiency was contagious. I found myself answering her questions with dispatch, and in a minute or two had given a description of myself—age, height, weight, coloring—and of what I would be wearing. "Now may I ask *you* some questions?" She laughed and said, "I was just going to ask if you had any." "The doctor is . . . ?" "He is a doctor and a surgeon. The operation will be performed in his office under a local anaesthetic. It will take about a half-hour. Anything else?" "I can't think of anything right now." "Well, if you have any further questions between now and Monday, just call the number you were given and we'll get back to you."

So it was finally settled. There was time: Although sev-

351

eral weeks had elapsed since my first attempts to find a doctor, I was still less than 2 months pregnant. And I still managed, in spite of my disappointment with Dr. Smith, to maintain a level of morale high enough to keep my family and friends from getting suspicious. It was a wonderfully great relief to have everything arranged, once and for all, to be able to say to myself, "Another 5 days and this will be over."

It didn't happen so easily.

* * *

The bus ride to Philadelphia takes 2 hours and the Greyhound bus leaves every hour at a quarter past. I had the choice of arriving at 7:15—uncomfortably early—or 8:15, dangerously late. I chose to be early, and took the 5:15 bus. The trip was not unpleasant. It was a mild day and there was a spectacular sunset over the Jersey meadows. A breeze ruffling the fields of ragweed made it look, through my greenish window, like soft, dense, downy fur. I felt sleepy and optimistic and not too nervous. We got in at 7:30, 15 minutes late, and for another 20 minutes I sat on a waiting-room bench reading a few paragraphs of a detective story. At 10 to 8 I took up my post outside the terminal. I was uncomfortably conscious of carrying a lot of cash (one can't, obviously, give an abortionist a check) and of being very much alone. Alone I remained. Two hours later I was still standing in front of the bus terminal. I don't think I need describe my anguish.

Early the next morning, back in New York, I got a phone call from a man who did not identify himself. He had been asked, he said, to "help me out," but he was going to be away for a day or two and would call me Thursday evening between 5 and 6. He sounded young, sincere, and scared. He did call on Thursday, but not until 7:30, by which time I was pretty thoroughly demoralized. We made an appointment for the following Saturday, and by that evening the ordeal was ended.

From this doctor I learned a few facts about the numbers I had been given in Dr. Smith's office. "Dr. Vincent" and "Dr. Charles" are of course nonexistent. Their numbers belong to answering services, and what they service is apparently a syndicate—an abortion ring. The reason I had not been met in Philadelphia was that the man there had "had a fatality." If I *had* been met, the doctor said, it would probably have been by a chauffeur who would have blindfolded me. "Blindfolded?" The doctor seemed to have a taste for sensationalism, but on further thought I'm not inclined to discount anything on the subject simply because it seems to belong to wildly cheap fiction. The fact is, I don't really know how close a brush I've had with extreme sordidness. That it exists I won't dispute. I am quite sure that there are thousands of women in New York who can tell stories a lot more hair-raising than this one. I can see that I got out of it quite lightly.

The doctor whom I finally contacted seemed honestly reluctant to involve himself. He had a successful practice and no need for the illegal fee. But he had apparently been told by the syndicate that I must be "taken care of." The syndicate had good reason to be worried. After my 2-hour sentry duty in Philadelphia, I was in no mood to feel protective of their interests. The doctor told me they demanded he turn over $150 of his fee (which was $500) to them to defray their costs. (Answering services cost around $15 a month.) He also told me a couple of disgusting little stories about enforced sexual activity exacted by two doctors from their patients. I cannot doubt that such things happen every day.

* * *

There are, I have read, nearly a million abortions performed annually in the United States, most of them upon married women. It is estimated that 5000 to 10,000 of these women die. (Not known is how many inadvertently kill themselves by trying to abort themselves with laundry detergents and other household soap-cleaners, though the *Current Medical Digest* says 40% who try it also die.) More than 10,000 women suffer permanent injuries.

This is a country that, for the most part, admits the element of choice in parenthood. Contraceptives are available. One needn't penetrate the underworld to buy a diaphragm. Why then should such an excursion be necessary if the diaphragm fails? Why should the privilege of choice be denied *then?* The laws are inconsistent to the point of absurdity. Eventually, they will be changed. When, as predicted, the population explosion reaches calamitous proportions (barring, of course, the holocaust), one can even imagine the large family's becoming the target of public-relations campaigns: "Is This Kid Necessary?" But between that grim future and our blessed times stretch years in which millions of women and girls will find themselves in trouble. Why can't the legislators of our enlightened democracy make that trouble a little easier to bear?

The Final Question

Introduction. At the root of the racial problem in America is the disgust and revulsion the average white man feels at the thought of a Negro's having sexual relations with a white woman, particularly if she happens to be the white man's daughter. The ban against miscegenation, Dr. Gordon Allport of Harvard writes in *The Psychology of Rumor*, is "the most sacred of taboos." St. Clair Drake and Horace R. Cayton have stated in *Black Metropolis* that "The ultimate appeal for the maintenance of the color line is always the simple . . . question, 'Would you want your daughter to marry a Negro?' To many white persons, this is the core of the entire race problem."

Public-opinion polls have confirmed this. Dr. Gunnar Myrdal interviewed people in all walks of life and found that "in the white man's rank order of discrimination . . . highest . . . is the ban against intermarriage and sexual intercourse involving white women" (*An American Dilemma*, 1944). More recently, a poll conducted by Louis Harris disclosed that 87% of American whites would mind if a close friend or relative married a Negro; 93% would mind if their teen-aged daughter dated a Negro; virtually 100% would mind if their daughter married a Negro (*Newsweek*, 10/21/63).

It's obvious that many people choke at the thought of intermarriage because right smack with it comes absolute equality with the Negro. Yet even this does not account for the fear and the revulsion white people feel. It does not explain why, just as the Jewish problem had its Final Solution, the Negro

357

problem has its Final Question: "Would you let your daughter . . . ?"

According to psychiatrists and sociologists, the reason that The Question is so electrifying is that it's not really one question at all, but four.

1. In our society, men generally become successful by forging their own careers. Women generally become successful when they *marry* someone successful. For parents, then, whom their daughter marries determines whether she's a social success or a social flop. And Negroes, as we all know, are rarely successes in our society: We tend to think of them as janitors, or window-cleaners (only 1% of American professional men are colored). Thus the Final Question also entails the question, *"Would you let your daughter marry a window-cleaner?"*

2. The American Negro is stereotyped not only as a window-cleaner. Many white people, when they think of the Negro, still summon up pictures of Jack Benny's witless friend Rochester, or the irresponsible Prissy in *Gone With the Wind,* or the jumpy chauffeur in all those Charlie Chan movies. Only recently have white people begun thinking in terms of Thurgood Marshall and Ruby Dee. The negative stereotypes have been ingrained in white people's minds by magazines like the *Reader's Digest,* radio programs like *Amos 'n' Andy,* novels like, yes, *Huckleberry Finn,* and—most of all—by the movie industry. Negro writer John Oliver Killens says,

I accuse Hollywood of being the most anti-Negro influence in this nation in the 20th century. . . . Hollywood has, more than any other institution, been responsible for the glorification of the South, past and present, and for creating the image of black inferiority. It created the lying, stealing, childish, eyeball-rolling, foot-shuffling, sex-obsessed, teeth-showing, dice-shooting black male, and told the world this was the real Negro in the U.S.A.

And so it is that another translation of the Final Question is, *"Would you let your daughter marry Jack Benny's Rochester?"* (It's interesting what happens when the question is changed a little: "If your daughter were Phyllis Diller, would you let her marry Harry Belafonte?")

358

3. Most white men are a little queasy about their daughter's marrying *anyone,* let alone Negroes. To a certain extent, all men are and have always been sexual rivals. They competed with their brothers and their fathers for their mother's attention and affection, with their school chums for their teachers', with other fellows for pretty girls'. When married, to some degree they lust after other men's wives and assume, knowingly or unknowingly, that other men reciprocate. But sexual competition with other white men is mitigated somewhat—by identification with them, by a desire for friendship with them, and by a wish to ingratiate themselves. None of these mitigating factors work well in the case of the Negro. Hence it is that the Negro emerges as the sex rival *par excellence,* naked and pristine. And therefore a Negro's having relations with a white man's daughter, his own precious virgin, is in effect a storming of the castle, the penultimate act of castration. Thus the Final Question is also translatable as follows: *"How would you like your daughter to have sexual relations with your worst enemy?"*

4. It's curious, but enemies of miscegenation habitually bandy about words like "immoral," "unnatural," and "incestuous." Indeed, in a famous legal decision even the Mississippi Supreme Court dubbed mixed marriages "incestuous"; commenting on this, Lerone Bennett Jr. called it "a strange choice of language." Perhaps the choice is not so strange.

By now, just about everybody is familiar with the scapegoat theory of Negro-white relations: White men project all their dark, evil impulses and fantasies—especially about sex—into the Negro. "Sex," says Dr. Allport, "is the source of heavy guilt feelings. . . . In the Negro, we perceive all the grabbing, climbing, and lewd behavior that we might indulge in if we let ourselves go. *He* is the sinner."

Less familiar perhaps is the fact that most men and women had incestuous wishes as children and still have them as adults. Dr. Irving B. Weiner, writing in the *Psychiatric Quarterly* (1962), maintains that "the existence of incestuous fantasies, both among children for their parents and parents for their children, has been repeatedly demonstrated. . . . Unconscious sexual seduction of children by parents, manifest in such activities as mutual bathing and allowing the child to sleep in the parental bed, appears to take place frequently."

The inference is clear: White men who have repressed their lust toward their daughters may have their memories refreshed when the Final Question is asked. Even if they have no daughters, incestuous fantasies toward sisters or mothers may be aroused. This shameful lust is then attributed to the traditional depository of the white men's shameful impulses: the Negro. *He* gets the hate we have toward our own feelings. And so the Final Question can be also interpreted as, *"Would you yourself like to marry your daughter?"*

* * *

Considering all it has going for it, it's not surprising that the miscegenation taboo is so strong that Calvin Hernton, in his *Sex and Racism in America,* can say that "before intermarriage becomes generally acceptable (especially between black men and white women), I am afraid there will be a bloody war."

Fact polled a number of well-known Americans about their own views on the subject, however, and it appears from this limited survey that the taboo may be easing—perhaps because the stereotype of the Negro is changing so rapidly, perhaps because the Sexual Revolution and the decline of Puritanism have done their bit.

Yet no one, it should be added, put the case *for* miscegenation as well as Mahalia Jackson once did:

Interracial marriage might bring about a closer fellowship of Mankind. I don't think it harms integration. It probably results in a better understanding on both sides. If a white man marries a colored woman and they have children, he is bound to have a better understanding of Negroes and the problems of being a Negro. The same thing happens if a white woman marries a Negro man. If they mingle, they will find that all human beings are the same.

—Warren Boroson

Nat Hentoff
writer

Of course I would let my children marry a Negro. I hope I bring up my kids strong enough not even to ask me when it comes time to make their own decisions. Would I object? Hell no!

Sure, I know there are Negro-white couples who get married for reasons other than love. They're rebelling, proving something to the world. But who am I to judge? If *that's* the way they want to work out their hang-ups, *fine*. You never know why two people get married anyway.

Listen, intermarriage is what it's all leading up to, and it's the best way to erase all traces of separatism and prejudice.

Henry E. Garrett, Ph.D.
professor emeritus of psychology, Columbia University

I think it would be ruinous generally to encourage intermarriage. Civilization is deteriorating fast enough as it is over here, and absorbing the Negro would just speed it up a little bit.

Genetic race differences which are well authenticated show the Negro to be very much lower in abstract intelligence than the white man. And his whole history of nonachievement in Africa, failure to develop any real civilization, failure to develop a written language, failure to domesticate an animal, and a number of other things would indicate that any marriage between Caucasians and Congoids would result in a general lowering of white civilization. Physically the Negro is strong (look at football and baseball players), he has a sense of rhythm, and he has an amiable disposition, but he simply doesn't have the ability to solve problems of a technical sort.

I don't think there is any way of changing the Negro. He'll remain a Negro as long as he doesn't mix with whites. In this country, of course, a considerable number of Negroes are mixed breed, as for instance Ralph Bunche, Thurgood Marshall, and the Rev. Adam Clayton Powell, that great man in New York there. He's almost white, of course, and I think he

361

could readily pass as a white man, but he gets a lot farther, politically at least, by pretending to be a Negro.

Ross Barnett
Governor of Mississippi

Well, I'm opposed to the whites and Negroes intermarrying, of course. You want to know why? Because their children will be mulattoes, and they will not be accepted by the whites nor the blacks. They'd be ostracized, you might say. Now that's just the way it happens.

No, that *isn't* all. It's just contrary to everything we ever stood for in the South, for the whites and blacks to court and go together, you know.

You're a white person, aren't you? You know God made you white, and you know why? He wanted you white and he intended for you to stay that way. He made a Negro black because he intended for him to stay that way. The good Lord was the first segregationist. You know why? Why, he put the white man in Europe first, he put the red man in America, he put the black man in Africa—all separated by oceans and huge deserts and mountains. Why didn't he put them together to begin with? Have you ever thought of *that*?

We don't stand for intermarriage down here. We put them in prison if they do it. It's just using good common sense. And people who are in favor of intermarriages don't have much sense. *They don't have much sense!* That's just the God's truth of it.

We respect Negroes highly down here, you understand that? We're good to them. We give them equal facilities in our schools. But we do not believe in intermarriage. We don't believe in that, and the one who does believe in that, they probably think he's insane.

Sheldon C. Reed, Ph.D.
geneticist, University of Minnesota

There's hardly any geneticist who thinks intermarriage will mean a deterioration of the races. To a geneticist, this is an insignificant matter, biologically.

I don't even think that Negroes and whites should avoid intermarriage because of the social problems. Intermarriage has been going on for 300 years and it will continue to go on, with or without the sanction of the law, and I would not recommend trying to slow it down.

Harry Golden
writer

How important a part of the racial problem is miscegenation? It's at the bottom. It's below the bottom.

The question "Would you let your daughter marry a Negro?" is only in the mind of the segregationist. No one else thinks of it. And it's a terrible, terrible degradation of the Negro. I've been in thousands of Negroes' homes, and nobody ever told me he desired white girls. First there's voting, next is employment, next is moving about as a free citizen, and so on. And I don't think miscegenation enters in.

Some whites think that all the Negro wants is some white gal. Well, it's a lot of bunk. Anyway, the *white man* has screwed Negro women all his life. He's screwed them and created a brand-new race, the brown race. So why in hell should he mind if the white woman is just as desirable to the Negro?

William Bradford Huie
writer

What would I do if a child of mine wanted to marry a Negro? Oh, I have no children. But I would be opposed to it. I wouldn't disinherit them, but I would be opposed to it. My personal experience today is that marriages, even in the best of conditions, are hard to make. I wouldn't oppose it on racial grounds: I'd oppose it on the grounds that that marriage would be less likely to succeed than one where people come from the same racial and religious background. I don't imagine there's a marriage counselor in America who would counsel a white and a Negro to be married.

Judy Collins
folk singer

Personally, I dig interracial marriage very much—if it's right. I mean, if the people are grooving with each other, that's all that counts.

Yes, it's an extremely important part of the whole racial question. Even the liberal who goes on marches has a funny feeling about racial intermarriages. When people get around to feeling groovy about such marriages, and stop thinking them odd, it'll be a big step, a very big step. But it's an attitude that doesn't wash away easily. It's as great a problem in the North as some of the more severe problems of voter registration are in the South.

Arthur Krock
political columnist

I have written that intermarriage is a bad racial combination in my judgment, and leads to the deteriorating of both races. I've seen evidences of it in the South.

I don't want to expand on this. I concede that it's a matter of dispute, and that some people can give studies in support of the other position. But I'm not impressed by these other studies, that's all. There's nothing more to discuss, because that's my observation and my conclusion.

Tallulah Bankhead
actress

I think intermarriage is truly personal, and it is up to the lady and gentleman. It has nothing to do with me, or anybody else as far as I can see.

Lillian Smith
writer

First, I think that fear of marrying outside of one's tribe is something that the human race has always had. It's basically a primitive fear that goes back perhaps 100,000 years to tribal life. And the fear of marrying strangers is still always there, in

364

the unconscious part of people's minds, to disturb them some-what. People have always tended to marry their next-door-neighbors and friends of the family, and so on. I would say that 80% of the fear of intermarriage comes from the fear of mar-rying outside your social group.

Now we come to this talk of intermarriage in the South, and much of it is hypocritical. I mean exactly that—hypo-critical! White men are always talking about intermarriage: "Would you want your sister to marry a Negro?" And yet many of these same white men have had children by Negro women. We have 6 million mixed children. And it still hap-pens, of course it does. It happened right down here in this country just 4 or 5 years ago. It happens everywhere.

What these men object to is not *mixed* children. What they object to is for the child to be *legal*. Now, I'm really giving it to you straight. That's why integration will lower the rate of mixed children. Because it will require marriage. And al-though our people have mixed children out of marriage very casually, they will not *marry* casually.

Integration is coming very fast, but it won't lead to an increase in intermarriage. People basically marry the image of their mother. I'm Freudian enough to believe that. A boy wants to marry a woman who reminds him of his mother. Therefore he will tend to marry one of his own kind.

So there's not going to be any amalgamation of the races and we are not going to be alike all over the earth. I *hope* not. Because it's in our differences that our possibilities lie. We all have the right to be different from each other. We don't have to be the same. Being the same, and being equal, are not the same thing. We don't have to mix and all become one color. And it would be a shame if we did. Why should we all become one color? Or one height? Such conformity would be rather horrible.

Now, when I make speeches, people ask me, "Would you want your niece to marry a Negro?" (They know I'm not mar-ried, so they say "niece.") I say, "I don't look at it that way. I want my niece to marry an intelligent, sensitive, healthy, tal-ented man. No matter *what*." Now I have some nieces who could take it beautifully. And I have some who couldn't take it at all. They'd crack up in 6 weeks. So I always say to an audience, "These things are very personal, and very individual, and I have some nieces to whom I'd say, 'My dear, I don't think you should try it because I don't think you've got the stamina to take this thing.' And I have other nieces to whom I'd say, 'Yes, you go ahead and do it and my blessings are with you. I know you're going to have a hell of a time, but I believe you're big enough to take it.' "

Westbrook Pegler
writer

I disapprove of it. I think the white race has advanced much further, so the white person has a heritage he must not sacrifice.

Ralph Ellison
novelist

Well, I'll say just this about miscegenation: It is not *my* problem—it is for *white* people to worry about. I believe that people should marry as individuals, and marry the person of their choice. Miscegenation is a personal problem, to be dealt with by individuals. Housing, jobs, schools are *political* problems. And interracial marriage is not nearly as important as these political problems.

The fact that there are social pressures on interracial couples has nothing to do with miscegenation itself. It's a serious problem for the individual who so marries, but if they're in love, why not? Let them take their chances.

If a child of mine wanted to marry a white, I would look at the individual he wanted to marry. Anyway, my child would know enough about the world not to have *that* kind of a problem.

Kenneth Clark, Ph.D.
professor of psychology, City College of New York

I don't know how important miscegenation is to the whole racial question. What's more, as a Negro I don't *care*—

except insofar as miscegenation laws reflect the total pattern of racism in this country and restrict the individual's freedom.

If a child of mine wanted to marry a *polka-dot* person, this is a decision my *child* has got to make. I didn't ask my parents whom I should marry—I *told* them. And if my child told me he was marrying a white and asked me for advice, the first thing I would say to him is, "If you're asking me about a *white,* then be sure your concern over race is not an unnatural one. And if you're asking me about a *person,* you obviously know more about this person than I do. It's your decision."

John Greenway, Ph.D.
anthropologist, University of Colorado

Speaking about prejudice, I used to live in Folcroft, Pennsylvania. I had built a house there myself and at that time it was a rather pleasant country town. And when I was in Philadelphia last week I took a visit to Folcroft. I had been rather shocked when I heard about this exclusion of a Negro family, and I couldn't imagine people there being so mean and prejudiced.

But on visiting Folcroft, I could see the reason. And that is, that a great number of Negroes from the South have moved in. Now, you know that these people are ignorant, they've got no education—we don't blame them for that, of course, we blame the whole complex of conditions and changes that were forced upon the Negro family. And I think anybody will admit that Negroes in Philadelphia live in an awfully bad section. And ever since so many Negroes have come in, they have completely taken over most of west Philadelphia and are now moving out to Delaware County. It reminds me very much of setting fire to a piece of paper: The burn spreads.

But it's not just a matter of Negro families coming in and acting like white families, but all the other concomitants of slum neighborhoods. That is, juvenile delinquency, bottles broken in the street, run-down houses. This has moved up almost to the edge of Folcroft. And the people who are living there are just defending themselves by refusing to let a Negro family move in. It gets finally to the point that one doesn't care about morality, about what is right, what is good for the country, or one's conscience. It just comes to a point, you just don't *want* it. And while I don't approve of it, of course, I'm living in Boulder, where we're able to make moral judgments because we're so far away from the situation. But if you lived in Folcroft and grew up there, as I did, you might feel differently about it.

Now, I'm in a minority opinion among anthropologists on this, because most of them are "liberals" and believe in what they think things *should be*, not as they *are,* and they maintain that there are some places in the world where there is no racial prejudice. I think, very frankly, that there are no such places. There is racial prejudice *everywhere.* And it is not always directed against Negroes. Sometimes it's Negro against the white, very often it's Negro against Pygmy, Pygmy against Negroes, Mongoloids against Negroes, Mongoloids against whites. I have evolved a sort of general statement, which is: Wherever you have two groups of people who can be distinguished either in reality or in imagination, you get prejudice. I don't think the racial question is biological at all. I think it's a social question. And it goes back to the in-group, out-group dichotomy. *Everybody* has this. I don't care if he's a hermit, he still has in-group, out-group feelings. It may show itself just in terms of a football game, where you root for one of the sides. But everybody belongs to these separate groups.

As for the so-called inferiority of the Negro, there's no evidence whatsoever to tell us whether one group is superior or inferior. We just don't have any information, and there's no way of getting it. Intelligence tests can't tell us anything at all because you cannot get the cultural factor out of them. It's impossible.

As for Negro sexuality, we have heard for a long time that the Negro is uninhibited as far as sex is concerned, but this is not true. The Negro is at least as inhibited as whites, and perhaps more so. On the other hand, the Negro may use sex today to bolster his self-esteem. I've seen this even in college. Negroes try to establish a rationale for their own superiority by a very blatant sexual expression. Of course, the idea of having sex with a white woman is not very frequent with them. But the desire to do so is stimulated because the white-beauty ideas have gotten over to the Negro as well—go through Harlem and you'll see ads for hair-straighteners and skin-whiteners. And having sex with a white woman is also a device to get back at whites. This kind of thing manifests itself in different ways. I'm told that the aborigines in Australia, if they get money, spend it on taking taxi rides. Now, why should they do that? Well, it's the only way they can put a white in a subservient position.

The myth of Negro sexuality, by the way, has gotten in the mind of white girls as well. On many campuses, you'll find "zebra" parties, as they're called. But physiologically, I don't think there's any sexual difference between the Negro and the white male.

How will we ever eliminate prejudice? By being invaded by Mars. That's the only thing that can get the whole human race feeling that it is *the* in-group. Because in-groups always find out you can't have one without the other: You always need an out-group.

I'm very discouraged by the prospects: I don't see how prejudice can possibly end. Man has to be aggressive against somebody—that's why I call Man a gregarious cannibal. He has to have the Negro to kick around, or he kicks his wife around, or somebody else. This is one of the defects of being a human being, I'm afraid. As far as I'm concerned, the sooner we put Man's destiny in the hands of machines, the better off we'll all be. Yes, I'm quite serious about that. Because it's emotions that cause all of the difficulties, not reason.

But I will tell you that with all my understanding of the situation . . . I wouldn't want to live in Folcroft.

Paul Goodman
sociologist

Sure, no qualifications—my daughter could marry a Negro. But I don't think, by the way, that love is the correct reason to get married. I think the reason to get married is you think you can bring up children well together and are compatible. I don't believe in American romantic marriages—it's idiotic.

Certainly, children of an interracial marriage have difficulties. Is there anyone who wouldn't say this? He'd be a moron. The parents face more difficulty too. So what? Life is difficult. Certainly it's a major problem, but life is full of major problems. You don't object to something because it's difficult. You object in terms of either taste or justice. Or a moral issue.

As for the idea of Negro sexual superiority, it's plain bullshit. Anytime a boundary is set up, people will project across the boundary. They will project whatever they are inhibiting in themselves. Now, in my own particular case, in my childhood my Negroes were Irish. The Irish were lusty, dirty,—all the nice things. But the Irish thought we *Jews* were dirty, lusty, and all the nice things. It's an inevitable psychological phenomenon —projection across an artificial boundary.

Harper Lee
novelist

The question wouldn't arise with me—I don't have any children. But I would think that two people who go into a marriage of that kind would have to be awfully mature emotionally and awfully sure of themselves. And people like that are pretty hard to find.

I mean, two people don't just marry each other, they in a sense marry the world. It depends on *who* they are and it depends on *where* they are, and where they want to live out their lives.

In the South, the part of the country with which I'm most familiar, frankly I think the social pressures are so loaded against a marriage like that to make it unfeasible. It would be dangerous for two people to try to enter into such a relationship. In the South, it would just be out of the question.

Murray Kempton
political writer

I assume there should be some restrictions on marriage— if two persons are certifiably insane, the state has reason to

370

raise a question if they decide to get married. But I'm certainly sure about what they call miscegenation: I don't see how the government can make *any* restriction on it. I imagine my *own* children will marry whom they please. It's not my business and it's not *society's* business to tell anybody who he or she should marry.

Setting aside everything else, I think that white people oppose miscegenation because they fear it will endanger their children's careers. Americans have a great fear about slipping back to peasantry, and I think this is one of the problems that underlies opposition to intermarriage.

Arthur Laurents
playwright

My personal views about interracial marriage? Well, the only thing I can say is that two of my closest friends are Lena Horne and Lennie Hayton.

An interracial marriage *does* create more difficulties. I think it's absurd to pretend otherwise. It's hard for anybody to adjust to *marriage,* let alone intermarriage. And if a mixed marriage *is* successful, the partners deserve more compliments than the partners in a so-called average marriage.

I think there's overt anti-Negroism in most people in this country. There are very few really unprejudiced people in this world, and if you're not prejudiced about one thing, you're prejudiced about another. This will never change. Watch children at play. There'll always be a scapegoat. I don't know whether people are born with prejudice or not. Maybe it comes from our own insecurity. We demand something to be superior to. And we demand someone to blame.

How can we stop it? Well, I don't know. But I think this is one of the reasons people turn to a God. It's an evasion of responsibility. "It's God's will" is the easy way out.

I think human beings will always demand a minority of one kind or another to feel superior to. At present the Jews are being replaced by the Negroes. I don't know what the Negroes will be replaced by, but they'll be replaced by something. In another 2000 years.

Lennie Hayton
musician

Surprisingly, I've found more opposition to intermarriage among Negroes than among whites. But, there's bigotry and prejudice on both sides.

There are more social pressures on the Negro and white couple than on so-called pure marriages. But this makes their marriage a little more interesting. When two people are in love with each other, I don't think it makes a difference *what* color they are. If they're seriously in love, they can rise above the obstacles.

Societal pressures are breaking down slowly, but much too slowly. They'll break down faster as the *white* people advance more.

Joseph H. Lewis
president, Freethinkers of America

I'm in favor of intermarriage. If people want to get married, I don't care *what* color they are. And if a child of mine came to me and was sincerely in love with a person of a different color, I would have to bless the union.

I think the reason so many people are against intermarriage is that the instincts in people are to go together. But I do think there's getting to be less and less antagonism to intermarriage, and if we keep our liberal attitudes about these matters, I don't see why the barrier against intermarriage shouldn't break down completely.

You mustn't forget that at one time Christians and Jews never married, and today they're getting married so much that the rabbis are crying to stop it. The antagonisms just wore away because Jews and Christians were living close to each other and meeting each other, and falling in love, and love is the strongest attachment two people can have.

The color barrier may be harder to break down than the religion barrier, but isn't it Sammy Davis who married a white girl? *That* marriage seems to be very successful, and it's going to be an example to other mixed couples, too.

---

producer and playwright

If my daughter had a choice of marrying a John Dillinger or a Ralph Bunche, I would be delighted if she would marry Ralph Bunche. It's not a question of intermarriage: It's a question of who the person is.

Mort Sahl
social critic

Well, first of all, the threat to white Southern males of who's going to marry their sister goes back to the folklore that Negro males have greater sexual endowments, which we know is nonsense. But it's the only nonsense that the civil-rights leaders haven't objected to. They're willing to live with that. That's my first point.

The second point I would make is that interracial sex affairs are the greatest arena for hostility—it's a great way to get your hostility across, and that's why it's always appealed to people. It's perfect psychologically. I've done it, I know.

Robert Shelton
Imperial Wizard, Knights of the Ku Klux Klan

I would certainly oppose any of my children, or any of the white race, in intermarrying with the Negro race, for the simple reason that you would destroy the heritage and background of either race, irregardless if it is white or black, and you'll have no leaders for the blacks or the whites. Amalgamation is ultimately the goal of the Communist element and also the leaders in the civil-rights movement, because it would destroy the morals of the people.

People who marry interracially do it for publicity, in most cases. Or in another case it is a lower element of either race that bring themselves together through matrimony. Love? If that is what you call "love"—that some white girl can lower her morals enough to marry a Negro man—well, I don't know if she had any religion or morals to start with.

Let me ask *you* a question. Would you object if you had a

daughter and she came home and told you she wanted to marry a Negro?

Dave Garroway
entertainer

Would I object if a child of mine wants to marry interracially? It would depend entirely upon the child. I don't think there's anything astonishing about President Truman's not wanting his daughter to marry a Negro. He knows his own daughter and he knows her emotional limitations. If my son said he wanted to marry a Negro, I would recommend it instantly. He grew up in France where interracial dating is common and he wonders what all the fuss is about over here. On the other hand, if my daughter asked me, "Daddy, should I start going out with a colored boy?" I'd say "No!" I know her well and she couldn't accept the trauma and social pressures of an interracial relationship. She's not that strong.

Norman Thomas
Socialist

I am by now a great grandfather, and my children are happily married. But I think that if I had been presented with the problem of interracial marriage, I would have said, "Go ahead—if you love each other and know what you're doing."

Rudy Vallee
entertainer

I think that if two persons love each other, race, religion, creed, or anything else shouldn't make any difference. And if it ever came around to me personally, I wouldn't care *what* society thought.

Godfrey Cambridge
comedian

Well, if my child wanted to marry a white, I would observe the relationship and make sure it was a mature relation-

374

ship based on real fact, you know, and then I would say, "Go right ahead."

See, what I'm concerned about is once I helped write a piece for the *Premise* which I called "The Sick Interracial Couple." It's the couple whose relationship depends entirely on other people's disapproval. So the scene opens and they come on together and she says, "Did you tell your mother?" And he says, "Yes, I did." "Oh, kiss me, Fred, oh kiss me!" So he says, "Did you tell your father?" And she says, "Oh yes, he nearly had a heart attack. Oh kiss me Fred! And you know my uncle, the one who's always a professional nice-guy and always says, 'Hi ya'? He said never darken his door again."

So everything is swinging and the next thing I have the parents coming in, and the kids are hugging each other and saying, "We don't care, we stand united together against the world." And the mother says, "Yes, we thought so, that's why we're giving you our permission." "We don't care, no matter what you say." So the mother says, "No, no, we're giving you our *permission*." "Oh well . . . that's great." Mother says, "Yes, we'll have a big wedding and everything will be fine, and I'll get you into the country club and everything will be fine." And then she says "Bye-bye, kiddies," and they're left in the room.

They look at each other and she says, "Kiss me Fred"— with no feeling—and he says, "I just did." And she says, "Well, kiss me anyway." He does, and she thinks about it and wipes it off her lips. And he says, "I'm going bowling." She says, "That's a good idea." He: "I'll see you." "Yeah, I'll see ya." And you know that "See you" is good-bye.

And he gets to the door and she says, "The butcher *hates* interracial couples! And the tailor *hates* us and my landlord will dispossess me!" And they get together and it's "Oh kiss me Fred!" and it starts all over again.

So it's this kind of sick relationship I'd be against. I've seen the couple who stand on the corner and wait for the people who disapprove, and she leans right up and starts kissing the guy and 7 feet of tongue is in his mouth—on the street corner! You realize it's his way of defying and her way of defy-

375

ing. "Yeah, what you got to say about *that*? I kissed one of your women!" Well, I feel sorry for these people. They become a source of embarrassment, a source of annoyance to me. Besides, I've *been* interracially involved. I went out with a chick once who was just out with me to punish her mother and father.

Sure, I know that intermarriage is one of the bigger bugaboos of the segregationists. "My God, they're going to marry white women"—that's their major thing. I can just hear the litany now. I know what's going on.

Let's face it, the problem of interracialism was settled years ago—by God. If He didn't want us to get together, we'd be built differently. Black and white physiologies would not be compatible. The root of the Negro sexuality problem comes from slave days when they would sell this Negro slave and say, "Oh, he can stud 97 women in 4 hours, so I want $6500 for him." And so the myth was built up. I don't feel necessarily that Negroes are better in bed than anybody. There's so much psychological conditioning. If a Negro cat gets on a Negro chick, and does what he does with a white chick, the Negro chick might say, "Oh honey, look, will you *please get off me*? I want to watch television. Go away." There is no conditioning going with him with this chick, no "Yes, oh my God! this is better" when the cat ain't doing nothing. The whole social structure of the South has been to keep Negro men away from white women, so white women became very, very curious, they heard all of these stories, and they got conditioned.

Look, if we're so oversexed, how come we're still a minority group?

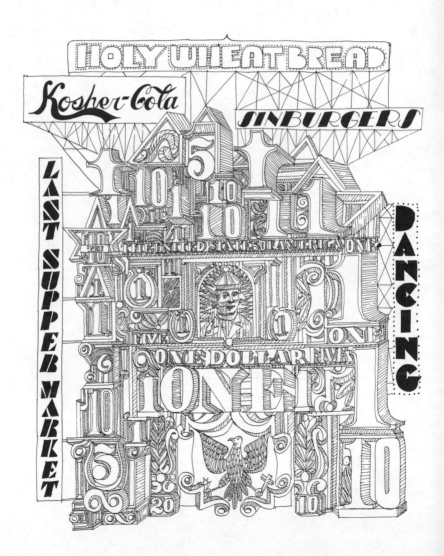

The Burgeoning Estates of the First Estate

By Edward Sylvester

There's no business like church business, and it's getting more and more profitable all the time.

Much church wealth, of course, is still invested in real estate: schools, hospitals, rectories, parsonages, temples, cathedrals, and those sure-fire money-makers, cemeteries. In addition, there are the traditional public offerings to church treasuries from the tithe, the collection plate, stock gifts, and bingo receipts.

But today all this is just a fraction of the economic empire of America's church groups. Today, the traditional house of worship is only one of the numerous assets of that vast holding company known as the church. The kingdom of heaven, nowadays, also includes a laundry in New Hampshire, a commercial office building in Chicago, the mortgage on the home of Billie Sol Estes (the convicted Texas mortgage manipulator), radio and TV stations in New Orleans, Yankee Stadium in New York, the Deseret book store in Salt Lake City (which calls itself the biggest book store in the West), two Mushroomburger restaurants in California, and a nightclub in Hawaii. Also, churches and their auxiliary organizations publish books, bake bread, pack meat, grow cattle, sell insurance, distill wine and brandy, and operate supermarkets, hotels, and factories.

Churches reap lovely profits from these enterprises, and manage to do so while thwarting that most resolute of the collectors—the Internal Revenue Service, as well as tax men at state, county, and local levels. Hiding behind a fortresslike tax

379

shelter, religious groups of all denominations are able to render unto God not only that which is God's, but that which is Caesar's as well.

It's little wonder then that, according to a recent study, the combined value of all church property of all denominations in the United States is an estimated $79.5 billion—which, to give you some idea of how fantastic a figure that is, represents 50% *more* than the full value of *all* real property (both taxable and tax-exempt) in the whole City of New York. This eye-opening study was conducted by Martin A. Larson and sponsored by the militant organization known as Protestants and Other Americans United for Separation of Church and State. In compiling the total, Mr. Larson put Jewish wealth at $7 billion, Protestant and miscellaneous groups' wealth at $28 billion, and Catholic wealth at $44.5 billion.

Not surprisingly, church wealth has been growing at a rate that should make any businessman green with envy. In the cities of Baltimore, Washington, Buffalo, and Denver (the cornerstones of the Larson study), for example, the combined church wealth was $40 million in 1906. In 1964, just the assessed valuation of church-owned real estate alone in the four cities was $469 million—an increase of 1100%. Another example: In 10 years the assets of the Baptist Foundation of Texas rose from $20 million to $53 million. And in New York City, in one decade church-owned, tax-exempt property increased in value from $408 million to $570 million.

Mr. Larson's estimate as to the wealth of the nation's churches may be a very rough one, but no better is available. Few churches will volunteer such information; some will not even disclose figures to their own members. The Internal Revenue Service, which might know, declines to estimate the extent of church wealth. Still no one can deny that their financial assets must be staggering. As one Catholic priest wrote a few years ago, "The Catholic Church must be the biggest corporation in the United States," with a branch office in nearly every neighborhood. "Our assets and real-estate holdings must exceed those of Standard Oil, AT&T and U.S. Steel combined.

And our roster of dues-paying members must be second only to the tax rolls of the United States government."

* * *

The churches' exemption from virtually all taxes is, of course, the main reason why they can succeed in business without really trying. It's a practice that has become so irritating to the Treasury Department that the T-men refer to a church enterprise by the irreverent nickname "monk business." All religious organizations are exempt from Federal taxes, and most state and local taxes too, even if the business is a profit-making venture and does not stem directly out of church activities. The only chance Uncle Sam has to put the tax bite on a church-run business is when it strays into commercial competition—and even then the chances are slim. "You've got to prove the venture is commercial and that the profits are not necessary to support the church's activities. And this is hard as hell to prove," one Internal Revenue official has said. "The courts are hesitant to take action against churches, so we stay away from them too if we possibly can. Church cases are nothing but headaches."

Two years ago, the tax-dodging opportunities of churches grew with the help of a Supreme Court decision, a decision that dealt with a scientific-research foundation but which could be applied to a church as well. The high court's ruling strengthened the "lease-back" tactic that for some time has been frequently used, and frequently abused, by crafty, investment-minded churchmen. Under this sale-and-lease-back maneuver, a church can take over a profitable business without laying out any cash. For example, in 1952 three churches in Bloomington, Illinois—First Baptist, First Christian, and Second Presbyterian—bought the Biltmore Hotel in Dayton, Ohio, from the Hilton Hotel Corporation for $3.5 million. The churches put up exactly $0.00 in cash. Immediately thereafter, the churches leased the hotel back to the chain to run, meanwhile using the rent they collected to gradually pay off the $3.5 million debt and the interest. Hilton benefited because its capital was freed for other uses. And, because of their tax exemption, the churches were able to swing a profit of $450,000 before transferring the property, 11 years later, to the original owners.

It was through a complex lease-back, among other maneuvers, that religion broke into organized baseball in 1953 when the Knights of Columbus, a Catholic fraternal order, acquired the land under Yankee Stadium. The ball-park site was just one more prize added to the K. of C.'s collection, which includes department stores, warehouses, and a steel-tube factory among its $200 million assets. Through lease-backs also, the Southern Baptist Annuity Board took over a textile mill; St. Andrew's R.C. Church of Chicago got into the hotel business.

Lease-backs are an "excellent hedge" against inflation, says J.C. Cantrell of the Baptist Foundation of Texas. This foundation's lease-back properties are also excellent earners—its supermarkets, service stations, etc., provide nearly 17% of its gross income of $2.8 million a year, though they make up only 14% of its investments.

Many religious groups plunge right into business without dawdling over lease-backs. The Self-Realization Fellowship, a religious sect, operates two successful Mushroomburger restaurants in California. The Congregational Church in Claremont, New Hampshire, runs a laundry. The Mormon Church in Hawaii is the impresario of a night spot that features Polynesian dancing. The First Methodist Church in Chicago rents out office space in a 22-story office building it owns in the Loop. And the Jesuits, through Loyola University in New Orleans, operate tax-free radio and TV stations that can afford to undercut all competition with cheap advertising rates. "Their rates are so cheap it's ridiculous," says the man who runs a competing TV station that must charge $50-a-minute more than the Jesuits for commercials during prime evening time. "There's a big difference between their dollar and ours," says the general manager, Louis Read. Read is a Catholic and a graduate of Loyola University. As a P.O.A.U. official says of the churches' tax exemption in general, "The irony is the competitive advantage it frequently gives a church over its own members."

* * *

Some of the most prosperous church enterprises are in the food field. Many began innocently enough with religious groups producing food specialties for their own needs and support. As their product caught on, they expanded beyond the cloister and the monastery and into the business world. One of the most celebrated is the Christian Brothers, a Roman Catholic order that began making sacramental wines in the 1880s and now sells a large portion of American wine—as well as *40%* of all American brandy. The St. Benedict's Monastery in Colorado every year sends almost 300 head of the Hereford cattle they raise to the Denver stockyards. The Seventh-Day Adventists, whose religion forbids them to eat meat, sell millions of dollars worth of vegetarian food products on the general market each year.

The Christian Brothers situation is one of the very few cases where a religious group has lost a tug-of-war with the tax collector.

On April 10, 1956, Paul Blanshard, special counsel for Protestants and Other Americans United, stood before an Internal Revenue Service hearing officer, raised high a bottle of brandy in one hand and muscatel wine in the other, and charged, "It is morally wrong and financially foolish to make Catholic religious orders tax-exempt on unrelated business income . . . when they are in competition with ordinary business." Thus P.O.A.U., along with other groups, launched its attack on the tax-exempt status of the Christian Brothers. The assault was part of lengthy litigation that ended 6 years ago with the Roman Catholic order's being forced to pay the government $4 million in back taxes. The revenuers made the Christian Brothers pay corporate taxes on profits, and the brothers filed suit for refund. In upholding the I.R.S. claim, the courts ruled that the Christian Brothers order is not a sacerdotal one. In other words, its members are not priests and are not qualified to perform the sacred rituals of the church. Moreover, the courts held that the wine and brandy profits were not necessary for the maintenance and operation of the school—the De LaSalle Institute of Napa, California—that the Christian Brothers run. With the decision came this opinion from Federal Judge Halbert in Sacramento: "It would be impractical to accord an exemption to every corporation which asserted itself to be a church." And for the argument by the brothers that their Constitutional rights had been invaded, the judge said: "If there were any Constitutional problems in this case, it would be the problem of whether any exemption of churches from the unrelated business tax could be justified."

This judgment was expected to open the way to similar suits, to a stricter attitude by the courts toward tax exemptions for church-owned businesses, and eventually to new tax laws that would remove any doubt about a church's obligation to pay taxes on business profits. But no such thing happened. Congressmen, ever fearful of antagonizing powerful religious groups in their home districts, kept out of the battle. The attitude of the courts remained lenient. And even the I.R.S. has been reluctant to press tax claims against churches. *"No one wants to be accused of being anti-religious,"* as one revenue man said.

Recently, the Treasury Department, in a report to Congress, asked for a sweeping overhaul of tax laws, with the aim of tightening tax-exemption loopholes for "charitable" foundations. It sought no such changes for churches. Apparently the Treasury Department wants to gain some ground against foundations before taking on the more formidable opponent.

In the long run, the tax fight against the churches has been ineffective. The City of Nashville levied a $140,000 impost on the headquarters building of the Baptist Sunday School Board, but the Tennessee Supreme Court ruled that only the building's cafeteria, snack bar, and parking lot, all used by employees, were taxable. In San Luis Obispo, California, the assessor imposed a tax on a church-owned swimming pool that charged admission and was never used for religious functions.

The county supervisors overruled the assessor and upheld the tax exemption. And a Minnesota court blocked an attempt by the State to collect property taxes from a publishing house and book store run by the Evangelical Free Church in America.

One of the most recent cases, and perhaps one of the most turbulent, is the one brought by Mrs. Madalyn Murray, the embattled atheist, late of Baltimore, but now living in Hawaii. Mrs. Murray, one of the successful plaintiffs in the fight to bar school prayers, sued the City of Baltimore and the State of Maryland to force them to collect taxes on church property. She argued that tax exemption for churches violates the Constitution's guarantee of separation of church and state. And, as a taxpayer herself, she contended that she is forced to pay an unfairly large portion of taxes because churches fail to pay their share for the public services they use, such as roads, police, and fire protection. Her lawyer estimated that the City of Baltimore alone would collect an additional $76 million annually by taxing church buildings. A Baltimore circuit court dismissed the case, and the U. S. Supreme Court, which has been resting on its vintage 1954 laurels, refused to consider an appeal.

True, the court is not always on the side of the church in such cases, but exceptions are rare and are considered oddities more than legal landmarks. A Denver woman, for example, bequeathed $7500 to Bishop Fulton J. Sheen of New York, and Colorado authorities hit him for inheritance taxes even though he wanted to give the money to the Society for the Propagation of the Faith. In 1960, the Pennsylvania Supreme Court ruled that church parking lots are subject to real-estate taxes, even though the church argued that parking space—whether for cars or for horses and buggies—is as important to freedom of worship as pews and prayer books.

Exemptions from real-estate and corporate-profits taxes may be the most valuable tax shelters for the church (and the most costly for the government), but there are other areas too where religion can duck the tax collector. If a nun, for example, teaches in a public school, her salary is safe from personal income tax if she gives it to her religious order. And the same principle could apply to a Jesuit priest who might serve as a bank president or corporation executive at a six-figure salary.

* * *

The government subsidizes religion in other ways besides tax exemptions. One practice, which rankles real-estate dealers in particular, is the selling of public lands to church groups without public bidding. The City of New York is being sued for this very thing. Under a New York City policy, a nonprofit organization—and this usually means religious groups—can buy any City land that is up for sale and pay only the "knockdown" price—that is, the minimum price for which the land could be legally sold, a price based on assessment values. A commercial dealer can't get his hands on the property, even if he's willing to bid twice as much.

Recently a New York builder named Arnold Tarshis was prepared to bid as high as $17,000 for a 30-foot-by-80-foot plot, which he was planning to combine with some adjacent land to build three houses. Instead, a rabbi representing a Jewish congregation got the property for $8500, although Mr. Tarshis topped the rabbi's bid as soon as the auction opened. The City lost not only the higher sale price, but potential real-estate taxes as well. Mr. Tarshis sued the City, citing the City Charter, the State Constitution, and the First and Fourteenth Amendments to the U. S. Constitution. His case was thrown out of court last summer, and he has filed an appeal.

* * *

Though Madalyn Murray and the P.O.A.U. are the most militant opponents of tax relief for church groups, opposition has come from other quarters as well. Businessmen are often outraged that they are competing with a rival that has an overwhelming economic advantage, and even churchmen have raised their eyebrows, and often their voices, at the practice.

The National Conference of Christians and Jews has called for a probe of tax exemption for church property and the correction of any abuses that may be found. The Baptist Joint Committee on Public Affairs has gone so far as to suggest that church businesses be taxed when they no longer concern themselves with religion. The expansion of church-owned businesses "is causing real damage to the image of the church, and it's high time businessmen themselves should be getting up in arms," says the Rev. Dean M. Kelley, an officer of the National Council of Churches of Christ, a group that encompasses most Protestant denominations. "I would love to see just one denomination spell out the tax-exempt properties it holds," he adds.

Some churches have even voluntarily shed the cloak of tax exemption, and some have never donned it at all. The Church of Jesus Christ of Latter-Day Saints (the Mormons), one of the most enterprising of all business-prone religions, prides itself on voluntarily paying all Federal, state, and local taxes. (The Mormon empire includes a department store, a sugar company, publishing houses, insurance firms, office buildings, and radio and TV stations, as well as the night spot in Hawaii.) And in Austin, Texas, not long ago, the Central Christian Church, uncomfortable at being cast in a huckster's role, stopped renting its parking lot to a funeral parlor for $1000 a month.

The most intense soul-searching on the whole problem has been done by one of the nation's leading clergymen, Dr. Eugene Carson Blake, stated clerk (chief executive) of the United Presbyterian Church and former president of the National Council of Churches of Christ. Writing for the magazine *Christianity Today,* Dr. Blake suggested that churches, for their own survival, initiate reforms. "A government with a mounting tax problem cannot be expected to keep its hands off the wealth of a rich church forever," he said, and went on to cite cases throughout history where a hungry state has pounced upon the property of a wealthy church: 16th-century England, 18th-century France, 19th-century Italy, and the Communist nations of the 20th century. And in America, says Dr. Blake, "One hundred years from now, the present pattern of religious tax exemption, if continued, may present the state with problems of such magnitude that the only solution will be revolutionary expropriation of church property."

Dr. Blake is bothered not only by the threat of government seizure, but also by the loss of church prestige that could come with its increasing wealth. As evidence, he points to the growing number of very simple store-front churches in poor neighborhoods. Apparently Dr. Blake believes that a wealthy, ornate church will have as much trouble commanding the respect of the poor as a camel would have in passing through the eye of a needle.

In his article, Dr. Blake asks rhetorically if there ought not to be a repeal of the Internal Revenue code that allows corporate tax exemption for church businesses not related to church purposes. And he offers one idea that could lead to nothing less than an economic Reformation. Suppose, wonders Dr. Blake, churches took the initiative and gave to local tax authorities 1% of the real-estate tax that would be due if their property were taxable, and suppose they increased the donation by 1% each year until they hit a ceiling of 10%? Unless something like this is done, Dr. Blake warns, "It is not unreasonable to prophesy that with prudent management, the churches ought to be able to control the whole economy of the nation within the predictable future."

Who Killed Kennedy?

Introduction. Remember those stories when Marilyn Monroe died, about her trying to telephone Bobby Kennedy? Or those rumors back in 1945 (noted in David J. Jacobson's *Affairs of Dame Rumor,* 1948) that FDR was "still alive, in a madhouse"? Remember when actor James Dean wasn't really killed in a motorcycle accident, but was laying low because he was hideously disfigured?

Maybe you also recall reading that Mrs. Warren G. Harding poisoned her husband because he was fooling around with Nanna P. Britton (Gaston B. Means, *The Strange Death of President Harding,* 1930). Huey Long wasn't shot by Dr. Carl Austin Weiss Jr., but by his own bodyguards (noted in Stan Opotowsky's *The Longs of Louisiana,* 1960). The Archduke Ferdinand, whose death triggered World War I, was assassinated by Freemasons (noted in Vladimir Dedijer's *The Road to Sarajevo,* 1966). John Wilkes Booth was never captured— the Secret Service killed the wrong man, then buried their mistake (*Dame Rumor*). Alternately, Booth's crime was instigated by Jesuits (Burke McCarty, *The Suppressed Truth About the Assassination of Abraham Lincoln,* 1922). President McKinley's assassination was masterminded by Emma Goldman, the anarchist (she was actually *arrested*). Woodrow Wilson's illness and death were the result of his being "a philanderer who had clandestine affairs" (*Dame Rumor*).

If you're up on the subject, you also know that Mozart was done in by Salieri, that Anastasia wasn't slain in Siberia (despite the history books), and that Jesse James lived to a ripe old age (despite Robert Ford). Joan of Arc burned at the stake? According to one historian, she recanted and ran off with a carpenter. Napoleon didn't die in 1821, on St. Helena, but in 1834, in England (American historian P.P. Ebeyer, in *Revelations Concerning Napoleon's Escape from St. Helena,* 1947, says a phony corpse was used).

The fact is that the untimely or unexpected death of almost every celebrated person sets the rumormongers mongering. Perhaps the sudden ending of a soaring career is so absurd that people must tamper with reality, or at least invent a more appropriate, magnificent death. Perhaps people need another shock to offset the first shock, according to the law that every emotional action has a reaction. And perhaps when the person who died was young and gifted, people simply cannot master their grief, and the event becomes a haunting obsession; and like all obsessions people mull it over and over again, in all sorts of new ways, hoping it will go away. The psychoanalysts have a phrase for it: the "working-through process."

The public's obsession with the death of President Kennedy will never go away. No other event in the lives of most people today was so tragic and traumatic. Three years later, while memorabilia still flourish and rumors are rife, jokes about the assassination are almost nonexistent.* We still have not mastered our grief. Anger remains, too: Blame Jack Ruby for taking away our scapegoat. And we are also afraid, for as Gordon W. Allport and Leo Postman note in *The Psychology of Rumor* (1947), ". . . anxiety is the power behind the macabre and threatening tales we so often hear. . . ." Our fear may be that, unless Kennedy's assassination was the result of a conspiracy, cleverly and thoroughly planned, other emotional earthquakes could hit just as easily.

Hence the rumors. We are trying to conquer our obsession; we are trying to assure ourselves that such an event is unlikely to recur (even if co-conspirators are lurking about, we are better prepared for them); and we are looking for someone to hate.

* Only two have been widely reported. (1) "What happened when the elephant walked into the Dallas police station?" "Nothing. Nobody saw it." (2) Oswald was "an Anarchist who finally decided to make an Existentialist commitment."

Easily the silliest and most far-fetched theory of all, judging by conversations at parties, is that Lee Harvey Oswald alone killed President Kennedy, but notwithstanding *Time* Magazine and William F. Buckley Jr. to the affirmative, it's probably true. It was his rifle and his palm print; he was seen in the building whence the shots came; his pistol killed Patrolman Tippit. He also had a motive—a pathological need for the self-esteem he never got from people, from his job, or from inner resources. Lee Harvey Oswald was a common American type: the creep. He appears in American literature as Wilmer Cook in Dashiell Hammett's *The Maltese Falcon* and in American films as Hunt Bromley in *The Gunfighter*. At 16, Oswald threatened to kill President Eisenhower. He had taken a potshot at General Walker, and his wife once had to stop him from taking potshots at Johnson, or Nixon. His widow and his half-brother concede he was the guilty man, and even his mother has said it was possible that Oswald assassinated the President, because as she said, "I am not the type mother to think that he is perfect. . . ."

Sure, a cop misidentified the rifle. But that cop was the all-American know-it-all. Sure, a lot of witnesses have since died violent deaths, but in Dallas, murder capital of the world, unnatural deaths are natural deaths. And yes, many people claim to have seen Oswald when they could not have seen him. But John Wilkes Booth was spotted 20 times after he was dead.

There *are* mysteries. Why was bullet 399 intact? How could a rifle be fired that quickly? For that matter, "How come the public didn't see him [FDR] dead, and why the constant guard over his grave?" (letter, New York *Daily News*, 3/24/46) "Why did [Harding] have that ptomaine poisoning? He didn't eat anything that all the rest of the party were not eating." (*Strange Death of President Harding*) "How, within six minutes of the shooting, 18 minutes before anybody in Baton Rouge knew who the assassin was, did a Washington newspaperman know his full name: Dr. Carl Austin Weiss, Jr? Why have neither friends nor foes of Huey Long seemed anxious to clear up the mystery once and for all?" ("Mystery in the Death of Huey Long," *Reader's Digest* 9/39) "Why wasn't the President effectively guarded on the night of April 14, 1865? . . . Why did Booth want to see Vice-President Johnson on that Good Friday? Why was the Vice-President so drunk the next day?" (Emmett McLoughlin, *An Inquiry into the Assassination of Abraham Lincoln*, 1963)

* * *

In a Louis Harris poll taken after the Warren Report was published, 54% of the respondents thought there "still may be some unanswered questions." Some 69% thought Oswald was the assassin, but only 34% thought he acted alone—46% believed there was a conspiracy and 20% were not sure. (Don't feel sorry for the Warren Commission. Holt, Rinehart and Winston editors report that Chief Justice Warren personally tried to prevent their publishing Mark Lane's *Rush to Judgment*.)

Fact's own poll of authorities and celebrities, published below, confirms the existence of widespread doubt about who killed President Kennedy. More important, *Fact*'s poll lends support to the various proposals that the assassination be investigated once again.

Whatever its make-up, such a committee could help scotch the assassination rumors. Psychologists have reported that the intensity of rumors (R) varies according to the importance of the topic (i) and the ambiguity of the evidence $(a) - R = i \times a$. In this equation, i cannot be reduced, but a can. And this is precisely what a new committee, devoted to unraveling the remaining mysteries, could accomplish.

—**Warren Boroson**

Paul Goodman
sociologist

I think that Mark Lane's book is definitely reasonable, and that the Warren Commission's report was poor. I think it's even likely that there was manufactured evidence—the FBI and the CIA have manufactured evidence before.

Certainly the whole case seems full of fabrication. It

seems unlikely that Oswald was the lone assassin of Kennedy, or that he was the assassin at all. And I think it's extremely stupid of the Warren Commission to try to hush up the thing.

Let's put it this way: I don't give a rap *who* killed Jack Kennedy, you know, one way or the other. You can quote me on that. I really don't care. I care *immensely* if the police and the government are involved in a fabrication, because that results in a complete loss of public trust. It becomes clear that, if in important matters like this we can't trust evidence that comes from the police, and such important police as the FBI, then there's no reason to have *any* public trust in *any* part of the government.

Cleveland Amory
writer

Where there's smoke, there's bound to be fire. There have now been five—no less than five—books criticizing the Warren Commission. If they are true, or even parts of them are true (and I believe they are), then you can add to the incredible failure of the Secret Service to protect the President to begin with, and add to the utterly incomprehensible shortcomings of the Dallas police in permitting Oswald to be shot by Ruby, a third and final outrage—that of the Warren Commission. If not actually inept, it was certainly hardly ept.

Arthur Miller
playwright

The evidence of the X-rays, which have been withheld, seems to throw doubt upon the description of the wounds as officially adopted by the Commission Report.

There's enough now to indicate that the bullets came from more than one direction.

John Updike
writer

I think there are some puzzling points in the official version, but I find the alternate reports less credible than the official one. Unless some additional information is brought out, I am inclined to think that Oswald was the lone assassin.

Harry Golden
writer and editor

I have an advantage. I have a big advantage. I was pretty close, and I still am pretty close, to Bobby Kennedy. I've worked for him, and so forth. You know, next to the widow he was the most devastated man in the world. Now, Senator Kennedy told me 2 months after the assassination, quote, "The family is satisfied there was this one fellow." He couldn't even mention Oswald's name!

Well, listen: that's only the Attorney General of the United States! And the brother! Who is *he* protecting? He'd go to the moon to get the guy.

You know, 50 years after the assassination of President Lincoln they were still charging a dime to see the mummified body of John Wilkes Booth. Now it's more expensive—these books about the assassination cost about five bucks each. But it's all a fake. And there'll be dozens of more books. People are titillated by it.

One fellow, Mark Lane, wrote a whole book wondering about how Jack Ruby had access to police headquarters. What Mark Lane doesn't know is that there's a Jack Ruby in every town in America. There's two or three of them *here,* in Charlotte. Guys with pockets full of courtesy cards, you know. Sheriff's courtesy cards. They follow the fire engines, and whenever there's an arrest, they're there.

Who is the Warren Commission supposed to be protecting? Another gunman? On what basis? Protecting the Far Right? The Far Right has signs all over America, IMPEACH EARL WARREN. Wouldn't that have been a nice time for Warren to smash 'em? Those fellows like Mark Lane are still showing the mummified body of John Wilkes Booth.

Melvin Belli
former lawyer for Jack Ruby

The real villain in this piece is that latter-day King Farouk, J. Edgar Hoover. Anything he gets his hands on becomes secret and covert. He has the ideology of a Louis XIV. Hoover had a lot of information he didn't make available, so blame the FBI. He brought suspicion on the Warren Commission to cover up the FBI's own shortcomings in the case. There's a lot of jealousy between him and the local law-enforcement officers. He has a lot on the Kennedy family and everybody else in this country (except me). The Kennedy family is afraid to move.

The Warren Report *is,* ultimately, proof. It was accurate, though perhaps the execution and the documentation left a lot to be desired. There *was* a lone assassin. There *was* a fair trial for him and Ruby. Ruby did *not* know Oswald.

As for Mark Lane, he's trying to promote alfalfa cigarettes as a cure-all for this country. I'll take Warren any day in the week, even though he's in the opposite political party. At least Warren never sold any alfalfa cigarettes.

Al Capp
cartoonist

I think that people are always willing to listen to all sorts of attacks on the Establishment, to listen to outrageous gossip. Good God, there's always been a market for that. And nowadays the surest way to make a buck is to attack the Warren Report.

We all adore detective stories and we all adore debunking and exposés, whether we believe them or not. Gee whiz, I remember there was a great debunker years ago who proceeded to debunk the myth of George Washington and the cherry tree —Woodward was his name. For years he wrote the most convincing cases against everything we believed in, and we were thrilled by it, we bought it and bought it. Now his books are no longer read, and everybody believes it about George Washington and the cherry tree.

Orson Bean
actor

I've always felt, right from the first few days, that it was this poor wretch Oswald. He was a wretch in every way—emotionally, mentally, and physically he was a *wretch*. So it's hard to believe he'd be in the pay of any scheming gang.

More often than not, when things are sloppy and messy in life, people want to put everything into order, tied up in a package. People are uncomfortable living with an untidy explanation, and they're anxious to have a slam-bang, pat one. So they're grasping at straws. But the fact is that a poor sick nut shot President Kennedy for no other reason than that he happened to be a poor sick nut.

Mark Lane's book and the others do raise questions in my mind, but I just feel it was a ridiculous series of coincidences that Oswald happened to be the way he was in the first place. If a plot ever is uncovered, I'd say fine, but did you know that it's never even been conclusively proven that Booth shot Lincoln? And I wonder what Lane's going to do if he discovered it was a plot of *Left* Wingers that killed Kennedy.

Mark Lane
author, Rush to Judgment

No, I hadn't heard that Justice Warren wanted my book suppressed. I know he's a friend of the president of Holt, Rinehart and Winston, but I don't believe it's true. It *is* true that the assistant director of the FBI called one publisher and asked him not to publish my book. But, after all, my book says that the FBI carried on at best like Keystone Cops, and at worst they were involved in subornation of perjury and extortion of witnesses.

The rumors about Johnson? Well, I've been on many radio and television telephone-format programs, where people call in, and at least 20% of the calls were from people who suggested Johnson was the assassin. I myself don't see any evidence that President Johnson was the assassin. I don't know *who* did it. I do know that the Warren Commission's conclusion that Oswald did it alone is ludicrous, but I don't know who did it. I'll have to leave the speculation to the Warren Commission.

As for my own book, if you consider the Warren Report

a prosecution document, mine—which is an answer to it—would be a defense brief. But it is really not even that because I don't say anywhere in the book that I believe Oswald was innocent. I only say that the evidence is not conclusive that he was *involved*. The evidence is conclusive that there were at least two people, but that's hardly a defense. If Oswald were alive, he would hardly be satisfied with a lawyer who said that about him.

The final truth might be in the national archives today. I think it's possible that there's material there that will not be made available until the year 2039. We have to convince the government that the evidence that might have been suppressed might be right there.

Kerry Thornley
writer

When the news of the assassination was first broken to me, somebody also told me that they had captured a suspect, and that he was a former Marine, and that he had been to Russia. So right away I said, "Was his name Oswald?" And of course it was, and then I immediately thought that he was innocent.

I knew Oswald in the Marines, and he was always the type of person who gets into trouble without really working too much at it. He knew how to, sort of, *look* suspicious, be in the wrong place at the wrong time, and say the wrong thing when he was questioned. And I thought, "Well, in a few days they'll find out he had nothing to do with it." Then I heard about all this evidence that was piling up, and I kept reading about it and I was really impressed, and I thought, "Gee whiz, if they have that much evidence on him, he must have done it." And I assumed Oswald was guilty.

Until I read the 26 volumes of testimony given to the Warren Commission. Because then I found that the Commission's Report was extremely inaccurate, and there are places in it where it's either a question of almost criminal carelessness, or a deliberate attempt to cover-up. I also have a friend, Dave Lifton, who spoke to one of the lawyers on the Commission, and that attorney said that the *only* kind of conspiracy they even seriously considered was that of a Communist conspiracy, and that was the *only* thing they attempted to debunk.

The newspaper reports about what kind of person Lee Harvey Oswald was just don't coincide with the person I knew. The newspapers were telling the American people what they thought would sell newspapers, what people wanted to hear— that Oswald was a troublemaker, an obvious psychopath, he was always getting in fights with other people. But the only time we ever discussed the subject of violence, Oswald expressed a great deal of distaste for it. He was talking about the Marines in the Far East beating up taxicab drivers and that sort of thing, and he was very upset about it, and although many times he got involved in arguments with other people, I never saw him personally involved in a fist-fight.

Oswald was a quiet individual, and he fitted very well the stereotype in our culture of the impractical intellectual. He read and kept to himself, and he resented authority, but he didn't particularly have an ax to grind, in the sense of going out and punching someone in the nose. I also feel that while, like most of us, he had his share of neuroses, he certainly was not obviously a madman.

He *did* take things too personally, though. Once the two of us were sitting around one Saturday morning, and there was going to be a parade. Now, many times Oswald had joked about his Marxist leanings, and he had referred to himself as "Comrade Oswald." Well, he was sitting there very quiet, and finally he said something about the stupidity of having a parade on a Saturday morning and getting everybody out of bed. I said, "Well, comes the revolution, you'll change all that. . . ." And he looked at me like I'd stabbed him or something, and he said, "Not *you* too, Thornley," and walked off. That was the last time we ever spoke to each other, because shortly thereafter I left for overseas.

At this point, I'm totally bewildered. I don't know whether Oswald was involved or not. I *am* profoundly skeptical of the lone-assassin theory now, however, but it is very possible that Oswald was involved. Obviously there's so much going on that I don't know about, that few individuals, if any, know about. . . .

On the other hand, I realize that the Honorable Earl Warren is a highly respected American with an immaculate reputation for integrity. So is the Honorable Richard B. Russell, the Honorable John Sherman Cooper, the Honorable Hale Boggs, the Honorable Gerald R. Ford, the Honorable Allen W. Dulles, and the Honorable John J. McCloy. "So are they all, all honourable men."

Kent Courtney
founder, Conservative Society of America

I often wonder why it is, when the Warren Commission mentioned Oswald's name, they forgot to mention that he was a member of an identified Communist-front organization, the so-called Fair Play for Cuba Committee. The press also refuses to mention it.

I have in front of me a big scrapbook containing all of the stories concerning the assassination, from the day before the assassination to the burial, from the Forth Worth and the Dallas newspapers. And I can tell you, just by rereading those as I do from time to time, that there were shots from at least *three* different places—one from the black bridge, one from the hill, and maybe one or two from where Oswald was.

So, just from reading of the press, I'd say there was a conspiracy that included Oswald and others, and I think that among these was Jack Ruby.

I think that one of the main reasons that Jack Kennedy was assassinated was that he had not been trying, during those years, to get the Congress to pass the foreign-aid-to-Communist-countries bills. I think Jack Kennedy was definitely putting the brakes on, and not pushing the Congress on legislation that favored Communists.

Carl Marzani
Marxist and publisher

The great, classic approach to crime detection goes back to Roman times—the phrase, *cui bono?* which means, To

whose benefit is it? Now, as Marquis Childs said in his syndicated column Oct. 19, 1963 (43 days before the assassination), President Kennedy was definitely considering removing
the depletion allowance. The depletion allowance is one of the
greatest boons to the oil business—the coal companies don't
get it, the copper companies don't get it, the mineral companies don't get it, timber people don't get it, only the oil companies. It's a complete steal from the tax-payers' funds. One of
the richest men in the world, oilman H.L. Hunt, according to
President Kennedy as reported by Childs, pays very little taxes,
for example. On top of that, Kennedy said, the 27% allowance
which Texas oil men get is used by them to finance Right Wing
activities, all tax exempt. Obviously, the assassination was to
the benefit of such people, because Johnson has not touched
the depletion allowance, and had no intention of doing so.

I feel quite positively that there was more than one person involved. If, in fact, Oswald was not alone, then immediately the question of a conspiracy arises, because it would be
incredible that two fanatics at the same time should both decide to kill the President. That being the case, you then have to
find somebody who planned the thing, and very definitely the
finger of suspicion points at those who benefited from it.

Now, the assassination would obviously not benefit the
Left Wing, for Kennedy was taking steps to abate the Cold
War, he'd made a promise to Castro that Cuba would not be
invaded. Further, with Kennedy killed, the Left got as a President a man known to be more conservative, so it's kind of silly
to knock off a young man who was on the road to softening
animosities internationally, and to get a guy who—we know
what we got now.

But from the Right Wing viewpoint, it makes a great deal
of difference. Skipping the depletion allowance, there is the
fact that the Right felt that Kennedy was pro-Communist, as
shown by the newspaper attack on Kennedy in Dallas. It's all
on the record that these people thought of Kennedy as a lefty,
as soft on Communism, and so on.

Now, mark my words: A break is going to come in this

case, like in the Dreyfus case. It took 12 years in France for the Dreyfus case to break open. It may not take that long in this one, because the pot is already boiling.

John Howard Griffin
writer, Black Like Me

Yes, I certainly do think that our society was responsible for the assassination. There is an atmosphere of violence in our country today, particularly in the South. In my own work, I've come across such a willingness to do away with a President that it's quite terrifying.

I also think that the possibility of another Presidential assassination is greater today than it was 5 years ago, or 3 years ago when it happened, because it seems to me that the climate of violence, in which people believe in force to accomplish their ends, has almost reached a peak in our country today.

Gordon Allport, Ph.D.
professor of psychology, Harvard University

We have to get an adequate reason for a disaster, and one little psychopath on the sixth floor doesn't look very adequate. Broadly speaking, systematic conspiracy theories would explain major disasters better. Your cause has to equal your effect, and the effect of the assassination was very great, and therefore people want an adequate cause.

David Rothstein, M.D.
psychiatrist

Maybe some of the people who prefer to believe that there was a conspiracy feel that there must be a reason for everything—the idea that chance was involved, or mental illness, or that there was no purposeful reason for the assassination might be upsetting to these people.

As for the Warren Commission, I was one of three psychiatrists who met with them on July 9, 1964, at the V.F.W. building in Washington. I feel they should have at least put

403

into their report the fact that they had *had* this discussion with us, and what some of the ideas were, even if they didn't commit themselves to saying that they were endorsing these ideas.

Renatus Hartogs, M.D., Ph.D.
psychiatrist

The Warren Report is, in my definite opinion, a serious and sincere, clumsy and ponderous effort to find the answer to the most hideous crime in recent American history. It mobilized extreme discomfort and anxiety among all those people who tremble in their boots when they have to face the undeniable fact that one single individual is able to plan and execute all by himself such a dastardly and monstrous deed of destruction.

While the Warren Report points the accusing finger clearly at that single man Oswald, who in his megalomanic power-hunger had to commit the world-shaking crime of his generation, agitated and frightened minds all over the world quickly had to write articles and books in an attempt to spread thin the responsibility for such a murderous deed by means of inventing and suspecting "conspirators." It would indeed be so much more soothing and anxiety-relieving if one could assume, or even prove, that such a murder was the result of a political conspiracy of many—rather than the frenzied product of a single, diseased mind.

My own early contact with the young Oswald left no doubt that I was psychiatrically dealing with an extremely violence-prone and exceedingly dangerous individual, filled with cold rage against the world around him. He was an isolate, always alone with his violent thoughts and not wanting to share his angry resentment and vindictive intentions with anybody. He was essentially a violent loner for whom a contact or alliance with conspirators was totally unthinkable and unacceptable.

Since I examined Oswald, I have encountered and diagnostically evaluated numerous such violence-prone individuals who—many years after the examination—actually committed very serious assaultive or homicidal crimes, but never got the

404

same publicity as Oswald did. These individuals with homicidal potential practically always act alone. They have—like the Texas tower-murderer or the Chicago nurses-killer—no conspirators, and do not need or want them. They plan their crimes carefully and cautiously and execute them with the cold precision, decisiveness, and the striking power we usually would not believe to find in a single individual. Yet they are and act alone in their closed world of hate and violence. They cannot tolerate any conspirators, because sharing the criminal responsibility and status would deprive them of the desired emotional impact, cathartic effect, and notoriety of their violent acting-out.

Even at the risk of frightening some soft-brained and tender-hearted rumormongers, we must state that Kennedy's death was "unfortunately" not a political assassination designed by a congenial group of conspirators, but a brutal murder with political impact, conceived, planned, and perpetrated by the morbid inner world-forces of a single, insanely destructive power-operator.

Albert Ellis, Ph.D.
psychologist

There is no certainty in the world. There's probably at least a 90 or 95% chance that the basic conclusions of the Warren Report are true. But there never will be absolute certainty, and many people demand absolute certainty.

I also feel that a large minority of people are paranoid, and paranoid people always think of things being a conspiracy. The Right Wing paranoiac suspects a conspiracy, as does the Left Wing paranoiac. These people always feel a little more comfortable with some kind of conspiracy because they feel, basically, that the world is against *them,* that there's a conspiracy against *them*—their own problems couldn't be their own doing, so it must be a plot. And they project this plot onto the socio-political scene.

The chances are 90 or 95 out of a hundred that Oswald did it alone, but there's always other possibilities, which will remain unprovable for all time. But I myself am willing to live in a world of probability and chance, where we pick the greatest possibility and don't expect certainty.

Warner Brown
psychoanalyst

First: Americans, because of their puritanical upbringing, are very apt to believe in wild rumors. Most Americans, as impressionable children, were exposed to a fantastic mystery: the mystery of sex. As the years went by, thanks to their parents' embarrassment, the mystery was not resolved. It deepened. Finally came the solution, strange and magical: sexual intercourse and childbirth. Thenceforward, whenever these people encounter any further mysteries, they are apt to look for fantastic and magical solutions—simply because the first mystery they ever encountered had that kind of solution.

My second point: All men, as children, at times wished that they had their mothers all to themselves, and they wish their fathers were out of the way—the Oedipus Complex. Naturally, these murderous impulses toward authority-figures carry over into adult life. And so you will find that whenever a leader of a country dies, whenever a father-figure dies, there is widespread guilt. People, in their unconscious minds, feel that they themselves are guilty. It's for this same reason that innocent people confess to crimes they did not commit: At one time or another, they *wanted* to commit that crime.

Now, the public's guilt over President Kennedy's assassination is manifested in the pathological mourning that followed, in the lavish gifts bestowed upon Officer Tippit's widow and Marina Oswald, the letters sent to Jacqueline Kennedy, and the adulation given to Bobby Kennedy. By giving Bobby Kennedy their votes and their cheers, people are proving that no, they didn't kill his brother. And perhaps they are proving that the President isn't dead after all—in the unconscious mind, it's easy to confuse the two brothers.

But the guilt is still there. And therefore many people want to prove, once again, that they didn't kill the President, and they are looking for other assassins.

My last point is that of all people, the Jews are the most vulnerable to the death of a leader. They feel more guilty than anyone else. One reason is that all their lives they have been blamed for the death of another father—God, Jesus Christ. Many of my Jewish patients told me how anxious they were until they found out that the assassin, Oswald, was a Protestant. It was natural for a Jew, Jack Ruby, in order to expiate his own feelings of guilt, to kill Oswald. And it is natural that Jewish intellectuals would try to find other guilty people besides Oswald: one Oswald is not enough to relieve their guilt. Mark Lane, Harold Popkin, Feldman, Harold Weisberg, Edward Jay Epstein—they are all looking for additional assassins, and they get their articles published in Jewish magazines like *Commentary* (run by Norman Podhoretz) and the *New York Review of Books* (run by someone name Epstein).

This may seem hard to believe, but a survey was made during World War II about credence given to wild rumors, and it was found that Jews, more than any other group, believed them. Of course, for historical and social reasons, the Jews have to pay more attention to frightening rumors than anyone else. But it is also true, I think, that Jews readily accept the guilt of any murder of a father-figure, and this explains why the inability to accept one lone assassin has come mainly from Jewish men and Jewish magazines.

Paul B. Sheatsley
director, Survey Research Institute
National Opinion Research Center

Jacob J. Feldman and I once conducted a survey on public reactions to the assassination, and a majority of the public expressed the belief that Oswald did not act alone, that other people were involved. The Anti-Defamation League of B'nai B'rith has attributed this conspiracy theory to the activities of extremist groups, which have been preaching about plots and conspiracies in American life for many years.

Daniel Bell has noted, "It takes a high degree of sophistication, Freud wrote, to believe in chance; primitive fears are allayed more easily by a devil theory of politics." Resort to a conspiratorial diagnosis would seem to be particularly appropriate in the case of the Kennedy assassination, because most people do not easily accept the concept of mental illness to explain behavior—especially if the person who is mentally ill displays self-control and appears to be rational. Moreover, the conclusion that mentally ill people—not responsible for their behavior—are at large among us, and are capriciously ending the life of even a President, is both bizarre and threatening.

Allen Ginsberg
poet

The 1966 published studies on the Warren Commission Report do confirm that, like most official documentation (whether of the death of President Kennedy or the reasoning behind the Vietnam war), language therein framed as a vehicle for perception and thought processes is not satisfactory human communication. Too much of the subjective data of the measuring instrument itself, that is, the Warren Commission or the Pentagon, is eliminated by terminological officialese. Norman Mailer's style of personal critique, for instance, carries more information than the inferior prose style of the Warren Commission Report.

Secondly, the "credibility gap" established by men in the government over the last decade has spread to cover almost all official statements, from FDA "fact sheets" on LSD (which are full of stereotype-language misinformation) to Rusk's analyses of the genesis of the Vietnam war (which differs so much from Walter Lippman's language or De Gaulle's). So who can believe anything said in "objective" jargon?

Close analyses published by Mark Lane and others have revealed crudities of procedure, discrepancies of information, and lacunae of association in Warren Commission texts. So that leaves all of us up in the air, in a bombing plane over Hanoi.

Mailer's proposal for a commission of literary persons whose goodness of temperament is more trustworthy than that of politicians makes simple common sense. The nation's in a mess. Dwight Macdonald's as trustworthy to straighten it out as LeRoi Jones or President Johnson.

Dwight Macdonald
journalist

Yes, I think there is a psychological explanation—more accurately a psycho-sociopolitical one—for why Americans have believed, before and after the Warren Report, that Oswald was either part of, or framed up by, a conspiracy that has not yet been uncovered, whether by chance or bungling or design. They are the young and/or the alienated, and they begin with a skepticism about the American Establishment and a suspicion of its motives for which they have many and good reasons—though not as many nor as good as they think they have. These assumptions have led them to seize on every contradiction, every obscurity, major or minor, in this most complex and murky affair, in order to justify their initial prejudice, which made it easy for them to believe, long before the Warren Report was published, on the shaky basis of newspaper stories and Mark Lane's lecture tours—his manipulation of The Facts was even more one-sided, for the defense, than that of his fellowlawyers on the Commission staff was for the prosecution—that "there must have been a conspiracy." The same assumption made it difficult, almost impossible, for them to believe that one peculiar individual might have done it all by himself for his own peculiar, personal reasons. I think this belief, or prejudice, would have survived, in this ambiance, even if the Warren Report had been a good deal more convincing than it was.

I must admit, however, that while I still find no difficulty in believing that Oswald did it all by himself and for his own peculiar, personal reasons, and that if I have to say *yes* or *no* to Oswald's sole guilt, I'd still say *yes,* I am more than a little shaken in this conclusion by some recent critical analyses of the Warren Report. When I wrote a critique of the Report in *Esquire* (March, 1965), soon after it was published, I found it a brief for the prosecution rather than what it pretended to be, an objective investigation. It seemed to me biased in favor of the hypothesis that Oswald had done it, all by himself. But I was convinced by the "hard" evidence of ballistics, handwriting, ownership of guns, analysis of paper fibers, presence on the scene, etc. Now we have a number of recent books which cast doubts on many of the Warren Commission's conclusions, on the basis of a more extensive study of the 26 volumes of testimony and exhibits than I had had time to make, since they were published only a few weeks before I finished my *Esquire* article.

More important, there is now a considerable body of what seems to me reasonable criticism of a crucial bit of "hard" evidence that I had accepted without thinking about it, had just assumed was Fact: the validity of the official autopsy on the President's body, which described the first wound as made by a bullet which entered his neck from the back and which could, therefore, also have completed its trajectory by wounding Governor Connally, who was sitting in front of him in the car. (If the same bullet didn't hit both men, there must have been a second assassin, since, for reasons everybody seems to accept, there couldn't have been time for the same rifle to have been fired, let alone aimed, twice.) This crucial point is made, with varying degrees of effectiveness, in recent books by Léo Sauvage, Harold Weisberg, Richard Popkin, and Mark Lane, but the one that really unsettled my previous assumptions was Edward Jay Epstein's *Inquest,* which not only turned up a lot of completely new data on it—and on other aspects of the Report—but also convinced me by his cautious, fair-minded, succinctly rational presentation of his material that his aim was quite simply, without any personal or political ax-grinding, to get at the truth rather than to score off the Commission's Report.

Finally, you ask: "Would you serve on a commission to investigate the assassination?" This puts me in a rather awkward position. Although I have been publicly nominated for such a post by Norman Mailer (see *Book Week,* August 28th last), with Edmund Wilson replacing Earl Warren as chairman, I have not yet received a formal invitation from the White House. All I can say at the moment—our President's

410

dislike of any premature "leaks" of his future appointments is well-known—is that my contacts in the Administration indicate that he, or He, is enthusiastic, image-wise, about Mailer's proposed Literary Commission To Revise The Warren Report. However, he (He) feels, with his subtle political sense, that the nominations should go "through channels," in this case a committee composed of Messrs. Rusk, Hoover, and McNamara. When this matter of form is complied with, I shall probably, *entre nous,* accept the appointment. I don't see how I or Mr. Wilson or Mr. Mailer could do worse than Mr. Warren's Commission has.

Marya Mannes
author and critic

I think the American public, exposed to movies, theater, and television, *want* a plot, and not one assassin who did it alone, by himself. To believe that more than one man did it is somehow more of a release. Yet most American assassinations have been committed by a single person. You really couldn't call the Lincoln assassination a conspiracy. It was one deranged man, one obsessed man.

The tremendous public interest in all these books is quite natural. The assassination of this particular President could be the major event of our time. It was a terrible emotional experience everybody went through, and I think there's a masochistic desire to somehow live through it all over again, and read anything and everything—even the most cock-eyed theories, whether you believe them or not. So far, the assassination was certainly the greatest tragedy of all for the current generation. I know that the young identified with him as they did with no one else.

I myself accepted Oswald as the lone assassin. Frankly, I have not read all these books, but I read the whole Warren Report, and I must say I came away from the long exercise pretty well convinced that indeed it was Oswald. Now I know that discrepancies have been discovered, which may or may not be important, and which may or may not involve others. If there is any final truth, one must certainly be open to it.

The assassination, I believe, was also related to the terrific underlay of violence in the American people. It worries me very much. I think it's very close to the surface, and I think it can be triggered by all sorts of things. I'm afraid that I do subscribe to the belief that there is a certain sickness in our society, the sickness of violence, and it troubles me deeply because I think it extends to the public's acceptance of the Vietnamese war, too. The acceptance of war as a necessary condition, for whatever aims, is a very frightening thing.

***

Thedore Bikel
actor and singer

First of all, it's very hard to reconcile oneself to a national tragedy, to as shocking an event as the assassination of a President revered as only F.D.R. was in this century. One is unwilling to accept tragedy—that's one reason many people don't accept the Warren Report. Another is that the explanation of the tragedy seems to be a facile one—too easy. It's all tied up with a neat blue ribbon.

I'm saying there's a possibility that it ain't so, and this possibility should have been mentioned more prominently than it has been. There are certain things that just don't fit the theory, and you can't just disregard the facts that don't fit your theory and press the ones that do. We're dealing with history here; we're also *not* dealing with children.

***

Godfrey Cambridge
comedian

The Warren Commission issued their report and people booed, right? Well, that's what people do. When something happens, from housemaid's knee to the stock market falling, people blame it on the Right—and people blame it on the Left.

Maybe in the year 2053 there'll be an obscure little professor with horn-rimmed glasses at the University of Minnesota who'll find an obscure diary and it will say that President Johnson actually had a remote-control set-up, and that when he pushed a button in his car—*choo!*—that was it. President

Johnson, Oswald, a Mexican peon, and a Negro bootblack. We have to get *all* races represented in there.

Sol Yurick
novelist, Fertig

Upon hearing the news, Malcolm X said that the chickens had come home to roost: it was an outrageous remark, widely misinterpreted: even Malcolm probably didn't know what he really meant. Malcolm thought the assassination merely a product of the racist struggle: Whitey's business.

The true meaning of Malcolm's words was that the act was an apotheosis of an American process; a purely American event was what killed Kennedy . . . Malcolm's sense of gloomy satisfaction meant that the killing, in the long run, was a just one.

Why just? Isn't such a speculation a little mad? What we fail to see is that Kennedy was a *sacrificial* figure whose death should have served to bring understanding of America and its corruption: a purification. This fact, in the later interpretation, was corrupted. The martyr became a martyr in name only: in the hands of the New Criticism, Kennedy's death became meaningless; sentimental.

What we dare not understand is that America is a corrupted land; its noble ideals have been denied or warped since the inception of the nation. America is a violent land which has been settled and developed by violent people, doing violence to one another on *all* levels. It is the veneer of pragmatic reasonableness, of consensus, that has disguised this fact because we have buried not only our victims, but the history of how we killed our victims. After all, we have gloated, this is no Germany, no Russia, no China; we have due process. But the seminal legend of frontier justice, the gun-hero cutting through red tape to redress grievances, pervades our culture. So every now and then, the whole implicit seethe of violence beneath the surface of our country comes to a head; some spectacular act is committed which is more in the nature of a national rite rather than a newspaper headline.

Now Kennedy was a good man, good by the pluralistic

413

standards of America: he was for civil rights, for an understanding with the iron-curtain countries, against poverty . . . he had all the right feelings. Yet he was the leader of the land and the very spirit of a hero-sacrifice consists of having the good man die for us, taking on our sins. And, according to legend, then there comes a Paul, or a Pauline council, to misinterpret the nature of the sacrifice in the interests of harmony. As has happened.

And the assassin? Only a kind of symbolic manifestation of the American process; an unwitting personification; a man drafted, so to speak, to be an executioner; a figure to fill all of our absurd, speculative projections.

Who then killed Kennedy? Not so much the political ultras, or the ultras of our dreams, but all of us who, in doing nothing, have given assent to the way things are . . . we were the assassin.

A Psychiatric Study of Jokes About Psychiatrists

By Warren Boroson

Everybody loves a lover—and hates a headshrinker. Not landlords, not undertakers, not even bill-collectors arouse the fear and the loathing that Americans feel when they hear that awful word, "psychiatrist." The Fright Wing, of course, cherishes the notion that psychiatrists are in league to put all of us into loony bins for the greater glory of Mother Russia, but even ordinary people may lose their cool when it comes to the men who deal in deep psychology. "Many studies," David Riesman and Donald Horton write in the *Sociological Quarterly*, "indicate that even today the great majority of Amcricans . . . view psychiatrists with a combination of fascination, malice, and ignorance. . . ."

Our mass media have helped spread the malice. In comic strips, from "Little Orphan Annie" to "Li'l Abner," psychiatrists are depicted as insane, and novels like Kingsley Amis's *The Anti-Death League* carry on the tradition. When they are not crazy, psychiatrists are sex-mad (John O'Hara's *From the Terrace*); bumbling and bungling (the Alan King play *The Impossible Years*, Virginia Woolf's *Mrs. Dalloway*, Lillian Ross's *Vertical and Horizontal*, F. Scott Fitzgerald's *Tender Is the Night*, the film *Move Over, Darling*); or cold and cruel (T.S. Eliot's *The Cocktail Party*, the Gregory Peck film *Mirage*, the film *A Fine Madness*, Arthur Koestler's *Arrival and Departure*). And then there are the three most famous fictional psychiatrists of all time—Dr. Lilith Ritter (in *Nightmare Alley*), who blackmails her patients; Dr. Forester (in Graham Greene's *Ministry of Fear*), who moonlights as a Nazi spy; and, of course, Dr. Charlotte Manning (in Mickey Spillane's *I, the Jury*), who not only blackmails her patients but occasionally murders them, to be shot in turn by Mike Hammer despite her efforts to distract him by doing a striptease. As for TV in general, psychiatrist Martin Meyers told the American Psychiatric Association recently, "It is doubtful if an evening goes by without a psychiatrist or patient being derided, lampooned, caricatured, or laughed at."

Yet our greatest repository of hatred for psychiatrists is not movies, novels, or TV, but cartoons and jokes. In the late 1940s, according to Fredrick C. Redlich of the Yale Medical School, one or two out of every 100 jokes in major magazines dealt with psychiatrists. After examining 100 such jokes, Dr. Redlich found they presented psychiatrists as "brutal, licentious, weak, anxious and helpless . . . aggressive, oversexed, and as abnormal as their patients" (*American Journal of Orthopsychiatry*). Today's cartoons and jokes about psychiatrists, I would say, haven't changed—except that there are more of them, one or two in 50.

Why do Americans seem to consider psychiatrists as one step removed from hatchet murderers? Psychiatrists give one answer:

All medicine is inextricably mixed with magic. The calling arose with witch-doctors, primitive "medicine men," and priests; today's physicians use strange instruments and marvelous potions, they speak and write a baffling language, and they effect miraculous cures. And "Within medicine," as psychiatrist Otto Fenichel has written, "psychiatry is not only the youngest branch of this magic-imbued science, but it is also the one most tainted with magic."

Now, the psychiatrist's job is to explore people's minds. But what is more, being magicians, they can (it is thought) peer right into our minds without any obstacle at all—and learn those horribly shameful things we don't want *anyone* to know: our evil impulses, our irrational ideas, our sexual fantasies, our wicked wishes. In short, psychiatrists are mind-readers; and by reading our minds, they can have us at their mercy.

It is a frightening idea. And just how frightening can be seen from the hundreds of nasty jokes told about psychiatrists.

Most of these jokes can be placed in five categories:

Psychiatrists are mad.

Perhaps the main reason for the myth of the mad psychiatrist is the application of the Brass Rule: Do unto others what you think they'd like to do unto you. The many people who are afraid of being judged mentally ill are, of course, tickled pink at the thought of their would-be judges becoming mentally ill. Everyone, likewise, is pleased when bluenoses get caught reading erotic books, when magistrates are arrested for speeding, and when dentists suffer from toothaches.

As a man happily trots down the street, stark naked, a woman sees him and shouts to her companion, "My God, George, that's my psychiatrist!"

A cartoon shows both the psychiatrist and his patient cutting out paper dolls. Says the psychiatrist, "Sure, you have the same speed—but yours aren't as *regular* as mine."

"Now, just how long have you had these hallucinations?" says the psychiatrist—to a couch with nobody on it.

Psychiatrist to patient: "I could easily cure you of your depression, but, as you say, everything seems so futile . . ."

A young psychiatrist is telling an older psychiatrist about his problems. "I ask a patient, What has delightful curves, wonderful form, and sometimes becomes uncontrollable?" "Sandy Koufax." "Right. I ask, What goes in hard and comes out soft and wet?" "A piece of gum." "Naturally. And I ask, What is a four-letter word meaning 'intercourse'?" " 'Talk,' " says the older man. "Of course! But you'd never *believe* the crazy answers I keep getting!"

Psychiatrists are money-mad.

Among physicians, psychiatrists are among the poorest paid. Most other specialists make several thousand dollars more a year. On the other hand, since a psychiatrist sees far fewer patients than other physicians do, for a far longer time, the psychiatrist must charge more per visit. Hence the complaints.

Hypno-analyst to patient: ". . . and when you wake up, Smedley, you bastard, you'll pay your bills *immediately*."

A woman tells her psychiatrist that recently she's been having obsessive impulses to kill herself, and she can't get these suicidal thoughts out of her mind. The psychiatrist purses his lips, reflects for a while, then says, "Well, that being the case, Mrs. Quackenbush, you won't mind paying your bills in advance?"

The businessman on the couch is dissolved in tears. The psychiatrist, holding his own head in his hands, groans aloud: "I know, I *know*. I've got stock in your company!"

Psychiatrists are cruel.

They certainly *could* be. By baring his mind as he never has before, the patient becomes terribly vulnerable: The psychiatrist becomes the Ultimate Judge. One girl told me after she had been in analysis 2 years, "One nasty word from that shrink, and I would have died." This fear that a psychiatrist might not protect his patient's sensitivities is very real, though actual cases of it happening are, of course, all but unknown.

"You don't have an inferiority complex," says the psychiatrist to his meek-looking, seedily-dressed patient. "You *are* inferior."

"You have two personalities," the psychiatrist tells his patient, "and neither is worth a plugged nickel."

Psychiatrist to parent: "Be gentle with him, but strict. Keep in mind at all times that you're dealing with a sensitive, high-strung, dirty son of a bitch."

"Mr. Davenport, I think I have the solution for you," says the psychiatrist, handing his patient a gun.

"Ridley," says the psychiatrist, "yours is a common enough personality problem. You're obnoxious."

After being institutionalized for 10 years, the patient is ready for release and visits the staff psychiatrist for his terminal interview. "Tell me, Canby," says the psychiatrist, "do

420

you promise henceforward to keep away from whiskey and women?" "Sure!" says the patient. The psychiatrist sighs and summons an attendant. "Lock this nut up, Henry, he's *still* crazy."

Patient: "Doctor, people think I'm boring." The psychiatrist behind her is snoozing.

Psychiatrist to patient: "Go out and mingle with other schizophrenics."

Psychiatrists are sex-mad.
For decades, psychiatry has been commonly and erroneously identified with sexual license, simply because psychiatrists in general have been rather outspoken about sex, have asserted the importance of sex, and have been somewhat tolerant of sexual freedom. Dr. Norman E. Zinberg, clinical associate in psychiatry at the Harvard Medical School, has written:

In no area has there been more conflict between [American] culture and psychiatrists than on the topic of candor about sex. The controversial libido theory, which outlined a broad definition of sexuality, led the earlier psychoanalysts to be seen as libertines. . . . In its emphasis on the person's relationship with himself, it takes individual release and gratification into account, and in that sense it is opposed to morality. . . . [Psychoanalysis rejects] morality in favor of a system of thought that considers what "fits," what "makes sense" for a person, rather than what is absolutely "right" or "wrong". . . .

When you add to this the fact that psychiatrists see female patients alone, for 50 minutes, with a couch, and listen to some very intimate matters, you discover whereof myths are made.

Outside a psychiatrist's office, a man hears this conversation: "Doctor, you've done so much for me, how can I ever repay you? The least I can do is give you a big kiss." "No, no!" shouts the psychiatrist, aghast. "Why, we shouldn't even be lying on this couch together!"

As the smirking psychiatrist hovers over his beautiful and buxom patient, he says, "Miss Carter, there's no such thing as a frigid woman . . ."

To a dried-up old spinster, the psychiatrist says matter-of-factly, "You're alone far too much. Go out, meet people, sleep around . . ."

Psychiatrists' patients are mad.

The butt of most jokes involving psychiatrists is not the psychiatrist, surprisingly, but the patient. After all, for many years people paid an admission charge to visit hospitals for the mentally ill to laugh at the loonies. The exhibitions at Bethlehem Hospital (Bedlam) in England are notorious, and they were abolished in only 1770. We Americans, of course, are quite different from the English: We kept up the practice until well into the 19th Century. In *The Mentally Ill in America*, Albert Deutsch writes:

It was customary, particularly on Sundays and holidays, for idlers and thrill-seekers to gather about the cell windows of the insane which stood at ground level and to take turns at "teasing the crazy people," with the aim of rousing them into raving fury.

Gradually the insane department of Pennsylvania Hospital became known as one of the show places of Philadelphia. . . . It was quite the thing for inhabitants to entertain their out-of-town guests by bringing them to observe, or to participate in, the sport of baiting the madmen.

Nowadays it's no longer socially acceptable to ridicule people who are sick, but the fear of the mentally ill remains with us. We fear the lunatic because to some degree we identify with everyone we meet, and identifying with a lunatic is frightening. (Many people get the same thrill of horror when they encounter cripples, or panhandlers.) So great is the fear of the mentally ill that some people, including one well-known psychiatrist, prefer to believe that mental illness does not even exist. Another defense is to laugh at the mentally ill—in jokes, where almost everything is acceptable. For by laughing at the lunatic, we are in effect saying, "That *is* not me, that could not *be* me."

"Everybody hates me," sobs the dejected patient. "My wife hates me, my children hate me, my employees hate me, even the neighbors hate me. Doc, I just can't, for the life of me,

422

understand why everyone hates me." "Er, what was that last phrase?" asks the psychiatrist. Answers the patient: "WHY DON'T YOU CLEAN THE WAX OUT OF YOUR EARS, STUPID?"

"I'm dead," announces the patient. "Look," the psychiatrist says, "dead men don't bleed, do they?" "Nosirree," answers the patient. Whereupon the psychiatrist sticks a pin into the man's finger and draws a drop of blood. Fascinated, the patient stares at the blood, then says: "What do you know? Dead men *do* bleed!"

Governor Romney once visited a state mental hospital, and observed that the men and the women lived in different buildings. To the doctor in attendance, he said: "Interesting that you've got the men and women separated." "Sure," replied the psychiatrist. "They're not *that* crazy."

"How long," asks the psychiatrist thoughtfully, "have you thought that you were a dog?" The patient reflects, then he says: "Well, I guess ever since I was a puppy . . ."

A man races into a psychiatrist's office, tobacco stuffed in both ears. "I see you need me," says the doctor. "Damn right!" the man says. "Got a match?"

Two men are waiting to see a psychiatrist. Both are dressed like Napoleon. Says one to the other, "What are you, some kind of nut?"

A man with a cat perched on top of his head walks into a psychiatrist's office. "What can I do for you?" asks the doctor. "Well, to begin with, I've got this man under me," says the cat.

Little Johnny was quite a problem. In public he was forever saying, "Look at the boobs on the blonde! Look at those knockers on that chick! Boyoboy, is that teenybopper built!" So his father took him to a psychiatric clinic in New York. After 2 months, the father came back for him, and began taking him home on a bus. Johnny was quite proper now, and glanced dully at all the women he saw. But suddenly he became excited. "Dad, dad!" he shouted. "What is it, son?" "Just look at the ass on that bus driver!"

All ready to be discharged from a mental hospital, the young man was explaining to a nurse his career plans. "You see, I have an M.D. and I can become a physician. With my law degree, I could try practicing law. And, of course, I could always try my hand at teaching." "Wonderful!" gushes the nurse. "It sounds like you're all ready to face the outside world." "And if none of that works out," continues the young man, "I can always be a teakettle."

The patient was convinced that, by sitting next to the window and sticking his tongue out, he was keeping lions and tigers away. Finally the psychiatrist got exasperated. "Look, Smedley," he said, "you've never actually *seen* any lions and tigers, have you?" "You see, doc? You *see*? It *works!*"

"Doctor, I have no problems, no problems at all," says the patient, who is dressed as Napoleon. "I'm the Emperor, undefeated in battle, women always give themselves to me, I'm fabulously wealthy. But there's one thing that bothers me—the Empress Josephine." "Hmmm," says the psychiatrist, "and what seems to be wrong with *her*?" "She thinks she's Mrs. Cohen."

The new arrival at the mental hospital was convinced that he was Abraham Lincoln. By coincidence, another patient there also thought he was Abraham Lincoln. So psychiatrists decided to put the two in the same room for one night to see if they could un-delude each other.

The next day, a psychiatrist went to see one of the men. "I'm not Abraham Lincoln! I'm not Abraham Lincoln!" the man was shouting. "What's your name, then?" Blushing coyly, the man says, "I'm *Mrs*. Lincoln."

"Baseball, baseball, that's all I ever dream about," says the new patient. "Interesting," says the psychiatrist. "You never dream about women, then?" "What, and lose my turn at bat?"

424

Patient on couch to doctor: "It all began when my team came in second in a toothpaste contest. . . ."

Three men are in a psychiatrist's waiting-room. One has a bandaged nose. "Which of you," says the psychiatrist, "is the woodpecker?"

"So your boy makes mud pies, does he?" says the psychiatrist. "Well, I happen to think that's perfectly normal." "Well, *I* don't think so," says the woman, "*he* doesn't think so, and his *wife* doesn't think so."

The patient is lying on the couch, with the mattress drawn up over him. Asks the psychiatrist: "Now, just what kind of sandwich do you think you are?"

The psychiatrist is lying on the couch, the patient is sitting in his chair—and saying, "Ever since I can remember, I've had this superiority complex . . ."

* * *

Of the 500 or so cartoons and jokes about psychiatrists I've tracked down, there were only a few that seemed somewhat favorable. One shows a tough, aggressive woman charging into a psychiatrist's office with her timid husband in tow. "Doctor," she bellows, "do for *him* what you did for *me*." In another, a man comes home and calls to his wife: "Darling, remember the psychiatrist you've been nagging me to see? Well, three guesses who he says is causing all my problems?" Finally, there is this cartoon: "Doctor," a beautiful young woman is saying, "you've been a great help, but [*taking out a gun*] you know too damn much."

These three jokes, significantly, were published quite recently. And it's significant, too, that a recent TV series, *Eleventh Hour,* had a psychiatrist as its hero, as did a recent novel, Leo Rosten's *Captain Newman, M.D.* (Gregory Peck played the movie's title role.) Then too, in the film *Blindfold,* the lead psychiatrist is portrayed by Rock Hudson. Obviously, things can't be all black when movie psychiatrists are being played by Messrs. Peck and Hudson.

425

But more: A few psychiatrists are even rather pleased by the number of nasty jokes about them. And with good reason. Psychiatry has swiftly gained influence in education, politics, history, literature, law, international relations, religion, and all other branches of medicine—in fact, throughout all of human society it is providing enlightenment and insight. Clearly, the rising number of jokes about psychiatrists is related to their growing influence on our lives. Dr. Redlich has written:

From the psychiatrist's point of view, the increasing number of cartoons depicting and deriding psychiatry should be welcome. . . . Psychiatrists have gained a status of respect and authority which is reduced through the unmasking process of caricature. . . . Since it is no fun to debunk someone unless he has already been placed on some kind of pedestal, it is interesting to note that during the period when the number of cartoons poking fun at psychiatrists has been increasing, the number poking fun at ministers has been decreasing.

Of Transcendental Beauty and Crawling Horror

By Ronald Weston

F our or five years ago I tried marijuana for the first time. I experienced a heightened visual awareness and a sort of nongenital sexuality. Every color I looked at was several degrees brighter than its usual luster, and my entire body had a delightful tingle, as if it were one undifferentiated erogenous zone. In the following months (this was in New York City, where pot is as easy to come by as tobacco if you have the right connections), I took marijuana several times, and once I made love to a girl while under the influence. It was the greatest orgasm I had ever had, and I could have become a confirmed pot-head then and there, except for one thing. A few weeks later I saw a friend go through the "pot horrors"—technically known as "hallucinogenic anxiety" or "psychotomimesis" (imitation psychosis). It was a wildly unpretty sight to see. My friend said later that it was the most unpleasant experience of his whole life, and watching it was certainly one of the most unpleasant experiences of mine.

A few years later, in California, at a party, I tried pot again. Nothing happened. I concluded later that this absence of reaction was caused by unconscious resistance: I still recalled my friend's experience and was afraid of repeating it.

* * *

One or two more years passed and I read a few things about the "hallucinogenic," or "psychedelic," drugs. I learned that many people under the influence of these drugs experience truly mystic states, comparable to religious visions, and that sometimes these effects are long-lasting and even permanent.

429

This is especially true of the chemical lysergic acid diethyla-mide (LSD), and of peyote, a drug obtained from a small cactus known as mescal; but it has been known to result from marijuana and even belladonna, a drug obtained from the poisonous plant. Many religious groups have used psychedelic drugs to induce visions of their gods. There is a peyote cult among the American Indians, a magic-mushroom cult among the Mexican Indians, a yage cult in South America, a marijuana cult among the Moslems. There was even a belladonna cult in Medieval Europe; its practitioners were burned as witches. Some theorists, notably Robert Graves and Alan Watts, have suggested that all religions can be traced to some group drug experience.

Over a year ago I heard of a place where peyote could be obtained easily. I knew that some people who take peyote have the horrors so bad that they have to be hauled off to a hospital, sometimes to remain for months, sometimes for years. Others have experiences of superhuman joy and blessedness. I am an artist and something of a mystic. I decided to take a chance.

I took the dose in the form of capsules. They were prepared in this way: The top of the peyote cactus was heated and dried until the moisture was removed (two complete cycles in a Laundromat drier did it). Then they were ground up into a fine powder by an ordinary wheat-grinding mill. The powder was then put into size 00 capsules. Twelve capsules makes a good dose. Fortunately, it takes a while to down 12 double-0 capsules, and you get a chance to decide whether you want to go through with it or not. I went through with it.

Nothing happened for about an hour.

Then anxiety began to creep over me. I began trembling and I felt nauseous. The wild idea that I had taken the wrong stuff and that I had been poisoned sent a chill through me. At the time I was in a farmhouse in a Midwestern state, and I walked outside to calm myself and get some fresh air. When I came back inside, a group of faces appeared at the window looking in at me. They were so patently sinister that I laughed at them. The laugh shifted the nature of the experience; the faces disappeared and I had no further anxiety. In a few moments I had my "marijuana symptoms": bright colors and sexual excitement. For another hour or so these symptoms continued and gradually increased until I was in a state far "higher" than anything I had reached on pot. The beauty of every object I turned to was now so great that I was in a continuous mood of childish awe and joy. I believe that a 2-year-old toddler who comes into a room and smiles softly at everything it sees has the kind of vision I had then. I was smiling and laughing continuously, and could only say, "It's all so *god*dam beautiful. . . ." A friend who had agreed to stay with me during this experiment says I looked exactly like one of the smiling Buddhas of China.

This was just after Christmas, and my friend suggested that, since ordinary objects were giving me such a charge, I ought to try looking at the Christmas tree in the next room. Neither of us had any idea of what that suggestion would produce.

I went into the living room and looked at the most beautiful Christmas tree I had ever seen. It was so lustrous, so multi-toned, so lovely, that I could not tear my eyes away from it. As I stood, literally stunned on the spot, the beauty began to focus and increase. This is, of course, impossible to verbalize. Crudely, let me say that marijuana-beauty is one foot above earth-level. In the past hour I had moved from that to about 10 feet high. Now, in about 2 or 3 minutes, I shot up dizzily to the height of Mount Everest. To express it another way, the words "transcendental," "supernatural," "more than human," "divine," "holy," etc., now have meaning for me. They mean precisely and exactly the millionfold beauty of that Christmas tree during those minutes.

I wept with joy. Yes, even that ridiculous cliché came true: I literally shook with sobs, and tears poured down my face, and I was happier than I have ever been before or since.

With the unleashing of the tears, something else happened. I know of no words that can describe that "something else," but I will try another analogy. I have been loved by two women in my lifetime, and that experience is something different in quality from the experience of being liked by the broad

431

you happen to be sleeping with at the time. By an even greater degree than love transcends sexual fondness, this experience transcended love. I am, as I said, a bit of a mystic, but I am a Buddhist mystic, not a Christian. Nevertheless, after this experience I can, almost, believe in a personal and very personalized god who loves and needs mankind maybe even more than mankind loves and needs him. The Catholic saint (I forget her name) who rolled around on the ground screaming, "Oh, the love, the love," was probably feeling what I felt then.

Bartolomeo Vanzetti wrote of how he once had a mystic experience looking at the night sky and felt "my soul go out from my body up." He was a very hard-headed, atheistical anarchist, and yet he needed this language to describe that experience.

For several hours thereafter I was in what I have come to call the Magic World. In that world, not only are colors supernaturally lovely, but *space is full*. I no longer saw beautiful objects: I saw one continuous beautiful unity.

Twelve hours after I had taken the capsules—that is, at 8 o'clock the next morning—I was back down to merely the marijuana level of beauty, and I finally began to feel sleepy. I slept most of the day and most of the next night, except for a few intervals of waking again in the Magic World. The next morning, Monday, I went into my regular job at the advertising agency where I work. Several people commented that I seemed happier than usual, but nobody thought I was acting crazy. I was well-oriented in space and time and had no bad after-effects.

For several weeks all colors were a little brighter than usual, and I was a little happier than usual.

Then another unexpected thing happened.

I fell in love, sexually, with a young boy.

I have never been homosexual in my life, and I am 34. In spite of that, and in spite of common sense and convention, I did not fear or reject my feelings. I let them develop and watched them with the fond tolerance I have for my children's carryings-on.

432

There was no doubting the reality, and the urgency, of the passion. I would get an erection just driving past the boy's house in a car.

The boy was definitely heterosexual and, I knew, would react to any advance with repugnance or fear. That realization alone—and no "moral" considerations at all—kept me from making a pass at him.

About a month after the "perversion" (if you want to call it that) began, it just as abruptly ended. Four months have passed since the ending of these homosexual impulses, and I have not had similar feelings toward that boy or any other male. I am very glad that I had this experience, though, for it has taught me to understand homosexuals a little better. It has also taught me why Freud was so fond of quoting the old proverb, "Nothing human is alien unto me."

Some time later I tried peyote again. Within a few hours I was back in the Magic World, and I stayed there, cozy and happy, for about 8 hours. Again, the color-awareness and the happiness lasted, in some degree, for several weeks.

I went back to peyote for the third time. I was in the Magic World for a while, then I went off into a different, nuttier world. I had visions of Donald Duck, of a Teddy bear I had slept with as a child and hadn't thought of for 30 years, of lollipops dancing, and of similar infantile things. Then I went outside and had the very spooky (but not frightening) experience of having the trees very definitely look back at me as I looked at them.

My wife tried some peyote and had a vision of Peyote Woman, an American Indian goddess. (Indians generally see either Peyote Woman or Jesus Christ during their peyote experiences, and my wife had been reading an anthropological study of these rites.) Peyote Woman spoke to my wife for several hours and made specific prophecies about various friends of ours. Most of the prophecies have come true.

A friend wrote to tell me that he and his girl had taken peyote together and were able to see each other's skeletons through the skin.

Another friend took peyote, got on the New York subway, and saw the figures in the advertisements acting out little dramas in 3-D.

I have read that biochemists have discovered that peyote, LSD, marijuana, and the other psychedelic substances have the same chemical basis as adrenochrome, a substance found in the blood of schizophrenics and diabetics. It is hypothesized that it is the adrenochrome that produces schizophrenic hallucinations and causes diabetics sometimes to act like schizophrenics. This hypothesis does not fully explain why schizophrenics almost always always have frightening hallucinations and peyote users almost always have joyous ones. Could it be that the nature of the hallucination depends upon the body-set before the substance is ingested (peyote) or produced by the body (adrenochrome)? The schizophrenic, before his first hallucination, generally has had several months, or years, of acute anxiety.

I was learning a great deal about religion and insanity, and about myself. I wanted to take more peyote and learn more. At this time, however, the U.S. Narcotics Bureau, after several years of effort, finally succeeded in getting the possession of peyote declared illegal.

If many of my friends might qualify as beatniks, and if I am in the privacy of my thoughts a superbeatnik and an anarchist, I nonetheless, for the sake of my wife and children, find it necessary to "pass" in the square world and hold a square job. I decided not to mess with the law and I decided to leave peyote alone. (You can dispose of marijuana easily, but peyote cacti are cumbersome.)

* * *

One day I heard that belladonna creates effects similar to peyote and can be purchased legally in any drug store. I investigated and found out that this was true. One dollar will buy you enough for ten experiences—but don't rush to the drug store until you've finished this article.

I took two teaspoons of belladonna at nine o'clock on a

434

Friday night, planning to have the whole week-end to recuperate.

In a few minutes I realized that something bad was happening. I saw a Hollywood monster coming at me across the yard. By the time this image faded, my legs and arms were trembling uncontrollably. I staggered indoors hoping that holding hands with my wife would calm me. Then I truly experienced high terror, for my wife, right in front of me, turned into a malignant, cannibalistic ghoul. And mixed with the terror I felt a profound sense of grief, for I knew that I was locked in the drug world for several hours at least, and it was going to be hideous. No words of comfort or reassurance from my wife would help, so long as they were coming out of that strange and satanic face.

In a few minutes, the words themselves were lost, for I could no longer hear her.

Somehow I found the sink and forced my finger down my throat. Again and again I provoked the vomit reflex. The fifth spasm brought up nothing—my stomach was empty—and the horrors continued. The drug, I knew, was in my bloodstream, and nothing now could stop its effects. I have never known a moment of greater despair.

I staggered around wildly, trying to get away from I-don't-remember-what. I banged into the wall again and again, and wondered if I'd end up with a concussion.

This was no ordinary fear. It was a billion-eyed crawling nameless Horror out of H.P. Lovecraft, orchestrated by Berlioz.

The sink was laughing. I knew water was running down the pipes, but I also knew that the sink was definitely laughing.

I was with a dwarf on a long journey through a dark woods. A knight in armor, shining like the Tin Woodman of Oz, attacked me with a lance.

I was crawling on all fours across white-hot coals.

A golden glow got my attention. I was on a bed—what bed?—in a supernaturally golden room. It was the Magic Land of peyote again! I turned my head and saw my wife, miraculously not looking like Lady Dracula anymore. Her face was the pretty, intellectual face I love above all others, but her hair was a new shade of red, lustrous and lovely beyond the vocabulary of a poet or even an ad man. I touched her hair and said, "It was worth all the terror to see you so beautiful. . . ."

They kept asking the same question over and over. I couldn't seem to make them understand. I tried again to explain: "We must all drink more milk," I said clearly and slowly, "for the Kennedy Administration in outer space of the Nuremberg pickle that exploded." I stopped, embarrassed, realizing I was making a fool of myself. That wasn't what I meant to say at all. "Where's the dwarf?" I asked testily.

Marv, a good friend who had suddenly appeared from nowhere, said quietly, "Don't you mean *The Ticket That Exploded*?"

"William Burroughs," I said. "Of course. All the literary critics will have to be shot because the cow is going dry again."

I was sitting in a chair, in my kitchen, talking to my wife and to Marv. "I've been off my head, haven't I?" I asked.

They started to assure me that it was all okay, that I was coming back to normal, don't worry . . . something more about the dwarf. . . .

Marv-the-Knight (now I knew him!) was walking me around the farm and I tried to show him the naked woman in the corn field. "Oh, of course," I said, giggling, "she's not really there." I wondered why he was smoking a cigarette (Marv never smokes) and asked him for one. He leered cruelly and said he didn't have any. No, he wasn't cruel: That was the drug. "But can I have a drag off the one you're smoking?" As soon as I asked it I realized that he wasn't smoking—I had hallucinated a cigarette in his mouth.

We were back in the kitchen, drinking coffee with my wife. "How long was I out of my head?"

"Five hours." They filled me in. Marv dropped by just shortly after I fell to the floor and started crawling. They got me into bed but I kept getting out. I kept lighting an imaginary cigarette and puffing on it with evident enjoyment. Then I re-

436

gressed to the aimless movements of infancy for an hour or so; I got up once and very carefully urinated into a bushel of tomatoes (which, undoubtedly, looked like a toilet bowl to me); for a few hours I was pushing away imaginary objects. I began to lecture on literature and Marxism, unintelligibly. That was when I began to be me again.

At dawn, we all went to sleep.

The next morning I was normal, but tired. Twice I had hallucinations. Once I saw a polar bear with a black-turtleneck sweater walk past the house, and once I saw a green Pan playing a flute in my vegetable garden.

That night I went to the movies. It was a melodrama. I began hallucinating, pleasantly enough during the black-and-white movie into Technicolor. Then a wave of anxiety swept over me and I had to leave the theater and walk a while to calm down.

The next day I was fine. That evening, however, the panic hit me again and lasted for half an hour. To neutralize it I concentrated on reciting to my wife the plots of old movies. By the time I was through *The Third Man, Citizen Kane, Odd Man Out,* and *Giant,* the sensation was neutralized . . . and then I recognized what it actually was. It was not the onset of the horrors: It was sexual excitement. Physically, it was the same sensation as sexual excitement! I went off into gales of laughter. The siege had been lifted.

* * *

"It's just like I found out in natural childbirth," my wife says. "A body-sensation can be felt as either pain or pleasure, depending on the brain's interpretation."

And it is just as Buddhism teaches: There is no beauty, no ugliness, no pain, no pleasure. It all depends on the mind.

This is the greatest lesson I have learned from my psychedelic research. It is also the last lesson I will learn, for I am leaving that field of investigation to the experts. I have learned a great deal about insanity, something about homosexuality, a little about Heaven and Hell, and an enormous amount about my own limitations. I think I will leave it at that.

437

Beyond the 25th Amendment

By Warren Boroson

O n June 14 of 1966, newspaper columnist Drew Pearson reported that Rep. L. Mendel Rivers (D., S.C.) had been unable to attend five consecutive meetings of the House Armed Services Committee, of which he is chairman. Because of his absence, the Committee had to delay approving an $18-billion bill to purchase military weapons. Pearson's explanation: Representative Rivers had been "drying out from a drunk. It was so serious that [he] had to be taken to Bethesda Naval Hospital."

On April 25, 1966, Reuters reported that Lord Charles Moran, Winston Churchill's physician, had asserted that the English Prime Minister's physical and mental exhaustion accounted for "much that is otherwise inexplicable in the last year of the war, for example the deterioration in his relations with President Roosevelt."

On June 10, 1966, a Philadelphia judge ruled that Kathryn E. Granahan, then Treasurer of the United States, was *not* incompetent, although at times she did become "shaken" by questions. Mrs. Granahan, who is recovering from brain surgery, was on leave of absence from her office. The petition to declare her incompetent was submitted by her own lawyers, and was then impounded by the court.

These news items appeared at a time when there is mounting concern in this country about what would happen if a powerful government leader succumbed to a mental disability. Fletcher Knebel's novel *Night of Camp David* tells of a President who gradually becomes paranoid. The film *Dr. Strangelove* features a crack-brained Army general who brings about nuclear annihilation. Recent articles in scholarly magazines—*Stanford Today, Medical Opinion & Review*, the *American Psychologist*—have given worried consideration to the chances of a President's becoming mentally disordered. In fact, one of the aims of the 25th Amendment to the Constitution is to facilitate the prompt removal of such a President from office.

Yet the 25th Amendment, though it does help clarify what the Constitution leaves vague, does not go far enough. While it empowers the Cabinet, the Vice-President, and the Congress to determine *if* the President is disabled, it doesn't indicate *how* a determination of disability is to be made. The Amendment does not specify that any medical authorities would be consulted. Nor is there any provision for removing a mentally-ill President over his objections. Obviously, more legislation is required.

There are compelling reasons for this additional legislation. Arnold A. Rogow, a professor of political science, has put it as succinctly as possible. Even with the 25th Amendment, he writes, if the President of the United States were to have a nervous breakdown ". . . it is entirely possible that the enormous power of the Presidential office will be exercised, at least temporarily, by someone who is mentally ill. . . ." Further, "Given the reality of increasing stress and strain in high office, the prospect is for increasing frequency of mental and physical breakdown. . . ." (*Stanford Today*, Summer, 1964) Ominously, Professor Rogow adds the clincher: ". . . the red telephone does not distinguish between sick Presidents and healthy ones. . . ." (*Medical Opinion & Review*, April, 1966)

As urgent as it is to quickly remove a mentally disabled President from office, noisy objections have been raised. Many people just pooh-pooh the possibility that a leader of this country could ever have a mental breakdown. Others, including a few psychoanalysts, argue that many grossly disturbed political leaders have actually proved quite capable. Still others are convinced that there simply is no practical way to go about diagnosing and removing a mentally-ill leader.

440

These may seem like valid objections. But on examination they prove to be baseless.

* * *

Just how common is mental disability among world statesmen? Psychologist Robert L. Noland of the University of Dayton has been trying to find out. In a study encompassing the last four centuries, he reports in the *American Psychologist* (March, 1966), he has so far come across 75 chief government figures who suffered "severe mental disturbances."

In modern times, key government figures who were clearly mentally disturbed include:

• Louis II, King of Bavaria, who ascended the throne on March 10, 1864, at the age of 18. He was formally declared insane on June 8, 1886, and 5 days later drowned both himself and his psychiatrist.

• Joseph Stalin of Russia. The distinguishing feature of Stalin's personality, according to Francis B. Randall's biography *Stalin's Russia,* was his paranoia. Khrushchev has reported that Stalin sometimes glared at him during Party meetings, demanding to know why he shifted his eyes and why he was afraid to look at him. Stalin had even loyal associates imprisoned and executed. In the Great Purge of 1937 and 1938, he had an estimated 900,000 people killed and an estimated 6 million people imprisoned. He took incredible precautions against assassination: While appearing in public in Red Square, he would have over a million people searched by security guards—twice. During these appearances, police airplanes had orders to shoot down any other planes flying overhead; in 1949 they shot down three Russian army transports that blundered over the area. "Just before his death," writes Professor Randall, "there were suspicious arrests of doctors and others, accompanied by rumors of a new purge of much or all of the high Party leadership. When last interviewed by a foreigner, the Ambassador from India, Stalin was allegedly seen doodling fierce pictures of wolves and heard to mutter, "None of them can be trusted!' "

There is no way of ascertaining, at this date, what

441

brought about Stalin's paranoia. But to engage in some speculation, it is true that paranoia is often linked with fear of homosexuality; and it is true that, while Stalin was attending a Christian seminary from ages 14 to 19, "There are vague hints in the record that Stalin may have had to avoid the advances of homosexual monks."

Professor Randall advances the theory that because Stalin was so short (about 5 feet 4), he may have "compensated for the slur upon his virility by a fanatical drive for political power over tall men. It is true that some of Stalin's most hated opponents, notably Trotsky, were taller than he. But so was Lenin. It is more strikingly true that practically all of Stalin's friends and political associates were as short as he, which cannot have happened simply by chance. Stalin liked to wear military boots, a kind of elevator shoe. He managed to avoid being photographed or seen in public standing next to taller men. . . ."

Another theory is that Stalin's personality stemmed from his "wretched father who could not earn as much as his wife, who drank, [and] who beat the child and beat his wife before his child's eyes. . . ." Professor Randall aptly observes: "The thought of Stalin with an Oedipus complex raises snickers from the skeptical, but he may have had one, and millions may have died in part because of it."

• Adolf Hitler of Germany. A walking textbook in psychopathology, Hitler has been psychiatrically described as a "psychopathic paranoid," an "amoral sadistic infant," an "overcompensatory sissy," a "neurotic laboring under the impulse to murder," and a "histrionic and hysterical adventurer." His symptoms included hallucinations and delirium (Hermann Rauschning, *The Voice of Destruction*), weeping fits, suicidal impulses, phobias, "universal suspicion, alternation of optimism and despair" (H.R. Trevor-Roper, *The Last Days of Hitler*), and temper tantrums (e.g., "His fists raised, his cheeks flushed with rage, his whole body trembling, the man stood there in front of me, beside himself with fury and having lost all self-control. . . . He was almost screaming, his eyes seemed about to pop out of his head, and the veins stood out

442

on his temples"—Gen. Heinz Guderian). Indeed, William L. Shirer reports that sometimes Hitler's frenzy was such that he would thrash about on the floor and chew the carpet.

Hitler never saw a psychiatrist, but for 9 years (1936-45) he consulted a physician named Theodore Morell, a quack who regularly gave him over 28 different drugs. These drugs included narcotics, hypnotics, stimulants, hormones, aphrodisiacs, sulphonamide (condemned by the pharmacological faculty at the University of Leipzig for harming the nerves), and Dr. Koester's Anti-Gas Pills, whose ingredients—belladonna and strychnine—were slowly poisoning him.

It's interesting that Gregory Zilboorg, an American psychiatrist, once wrote that "primitive infantile intransigence . . . seems to pervade Hitler's personality. . . . I suspect he shows certain precursory signs of true psychological inability to cope with himself . . . a purely pathological outcome is not at all excluded." That prediction was published on April 26, 1939.

• Rudolf Hess was Hitler's "closest personal confidant, the deputy leader of the Nazi Party, the second in line to succeed him after Goering. . . ." (Shirer, *The Rise and Fall of the Third Reich*) In May, 1941, convinced by an astrologer that he was fated to bring about peace, Hess flew to Scotland to urge England to stop the war. Hitler himself concluded that Hess was mad, and ordered him shot if he returned. Indeed, in prison Hess tried to kill himself twice, and experienced long stretches of amnesia. Recently an appeal was made for his release (*Times*, 5/24/66), and Hess's lawyer argued that his client was suffering from "latent schizophrenia."

• Viscount Castlereagh was British Foreign Minister from 1812 to Aug. 12, 1822, when "he could no longer endure the strain to which he had been subjected. . . . Castlereagh cut his throat with a small penknife and died immediately. . . ." (*Encyclopedia Britannica*)

Other statesmen who have committed suicide include Jan Masaryk, Foreign Minister of Czechoslovakia, on March 10, 1948 (according to one view, though, he was murdered); Erich Apel, Deputy Premier of East Germany, on Dec. 3,

1965, as a result—according to news reports—of a nervous breakdown; Samuel Whitbread, a Member of Parliament, in 1815; Sir Samuel Romilly, a member of the House of Commons, in 1818; Lee Ki Poong, Vice-President of Korea and chosen successor to Syngman Rhee, in 1960 with his entire family; E. Herbert Norman, Canadian Ambassador to Egypt, in 1957; and Getulio Vargas, President of Brazil, who on June 26, 1954, shot himself through the heart.

* * *

But in spite of these cases and others, there is a powerful myth in this land which holds that *Americans* in high office are immune to mental illness. According to this myth, to quote Professor Rogow, "while ordinary people holding ordinary jobs can and do become psychotic, VIP's do not. It also follows that ordinary people who can afford it visit psychiatrists, but not VIP's. Finally, it follows that ordinary people may spend some time in mental hospitals, but never VIP's. These and other themes constitute the mental-health mythology of official Washington—despite the fact that Washington has more psychiatrists in proportion to population than most other cities in the world."

The truth is that Very Important People do become mentally ill, and some of them *have* been Americans. At least four Presidents, one Defense Secretary, three Governors, and six Congressmen have been emotionally disturbed while in office. Assuming that alcoholism and suicidal tendencies are presumptive evidence of an underlying psychological disturbance, a list of these Americans would include:

• John Winant, former Governor of New Hampshire, Ambassador to Great Britain, and representative to UNESCO, who committed suicide on Nov. 3, 1947, as a result of "A nervous breakdown resulting from overwork and 'the growing disillusionment of today. . . .' " (*Times*, 11/5/47)

• Army Col. Charles S. Cumings Jr., who was once a member of the Policy Planning Council, the nation's highest foreign-policy-making group. In October, 1965, Colonel Cumings was found in Washington slumped over the wheel of his

444

automobile, nude. A loaded pistol lay on the front seat, next to a bottle of vermouth. A second weapon was found in the glove compartment. The police charged Colonel Cumings with carrying a dangerous weapon without a license, and with being drunk. At the time of his arrest, the Colonel had access to classified information and was on duty with the State Department. (*New York Post*, 10/24/65)

• George Wallace of Alabama, prior to becoming Governor in 1962, served as his State's Assistant Attorney General, as a legislator, and as a circuit-court judge. In September, 1945, according to medical records of the Veterans Administration, Wallace was hospitalized because of a "severe anxiety state, chronic, manifested by tension states, anxiety states, anorexia [loss of appetite], and loss of weight." In December, 1946, Wallace began receiving disability payments of $20 a month "for psychoneurosis." He was examined again by the Veterans Administration in November, 1956, and the report stated that he was "tense, restless, and ill at ease, frequently drummed the desk with his fingers, changed position frequently, sighed occasionally, and showed a tendency to stammer, resulting in the diagnosis of anxiety reaction." The disability payments were continued. (*Times*, 9/6/63)

• John M. Spencer, Democratic State Chairman of Vermont, went before the State Democratic Committee in 1964, announced he was an alcoholic, and resigned. (Rogow, *Stanford Today*)

• The late William C. Marland was the youngest Governor ever elected to the State of West Virginia. In 1961 he voluntarily entered the alcoholic ward of a mental hospital. Marland confessed that he had been an alcoholic while he was Governor (1953-57), and then the problem grew into "a 24-hour proposition, with all the attendant evils and a significant reduction in ability to handle my duties." (*Times*, 11/27/65)

• John S. Little, Governor of Arkansas, in 1907 suffered a nervous breakdown so disabling that, for the balance of his term, his duties had to be performed by the president of the Senate and the president pro tem. (Richard H. Hansen, *The Year We Had No President*, 1962)

• Former Gov. Earl Long of Louisiana. In 1959, after he had burst into profanity on two occasions in front of the State Legislature, Governor Long was hospitalized, examined, and declared mentally ill. His wife, Blanche, requested that he be held in protective custody in a hospital.

Soon after, the Governor escaped from one hospital, then was committed to another, Southeast Louisiana State Hospital at Mandeville. The Governor filed suit for a legal separation from his wife, so she could no longer commit him; fired the Director of State Hospitals; and fired the superintendent of the Mandeville hospital. He then named a new director of hospitals and a new superintendent. They declared him sane, and he was a free man. Unfortunately, according to Richard Hansen of the University of Nebraska, Long's "mental and physical condition deteriorated."

• Fred R. Zeller was the State Controller of Connecticut from 1938 to 1958, and ran for Governor on the Republican ticket against Abraham Ribicoff in 1958. On June 24, 1966, he was sentenced to 1 to 3 years in prison for having embezzled $26,297 from a church. The charges covered the period 1962-65; other charges going back to 1954 were dropped because of the statute of limitations. At the trial, Zeller's lawyer contended that a psychiatric examination of his client showed that he was a manic-depressive.

• Sen. Lester C. Hunt (D., Wyoming), a former Governor, was completing his first term in the Senate when—on June 19, 1954—he shot himself in the right temple with a .22-calibre rifle at his desk in the Senate Office Building.

• Sen. Frank B. Brandegee (R., Conn.) was the chairman of the Senate Judiciary Committee and had been a leader in the fight against this country's entering the League of Nations. On the night of Oct. 14, 1924, worried about his real-estate investments, he killed himself by inhaling illuminating gas.

• Rep. Douglas H. Elliott (R., Pa.) killed himself on June 19, 1960, by inhaling carbon monoxide.

• Rep. Marion A. Zioncheck (R., Wash.) was, at 34, known as "Peck's Bad Boy" of the House. In early 1936, he took over the switchboard of an apartment house while intoxi-

446

cated, and rang all the bells (it was New Year's Eve); he was arrested several times for speeding, and also for throwing bottles from a window; with his new bride, he waded through the fountain in Rockefeller Center; and he was ejected from a hotel "for lapping his soup from a plate and drinking a rum and hair-tonic cocktail" (*Times*, 8/8/36). Hospitalized, he was declared "dangerously insane." He escaped from a hospital in Maryland, fled to Seattle, and on Aug. 7, 1936, leaped to his death from the fifth floor of his office, his body landing a few feet from the car in which his horrified bride was waiting for him.

• Sen. Key Pittman of Nevada was chairman of the Foreign Relations Committee from 1932 to 1940. "During his eight years as chairman," Fred L. Israel writes in *Nevada's Key Pittman* (1963), "the Senator's addiction to alcohol grew progressively worse. He had a refrigerator installed in the committee room in which liquor was stored. At meetings or hearings he always had a glass before him and continually sipped whiskey. . . ."

The Senator also had episodes of uncontrollable aggressiveness. In a letter to his wife (quoted by Israel), he once wrote:

I was and had been for years, a periodical drunkard . . . . a mania seized me,—you cannot understand it, and no one can explain,— . . . . All of the savage in me asserted itself in me—I longed for, and nothing satisfied me but, the most intense excitement—I longed to murder kill and howle [sic] with delight at the sound of death dealing instruments and the sight of human blood . . . . It was Mental disease, strong and terrible.

In *The Coming of the New Deal*, Arthur M. Schlesinger Jr. tells of a time when Senator Pittman chased a technical advisor down the corridors of the Claridge Hotel with a bowie knife. (The advisor later bought a pistol to protect himself.) According to biographer Israel, "When Washington hotels and bars refused to serve him, the Senator would whip out his silver pistol, which he almost always carried with him, and threaten to 'shoot up' the establishment."

In 1933, Senator Pittman attended the World Economic

and Monetary Conference in London. "Throughout the conference," reports Fred Israel, "especially at crucial moments, he would get drunk. While in this condition, his favorite method of amusing himself was to pop the London street lights with his six-shooter. Secretary Hull and Governor Cox were outraged at Pittman's behavior. . . ."

• James Forrestal, Secretary of Defense (1947-49), seems to have been a typical Authoritarian Personality. His father, according to Professor Rogow's biography *James Forrestal* (1963), was distant; his mother was cold, overly protective, and strict. ". . . to Forrestal his father must have appeared weaker than his mother, perhaps even less masculine. . . . The young Forrestal, who was often ill, ashamed of his physique, and perhaps uncertain of his masculinity, would, all his life, exercise strenuously, emphasize body-contact sports, and try to appear 'tough.' . . . Regarding . . . passivity as a feminine attribute, Forrestal may have felt, consciously or unconsciously, that he would have to struggle more than most men to establish his essential masculinity. . . ."

After a brilliant career in business, Forrestal became Undersecretary of the Navy, Secretary of the Navy, and then, under Truman, Secretary of Defense. Early in 1949 he began complaining that his phone was being tapped and that he was being followed. President Truman asked Secret Service Chief U.E. Baughman to investigate. Baughman did, and reported that Forrestal was suffering from "a total psychotic breakdown . . . characterized by suicidal features."

Forrestal's resignation was called for, and shortly afterwards he entered Bethesda Naval Hospital. The chief psychiatrist there diagnosed his illness as involutional melancholia. Against the psychiatrist's advice, Forrestal was shifted from a room on the ground floor to one on the sixteenth floor. On the night of May 22, 1949, he fell from the window to his death, becoming "the highest-ranking American official to have committed suicide."

• Sen. Joseph McCarthy. According to one psychiatric textbook, a *psychopath* is "an adventurer in the service of absurdity who behaves as though he were consciously trying to undermine the moral order of our society. . . . His gratuitous acts are not gestures of a mighty defiance, but the outgrowth of shamelessness and lack of restraint . . . He knows what the ethical rules are . . . but they are void of meaning to him."

Such seems to have been Senator McCarthy. The Senator, as seen by biographer Richard Rovere, "operated far outside the framework of American political morality. . . . Cheating of one sort or another is, of course, tolerated in politics. But there are limits of tolerance, and it was one of McCarthy's distinctions . . . that he simply did not consider that the No Trespassing signs were for him. . . . The man was a moral vacuum. . . . He faked [his passions] and couldn't understand anyone who didn't."

In his last days, McCarthy also came close to being an alcoholic. He was, says Richard Rovere, "drinking more and holding it less well. . . . He would come into the Caucus Room late, interrupt a line of questioning with questions of his own, some of which were incoherent, and after twenty minutes or so wander out in an almost trance-like state." He died of cirrhosis of the liver.

• John Adams, President. According to Richard Hansen, "John Adams . . . had such a suspicious disposition that it would be diagnosed as a persecution complex if he lived today. There is no doubt that his inordinate distrust of people affected his judgment at times, particularly in connection with this country's relations with England."

• Abraham Lincoln, President. Throughout his life, Lincoln was subject to gloomy depressions and strong suicidal yearnings.

According to Lincoln's friend and law partner, William Herndon, when Anne Rutledge—Lincoln's first sweetheart—died in 1835, Lincoln "had fits of great mental depression and wandered up and down the river and into the woods woefully abstracted—at times in the deepest distress. If . . . we do not conclude that he was deranged, we must admit that he walked on that sharp and narrow line which divides sanity from insanity."

Six years later, Herndon reports, Lincoln failed to appear for his wedding to Mary Todd (whom he did marry eventually). When his friends found him, Lincoln's depression was so deep that "knives and razors, and every instrument that could be used for self-destruction, were removed from his reach. Mrs. Edwards [Lincoln's eventual sister-in-law] did not hesitate to regard him as insane, and of course her sister Mary shared in that view."

While he was a member of the Illinois Legislature, Lincoln told a colleague—again according to Herndon—that at times his depressions were so severe that he dared not carry a pocket knife.

One of the most persuasive psychological studies of President Lincoln has been made by Dr. Edward J. Kempf. In "Abraham Lincoln's Organic and Emotional Neurosis" (*Archives of Neurology and Psychiatry*, 1952), Dr. Kempf points out that when Lincoln was 10 years old, he was kicked in the head by a horse. For hours he lay unconscious, and some bystanders even thought he was dead. Because the nearest physician was many miles away, even when Lincoln recovered he received no treatment. According to Dr. Kempf, "fracture of the skull and cerebral after-effects were never suspected, or at least never reported by physicians, although after the age of 30 he consulted several for melancholia and other nervous symptoms."

From studying the many photographs of Lincoln, and the Volk life mask made in 1860, Dr. Kempf concludes that Lincoln had suffered a skull fracture, which led to visual and nervous disintegration. "A person with this type of cerebral lesion," Dr. Kempf writes, "in order to remain mentally alert, would have to be involved, or keep himself involved, in emotionally stimulating situations . . . in an endless fight to overcome the tendency to lapse into a rut of sad, gloomy, suicidal preoccupations."

• James A. Garfield, President. On July 2, 1881, President Garfield was shot by an assassin. He died 80 days later, Before his death he recovered somewhat, but—to quote Richard Hansen—"During this last month of his illness he had hallucinations and was completely out of his mind."

• Woodrow Wilson, President. Like Lincoln and Garfield, President Wilson's mental disorder seems to have been organically induced. In December, 1918, Wilson sailed for Europe to attend the peace conference concluding World War I. While in Paris, he was bothered by a nervous stomach. According to Gene Smith's *When the Cheering Stopped,* he showed other signs of strain—talking incessantly, irritability, loss of weight, and facial twitches. Finally he collapsed. His condition was diagnosed as influenza.

When Wilson began recovering, he started showing signs of paranoia. According to Ike Hoover, a member of his entourage,

Even while lying in bed he manifested peculiarities, one of which was to limit the use of all the automobiles to strictly official purposes, when previously he had been so liberal in his suggestions that his immediate party should have the benefit of this possible diversion, in view of the long hours we were working. When he got back on the job, his peculiar ideas were even more pronounced. He now became more obsessed with the idea that every French employee about the place was a spy for the French government. Nothing we could say would disabuse his mind of this thought. He insisted they all understood English, when, as a matter of fact, there was just one of them among the two dozen or more who understood a single word of English.

About this time he also acquired the peculiar notion that he was personally responsible for all the property in the furnished palace he was occupying. He raised quite a fuss on two occasions when he noticed articles of furniture had been removed. Upon investigation—for no one else noticed the change—it was learned that the custodian of the property for the French owner had seen fit to do a little re-arranging. Coming from the President, whom we all knew so well, these were very funny things, and we could but surmise that something queer was happening in his mind.

Almost beyond doubt Wilson had suffered the first of a fatal series of cerebral thromboses, which accounted for his ever-increasing suspiciousness, petulance, and absent-mindedness.

In September, 1919, Wilson collapsed in Pueblo, Colorado, while on tour to persuade Americans of the need for a League of Nations. He was rushed to the White House, where on October 2 he had a third attack, this time diagnosed as a cerebral thrombosis. His left side was paralyzed. Dr. Cary T. Grayson, Wilson's personal physician, and a small group of specialists gathered hastily at the White House, and realizing that "serious brain damage had been sustained" (Smith), told Mrs. Wilson that her husband must have absolute rest.

Wilson was unable to concentrate on any one subject for more than a short time. He could not dictate for more than 5 minutes. He could not work more than an hour or two a day. Dr. Grayson reported that he had a "nervous breakdown." Warren G. Harding, Wilson's successor, wrote: "He has an extreme case of nervous breakdown with hysterical symptoms and unmistakable flights of mental disturbance. . . ."

Yet Mrs. Wilson and Dr. Grayson got together and decided to suppress the truth about the President's condition! Thus began what has been called "Mrs. Wilson's Regency." Mrs. Wilson had just 2 years of formal schooling, yet—as Dr. Noah D. Fabricant has written—"During the critical phase of Wilson's illness, his wife was for all practical purposes the President of the United States." Even when Wilson recovered somewhat, for many months he was "an intensely sick, part-time President. . . . Invalidism made Wilson querulous and emotionally unstable," writes Dr. Fabricant (*13 Famous Patients*). "His moods alternated between melancoly to the point of tears, brooding, and unreasonable obstinacy. His judgment was no longer reliable, and his illusions became delusions. He evolved a fantastic scheme whereby opposition Senators would resign in a body. . . ." This appalling situation continued until the end of Wilson's term of office.

* * *

By no means does this list exhaust the names of all American political leaders who have been mentally disturbed. We simply have no way of knowing about any others. Professor Rogow

452

wonders what the state of General MacArthur's health was "when he urged that a 2,000-square-mile belt of radioactive cobalt be laid across Korea . . ." and inquires about Roosevelt's health at the Yalta Conference. Indeed, Professor Rogow adds, there are reports that Eisenhower, for his heart condition, was given a drug the side-effects of which "include mental states not conducive to rational thinking." Another President, Professor Rogow notes, reportedly "took Miltown in a rather impressive dosage. . . ." There have been persistent reports that Adlai Stevenson was seeing a psychoanalyst. President Johnson, in late 1965, confided to a *Time* Magazine reporter that "he had been taking tranquilizers ever since his heart attack ten years ago. . . ." Incomplete as the above list may be, however, it does demonstrate beyond question that Very Important People, including Americans, do become mentally ill.

There are several important corollaries.

One is that a *mentally-ill government leader is not necessarily removed from office*. Governor Little of Arkansas served out his term. So did Woodrow Wilson. So did Earl Long.

A second is that a *mentally-ill government leader may even be re-elected*. His symptoms may be flatly denied, or unapparent to the general public. Key Pittman stood for re-election in 1940. According to Fred Israel, "During the last weeks of the contest, he drank very heavily and was in an almost continuous stupor. Four days before the election, he entered Reno's Washoe Hospital. On November 5, his fellow Nevadan's re-elected him by 6,000 votes. . . ." Five days later, Pittman was dead. In 1960, Governor Long ran for Congress and was elected. He died 9 days later.

The third corollary is the most important. *While in office, some mentally-ill government leaders have done great harm.*

Senator Pittman's alcoholism may have contributed to his "vacillation and lack of leadership in the Foreign Relations Committee. . . ." (Israel) It may have also provoked his "intemperate statements," such as that our World War II Allies,

453

France and England, were "sullen, defaulters, and double-crossers," and that it was futile for England to resist Hitler's onslaught.

Franklin D. Roosevelt's illness at the Yalta Conference in 1945 may have been responsible for the unwise concessions he made to Russia. According to Edward S. Corwin and Louis W. Koenig's book *The Presidency Today* (1956),

. . . there is impressive evidence that he was a very sick man in the last months of his life. His trusted secretary, William D. Hassett, has written that he "had started to weaken at least a year before his death" and that it was clear before the fourth-term nomination that "the boss was leaving us." A study of the Yalta papers shows F.D.R. so far short of his normal vigor that he had left undone much of his homework and failed to gain the mastery of the essential briefing papers without which a negotiator is at the mercy of a hard bargainer; that his top advisers had difficulty in seeing him and getting his attention for what they had to say and what he needed to know; and that he showed lack of vigor, zest, and sustained concentration in the Yalta discussions.

In addition, William C. Bullitt, former Ambassador to Russia, has written that "At Yalta, Roosevelt was more than tired. He was ill. . . . Frequently he had difficulty formulating his thoughts, and greater difficulty in expressing them consecutively." Reporter John Gunther noted that Roosevelt's exhaustion "was so complete that, on occasion, he could not answer simple questions and talked what was close to nonsense."

An English physician, Hugh L'Etang, suggests that the three Prime Ministers who dealt so feebly with Hitler "were sick men, rather than sinners" ("The Health of Statesmen and Affairs of Nations," *Practitioner,* 1/58).

J. Ramsay MacDonald was Premier from 1929 to 1935. Lord Attlee had described his decline thus: "His speeches became increasingly incoherent and for the last years of his life he was only a melancholy passenger in the Conservative ship." A Member of Parliament, Hugh Dalton, says of MacDonald: "It had long been clear to all, not only that his general health was bad, but that his mental powers were in decay."

Stanley Baldwin was Premier from 1935 to 1937. An intimate friend, Thomas Jones, wrote during this time that he showed "little mental resilience" and was "already brooding apprehensively on coming burdens and responsibilities." Again: "He lost his nerve, and every burden became a nightmare." L'Etang observes, "This was a Prime Minister who had to face the increasing threats of Hitler and Mussolini."

Neville Chamberlain succeeded Baldwin in 1937. In December, 1939, according to his biographer, Keith Feiling, ". . . it is possible to detect a weariness, an added sensitiveness, a disposition to identify criticism with faction. . . . Some of this may have come from the physical machine slowing down, for the letters speak of much gout and minor ailments."

As for Woodrow Wilson, in the nearly 2 years that he was incapacitated, 28 Acts of Congress became law because of his failure to sign or veto them. In the fall of 1919, race riots broke out, but the President, if he knew about them, did nothing. A high official was accused of graft: Again nothing was done. The British Ambassador spent 4 months in Washington waiting to be received by the President. New governments, notably Costa Rica's, were not recognized. Vacancies—the Secretaries of the Treasury and Interior, the Assistant Secretary of Agriculture, and diplomatic appointments—were never filled. Nor were resignations acknowledged, so that when new men *were* chosen, they filled posts that, technically, had never been vacated. Finally, L'Etang observes: ". . . in his early dealings with Lloyd George, Clemenceau, and Orlando in Europe, and with the Republican Senators at home, he exhibited poor judgment, inflexibility of mind, and at times a dour obstinacy . . . his actions destroyed any hope of the American Senate ratifying the peace treaty and agreeing to enter the League of Nations. These measures were finally defeated in the Senate on March 19, 1920."

All this, though, is not to deny that pathology can sometimes produce excellence, an objection that even psychologists may make when the subject of mental illness among government leaders is brought up. A person driven by gnawing emotional needs may vastly outproduce people who are "normal." Even someone with a latent psychosis may function magnificently most of the time. Along with a Wound, in Edmund Wilson's imagery, there often goes a Magic Bow.

One psychoanalyst told a *Fact* researcher: "I know a surgeon on the staff of a hospital in New York, who is the head of a certain type of surgery. In my opinion, this man is psychotic. If, however, I required the kind of surgery this man performs, I would not hesitate to have him operate. His psychosis does not prevent him from being an excellent surgeon."

Similarly, in part to prove how tough he was, Forrestal worked like a demon, and made the U. S. Navy the best in the world. Lincoln, despite or because of his tortured soul, became a great humanitarian. Stalin's drive for power helped make Russia a powerful nation.

* * *

To this objection that the mentally disturbed may prove to be overachievers, if not positive geniuses, there are three answers.

First, a distinction should be made between the mentally disturbed who can continue functioning normally, and those who cannot. A psychotic surgeon whose symptoms have subsided can certainly go on doing his job. So can people who have character disorders—psychopaths like McCarthy and paranoiacs like Stalin. On the other hand, people with full-blown psychoses like Forrestal, people with symptoms like hallucinations, severe depression, and disordered thinking, can no longer function properly, and provision must be made to remove *them,* at least, from office as quickly as possible.

Second, the office of the Presidency—and other key posts —can no longer be entrusted to someone on a double-or-nothing basis. No longer can we afford the luxury of gambling that a person with a conflicted personality will, once in office, surmount his problems. The stakes have gotten too high. Unless we put our money on a pretty sure thing, we may be wiped out.

Professor Rogow writes:

Clearly, no nation <u>now</u> can afford the breakdown in office of high officials in a world where the difference between a first and second strike, between a nuclear initiative and a nuclear response, is a mat-

ter not of days or hours, but of minutes and seconds. The policy process . . . is difficult enough assuming the sanity and rationality of those involved. Assuming that sometime, somewhere, a decision will be made by one or more persons suffering from certain types of mental illness, eventual annihilation is assured.

And Richard Hansen points out:

The President's powers and responsibilities in the field of foreign affairs are such that the necessity for keeping the President fit, physically and mentally, is synonymous with national survival. The nature of these responsibilities is symbolized by a large leather pouch, with a double lock. Guarded by five United States Army warrant officers, this pouch contains all the super-secret messages and codes to put the nation's key emergency plans into effect. These are the plans which only the President can initiate. . . .

On the President's desk sits a "crash" telephone. A President has only to reach for that telephone, speak a few words in the mouthpiece, and our nuclear deterrent is unleashed. The law as it now stands increases the risk that a sick President either might use that phone prematurely or be unable to use it at all.

Third, in cases where government leaders have, despite their problems, turned out to be top-notch, we have been extraordinarily lucky. Forrestal, in his last months, was convinced that Russia was planning to invade the United States. "Suppose," asks Professor Rogow, "Forrestal had not been Secretary of Defense but President? Suppose, further, that the nation's military capability had been based on missiles rather than manned aircraft? Suppose, finally, that push-button warfare had achieved the development stage then that it has since achieved?"

As for Stalin, his pathology may have contributed to making Russia a powerful nation, but it also contributed to making him, in Professor Randall's words, "on balance, one of the two or three worst men who ever lived."

And as for Lincoln, very few people really know how lucky this country was. In early 1863, Lincoln received—in short succession—news of the Army of the Potomac's defeat on the Virginia peninsula, two defeats at Bull Run, another at Fredericksburg, and one at Chancellorsville. To quote Edward R. Ellis and George N. Allen's book *Traitor Within,*

457

When the news reached Lincoln, he paced up and down, his hands clasped behind his back, muttering: "My God! My God! What will the country say! What will the country say!"

The President was reported to believe firmly that this disaster would be more injurious, at home and abroad, than any previous event of the Civil War. It preyed on his mind to such an extent that he lost all hope. His Secretary of War, Edwin M. Stanton, later reported: "Mr. Lincoln had fully made up his mind to go to the Potomac River, and there end his life, as many a poor creature—but none half so miserable as he was at the time—had done before him." Stanton added that he was afraid to leave Lincoln alone. He told the President to be brave, to try to sleep, and then to consider visiting the army. . . .

What would have been the most devastating suicide in American history was narrowly averted. . . .

*   *   *

To make sure that a mentally-ill President is promptly removed from office, Congress must do two things. First: establish a Disability Commission.

Such a Commission, as recommended by New York Supreme Court Justice Samuel H. Hoffstadter and lawyer Jacob M. Dinnes, would function as follows: Within 10 days after his Inauguration, the President would appoint nine members to the Commission—three from his Cabinet, two from the Senate, two from the House, and two from the Supreme Court. The Commission would have final authority to certify that the President was unable to serve, and also that he was fit to resume his duties.

The second step needed is for Congress to set up regular physical and psychiatric examinations of the President.

As it is now, the President is not required to consult *any* physician while in office. Nor is he required to inform the Vice-President, the Cabinet, the Congress, or the public about the findings of any medical examination. The same goes for other high government officials. "As a consequence," writes Professor Rogow, "we do not know what proportion of Cabinet officers, Senators and Representatives, generals and admirals, avail themselves of psychiatric services, and for what purposes. We do not know how many suffer from ulcers and other ailments of a psychiatric nature. The number of those who consume tranquilizers has not been totaled, and we know even less about the significance of alcohol and marijuana in the relief of tensions arising from everyday Washington life. . . . The point is not that alcohol, narcotics, tranquilizers, and other drugs have played a role in this or that policy decision. The point is: *We do not know.*"

Any physician or psychiatrist that a President does consult must not be a personal friend, "biased in his favor to a greater or lesser extent," as Richard Hansen has observed. Dr. Cary T. Grayson told a series of half-truths to Wilson's Cabinet about the President's health. President Cleveland's cancer operation was kept from all but one member of the Cabinet. Franklin Roosevelt did not even inform his own physician of two seizures he had had. "Surely these lessons of history and human nature," concludes Mr. Hansen, "point to the necessity of enacting legislation requiring periodical physical examinations of the President by a board of physicians."

Hansen recommends that such a board examine the President four times a year. As for its make-up, "The Secretary of Health, Education and Welfare would select the doctors on a rotating basis from a list provided by the Civil Service Commission."

And on that board, needless to say, there should be at least one psychiatrist.

Professor Rogow suggests that the psychiatrist's responsibility would be to make recommendations to the President regarding treatment, if treatment were warranted, and then to present his findings to the Disability Commission. "The matter would properly come to the Disability Commission only if the psychiatrist were convinced beyond any doubt that the man he had examined was in such a state of mind that without treatment he would be likely to do grave harm to his country, to himself, or both. The Commission would be free to accept or reject psychiatric opinion and would have authority to make its own inquiry."

* * *

Once Congress has set up a board of physicians to report on the President's mental and physical condition to a Disability Commission, the same principle can easily be enlarged. A psychiatrist might be empowered to concern himself not only with incipient breakdowns, but with character disorders as well. A Presidential *candidate* might be required to go before such a board of physicians, and the board's findings be made public. (A Los Angeles psychiatrist, Isidore W. Ruskin, observes: "Psychological examinations to determine emotional fitness are commonly used in hiring police officers, corporation executives, and candidates for the U. S. armed forces. It is time it caught up with political aspirants.") Professor Rogow even suggests "regular psychiatric check-ups for *all* policy personnel, and disability commissions which will determine, in the last resort, whether an official was mentally and physically able to continue in the government service."

All this is obviously far in the future. Right now, the question of the President's mental health is the most pressing issue. As one government leader has said,

While we are prepared for the possibility of a President's death, we are all but defenseless against the probability of a President's incapacity by injury, illness, senility, or other affliction. A nation bearing the responsibilities we are privileged to bear for our own security—and the security of the free world—cannot justify its appalling gamble of entrusting its security to the immobilized hands or uncomprehending mind of a Commander-in-Chief unable to command.

The source of that statement: Lyndon B. Johnson.

Is America a Dying Country?

Something is radically wrong.

Throughout America people are strangely uneasy and fretful. They are, above all, tense, as if they had glimpsed flashes of lightning some time ago and were now waiting, not quite consciously, for the terrible thunderclaps. There has been much abstruse analysis of this eerie American malaise; much Fall of the Roman Empire talk. Only the dim-witted, or those insulated by self or circumstance, can have failed to notice it.

Our writers have noticed it. Bruce Jay Friedman says: "If you are alive today, and stick your head out of doors now and then, you know that there is a nervousness, a tempo, a near-hysterical new beat in the air, a punishing isolation and loneliness of a strange, frenzied kind." Nelson Algren writes: "Though ten thousand voices announce our national contentment coast to coast, every hour on the hour, through editorial, headline and the fashion magazines, actually we are living today in a laboratory of human suffering as vast and terrible as that in which Dickens and Dostoevsky wrote." Norman Mailer has written, simply, "The country is in disease."

Many others have remarked this strange new American malaise. "Living," says Karl Menninger, the psychiatrist, "in spite of all the multiplying mechanical aids, grows daily more difficult, complicated, and restrictive." Philosopher Charles Frankel maintains that anxiety has become our "way of life." James Reston, *The New York Times* writer, notes that "There is scarcely a philosopher in the nation or a serious historian who is not full of anxiety about the political or spiritual derangement of the free world" led by the United States. Before his death Adlai Stevenson wrote: "An air of disengagement and disinterest hangs over the most powerful and affluent society the world has ever known. Neither the turbulence of the world abroad nor the fatness and flatness of the world at home are moving us to more vital effort." The dean of the Harvard Divinity School, Samuel H. Miller, has said, "Make the rounds of people on any level. Something's wrong with America, they all say. In our work, we find no purpose. In our frenzy, there is no direction." Richard N. Goodwin, formerly one of Johnson's aides, has said that there is a "growing discontent with what we have, dissatisfaction with the life we have created, unhappiness and restlessness."

America, in short, seems to be on the verge of a nervous breakdown. Perhaps, as some say, the trouble is that our country lacks a goal, a common, elevating, national purpose; that —in this age of the anti-novel and the anti-hero and even anti-matter—America has only an anti-purpose, namely, fighting Communism.

Perhaps, as others say, we are in the throes of the Newer Nihilism. God has died and not been succeeded, and the result is that the entire framework of traditional morality has come crashing to the ground. Love, generosity, and trust seem to have fled our shores.

And perhaps, as still others say, the trouble is just a single overriding problem, like the Bomb, or overpopulation, or automation, and all our other anxieties are simply displacements of our worry over this one main problem.

But that may suggest the real root of the new American malaise: Too damn many problems. Our 18th-century political machinery, our Enlightenment machinery, as de Tocqueville feared, may be simply inadequate to cope with the continual crises of these new Dark Ages. Especially since resolving our problems would mean, in many instances, that a powerful, special-interest group would have to get burned. Especially since our problems seem sickeningly unending: unemployment; mental illness; dishonesty in labor unions, big business, and everywhere else; the crumbling wall between Church and

State; the erosion of civil liberties; the growing power of Birch-type groups; poverty that President Johnson's program won't begin to eradicate; state legislatures that are a joke; a national Congress that finds legislation so complex it leaves law-making to lobbyists; manufacturers of cars and cigarettes and food and drugs who care not for safety but for sales; a crime rate that is increasing at almost 6 times the rate of the population; alcoholism; drug addiction; homosexuality; mass media that kowtow not to consumers but to advertisers; tax laws that favor the rich; traffic congestion; school drop-outs; air and water pollution; vanishing parks and playgrounds; slums; problems of disarmament; problems, problems, problems.

It is not only that America's house is on fire. The house is burning, yes, but gas is also escaping in the kitchen, the baby is drowning in the bathtub, and the village idiot is fiddling with the family car. Meanwhile, the cops, the firemen, and the politicians are wrangling over what color to paint the porch—and how to fix it so they get a rake-off. No wonder that a totalitarian country with its crackerjack efficiency can sometimes make our country look bumbling and senescent; no wonder that one patriotic and forthright American, former Soviet Ambassador George F. Kennan, can confess: "If you ask me whether a country—with no highly developed sense of national purpose, with the overwhelming accent of life on personal comfort, with a dearth of public services and a surfeit of privately sold gadgetry, with insufficient social discipline—has, over the long run, good chances of competing with a purposeful, serious and disciplined society such as that of the Soviet Union, I must say that the answer is no."

* * *

To find out whether people in general share Professor Kennan's pessimism, whether they suffer themselves from the new American malaise and whether they are concerned about it, *Fact* telephoned and wrote to well-known citizens of this country. They were asked, right off the bat, whether they thought America was a dying country or not. Some were contemptuous of the question, some got enraged at the very idea, some were

465

perplexed. But a goodly number, a heartening number, were found to be genuinely concerned.—**Warren Boroson**

Christopher Isherwood
writer

I think America is in a very bad way. We've simply got to stop the breeding; we've got to control the population. All our evils come from that. There are more people, so we've got to put up this hideous building, that dreadful place, this causeway, that freeway . . . that everything! You go to India and you see what America is going to be like soon—a nightmare. And how any *decrease* in population will happen, whether by some terrible natural disaster or by a manmade war or simply by common sense, I just don't know.

New York, for example, is a doomed city. I was there the other day. Everybody there is half-mad. People laugh, but it's quite an effort. They don't see the sky—and that's serious. Here in California we can still make it out—so far. Out of one window I can see the ocean. Very big still—but very soon they're going to build a huge causeway right across the bay. As for New York, sooner or later it will have to be evacuated and left for the sea gulls, for the simple reason that it's uninhabitable. I would take down everything except the skyscrapers and leave the island—it would make a very pretty national monument.

Overpopulation is a threat psychologically as well as physically, because you can control enormous populations only through totalitarianism. Any idea that you can do anything else is idle. In one way or another, you're going to have to start ordering them around. This is what leads to totalitarianism, either of the Left or of the Right, and this is what I find so absolutely appalling.

Robert Lowell
poet

A dying country? That's a lot in a mouthful. Well, it's not dying in the *arts*. I don't think so, particularly in poetry. Good poets are coming up.

466

I do think it's a time of crisis. I think it's sort of a very important, questionable time, a time when we could go very wrong. There's great danger of our going very wrong, but I just don't know what's going to happen.

Wayne Morse
U.S. Senator (Dem., Ore.)

I don't share the view of some that neither our country nor our leaders have any goals. Our leaders certainly have goals—but I think the American people should evaluate them with much greater care. This is especially true with respect to foreign policy.

I'm afraid that we're making the same mistake in the field of foreign policy that practically all the other countries of the world are making. We, too, rationalize our foreign policy by saying, in effect, "This particular course of action is in our best national interest, and the rest of the world can like it or else." It is such a course of action that we have been following in Southeast Asia, with the result that today we are on the verge of a massive war.

But I am satisfied that, at the grassroots of America, people are opposed to unilateral military action on the part of the United States. After all, foreign policy does not belong to the President of the United States under our Constitutional system. It belongs to the American people. Their medium for expressing that right is the ballot box, and I think that the American people are going to repudiate our gunboat foreign policy.

Sometimes I do become a little discouraged. It does worry me to see various economic groups within our society place their selfish interests above the general welfare. It does disappoint me to see political officeholders place their selfish political interests above the public welfare in order to gain favor with some particular economic or political group. And I have noted that many, many times a citizen may be very objective about an issue in the abstract, but when it affects his pocketbook he tends to become a special pleader.

Recently, I listened to representatives of American banks and loaning institutions testify in opposition to the Federal

Government's lending money at low-interest rates to students to complete their education.

Why were they opposed to the Government-loaning section of the student-aid bill? They wanted the money to be loaned to these students at a 6% interest rate. In fact, one witness said, in effect, that this was one way to teach the students to understand and appreciate the private-enterprise system! What happened to the citizen-statesmanship of these money changers? They subordinated it to their selfish interests.

However, I am always optimistic about the final judgment of public opinion. It is my faith and confidence that the American people, once they understand the facts, will arrive at the right ultimate judgment.

Jack Douglas
humorist

Well, I think people don't seem to be too proud of their jobs anymore. So they goof off. I was born in New York and I've lived here now for 8 years, and I think this city is one of the most goof-off cities I've ever lived in. I mean, everything you have done you almost have to have done twice to have it done right.

A guy's a vacuum-cleaner repairman, he seems to resent it he's not a bank president or something like that. Nobody's proud even to be working anymore. You pick up a magazine that has these big glossy ads and you read them and Jesus Christ, you see guys posing around the deck of a 41-foot cabin cruiser and other guys parked by their Rolls-Royce in front of some fancy club somewhere where the jet set's supposed to be gathered. What's a Rolls-Royce anyway? Personally, I think it's a lousy car. Work? They wouldn't go near the stuff.

A lot of people do seem unhappy, and I think communication's got a lot to do with it. Say, 60 years ago—or whenever the hell the telephone started—we didn't know what was going on in these goddam countries that are always fighting each other. Jesus, the Arabs and the Jews and the tribes in Africa are always fighting. We never heard about this then, so consequently it didn't bother us at all. Now, in 5 seconds we know when something's happening somewhere, even if it's just a little brush war with two gunboats taking pot-shots at one another and missing in the Gulf of Tonkin. It hits home. Or you pick up the paper and you see this guy got slugged, that guy got killed on Second Avenue a couple of nights ago—Jesus Christ, it scares the hell out of you.

But once upon a time you didn't hear about these things. You lived on a farm or in the suburbs, and news didn't travel so fast. Ignorance was bliss.

And all this hubbub about pornography—it's a crock of shit. I love pornography. I really do. And I'm not a sex fiend and never was. I always thought sex was a pretty good idea, but I never grabbed any girl on the street. *Honest.*

All in all, we're still the most powerful nation on earth, no matter what anyone else says. So I don't think there's anything to worry about.

Nat Hentoff
writer

It's difficult for me to think in terms of whether America has a national purpose or not because I'm utopian enough to hope that eventually—if we're not all blown up—we'll see an international society. With our resources, we have the capacity to point the way to an international society, and that would mean the *obverse* of what we've done in Vietnam and the Dominican Republic. It would mean allocating our resources both here and abroad to eliminate poverty. But there's no real sign of our doing that. So I suppose that the answer is that our national purpose is insular, self-protective, aggressive, and increasingly messianic—as if we were the savior of the world instead of its potential destroyer.

It was C.P. Snow who said that it is a mathematical certainty that there will be a nuclear war in a decade or so unless there is a real *détente*. Instead, we seem to be locked in a self-destructive pattern. And I think there's going to *be* suicide.

The only hope I see comes from people in the streets—like S.N.C.C., the Northern Student Movement, Students for a Democratic Society, and the various totally indigenous groups in ghettos around the country. Mostly, at present, the black ghettos. I mean the people who are going beyond civil rights into politics and who are working on the conviction—which I share—that the institutions in this country have to be changed, that power has to be redistributed and transformed.

I do see changes. They're not big yet, but I'm heartened that in some cities—like Detroit and Newark—the so-called voiceless poor are now getting up and telling War on Poverty bureaucrats that they know they are being conned, and in some cases they're getting some authority over their own lives. Sure, it's small next to nuclear escalation.

But it's something.

Kennoth Rexroth
poet and critic

Everybody's days are numbered and so are every nation's. Yes, I suppose that the world hegemony of the United States is either over, or would have to be reasserted by force of arms. I don't think America can rule the world anymore, and back when it could it didn't do such a very good job of it.

Politics aside, I think there is a general disintegration of society's morals. There's nothing corny about morals. I mean, Cincinnatus didn't call up Marcus and say, "Well, like I don't want to use a corny word like 'morals,' but—" And I don't mean *sexual* morals. I mean bona-fide, trustworthy, interpersonal relationships are breaking down. And it's universal. It's just as bad, if not worse, in Jakarta and Manila. And it's just as bad in the Iron Curtain countries, and certainly worse in the newly liberated countries.

This breakdown in morals is possibly due to just population pressures—like those rats, you know, that that guy made delinquent just by overcrowding them. It may be just that, but it's certainly *true*.

I suppose one of the most important indications that something is wrong is the complete rejection of our civilization by its creative, growing, and intellectual community, and this is true in all countries where free expression is permitted at all. In the first half of this century, this was by and large a rejection of the official values in favor of values which the creative community was developing for itself. Now this is no longer true. Now there is total rejection. That is, Picasso or Kandinsky stand for very clearly defined values, though they may not be those of the man in society. But this fellow who presses automobiles, or Yves Klein, they stand for nothing at all, they stand for total nihilism. And it's caused, I think, by the loss of the primary virtues in human relationships—of courage and trustworthiness and generosity. . . .

A lot of people talk about the tremendous increase in homosexuality, but it's increased only because society has generally become more permissive. But that's not what I'm really talking about. The increase in homosexuality's not important. What's important is that there are more and more people who believe you can take a middle-aged homosexual off on the edge of a wharf, take his money away from him on sexual pretenses, hit him over the head, dump him into the water—and that you can do this every week-end. It's called "stud-busting," the murder of homosexuals. These fellows wear a regular uniform: skin-tight Levis, boots, leather jackets. It's just a complete breakdown of ordinary human relationships. And you can take any department of life and you see this.

But America is not a dying country. It's a sick one, but not dying. The world has changed and our society hasn't changed with it. So today we fight battles of gunboat imperialism as though we were still able to establish banana republics. And these things are senseless because they're not even profitable. I mean, imperialism no longer even pays. And yet we go on blindly, landing Marines.

The same thing is true of our internal programs. We set up things that are simply glorified W.P.A.s which will employ immense numbers of Phi Beta Kappas and which will make no essential difference to the actual poverty of the backwoods of the countryside or the slums of the city. This just becomes another hustle. *Hustle!* A social worker—Ph.D., rather, not a social worker, just an executive—connected with HARYOU said to me once, "You know what's happening to all these boys? They just talk about their social workers and their advisers just the way they talk about gambling and dope and the numbers game. We don't make any impression." And I said, "You know, that's right, it's just another hustle." And she said, "What?" And I said, "You know. *Hustle.*" "Yes," she said, "that's right." And I said, "Yeah, honey, and it's the same thing for you. It's just another hustle for you. You just use different language. Just what the hell do you think you're doing? And all your friends, from Kenneth Clark on down? They're doing the same thing. It's just another hustle. And it has no essential meaning."

And of course our whole society is sick this way. We are still fighting the battles of the industrial revolution and capitalism and the labor theory of value and all that stuff. We're still living as if this were the world of classical economics when actually we're living in an electronic world in which the sources of power and the means of using it are entirely different. I mean the people who run what Jim Baldwin called the Power Structure—they're living in another age. They're fighting the Crimean War. Or they're colonizing South Africa. Or they're setting up Toynbee's father's project in the East End of London to redeem the worthy poor. Hell, all that took place in the '80s. And this is the real cause of the sickness of society, and it could kill the society if it got out of hand. Of course, the sickness can be cured. But the point is that the power and technology are in the hands of these crazy people. And it's a race between a life of universal leisure and complete democratization of culture—and radioactive dust and a new nova in the sky. And you have to believe in the inherent goodness of man to believe that the nova is not the more likely possibility.

John Rechy
novelist

I don't know whether our days are numbered or not, but I do feel something impending—not exclusively the Bomb, but something uglier than that, of which the Bomb is merely a representation. It has more to do with what's happening to people, inside. So instead of coping with this thing inside, we go off to Vietnam and fight in the jungle.

True morality is a possible way to keep our sanity (not morality in the overemphasized, restrictive sense of sex, but in the sense of living as if there *is* some meaning, some hope—as if God exists, whether he does or not). For this reason, I don't necessarily put down organized religion, when it isn't being itself—as it so sadly often is—a part of the hungry viciousness.

We've definitely become too cool for our own good, and I would say that my own book *City of Night* reflects a great deal of this "too-coolness" which has by now become frozen. Hubert Selby Jr.'s *Last Exit to Brooklyn* is certainly another manifestation of this. Yet the very publication of books like these, revealing icy despair, is a *hope*, a chance to stare at things as they are, not to hide them.

Hubert Selby Jr.
novelist

I certainly do feel there is a drastic change in the air—in addition to the smog. There certainly is a lot of tension.

In human terms, what's dying around us is simply—love. Of course, there'll always be some semblance of the man-woman type of love, just to keep the race going. That's a biological thing. Lust can always be felt as love. As a matter of fact, most of the time that's *really* what people are thinking about when they use the word "love."

As an example of the dehumanization of the race, the other night a kid was killed and ten people sat there and watched it. The Industrial Revolution was a very important aspect of the dehumanization of the race. I think that directly or indirectly this dehumanization is responsible for our preoccupation with such things as sado-masochism—suddenly *s* and *m* have become a topical joke, like it's a household word, which is pretty fantastic when you think about it. It wasn't so very long ago when people didn't even know what the word "sadism" meant. Twenty years ago, I just thought of "sadistic" as—like in the movies—the "sadistic" bad guy tortures the good guy.

And there's all this hatred of homosexuals. You know how people are always talking about goddam fag this and god-

473

dam fag that, for no reason at all, simply because they're a fag? In my novel I was trying to say, well, we're all people, fag or not, it doesn't make any difference, we all supposedly deserve the same breaks, and let's try to look at them as people and not some kind of freak.

If it is true that homosexuality is a psychological and not a physiological disease, then it certainly does make a very definite statement about our society and our culture, and it's not a very complimentary one. Not that I mean that a fag is no good because he's a fag, but simply that it is *contra naturam,* homosexuality isn't a natural thing. Nature intended things to be different. And if you have that many people who are contrary to the laws of nature, then something must be wrong with the society that produces them.

John Updike
writer

Living as I do up here in Massachusetts, I can't speak for the rest of the country. But there has been a general apocalyptic quality in much of the arts since the early '50s, I'd say. At least, it appears in writing as the kind of doom-mongering you find in Baldwin and Mailer, a kind of rhetoric, really, which is linked loosely with words like the "Bomb" and whatnot. I've never worried too much about the Bomb for some reason. . . .

I'll tell you what I think. There probably *is* some sort of disaster imminent just by dint of the 25-year rhythm that seems to space most world disasters. In the last 2 years, ever since we successfully maneuvered through the Cuban crisis, there's been a slight complacency, a sort of "get tough" attitude that you see in Vietnam. And just going by the principle that the reverse is always likely to happen, I'm a little worried that there isn't *enough* pointed anxiety about the international scene.

I would say, in the arts, it's more of a technical issue. Painting has moved with great speed to a number of increasingly radical and in some ways surprising modes, whereas prose has, if anything, receded from the great rebel experiments of the '20s, so that there is a kind of technical feeling of inferiority that outs in a curious sloppiness. It seems to stem from just an impatience with the tedium of writing intelligible prose. All that the Grove Press school of writing is a symptom of is Grove Press's desire to keep on topping itself.

Does America lack a goal? America is striving toward the survival of the happiness of its citizens. That's a worthy enough goal.

As for those doctors who are against Medicare, and a supposed decline in virtue, I suppose it's a mixture, as it's always been. Medicare seems to be debatable. I know if there was a similar attempt to socialize writing, I'd be fairly distressed. And as for automation, I think there are worse dangers. It doesn't frighten me much. I don't think a machine can be a Mozart. And what *about* water pollution? I think it's a pity if water is polluted. I am firmly against water pollution. I am foursquare against water and air pollution.

This is not a monolithic state, and it's correct that there be a certain limit on what a centralized authority can do. It seems to me that the basic notions behind the founding of this country carry with them a price of inefficiency. Yes, even now I think we can afford this inefficiency.

Dizzy Gillespie
jazz musician and composer

The Negro revolution that's going on today is the best thing that could possibly happen to America. Within 10 years, I think that America will be in the greatest era of prosperity in its history, because by then we may have solved our racial differences. On the other hand, if we don't, I think America has reached its potential as far as the white citizens are concerned.

The black people are becoming more and more dissatisfied. And if changes don't take place within 10 years, there'll be a revolution. Someone might lead up the masses of the poor, where the power really comes from. So we ain't seen nothing yet.

White America has gone as far as it can go. But our culture ain't dying. There's so much energy left. You know the old thing. Somebody says, "I got class." And somebody else says, "*I* got class I ain't even *used* yet!" You heard that saying? Well, we've got *culture* that ain't even been tapped yet.

Tom Paxton
folk singer

Maybe the Negro revolution in this country is precisely the thing that's going to keep the country alive. I think we're really hitched to their wagon now, we're really attached to their star. If the Negro revolution succeeds, it will revitalize the whole country. We'll have all that new talent that we haven't been using up to now.

But if the Negro revolution fails, this country's dead beyond a doubt. If it fails, there'll be a blood bath. And I'm reluctantly pessimistic. There are an awful lot of rednecks in America.

Robert Osborn
artist

I have the feeling that for the first time we have a President who is talking about the Great Society, and I like it.

O.K., I take this to be a very good sign.

However, it seems to me that the forces of violence—the naked use of power out there in Vietnam, guys running around on motorcycles who are willing to rape every woman they find, kids being stabbed in the subway, the woman stabbed and nobody doing anything about it—I find that perhaps the release of the forces of violence may be increasing faster than these other, more admirable efforts. There is this love-side of us and this hate-side of us—this animal, black, id quality in us. There are almost no permissible outlets for this. In Spain, you go to a bullfight Sunday afternoon, and boy! you come home just wrung out, you've had just about as much violence as you can take. They're *recognizing* violence. They're not a puritanical, goody-goody society. They're admitting that there's this terrible, black, violent side to us. Here, what do you do on a Sunday afternoon? Me, I go shooting—I take a lot of it out on the poor game birds. I hunt good and hard, also fish —but I'm really kind and decent with my wife. I've talked to Ben Spock about this, and he says he's not absolutely sure that the good part of us is going to win out. All that we do is so ugly, so violent, so selfish—and maybe these things may win out.

Eugene Burdick
writer and teacher

The only Americans I see at close-hand are the kids here at Berkeley in San Francisco, and they don't have any apocalyptic view. They're always protesting one thing or another and seem to be pretty purposeful.

But this is only half the story. A number of British writers have been pointing out that we've outlasted the 20-year cycle which is supposed to separate all major wars. The war rhythm has been suspended, and the reason might be that the Bomb is so awesome an alternative. But we're still left with all that emotional energy. And a lot goes into the free-speech movements, a lot into the civil-rights movement.

Having myself been witness to a lot of these demonstrations, it's my distinct impression that a hell of a lot of it is a very unwholesome kind of energy. When the kids go limp just as they're being arrested, you can see they'd just love to turn and go violent against the cops. And in every demonstration I've witnessed or participated in, there's been an awful moment like that, when you just *sense* that the whole group was really in a brutal mood. They get a kind of catharsis out of it.

The people who are really in trouble are *not* these kids but the men and women who have no outlets at all. I mean, what is the middle-class executive doing for kicks these days? He probably can't even get a girl to whip—unless his wife submits. These older people—lawyers, small-town politicians, what have you—are really getting worked up. Look how hysterical those legislators got about the free-speech movement. Their mood was generally more savage than that of the kids. The kids let it go in little doses day after day on the Berkeley plaza as they listened to Savio speak. But the oldsters have no emotional outlets at all.

Saul Bellow
novelist

A good deal of this Fall of the Roman Empire talk may be just cocktail-party chatter, but there's no reason why cocktail-party chatter can't contain any germs of truth.

Still, I think that a lot of the doom-crying in our theater and art is just cant. It's the product of very solid and comfortable people who are very well rewarded for their efforts as doom-criers. Our modern, way-out art and theater just represent the end of an art movement rather than the end of the country. Simply because these people don't have the originality to begin something new, they are exploiting what is left of the vanguardism of the earlier part of the century.

These doom-criers are sought out by a new class of prosperous people who don't feel secure in their prosperity. They feel very uneasy about their comfort; they feel a great guilt over it, which the doom-criers help provide catharsis for. They're Pharisees in their social position and in their income. But they don't have the healthy obstinacy or self-confidence of real Pharisees.

Yet I do think that people are very pessimistic about the future, consciously or unconsciously. Twice in this century we've depended on the good sense of politicians when we've been on the brink of war, and twice we've had these wars. So it's hard to depend upon the good sense of politicians any more. Now, we have no guarantee, so how can we rationally think that just because the Bomb is so horrible, we won't have another war?

Philip Wylie
author

People are apprehensive today, sure—who wouldn't be? The main source of this apprehension is the fear of thermonuclear extermination. But it's psychologically inevitable that, in-

478

stead of worrying about the Bomb, people pick what seems to them the *next* most likely source of anxiety. A neurotic person doesn't live out the cause of his neurosis; he lives out some psychologically converted form of it.

A good example is the Birch Society. This is an age to which they haven't adjusted, but their real fears have been replaced by *symbolic* ones, such as that "Earl Warren is a card-carrying Communist." And when you're in that position psychologically, boy, you're *sick*.

Herman Kahn
economist

The intellectuals are very unhappy. It's a bad thing, but it's not a disaster necessarily. I myself see a lot of problems in our society, but they are an almost inevitable complement to economic progress. Every decade has new and different problems.

There *are* very strong analogies to be made between the United States and the Roman Empire. But let's remember that Rome lasted 400 years even after it began decaying. Rome from 200 B.C. *on* was no longer the country it had once been. The fact is, decay is not an immediate process—everything is decaying. My God, you can see signs of aging in a new-born infant.

The United States does have a great scientific and industrial vigor. But this vigor is today being challenged by the rise of other areas of the world. Relative to these other areas the United States seems to be declining, but not relative to itself. It displays an impressive intellectual and economic vigor, and within the next decade I can't envision any country overtaking the United States.

Pamela Tiffin
actress

Oh yeah, into the politics again. Here we go again.
I don't know anything about politics.

479

I don't know if America's dying. Is it? What's a dying country?

I mean there's one thing I know. I think we should just live and have a good time.

Mrs. Bonaro Overstreet
writer

I would say that throughout America there is a definite mood of expectation—not necessarily of disaster, but rather of change. Now, whether this expectation induces in people a sense of impending disaster, or of new possibilities, is largely a matter of whether or not the person feels he can *control* these changes.

Today, both the Right and the Left are dissatisfied. And if you couple this feeling of dissatisfaction with someone's also feeling he *ought* to be doing something about it, that person is likely to be a very frustrated and unhappy soul. And he's likely to go out and do the wrong thing.

So we're in a real mess. I think that about sums it up.

Vance Packard
writer

The fact is that today we are facing a situation unique in the history of mankind. All throughout history, man has been struggling to get a little bit more in the way of abundance and a little bit more in the way of leisure. Now we've had a big breakthrough. And the big challenge is to adjust to this abundance and this leisure, and to the technology and giant organizations that go with them.

But America is not ready to be counted out yet, by any means.

Bruce Catton
historian

I don't think our society is falling apart. On the contrary, all of the troubles we're having are simply part of the process of coming together—growing pains. Folks are just as good as they ever were, if not a little bit better, and I have yet to see any signs that they're getting discouraged.

Some of us bright guys worry just a little too much.

***

Hans Morgenthau
political scientist

I think we have gone back to a primitive type of crusading foreign policy which, if continued, is going to lead to disaster. Anti-Communism is the hallmark of that policy. And this kind of indiscriminating crusade is completely inappropriate to the present age, when you find different types of communism which have to be dealt with on their own merits. Also, it can't be pursued consistently because no nation has the power to do it.

***

Tallulah Bankhead
actress

Christ, not *another* one of those *Fact* Magazine polls! Look, darling, I'm having my nails done and everything else. You can't ask me something like that right off the hook like that.

***

Charles Schulz
cartoonist

Is America a dying country? Good grief, no! That's the most ridiculous thing I ever heard. I'm optimistic about the future of the country, and I think we've got a good man at the helm. I think America has many years to go.

But let me know, though, if anything happens, will you?

***

Dagmar Wilson
president, Women's Strike for Peace

Frankly, I wish there *were* some pessimism—pessimism in the sense of feeling we've got to find a new direction. I think that among the socially conscious there may be such a feeling, but I don't think the man in the street is yet aware of the difficulties we are in. And I regard them as basically economic difficulties. Perhaps if the man in the street *were* a little more pessimistic, he'd have less to be pessimistic about.

Society is always changing. There's no permanent solution to economic or social problems. And so what was once a new and hopeful and revolutionary idea—and I think the American idea was—becomes obsolete because of normal changes. And when we make our original hope into a doctrine, something more sacred than God—as our free-enterprise system is—then we're in trouble. And that's when we try to impose it on other people. It's an overcompensation for our growing doubts. We silence these doubts by shouting, "This is the only way!"

In my pessimistic moments I do think we will have a nuclear war. It won't be too big a one. On the other hand, looking at mankind's past, I also think of Thornton Wilder, who wrote a play called *The Skin of Our Teeth*. And I think he illustrated very, very beautifully that somehow or other, mankind has survived crisis after crisis by the skin of his teeth. I am still trusting in mankind's ability for self-preservation, which will again save us—by the skin of our teeth.

Index

A

abortion, 347-357
advertising pressure on news media, 183-194, 197, 209
Albee, Edward, 153
alcoholism, media treatment of, 193-194
Alka-Seltzer, 304
Allen, George E., 167-168
American Bar Association, 313-314, 322
American Cancer Society, 186, 187
American character, 32-33
American Civil Liberties Union, 256-257, 269, 275
American malaise, 463-482
American Nazi Party, 13, 19, 20. *See also*
Rockwell, George Lincoln
Americans for Democratic Action, 48
Anacin, 304, 305
Anti-Defamation League, 15, 407
aspirin-type remedies, 304-305
Atterbury, General W. W., 203

B

Baker, Russell, 213-214
Bayer aspirin, 303-308
belladonna, 434-437
Bellevue Psychiatric Hospital, 137, 138, 139-147
Belli, Melvin, 218, 311-328
Black Muslims, 20
Blatnik, Representative John A., 187, 188
Blume, Helmut, 213, 215
Bomb, the, 472, 474, 477, 479
breakdown in morals, 470, 473
Bristol-Myers, 306
brutality
    in mental hospitals, 138, 140-146, 147
    police, 56-57, 267-280

H

I

J

K

prison
   gambling in, 82
   life in, 81-82
   homosexuality in, 82, 83-90
   sex in, 81, 82
psychedelic drugs, 429
psychiatry, jokes about, 417-426

R

Reader's Digest, 185, 187, 188, 190, 192-193, 258, 262
Reuther, Walter, 16, 17
Riesman, David, 146, 148-149, 417
Rockefeller, Governor Nelson A., 17
Rockwell, "Doc," 21
Rockwell, George Lincoln, 13-25, 343
Roosevelt, Eleanor, 20
Roosevelt, President Franklin D., 16, 20, 205,
206-207, 453, 454, 459
Ruby, Jack, 317, 318, 323, 324, 325, 392, 397, 407
Russia, 1, 2, 5, 6-7, 27, 29, 30, 33, 35
Russo-China feud, 6-7, 8

S

St. Joseph's aspirin, 303, 305
Saturday Review, 261
Schonberg, Harold, 213, 218
Schulberg, Budd, 178-179
Shahn, Ben, 213, 218
sick children, 71-72
Slater, Stanley, 267
smegma, human, 333
Society of Friends, 240
South Vietnam, 3, 7
Soviet Union, *see* Russia
Spiegel, Sam, 178-179
Stalin, Joseph, 441-442
Stapleton, Luke, 237, 238-240, 251-252, 255, 256
Sterling Drug Inc., 303, 305, 306
Stevenson, Adlai, 168, 453, 464
syndicated newspaper features, 201-202

T

U

V

W